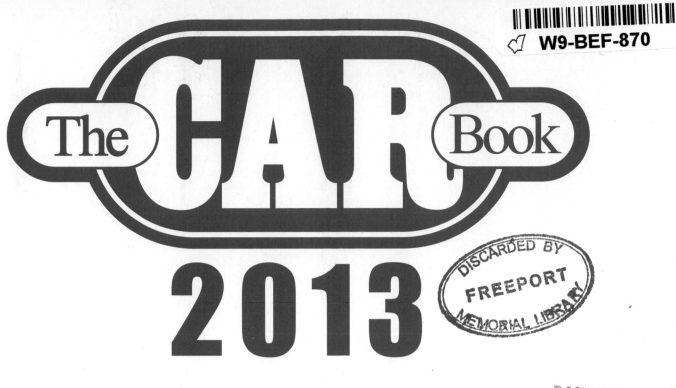

The CAR Book

2013

by
Jack Gillis

with
Amy Curran,
Peter Kitchen
and
Michael McQuiller

Foreword by
Clarence Ditlow
Center for Auto Safety

A Center for Auto Safety Publication

ACKNOWLEDGMENTS

In the 33 years we've been publishing *The Car Book* I've been blessed with some remarkable co-author researchers and this year is no exception as Peter Kitchen stepped in to ably manage and organize this extraordinary effort. It's a huge job to acquire and sift through the massive amount of data needed to compile the book and Peter did so with great competence. For 22 years, Amy Curran has been expertly preparing all the graphics necessary to clearly present the data, managing the logistics necessary to get a printed book in the hands of the public, and keeping the project on track. This year we added Mike McQuiller to the team. He effectively "dug up," compiled and analyzed an amazing amount of vehicle data. Thanks to Amy, Peter, and Mike, consumers have the information they need to make a smart, sensible new car choice.

As has been the case for 32 years, this year's edition would not have been possible without the essential contributions from Clarence Ditlow and the staff of the Center for Auto Safety, including Michael Brooks and Jon Robinson.

As always, the most important factor in being able to bring this information to the American car buyer for 33 years is the encouragement, support, and love from my brilliant and beautiful wife, Marilyn Mohrman-Gillis. For her and four terrific children–Katie, John, Brian and Brennan– I am eternally grateful.

—*J.G.*

As Always,

for Marilyn &
Katie, John, Brian, and Brennan

ISBN-13: 978-0-9841734-3-3 ISBN-10: 0-9841734-3-9

CLARENCE DITLOW

The Center for Auto Safety has watch dogged the National Highway Traffic Safety Administration (NHTSA) and the auto industry for over 40 years. NHTSA is a wonderful agency with a vital mission but it is woefully underfunded, understaffed and outgunned by the industry it regulates.

To expect today's NHTSA to adequately regulate the trillion dollar auto industry is like asking a high school football team to beat the Super Bowl champion Baltimore Ravens. GM's third quarter 2012 income was $37.6 billion compared to NHTSA's annual vehicle safety budget of less than $200 million. Unlike such other public health and safety agencies as FDA and EPA, NHTSA doesn't even have its own research facility. Instead it must rent space owned by Honda, one of the companies it regulates.

The history of NHTSA since its creation in 1966 has been one of an agency where Congress has to intervene as one major safety issue after another emerges that the agency is unable to resolve or lacks authority to take action. Some examples of Congressional intervention are:

1970 - Inclusion of Tires in Recall Program

1974 - Free Recall Repairs, Doubled Civil Penalty, Fuel System Integrity, Schoolbus Safety Standards, Public Defect Petitions, Doubled Civil Penalty

1991 - Full Front Seat Airbags, Head Injury Protection

1998 - Improved Airbag Rule

2000 - Tire Safety Standards, Early Warning Reporting System, Increased Civil Penalty to $15 Million

2002 - Booster Seat, Lap & Shoulder Belt Rules

2005 - Rollover Prevention, Side Impact, Roof Crush, Occupant Ejection, Crashworthiness Ratings & 15-Passenger Van Safety

2007 - Backover, Power Window, Brake Shift Interlock

2010 - Increased Civil Penalty to $35 Million

NHTSA's inability to impose significant penalties on the auto industry makes it a paper tiger. Although Ralph Nader urged Congress to put criminal penalties in the 1966 Vehicle Safety Act, the auto companies successfully fought to keep them out. Congress capped NHTSA civil penalties at $400,000. Spurred by the Ford-Firestone recalls in 2000, Congress raised the penalty to $15 million. Spurred again by Toyota sudden acceleration, Congress raised the penalty to a still inadequate $35 million effective July 2013 and again refused to add criminal penalties.

In contrast, EPA imposed a $1.4 billion penalty against Transocean in the BP Oil Spill; BP paid a $525 million SEC fine for understating the amount of oil spilled with an even larger one from EPA pending. Fines against pharmaceutical companies for violating FDA regulations run into the many billions with GlaxoSmithKline paying $3 billion, Pfizer $2.3 billion, Abbott $1.5 billion and Eli Lilly $1.4 billion in the last 3 years.

So how does a $17.35 million NHTSA fine against Toyota stack up - it's chump change. The largest penalty against an auto company is $185 million imposed by the SEC on Daimler AG for vehicle kickbacks in foreign countries. So bribing foreign officials to sell luxury cars results in a penalty 10.7 times higher than the highest fine ever imposed by NHTSA to save lives. That's wrong.

NHTSA's history has two big lessons to drive highway deaths down to CAS' Vision of Zero Deaths. First, the agency needs the resources, skills and laboratories to anticipate and lead developments in automotive technology rather than react to changes. Second, the agency needs the enforcement clout to bring auto companies back onto the road to safety when they veer off.

Advanced safety features like lane departure, radar braking, adaptive cruise control, active pre-crash safety, blind spot detection, and backup cameras are appearing in some models but not as swiftly or as functionally as they could be if they had guiding regulations. The Federal Communications Commission requires cell phones with expired service plans to be able to call 911. Yet NHTSA has not required vehicles with lifesaving automatic crash notification to call Emergency Responders in crashes after their service plans have expired. Talk about callous disregard for human life.

Buying the *Car Book* helps you buy a safer car and helps CAS reach our Vision of Zero Traffic Deaths. The Center for Auto Safety works every day on your behalf for safer and more reliable vehicles. Go to our Website www.autosafety.org and find out how you can support the Center and have CAS be your safety and lemon insurance.

JACK GILLIS

The car makers are back and the choices are better than ever before. And, you've got the 33rd edition of *The Car Book* to guide you to the best choice possible!

Not only will our "*Car Book* Best Bets" lead you to some excellent vehicles, but there are numerous other choices that, while not making our top lists, will do well in meeting your demands for efficient, safe and intelligently designed vehicles. You can confidently let *The Car Book* be your guide to the best for 2013.

Working closely with the Center for Auto Safety's Clarence Ditlow and his staff, the information in *The Car Book* has significantly improved the way carmakers build their vehicles. This is because we have always believed that if *you* knew that one car was safer than another you'd buy the safer car. We believed that your action would put enormous pressure on the auto makers to improve safety. It worked and cars today are safer than ever before!

As it has been for 33 years, my goal is to sift through the myriad of government and industry data on cars and present the information so you can actually use it. Thirty-three years ago, *The Car Book* was the first publication to give consumers the ability to make an informed choice on one of the most important and complex items that they will ever purchase. Today, thanks in large part to the efforts of the Center for Auto Safety in Washington, DC, our mission has never wavered.

In setting out to change the way people buy their cars, *The Car Book* was able to change the way car companies made them.

This is the second year of the government's improved crash test program on which we base our all-important and unique safety ratings. In keeping with *The Car Book*'s philosophy of making it as easy as possible to identify the truly good performers in the government crash tests, we provide a unique *Car Book* Combined Crash Test Rating which combines all of the complex government testing into a simple, straightforward number. In addition, we take the step of comparing the vehicles on a relative basis to each other so you can easily tell the best performers from the worst.

While making improvements to the crash test program (see page 18) is a good thing, not all of the 2013 vehicles have been tested. While we (and you!) look forward to the day when all of your choices have been tested, our safety ratings will provide a good indication of which cars can be expected to best protect you.

Before *The Car Book*, consumers had no idea which warranties were better, what you could expect to pay for typical repairs, which cars cost the most and least to insure, or how they stacked up in government complaints. Now you have this information all in one place.

Our exclusive car-by-car ratings at the end of the book provide an overview of all the criteria you need to make a good choice. Here, you'll be able to quickly assess key features and see how the car you're interested in stacks up against its competition so you can make sure your selection is the best car for you.

Even though the choices get better each year and safety is improved, it's still a challenge to separate the lemons from the peaches. There are notable differences in how cars protect you in a crash, how much they cost to maintain, the benefits of their warranties, and how far they'll go on a gallon of expensive gasoline. Nevertheless, if you use the information in *The Car Book*, there is no reason why your next car should not last *at least* 150,000 miles.

Buying a car means staying on your toes and not being "schnookered" in the showroom. *The Car Book* will help you do just that. It's not easy matching wits with a seasoned salesperson, but our "Showroom Strategies" section will give you the keys to getting the best deal. In spite of all the new car technology and the Internet, the fundamentals of buying a good, safe, reliable car remain the same: do your homework; shop around; and remember that car dealers need you more than you need them!

The information in *The Car Book* is based on data collected and developed by our staff, the U.S. Department of Transportation, and the Center for Auto Safety. With all of this information in hand, you'll find some great choices for 2013.

—*Jack*

USING THE BUYING GUIDE

T he "Buying Guide" provides a quick comparison of the 2013 cars in terms of their safety, warranty, fuel economy, complaint rating, and price range—arranged by size class. To fully understand the information in the charts, it is important to read the related section in the book.

Overall Rating: This shows how well this car stacks up on a scale of 1 to 10 when compared to all others on the market. Because safety is the most important component of our ratings, cars with no crash test results at printing are not given an overall rating.

Combined Crash Test Rating: This indicates how well the car performed in the government's frontal and side crash test programs compared to this year's vehicles tested to date. See page 18 for details.

Warranty Rating: This is an overall comparative assessment of the car's warranty.

Fuel Economy: This is the EPA city/highway mpg for, what is expected to be, the most popular model.

Complaint Rating: This is based on complaints received by the U.S. Department of Transportation. If not rated, the vehicle is too new to have a complaint rating.

Price Range: This will give you a general idea of the "sticker," or suggested retail price.

Indicates a *Car Book* Best Bet. See page 13.

ABOUT THE CAR BOOK BEST BETS

TIP

It is important to consult the specific chapters to learn more about how *The Car Book* ratings are developed and to look on the car pages, beginning on page 81, for more details on these vehicles. In order to be considered as a "Best Bet" the vehicle must have a crash test rating as safety is a critical factor in gaining that recognition. Vehicles with "Poor" (3 or 4) or "Very Poor" (1 or 2) in Combined Crash Tests, "Very Poor" in Front or Side Crash Test Ratings, or an additional injury warning were not considered a "Best Bet." Because most people are considering vehicles in the same size category, the "Best Bets" are by size—indicating how these vehicles compared against others in the same size class.

Vehicle	Page #	Overall Rating	Combined Crash Test Rating	Warranty Rating	Fuel Economy	Complaint Rating	Price Range
Subcompact							
Chevrolet Sonic	118	10	Very Good	Average	25/35	Very Poor	$14-$21,000
Fiat 500	133	8	Poor	Good	30/38	Poor	$15-$22,000
Ford Fiesta	140	4	Good	Very Poor	29/39	Very Poor	$13-$18,000
Honda Fit	151	4	Poor	Very Poor	27/33	Good	$15-$19,000
Hyundai Accent	156	8	Poor	Very Good	28/37	Good	$14-$17,000
Hyundai Veloster	163			Very Good	28/37	Very Poor	$17-$22,000
Kia Rio	177	8	Poor	Good	28/36	Very Good	$13-$17,000
Kia Soul	179	6	Average	Good	25/30	Poor	$14-$19,000
Mazda Mazda2	189			Very Poor	28/34		$14-$17,000
Mazda MX-5 Miata	195			Very Poor	21/28	Very Good	$23-$30,000
Mini Clubman	202			Very Good	27/35		$21-$32,000
Mini Cooper	203			Very Good	28/36	Poor	$19-$35,000
Mini Countryman	204			Very Good	25/30	Average	$22-$35,000
Nissan 370Z	208			Very Poor	18/26	Good	$33-$45,000
Nissan Versa	223	4	Very Poor	Very Poor	26/35	Good	$10-$18,000
Scion iQ	228	3	Very Poor	Very Poor	36/37	Very Good	$15-$15,000
Scion xB	230			Very Poor	22/28	Poor	$16-$17,000
Scion xD	231			Very Poor	27/33	Very Good	$15-$16,000
Smart ForTwo	232			Very Poor	34/38	Poor	$12-$17,000
Suzuki SX4	240	1	Very Poor	Poor	23/29	Poor	$13-$20,000
Toyota Yaris	257	5	Poor	Very Poor	30/37		$14-$17,000
Volkswagen Beetle	258	5	Average	Good	22/29	Very Poor	$19-$24,000
Compact							
Acura ILX	81	8	Good	Poor	24/35		$25-$34,000
Audi A3	86			Very Good	21/24	Very Poor	$27-$32,000
Audi A4	87	10	Good	Very Good	22/32	Very Good	$33-$47,000
BMW 1 Series	94			Very Good	18/27	Very Poor	$31-$47,000
BMW 3 Series	95	10	Good	Very Good	22/33		$36-$60,000
Buick Verano	105	10	Very Good	Average	21/32	Good	$23-$26,000
Cadillac ATS	106	9	Very Good	Good	22/32		$33-$47,000
Chevrolet Cruze	113	9	Very Good	Average	22/35	Poor	$17-$23,000
Chevrolet Volt	122	9	Average	Average	35/40	Very Poor	$39-$39,000

Vehicle	Page #	Overall Rating	Combined Crash Test Rating	Warranty Rating	Fuel Economy	Complaint Rating	Price Range
Compact (cont.)							
Dodge Dart	129	9	Very Good	Average	24/34		$15-$19,000
Ford C-MAX	134			Very Poor	47/47		$25-$28,000
Ford Focus	142	6	Good	Very Poor	27/38	Very Poor	$17-$39,000
Honda Civic	148			Very Poor	28/39	Average	$15-$26,000
Honda Civic Coupe	149			Very Poor	28/39		$15-$23,000
Honda Insight	152			Very Poor	41/44	Poor	$18-$23,000
Hyundai Elantra	158	9	Good	Very Good	28/38	Good	$16-$20,000
Kia Forte	175	7	Very Poor	Good	26/36	Good	$15-$19,000
Lexus CT	182			Average	43/40	Very Good	$31-$32,000
Mazda Mazda3	190	5	Average	Very Poor	24/33		$16-$25,000
Mercedes-Benz C-Class	196	4	Very Poor	Poor	18/25	Very Good	$35-$62,000
Mitsubishi Lancer	205	6	Poor	Very Good	25/34	Average	$15-$40,000
Nissan Altima Coupe	210			Very Poor	23/32		$24-$24,000
Nissan Cube	212			Very Poor	27/31	Very Good	$14-$18,000
Nissan Leaf	215	7	Good	Very Poor	106/92	Very Poor	$35-$37,000
Nissan Sentra	221			Very Poor	30/39		$17-$20,000
Scion FR-S	227			Very Poor	22/30		$24-$25,000
Scion tC	229	8	Good	Very Poor	23/31	Very Good	$18-$22,000
Subaru BRZ	233			Very Poor	22/30		$25-$28,000
Subaru Impreza	235	4	Poor	Very Poor	25/34	Average	$17-$38,000
Suzuki Kizashi	239			Poor	23/30	Very Good	$19-$28,000
Toyota Corolla	244	4	Average	Very Poor	26/34	Very Poor	$16-$19,000
Toyota Matrix	247			Very Poor	25/32	Poor	$19-$22,000
Toyota Prius	248	7	Good	Very Poor	51/48	Very Poor	$23-$39,000
Toyota Prius C	249			Very Poor	53/46		$18-$23,000
Toyota Prius V	250			Very Poor	44/40		$26-$30,000
Volkswagen Golf	260			Good	24/31	Very Poor	$17-$26,000
Volkswagen Jetta	261	6	Average	Good	24/31	Poor	$15-$26,000
Volvo C70	266			Very Good	19/28	Very Good	$41-$41,000
Intermediate							
Acura TL	84	5	Very Poor	Poor	20/29	Good	$35-$45,000
Acura TSX	85			Poor	22/31	Good	$30-$39,000
Audi A5	88			Very Good	20/30	Good	$37-$57,000
BMW 5 Series	96	9	Average	Very Good	24/34	Very Poor	$47-$64,000
Buick Regal	104	7	Good	Average	25/36	Poor	$29-$34,000
Cadillac CTS	107	9	Very Good	Good	18/27	Average	$38-$63,000
Chevrolet Camaro	111	8	Very Good	Average	18/27	Average	$24-$59,000
Chevrolet Corvette	112			Average	14/21	Poor	$49-$111,000

Vehicle	Page #	Overall Rating	Combined Crash Test Rating	Warranty Rating	Fuel Economy	Complaint Rating	Price Range
Intermediate (cont.)							
Chevrolet Malibu	116	9	Good	Average	22/34		$22-$27,000
Chrysler 200	123	3	Very Poor	Good	21/30	Very Poor	$18-$32,000
Dodge Avenger	126	2	Very Poor	Average	21/30	Poor	$18-$25,000
Ford Fusion	143			Very Poor	22/34		$21-$32,000
Ford Mustang	144	2	Poor	Very Poor	19/31	Very Poor	$22-$59,000
Honda Accord	146	9	Good	Very Poor	27/36		$21-$33,000
Honda Accord Coupe	147			Very Poor	26/35		$24-$32,000
Hyundai Azera	157			Very Good	20/29	Very Poor	$32-$32,000
Hyundai Genesis	159			Very Good	18/28	Poor	$34-$46,000
Hyundai Sonata	161	9	Good	Very Good	24/35	Very Poor	$20-$27,000
Infiniti G	166			Average	19/27	Very Good	$32-$52,000
Infiniti M	168	6	Average	Average	18/26	Very Poor	$48-$63,000
Kia Optima	176	7	Good	Good	24/35	Poor	$21-$30,000
Lexus ES	183	8	Good	Average	21/31		$36-$38,000
Lexus GS	184			Average	19/28		$46-$58,000
Lexus IS	185	7	Average	Average	21/30	Good	$35-$46,000
Lincoln MKZ	188			Average	19/28		$34-$36,000
Mazda Mazda6	192	4	Very Poor	Very Poor	21/30		$20-$29,000
Mercedes-Benz E-Class	197			Poor	20/30	Very Good	$51-$92,000
Nissan Altima	209	7	Poor	Very Poor	27/38	Good	$21-$30,000
Nissan Maxima	216	4	Very Poor	Very Poor	19/26	Very Good	$32-$35,000
Subaru Legacy	236	3	Poor	Very Poor	24/32	Poor	$20-$28,000
Subaru Outback	237	2	Poor	Very Poor	24/30	Poor	$23-$32,000
Toyota Avalon	242			Very Poor	21/31	Very Poor	$33-$36,000
Toyota Camry	243	4	Very Poor	Very Poor	25/35	Good	$22-$30,000
Volkswagen CC	259			Good	22/31	Good	$30-$41,000
Volkswagen Passat	262	9	Very Good	Good	22/31	Good	$20-$33,000
Volvo S60	267	10	Very Good	Very Good	18/25	Average	$31-$43,000
Large							
Audi A6	89			Very Good	25/33	Average	$42-$56,000
Audi A7	90			Very Good	18/28		$60-$66,000
Audi Allroad	91	9	Good	Very Good	20/27		$39-$48,000
BMW 7 Series	97			Very Good	16/24	Average	$73-$140,000
Buick LaCrosse	103	8	Good	Average	25/36	Average	$31-$39,000
Cadillac XTS	109	8	Very Good	Good	17/28		$44-$60,000
Chevrolet Impala	115	6	Average	Average	18/29	Average	$25-$30,000
Chrysler 300	124	5	Average	Good	19/31	Average	$29-$47,000
Dodge Challenger	127	3	Good	Average	18/27	Poor	$25-$43,000

Vehicle	Page #	Overall Rating	Combined Crash Test Rating	Warranty Rating	Fuel Economy	Complaint Rating	Price Range
Large (cont.)							
Dodge Charger	128	7	Good	Average	18/27	Average	$25-$44,000
Ford Taurus	145	5	Good	Very Poor	19/29		$26-$39,000
Jaguar XF	170			Poor	18/28	Very Poor	$46-$83,000
Lincoln MKS	187	6	Good	Average	18/27	Average	$42-$49,000
Mercedes-Benz S-Class	201			Poor	15/25	Very Good	$92-$212,000
Volvo S80	268			Very Good	19/28	Good	$38-$42,000
Minivan							
Chrysler Town and Country	125	5	Average	Good	17/25	Very Poor	$29-$39,000
Dodge Grand Caravan	131	5	Average	Average	17/25	Poor	$19-$29,000
Honda Odyssey	153	7	Good	Very Poor	18/27	Poor	$28-$43,000
Mazda Mazda5	191			Very Poor	22/27	Very Good	$19-$24,000
Nissan Quest	219			Very Poor	19/25		$27-$41,000
Toyota Sienna	253	3	Average	Very Poor	18/25	Poor	$26-$41,000
Volkswagen Routan	263			Good	17/25	Very Poor	$27-$44,000
Small SUV							
Acura RDX	83			Poor	19/27		$34-$39,000
BMW X1	98			Very Good	18/27		$30-$38,000
Buick Encore	102			Average	25/33		$24-$29,000
Ford Escape	136	7	Average	Very Poor	22/31		$22-$32,000
Honda CR-V	150	7	Average	Very Poor	22/30	Good	$22-$30,000
Hyundai Tucson	162	7	Poor	Very Good	22/29	Average	$20-$26,000
Infiniti EX	164			Average	17/25	Average	$36-$40,000
Jeep Compass	171	1	Very Poor	Poor	21/27	Poor	$19-$26,000
Jeep Patriot	173	1	Very Poor	Poor	21/26	Very Poor	$15-$25,000
Jeep Wrangler	174			Poor	17/21	Very Poor	$22-$33,000
Kia Sportage	162	7	Average	Good	21/28	Average	$19-$28,000
Mazda CX-5	193	6	Good	Very Poor	25/31		$20-$28,000
Mitsubishi Outlander Sport	207	4	Poor	Very Good	24/31		$19-$23,000
Nissan Juke	214	5	Very Poor	Very Poor	27/32	Very Good	$19-$26,000
Subaru Forester	234	3	Poor	Very Poor	21/27	Good	$21-$29,000
Subaru XV Crosstrek	238			Very Poor	25/33		$21-$26,000
Toyota RAV4	251			Very Poor	21/27		$22-$28,000
Volkswagen Tiguan	264	4	Very Poor	Good	21/26	Poor	$22-$36,000
Mid-Size SUV							
Acura MDX	82	8	Average	Poor	16/21	Very Good	$43-$54,000
Audi Q5	92			Very Good	20/28	Very Good	$35-$53,000
BMW X3	99			Very Good	19/26	Average	$38-$43,000
BMW X5	100	6	Poor	Very Good	16/23	Good	$47-$88,000
Cadillac SRX	108	7	Very Good	Good	17/24	Average	$37-$50,000

Vehicle	Page #	Overall Rating	Combined Crash Test Rating	Warranty Rating	Fuel Economy	Complaint Rating	Price Range
Mid-Size SUV (cont.)							
Chevrolet Equinox	114	5	Poor	Average	22/32	Poor	$23-$32,000
Dodge Journey	132	1	Poor	Average	16/24	Very Poor	$18-$30,000
Ford Edge	135	4	Very Poor	Very Poor	19/27	Good	$27-$39,000
Ford Explorer	138	6	Very Good	Very Poor	17/23	Very Poor	$28-$40,000
GMC Terrain	114	4	Poor	Poor	22/32	Average	$26-$36,000
Honda Pilot	154	4	Poor	Very Poor	17/24	Good	$29-$41,000
Hyundai Santa Fe	160	9	Very Good	Very Good	21/29		$24-$29,000
Infiniti FX	165			Average	16/22	Very Good	$44-$60,000
Kia Sorento	178	3	Poor	Good	21/29	Very Poor	$23-$33,000
Land Rvr Range Rv r Evoque	181			Poor	18/28		$43-$52,000
Lexus RX	186	5	Poor	Average	18/24	Good	$39-$47,000
Lincoln MKX	135			Average	17/23	Good	$39-$41,000
Mazda CX-9	194			Very Poor	25/31	Very Good	$29-$35,000
Mercedes-Benz GLK-Class	199			Poor	19/24	Very Poor	$37-$39,000
Mercedes-Benz M-Class	200			Poor	18/23	Very Good	$47-$96,000
Mitsubishi Outlander	206	2	Very Poor	Very Good	23/28	Average	$22-$28,000
Nissan Murano	217	3	Very Poor	Very Poor	18/24	Good	$29-$39,000
Nissan Pathfinder	218	5	Average	Very Poor	19/25		$28-$43,000
Nissan Rogue	220	5	Average	Very Poor	22/27	Very Good	$22-$26,000
Nissan Xterra	224			Very Poor	15/20	Poor	$24-$30,000
Porsche Cayenne	225			Good	17/23	Poor	$48-$107,000
Toyota FJ Cruiser	245			Very Poor	17/20	Very Poor	$26-$28,000
Toyota Highlander	246	2	Poor	Very Poor	17/22	Average	$28-$46,000
Toyota Venza	256	3	Good	Very Poor	20/26	Average	$27-$38,000
Volkswagen Touareg	265			Good	17/23	Average	$43-$62,000
Volvo XC60	269	9	Very Good	Very Good	17/23	Poor	$34-$44,000
Volvo XC90	270			Very Good	16/22	Poor	$39-$44,000
Large SUV							
Audi Q7	93			Very Good	16/22	Average	$46-$66,000
Buick Enclave	101	7	Very Good	Average	17/24	Average	$38-$47,000
Cadillac Escalade	120	6	Very Good	Good	13/18	Very Good	$63-$86,000
Cadillac Escalade ESV	119	7	Very Good	Good	13/18	Very Good	$66-$85,000
Cadillac Escalade EXT	110			Good	13/18	Average	$63-$74,000
Chevrolet Suburban	119	7	Very Good	Average	15/21	Good	$42-$58,000
Chevrolet Tahoe	120	8	Very Good	Average	15/21	Good	$39-$56,000
Chevrolet Traverse	121	8	Very Good	Average	17/24	Very Good	$30-$42,000
Dodge Durango	130	5	Poor	Average	16/23	Good	$28-$42,000
Ford Expedition	137	4	Poor	Very Poor	13/18	Average	$36-$50,000
Ford Flex	141			Very Poor	18/25	Poor	$30-$43,000

Vehicle	Page #	Overall Rating	Combined Crash Test Rating	Warranty Rating	Fuel Economy	Complaint Rating	Price Range
Large SUV (cont.)							
GMC Acadia	121			Poor	17/24	Average	$34-$45,000
GMC Yukon	120	3	Very Good	Poor	15/21	Good	$40-$63,000
GMC Yukon XL	119	6	Very Good	Poor	15/21	Good	$44-$61,000
Infiniti JX	167	5	Average	Average	18/23		$40-$41,000
Infiniti QX	169			Average	14/20	Average	$58-$61,000
Jeep Grand Cherokee	172	5	Average	Poor	17/23	Good	$27-$59,000
Land Rover Range Rover	180			Poor	12/17		$80-$126,000
Lexus GX	241			Average	15/20	Good	$53-$58,000
Lincoln Navigator	137	5	Poor	Average	13/18	Very Good	$58-$61,000
Mercedes-Benz GL-Class	198			Poor	14/19	Good	$62-$86,000
Nissan Armada	211			Very Poor	12/18	Poor	$38-$53,000
Toyota 4Runner	241	4	Poor	Very Poor	17/21	Very Good	$31-$40,000
Toyota Sequoia	252			Very Poor	13/17	Good	$41-$62,000
Compact Pickup							
Nissan Frontier	213			Very Poor	14/19	Average	$18-$32,000
Toyota Tacoma	254	1	Very Poor	Very Poor	16/21	Average	$17-$28,000
Standard Pickup							
Chevrolet Avalanche	110			Average	14/20	Average	$35-$47,000
Chevrolet Silverado	117	7	Good	Average	15/21	Very Good	$22-$43,000
Ford F-150	139	5	Poor	Very Poor	14/19	Very Good	$23-$52,000
GMC Sierra	117	4	Good	Poor	15/21	Very Good	$23-$49,000
Honda Ridgeline	155			Very Poor	15/21	Good	$29-$37,000
Nissan Titan	222			Very Poor	12/17	Very Poor	$27-$40,000
Ram 1500	226	2	Poor	No Index	17/25	Average	$22-$47,000
Toyota Tundra	255	2	Average	Very Poor	14/19	Good	$25-$48,000

BEST BETS

T he following is our list of the highest rated vehicles in each size category. The ratings are based on expected performance in nine important categories–Combined Crash Rating, Safety Features, Rollover, Preventive Maintenance, Repair Costs, Warranty, Fuel Economy, Complaints, and Insurance Costs–with the heaviest emphasis placed on safety. (See box on previous page.)

CHEVROLET SONIC
SUBCOMPACT

Page 118

Combo Crash Tests 10	Warranty 6
Safety Features 9	Fuel Economy 8
Rollover 6	Complaints 2
PM 7	Insurance 8
Repair Costs 10	**OVERALL RATING . . 10**

AUDI A4
COMPACT

Page 87

Combo Crash Tests 8	Warranty 9
Safety Features 6	Fuel Economy 6
Rollover 9	Complaints 9
PM 5	Insurance 8
Repair Costs 4	**OVERALL RATING . . 10**

BMW 3 SERIES
COMPACT

Page 95

Combo Crash Tests 8	Warranty 9
Safety Features 8	Fuel Economy 6
Rollover 9	Complaints . . . . –
PM 10	Insurance 8
Repair Costs 3	**OVERALL RATING . . 10**

BUICK VERANO
COMPACT

Page 105

Combo Crash Tests 10	Warranty 5
Safety Features 10	Fuel Economy 6
Rollover 7	Complaints 8
PM . . . . –	Insurance 8
Repair Costs . . . . –	**OVERALL RATING . . 10**

CADILLAC ATS
COMPACT

Page 106

Combo Crash Tests 10	Warranty 8
Safety Features 10	Fuel Economy 6
Rollover 8	Complaints . . . . –
PM 3	Insurance 5
Repair Costs 3	**OVERALL RATING . . . 9**

CHEVROLET CRUZE

COMPACT

Combo Crash Tests	10	Warranty	6
Safety Features	10	Fuel Economy	7
Rollover	7	Complaints	4
PM	3	Insurance	1
Repair Costs	10	**OVERALL RATING**	**9**

Page 1113

CHEVROLET VOLT

COMPACT

Combo Crash Tests	6	Warranty	6
Safety Features	9	Fuel Economy	10
Rollover	9	Complaints	1
PM	5	Insurance	5
Repair Costs	10	**OVERALL RATING**	**9**

Page 122

DODGE DART

COMPACT

Combo Crash Tests	9	Warranty	5
Safety Features	7	Fuel Economy	7
Rollover	8	Complaints	–
PM	4	Insurance	–
Repair Costs	9	**OVERALL RATING**	**9**

Page 129

HYUNDAI ELANTRA

COMPACT

Combo Crash Tests	7	Warranty	10
Safety Features	2	Fuel Economy	9
Rollover	7	Complaints	7
PM	5	Insurance	1
Repair Costs	9	**OVERALL RATING**	**9**

Page 158

BMW 5 SERIES

INTERMEDIATE

Combo Crash Tests	6	Warranty	9
Safety Features	9	Fuel Economy	7
Rollover	9	Complaints	1
PM	10	Insurance	10
Repair Costs	1	**OVERALL RATING**	**9**

Page 96

CADILLAC CTS

INTERMEDIATE

Combo Crash Tests	9	Warranty	8
Safety Features	8	Fuel Economy	3
Rollover	8	Complaints	5
PM	3	Insurance	8
Repair Costs	3	**OVERALL RATING**	**9**

Page 107

CHEVROLET MALIBU

Page 116

Combo Crash Tests	8	Warranty	6
Safety Features	10	Fuel Economy	6
Rollover	7	Complaints	–
PM	3	Insurance	3
Repair Costs	8	**OVERALL RATING**	**9**

HONDA ACCORD

Page 146

Combo Crash Tests	8	Warranty	1
Safety Features	4	Fuel Economy	9
Rollover	9	Complaints	–
PM	5	Insurance	8
Repair Costs	8	**OVERALL RATING**	**9**

HYUNDAI SONATA

Page 161

Combo Crash Tests	8	Warranty	10
Safety Features	5	Fuel Economy	8
Rollover	9	Complaints	1
PM	6	Insurance	1
Repair Costs	9	**OVERALL RATING**	**9**

VOLKSWAGEN PASSAT

Page 262

Combo Crash Tests	9	Warranty	7
Safety Features	3	Fuel Economy	6
Rollover	8	Complaints	8
PM	8	Insurance	3
Repair Costs	6	**OVERALL RATING**	**9**

VOLVO S60

Page 267

Combo Crash Tests	10	Warranty	10
Safety Features	9	Fuel Economy	3
Rollover	8	Complaints	5
PM	6	Insurance	5
Repair Costs	5	**OVERALL RATING**	**10**

AUDI ALLROAD

Page 91

Combo Crash Tests	8	Warranty	9
Safety Features	8	Fuel Economy	4
Rollover	8	Complaints	–
PM	–	Insurance	–
Repair Costs	4	**OVERALL RATING**	**9**

BUICK LACROSSE

The CAR Book BEST BET

LARGE

Page 103

Combo Crash Tests	8	Warranty	5
Safety Features	8	Fuel Economy	8
Rollover	6	Complaints	5
PM	3	Insurance	8
Repair Costs	4	**OVERALL RATING**	**8**

CADILLAC XTS

The CAR Book BEST BET

LARG

Page 109

Combo Crash Tests	10	Warranty	8
Safety Features	10	Fuel Economy	3
Rollover	6	Complaints	–
PM	3	Insurance	–
Repair Costs	3	**OVERALL RATING**	**8**

HONDA ODYSSEY

The CAR Book BEST BET

MINIVAN

Page 153

Combo Crash Tests	7	Warranty	1
Safety Features	7	Fuel Economy	3
Rollover	6	Complaints	4
PM	5	Insurance	10
Repair Costs	9	**OVERALL RATING**	**7**

FORD ESCAPE

The CAR Book BEST BET

SMALL SUV

Page 136

Combo Crash Tests	6	Warranty	2
Safety Features	6	Fuel Economy	6
Rollover	2	Complaints	–
PM	7	Insurance	8
Repair Costs	10	**OVERALL RATING**	**7**

HONDA CR-V

The CAR Book BEST BET

SMALL SUV

Page 150

Combo Crash Tests	7	Warranty	1
Safety Features	4	Fuel Economy	6
Rollover	3	Complaints	8
PM	6	Insurance	8
Repair Costs	9	**OVERALL RATING**	**7**

KIA SPORTAGE

The CAR Book BEST BET

SMALL SUV

Page 162

Combo Crash Tests	6	Warranty	7
Safety Features	5	Fuel Economy	5
Rollover	4	Complaints	5
PM	5	Insurance	5
Repair Costs	8	**OVERALL RATING**	**7**

ACURA MDX

Page 82

MID-SIZE SUV

Combo Crash Tests	5	Warranty	4
Safety Features	8	Fuel Economy	1
Rollover	5	Complaints	10
PM	7	Insurance	10
Repair Costs	5	**OVERALL RATING...**	**8**

HYUNDAI SANTA FE

Page 160

MID-SIZE SUV

Combo Crash Tests	9	Warranty	10
Safety Features	7	Fuel Economy	5
Rollover	4	Complaints	–
PM	5	Insurance	8
Repair Costs	3	**OVERALL RATING...**	**9**

VOLVO XC60

Page 269

MID-SIZE SUV

Combo Crash Tests	10	Warranty	10
Safety Features	9	Fuel Economy	2
Rollover	3	Complaints	4
PM	6	Insurance	10
Repair Costs	4	**OVERALL RATING...**	**9**

CHEVROLET TAHOE

Page 120

LARGE SUV

Combo Crash Tests	9	Warranty	6
Safety Features	8	Fuel Economy	1
Rollover	1	Complaints	8
PM	3	Insurance	10
Repair Costs	5	**OVERALL RATING...**	**8**

CHEVROLET TRAVERSE

Page 121

LARGE SUV

Combo Crash Tests	9	Warranty	6
Safety Features	8	Fuel Economy	2
Rollover	3	Complaints	9
PM	3	Insurance	10
Repair Costs	4	**OVERALL RATING...**	**8**

CHEVROLET SILVERADO

Page 117

STANDARD PICKUP

Combo Crash Tests	8	Warranty	6
Safety Features	6	Fuel Economy	1
Rollover	2	Complaints	10
PM	3	Insurance	8
Repair Costs	6	**OVERALL RATING...**	**7**

CRASH TESTS

Safety is likely the most important factor that most of us consider when choosing a new car. In the past, evaluating safety was difficult. Now, thanks to the information in The Car Book, it's much easier to pick a safe vehicle. The bottom line: For the greatest protection, you'll want the maximum number of safety features (pages 78-79) and good crash test results (the following tables).

A key factor in occupant protection is how well the car protects you in a crash. This depends on its ability to absorb the force of the impact rather than transfer it to the occupant. In 2011, the government began a new crash test program with more sophisticated dummies, additional test measurements, and a small female dummy.

In the frontal test, the vehicle impacts a solid barrier at 35 mph. In the side test, a moving barrier is crashed into the side of the vehicle at 38.5 mph. A second side test, new in 2011, simulates hitting a tree or roadside pole by smashing a vertical pole into the driver side door at 20 mph. The only occupant in this side pole test is a small female dummy in the driver seat.

In all crash tests the dummies are securely belted. Therefore, these test results do not apply to unbelted occupants. The new dummies measure impact on a different scale from previous tests, and the new test measures neck injuries and chest deflection which were not included in the previous tests. In addition, these new test results cannot be compared with older results.

Because of the new test procedures not all 2013 vehicles have undergone the new tests. The good news is that by carrying forward new 2011 tests from cars that haven't changed, we can predict results for 111 2013 models. The bad news is that there are 79 models for which we don't have crash test results.

How the Cars are Rated: The combined crash test ratings are based on the relative performance of the vehicles tested to date using the new test. It is best to compare the results within the size class.

The first column provides The Car Book's Combined Crash Test Rating. The cars are rated from 10 Best to 1 Worst. The front is weighted 60%, the side 36%, and the pole test 4% with results compared among all new 2013 crash tests to date.

Next are the individual front and side tests. Again, relative to all other 2013 vehicles tested, we indicate if the vehicle was Very Good, Good, Average, Poor or Very Poor. For side tests, the cars are rated separately from the trucks. Because of their construction the dynamics of a side test are different in cars and trucks.

The next five columns indicate the likelihood of the occupant sustaining a life-threatening injury. The percent likelihood is listed for the driver and front passenger in the front test, the driver and rear passenger in the side test, and the driver in the side pole test. Lower percentages mean a lower likelihood of being seriously injured. This information is taken directly from the government's analysis of the crash test results.

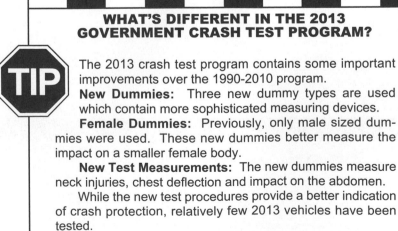

WHAT'S DIFFERENT IN THE 2013 GOVERNMENT CRASH TEST PROGRAM?

The 2013 crash test program contains some important improvements over the 1990-2010 program.

New Dummies: Three new dummy types are used which contain more sophisticated measuring devices.

Female Dummies: Previously, only male sized dummies were used. These new dummies better measure the impact on a smaller female body.

New Test Measurements: The new dummies measure neck injuries, chest deflection and impact on the abdomen.

While the new test procedures provide a better indication of crash protection, relatively few 2013 vehicles have been tested.

CRASH TESTS

Crash Test Performance (10=Best, 1=Worst)	Combined Car Book Crash Test Rating	Test Type	Car Book Crash Test Rating - Index (Lower numbers are better)	Likelihood of Life Threatening Injury				
				Front Fixed Barrier		Side Moving Barrier		Side Pole
				Front Driver	Front Pass.	Side Driver	Side Pass.	Pole Driver
Subcompact								
Chevrolet Sonic	10	Front	Very Good-165	8.5%	8.8%			
		Side	Good-113			7.0%	4.6%	7.0%
Fiat 500	4	Front	Poor-256	11.4%	16.0%			
		Side	Average-148			5.3%	8.0%	15.8%
Ford Fiesta[1]	7	Front	Good-199	8.2%	12.8%			
		Side	Good-121			10.1%	1.8%	11.8%
Honda Fit	4	Front	Average-202	9.6%	11.7%			
		Side	Very Poor-240			15.5%	8.1%	24.1%
Hyundai Accent	4	Front	Average-209	9.2%	12.9%			
		Side	Very Poor-234			8.5%	17.0%	4.3%
Kia Rio	4	Front	Poor-231	10.9%	13.8%			
		Side	Poor-178			13.6%	7.0%	3.4%
Kia Soul	6	Front	Average-218	12.7%	10.5%			
		Side	Good-126			8.6%	5.3%	3.9%
Nissan Versa	1	Front	Very Poor-294	12.2%	19.6%			
		Side	Very Poor-256			16.4%	13.5%	4.7%
Scion iQ	1	Front	Very Poor-258	12.1%	15.6%			
		Side	Very Poor-294			14.8%	18.7%	6.7%
Suzuki SX4	2	Front	Poor-251	11.9%	15.1%			
		Side	Very Poor-331			9.5%	25.0%	16.0%
Toyota Yaris	4	Front	Average-216	9.8%	13.1%			
		Side	Poor-159			7.3%	8.7%	10.1%
Volkswagen Beetle	6	Front	Average-216	9.6%	13.2%			
		Side	Good-125			7.3%	6.0%	5.3%
Compact								
Acura ILX	7	Front	Good-193	9.3%	11.0%			
		Side	Average-139			8.0%	5.2%	13.9%
Audi A4	8	Front	Very Good-178	9.5%	9.1%			
		Side	Average-152			12.8%	4.8%	3.8%

[1] Additional Injury Potential: Due to the intrusion of the left rear door during the side impact test, the interior door panel struck the torso of the driver dummy, causing impact on lower spine acceleration to exceed the government limit, resulting in a higher likelihood of thoracic injury.

CRASH TESTS

Crash Test Performance (10=Best, 1=Worst)	Combined Car Book Crash Test Rating	Test Type	Car Book Crash Test Rating - Index (Lower numbers are better)	Likelihood of Life Threatening Injury				
				Front Fixed Barrier		Side Moving Barrier		Side Pole
				Front Driver	Front Pass.	Side Driver	Side Pass.	Pole Driver
BMW 3 Series	8	Front	Good-195	11.6%	8.9%			
		Side	Very Good-109			8.0%	4.3%	2.3%
Buick Verano	10	Front	Very Good-155	7.5%	8.7%			
		Side	Very Good-75			6.1%	1.9%	4.3%
Cadillac ATS	10	Front	Very Good-162	8.2%	8.7%			
		Side	Very Good-111			4.7%	6.6%	5.2%
Chevrolet Cruze	10	Front	Very Good-161	8.0%	8.8%			
		Side	Good-114			7.1%	4.8%	6.6%
Chevrolet Volt	6	Front	Average-205	8.8%	12.9%			
		Side	Average-141			7.9%	7.9%	2.0%
Dodge Dart	9	Front	Good-188	9.2%	10.6%			
		Side	Very Good-78			4.1%	4.1%	2.4%
Ford Focus	8	Front	Good-192	8.1%	12.1%			
		Side	Good-116			10.3%	3.0%	3.4%
Hyundai Elantra	7	Front	Good-199	9.7%	11.3%			
		Side	Average-146			12.0%	3.9%	7.8%
Kia Forte[2]	2	Front	Poor-246	9.0%	17.2%			
		Side	Very Poor-235			17.1%	6.2%	23.7%
Mazda Mazda3	5	Front	Good-186	7.2%	12.3%			
		Side	Very Poor-311			13.2%	19.9%	16.7%
Mercedes-Benz C-Class	2	Front	Very Poor-302	12.7%	20.1%			
		Side	Poor-162			3.1%	12.2%	10.3%
Mitsubishi Lancer	4	Front	Average-215	9.4%	13.4%			
		Side	Poor-199			4.0%	16.3%	5.5%
Nissan Leaf	7	Front	Average-202	10.4%	10.9%			
		Side	Very Good-109			6.7%	3.8%	10.2%
Scion tC	8	Front	Good-201	9.1%	12.1%			
		Side	Very Good-89			2.7%	6.1%	4.0%
Subaru Impreza	3	Front	Poor-229	9.3%	15.0%			
		Side	Very Poor-259			8.4%	18.3%	12.8%

[2]Additional Injury Potential: Due to the intrusion of the left rear door during the side impact test, the interior door panel struck the torso of the driver dummy, causing impact on lower spine acceleration to exceed the government limit, resulting in a higher likelihood of thoracic injury. Although not included in the rating, the rear passenger dummy's thoracic rib deflection reading was elevated.

CRASH TESTS

| Crash Test Performance
(10=Best, 1=Worst) | Combined Car Book Crash Test Rating | Test Type | Car Book Crash Test Rating - Index (Lower numbers are better) | Likelihood of Life Threatening Injury | | | | |
| | | | | Front Fixed Barrier | | Side Moving Barrier | | Side Pole |
				Front Driver	Front Pass.	Side Driver	Side Pass.	Pole Driver
Toyota Corolla	5	Front	Average-210	8.8%	13.4%			
		Side	Poor-175			6.0%	9.9%	18.2%
Toyota Prius	7	Front	Good-191	9.1%	11.0%			
		Side	Average-137			5.6%	8.2%	7.2%
Volkswagen Jetta	5	Front	Good-201	10.1%	11.1%			
		Side	Poor-181			10.6%	9.6%	4.7%
Intermediate								
Acura TL	2	Front	Poor-258	12.0%	15.7%			
		Side	Poor-232			16.0%	11.3%	3.4%
BMW 5 Series	6	Front	Poor-233	13.1%	11.7%			
		Side	Very Good-85			8.4%	0.8%	5.5%
Buick Regal	8	Front	Good-199	9.9%	11.1%			
		Side	Good-115			4.0%	7.8%	4.2%
Cadillac CTS	9	Front	Very Good-170	8.9%	8.8%			
		Side	Good-130			5.4%	7.6%	7.6%
Chevrolet Camaro	10	Front	Very Good-171	9.7%	8.2%			
		Side	Very Good-67			5.7%	1.5%	3.2%
Chevrolet Malibu	8	Front	Very Good-177	8.5%	10.1%			
		Side	Average-141			5.8%	8.2%	9.4%
Chrysler 200	2	Front	Poor-245	10.5%	15.6%			
		Side	Very Poor-281			8.9%	10.3%	63.7%
Dodge Avenger	2	Front	Poor-239	9.9%	15.5%			
		Side	Very Poor-245			16.6%	8.8%	20.1%
Ford Mustang	4	Front	Average-211	12.4%	9.8%			
		Side	Very Poor-260			7.7%	18.6%	14.7%
Honda Accord	8	Front	Average-201	11.0%	10.2%			
		Side	Very Good-60			3.4%	2.9%	2.6%
Hyundai Sonata	8	Front	Good-197	8.9%	11.9%			
		Side	Very Good-103			7.6%	2.6%	9.2%

CRASH TESTS

Crash Test Performance (10=Best, 1=Worst)	Combined Car Book Crash Test Rating	Test Type	Car Book Crash Test Rating - Index (Lower numbers are better)	Likelihood of Life Threatening Injury				
				Front Fixed Barrier		Side Moving Barrier		Side Pole
				Front Driver	Front Pass.	Side Driver	Side Pass.	Pole Driver
Infiniti M	6	Front	Poor-227	9.8%	14.3%			
		Side	Very Good-107			8.4%	3.9%	1.8%
Kia Optima	7	Front	Very Good-174	8.6%	9.6%			
		Side	Poor-167			16.8%	2.0%	7.9%
Lexus ES	8	Front	Good-187	9.7%	9.9%			
		Side	Good-134			11.7%	2.9%	6.9%
Lexus IS	5	Front	Average-221	12.4%	11.2%			
		Side	Average-155			11.1%	4.9%	11.2%
Mazda Mazda6	2	Front	Very Poor-286	12.0%	18.9%			
		Side	Poor-219			9.7%	11.9%	17.6%
Nissan Altima	3	Front	Poor-234	10.6%	14.3%			
		Side	Poor-181			12.7%	8.0%	3.8%
Nissan Maxima	2	Front	Very Poor-298	11.2%	21.0%			
		Side	Poor-168			15.6%	4.0%	4.3%
Subaru Legacy	3	Front	Poor-227	12.2%	12.0%			
		Side	Poor-222			8.3%	13.7%	15.8%
Subaru Outback	3	Front	Poor-227	12.2%	12.0%			
		Side	Poor-222			8.3%	13.7%	15.8%
Toyota Camry	1	Front	Very Poor-305	13.2%	19.9%			
		Side	Very Poor-355			9.1%	27.2%	20.7%
Volkswagen Passat	9	Front	Very Good-154	7.7%	8.4%			
		Side	Good-137			13.1%	2.7%	3.9%
Volvo S60	10	Front	Very Good-157	8.3%	8.1%			
		Side	Good-120			9.9%	3.7%	3.2%
Large								
Audi Allroad	8	Front	Very Good-178	9.5%	9.1%			
		Side	Average-152			12.8%	4.8%	3.8%
Buick LaCrosse	8	Front	Very Good-169	8.0%	9.7%			
		Side	Average-158			5.0%	10.4%	10.3%
Cadillac XTS	10	Front	Very Good-160	7.6%	9.1%			
		Side	Very Good-88			4.2%	4.3%	6.7%

CRASH TESTS

Crash Test Performance (10=Best, 1=Worst)	Combined Car Book Crash Test Rating	Test Type	Car Book Crash Test Rating - Index (Lower numbers are better)	Likelihood of Life Threatening Injury				
				Front Fixed Barrier		Side Moving Barrier		Side Pole
				Front Driver	Front Pass.	Side Driver	Side Pass.	Pole Driver
Chevrolet Impala	5	Front	Good-194	8.4%	12.0%			
		Side	Poor-230			22.8%	4.7%	5.0%
Chrysler 300	5	Front	Average-207	11.2%	10.7%			
		Side	Average-152			7.4%	8.8%	5.5%
Dodge Challenger	8	Front	Very Good-172	9.1%	8.9%			
		Side	Average-154			11.9%	0.7%	26.3%
Dodge Charger	8	Front	Good-190	9.7%	10.3%			
		Side	Good-127			13.4%	0.7%	7.0%
Ford Taurus	8	Front	Very Good-164	8.4%	8.7%			
		Side	Average-154			8.3%	8.3%	5.8%
Lincoln MKS	8	Front	Very Good-164	8.4%	8.7%			
		Side	Average-154			8.3%	8.3%	5.8%
Minivan								
Chrysler Town and Country	5	Front	Average-207	11.2%	10.7%			
		Side	Poor-152			7.4%	8.8%	5.5%
Dodge Grand Caravan	5	Front	Average-207	11.2%	10.7%			
		Side	Poor-152			7.4%	8.8%	5.5%
Honda Odyssey	7	Front	Very Good-176	8.6%	9.9%			
		Side	Poor-96			6.0%	3.5%	7.6%
Toyota Sienna	5	Front	Poor-234	8.4%	16.4%			
		Side	Average-80			4.5%	2.2%	11.5%
Small SUV								
Ford Escape	6	Front	Poor-230	10.9%	13.5%			
		Side	Very Good-60			2.0%	3.5%	5.0%
Honda CR-V	7	Front	Good-189	10.3%	9.5%			
		Side	Average-84			4.1%	3.9%	7.5%
Hyundai Tucson	4	Front	Poor-231	11.5%	13.2%			
		Side	Poor-104			8.5%	2.3%	7.5%
Jeep Compass	1	Front	Very Poor-314	17.4%	16.9%			
		Side	Very Poor-267			5.8%	21.0%	13.0%

CRASH TESTS

Crash Test Performance (10=Best, 1=Worst)	Combined Car Book Crash Test Rating	Test Type	Car Book Crash Test Rating - Index (Lower numbers are better)	Likelihood of Life Threatening Injury				
				Front Fixed Barrier		Side Moving Barrier		Side Pole
				Front Driver	Front Pass.	Side Driver	Side Pass.	Pole Driver
Jeep Patriot	1	Front	Very Poor-295	18.6%	13.4%			
		Side	Poor-127			2.7%	7.4%	18.2%
Kia Sportage	6	Front	Good-185	8.9%	10.5%			
		Side	Poor-101			7.8%	3.5%	3.2%
Mazda CX-5	7	Front	Average-215	7.8%	14.8%			
		Side	Good-64			2.2%	3.4%	7.0%
Mitsubishi Outlander Sport	4	Front	Average-203	10.0%	11.3%			
		Side	Very Poor-200			6.6%	13.7%	9.9%
Nissan Juke	1	Front	Very Poor-289	12.5%	18.8%			
		Side	Very Poor-186			11.8%	9.2%	4.8%
Subaru Forester	4	Front	Good-200	11.6%	9.5%			
		Side	Very Poor-236			7.1%	12.3%	36.2%
Volkswagen Tiguan	2	Front	Very Poor-339	15.9%	21.4%			
		Side	Average-86			3.3%	4.2%	10.0%
Mid-Size SUV								
Acura MDX	5	Front	Poor-227	9.3%	14.8%			
		Side	Average-84			4.4%	3.4%	7.9%
BMW X5	4	Front	Very Poor-307	18.2%	15.3%			
		Side	Very Good-56			2.3%	2.0%	9.4%
Cadillac SRX	9	Front	Very Good-184	8.2%	11.1%			
		Side	Good-67			2.6%	1.7%	14.9%
Chevrolet Equinox	4	Front	Average-216	9.5%	13.4%			
		Side	Poor-120			11.7%	2.0%	4.5%
Dodge Journey	3	Front	Average-222	9.6%	14.0%			
		Side	Very Poor-168			3.7%	11.9%	13.5%
Ford Edge	2	Front	Very Poor-313	16.1%	18.1%			
		Side	Average-81			5.3%	2.3%	8.3%
Ford Explorer	9	Front	Very Good-183	10.4%	8.8%			
		Side	Good-63			4.2%	1.6%	7.1%
GMC Terrain	4	Front	Average-216	9.5%	13.4%			
		Side	Poor-120			11.7%	2.0%	4.5%

CRASH TESTS

Crash Test Performance (10=Best, 1=Worst)	Combined Car Book Crash Test Rating	Test Type	Car Book Crash Test Rating - Index (Lower numbers are better)	Likelihood of Life Threatening Injury				
				Front Fixed Barrier		Side Moving Barrier		Side Pole
				Front Driver	Front Pass.	Side Driver	Side Pass.	Pole Driver
Honda Pilot	3	Front	Average-222	9.4%	14.1%			
		Side	Very Poor-185			6.4%	12.3%	9.9%
Hyundai Santa Fe	9	Front	Very Good-184	9.2%	10.1%			
		Side	Good-71			3.6%	3.2%	6.3%
Kia Sorento	4	Front	Average-221	9.4%	14.0%			
		Side	Poor-136			5.0%	8.8%	6.6%
Lexus RX	3	Front	Poor-234	11.5%	13.4%			
		Side	Poor-148			3.2%	10.8%	9.9%
Mitsubishi Outlander	1	Front	Very Poor-268	12.8%	16.1%			
		Side	Very Poor-200			6.6%	13.7%	9.9%
Nissan Murano	1	Front	Very Poor-270	13.3%	15.8%			
		Side	Very Poor-165			4.4%	11.5%	10.7%
Nissan Pathfinder	5	Front	Poor-233	9.6%	15.2%			
		Side	Good-69			4.5%	2.8%	3.1%
Nissan Rogue	5	Front	Poor-238	10.3%	15.1%			
		Side	Good-65			3.8%	3.0%	2.9%
Toyota Highlander	3	Front	Very Poor-260	14.9%	13.1%			
		Side	Average-77			3.0%	4.0%	7.2%
Toyota Venza	7	Front	Good-196	9.4%	11.2%			
		Side	Good-65			3.9%	1.7%	9.0%
Volvo XC60	10	Front	Very Good-165	8.2%	9.0%			
		Side	Very Good-60			4.0%	2.1%	4.0%
Large SUV								
Buick Enclave	9	Front	Good-193	9.3%	11.0%			
		Side	Very Good-49			2.1%	2.2%	5.2%
Cadillac Escalade	9	Front	Good-185	9.3%	10.1%			
		Side	Very Good-53			4.7%	0.3%	\6.5%
Cadillac Escalade ESV	10	Front	Very Good-181	9.0%	9.9%			
		Side	Very Good-33			2.2%	0.3%	6.3%

CRASH TESTS

Crash Test Performance (10=Best, 1=Worst)	Combined Car Book Crash Test Rating	Test Type	Car Book Crash Test Rating - Index (Lower numbers are better)	Likelihood of Life Threatening Injury				
				Front Fixed Barrier		Side Moving Barrier		Side Pole
				Front Driver	Front Pass.	Side Driver	Side Pass.	Pole Driver
Chevrolet Suburban	10	Front	Very Good-181	9.0%	9.9%			
		Side	Very Good-33			2.2%	0.3%	6.3%
Chevrolet Tahoe	9	Front	Good-185	9.3%	10.1%			
		Side	Very Good-53			4.7%	0.3%	6.5%
Chevrolet Traverse	9	Front	Good-193	9.3%	11.0%			
		Side	Very Good-49			2.1%	2.2%	5.2%
Dodge Durango	4	Front	Very Poor-275	11.7%	17.9%			
		Side	Good-63			6.4%	0.6%	2.9%
Ford Expedition	4	Front	Poor-248	15.6%	10.9%			
		Side	Average-74			2.7%	1.2%	20.7%
GMC Yukon	9	Front	Good-185	9.3%	10.1%			
		Side	Very Good-53			4.7%	0.3%	6.5%
GMC Yukon XL	10	Front	Very Good-181	9.0%	9.9%			
		Side	Very Good-33			2.2%	0.3%	6.3%
Infiniti JX	5	Front	Poor-233	9.6%	15.2%			
		Side	Good-69			4.5%	2.8%	3.1%
Jeep Grand Cherokee	6	Front	Good-196	9.9%	10.8%			
		Side	Average-94			8.4%	2.3%	2.4%
Lincoln Navigator	4	Front	Poor-248	15.6%	10.9%			
		Side	Average-74			2.7%	1.2%	20.7%
Toyota 4Runner	4	Front	Poor-255	11.9%	15.5%			
		Side	Average-79			6.9%	0.5%	9.7%
Compact Pickup								
Toyota Tacoma	2	Front	Very Poor-283	14.9%	15.8%			
		Side	Poor-134			11.5%	1.9%	12.9%
		Side	Very Good-28			1.6%	0.6%	4.7%

CRASH TESTS

Crash Test Performance (10=Best, 1=Worst)	Combined Car Book Crash Test Rating	Test Type	Car Book Crash Test Rating - Index (Lower numbers are better)	Front Fixed Barrier		Side Moving Barrier		Side Pole
				Front Driver	Front Pass.	Side Driver	Side Pass.	Pole Driver
Standard Pickup								
Chev. Silverado/GMC Sierra Crew Cab[3]*	8	Front	Average-213	10.7%	11.9%			
		Side	Very Good-52			4.5%	0.4%	6.3%
Regular Cab		Front	Poor-228	9.9%	14.3%			
		Side				2.8%		8.6%
Extended Cab	6	Front	Poor-228	9.9%	14.3%			
		Side	Very Good-46			2.8%	0.7%	8.6%
Ford F-150 Super Cab*	4	Front	Very Poor-277	12.4%	17.4%			
		Side	Very Good-58			2.2%	1.4%	13.9%
Regular Cab		Front	Very Poor-277	12.4%	17.4%			
		Side				2.2%		13.9%
Super Crew	4	Front	Very Poor- 309	14.3%	19.3%			
		Side	Very Good-37			1.4%	0.7%	9.7%
Ram 1500 Crew Cab[4]*	3	Front	Very Poor-228	12.6%	11.6%			
		Side	Poor-183			6.2%	0.4%	65.1%
Regular Cab		Front	Very Poor-389	15.5%	27.7%			
		Side				7.6%		54.5%
Quad Cab	4	Front	Average-214	10.7%	11.9%			
		Side	Very Poor-173			7.6%	0.3%	54.5%
Toyota Tundra Crew Cab*	5	Front	Very Poor-293	13.8%	18.0%			
		Side	Very Good-28			1.6%	0.6%	4.7%
Regular Cab		Front	Very Poor- 270	18.3%	1.6%			
		Side				1.6%		9.5%
Extended Cab	5	Front	Very Poor-270	10.6%	18.3%			
		Side	Very Good-40			1.6%	0.9%	9.5%

[3]Chevrolet Silverado/GMC Sierra crash test ratings are for the 1500 trim only.

[4]Additional Injury Potential: Due to the intrusion of the driver door during the side impact pole test, the interior door panel struck the torso of the driver dummy, causing impact on lower spine acceleration to exceed the government limit, resulting in a higher likelihood of thoracic injury. Although not included in the rating, the driver dummy's abdomen rib deflection readings were elevated.

*Results used to calculate vehicle's overall rating on the Car Pages, Buying Guide and Best Bets.

AUTOMATIC CRASH PROTECTION

The concept of automatic safety protection is not new. Automatic fire sprinklers in public buildings, oxygen masks in airplanes, purification of drinking water, and pasteurization of milk are all commonly accepted forms of automatic safety protection. Airbags provide automatic crash protection in cars.

Automatic crash protection protects people from what is called the "second collision," when the occupant collides with the interior of the vehicle. Because the "second collision" occurs within milliseconds, providing automatic rather than manual protection dramatically improves the chances of escaping injury.

Automatic crash protection comes in two basic forms, airbags and automatic control of safety features.

Since airbags were introduced over 30 years ago, they have been so successful in saving lives that car makers now include a variety of types which deploy from 4 to 8 different points.

The automatic control of safety features was first introduced with anti-lock brakes. Today, Electronic Stability Control (ESC) and other automatic functions are improving the safety of new cars.

Electronic Stability Control (ESC) takes advantage of anti-lock brake technology and helps minimize the loss of control. Each car maker will have its own name for this feature, but they all work in a similar fashion.

For ESC, anti-lock brakes work by using speed sensors on each wheel to determine if one or more of the wheels is locking up or skidding. ESC then uses these speed sensors and a unit that determines the steering angle to monitor what's happening with the vehicle. A special control device measures the steering and rotation of the tires in order to detect when a vehicle is about to go in a direction different from the one indicated by the steering wheel–or out of control! This will typically occur during a hard turn or on slippery surfaces. The control unit will sense whether the car is over-steering (turning sharper than you intended resulting in the back wheels slipping sideways) or under-steering (continuing to move forward despite your intended turn). When either of these events occur, the control unit will automatically apply the brakes to the appropriate wheels to correct the situation and, in some cases, automatically slow down the engine.

As amazing as this device is, it will not keep the vehicle under control in severely out of control situations. Nevertheless, according to the IIHS, ESC can reduce the chance of a single vehicle crash by over 50%. Its benefit is that it will prevent more typical losses of control from escalating into a crash. It is an extremely important and recommended safety feature.

TELEMATICS

Telematic systems are subscription-based services ($200-$300 per year) that use a combination of cellular technology and global positioning systems to provide a variety of safety and convenience features. The main safety feature is automatic crash notification (ACN) which connects the vehicle's occupants to a private call center that directs emergency medical teams to the car. This system can be activated by pressing a button on the dash or rear view mirror or it is automatically activated if the airbag deploys. Once the system is activated, the call center receives the exact location of your vehicle and notifies the local emergency response team. This can potentially reduce the time it takes for an emergency team to reach your vehicle. Other safety features can include roadside assistance, remote door unlocking, stolen vehicle tracking, and driving directions.

Caution! Some manufacturers are adding cell phone capability to the ACN system which increases the risk of a crash 4-fold when talking on the ACN cell phone. This is about the same effect as drinking and driving. Don't drink and drive or telephone and drive!

CHILD SAFETY

Seat Belts for Kids: How long should children use car seats? For school-age children, a car seat is twice as effective in preventing injury as an adult lap and shoulder harness—use a booster as long as possible. Most children can start using seat belts at 4'9" and when tall enough for the shoulder belt to cross the chest, not the neck. The lap section of the belt should be snug and as low on the hips as possible. If the shoulder belt does cross the face or neck, use a booster seat.

Never:

☒ Use the same belt on two children.

☒ Move a shoulder belt behind a child's back or under an arm.

☒ Buckle in a pet or any large toys with the child.

☒ Recline a seat with a belted child.

☒ Use a twisted seat belt. The belt must be straight and flat.

☒ Use pillows or cushions to boost your child.

☒ Place a belt around you with a child in your lap. In an accident or sudden stop, your child would absorb most of the crash force.

Incorrect Installation: Surveys show up to 85 percent of parents do not install their child seats properly. Incorrect installation of a child safety seat can deny the child lifesaving protection and may even contribute to further injuring the child. Read the installation instructions carefully. If you have any questions about the correct installation in your particular car, contact the National Highway Traffic Safety Administration's website at www.nhtsa.gov. They can direct you to the nearest child seat inspection station that will check to see if you have installed your child seat correctly and instruct you on the proper way to install the seat if you have any questions. There is no charge for this service.

Following are some common mistakes parents make when installing a child safety seat.

☒ Infant is in safety seat facing forward, rather than to the rear.

☒ Child safety seat in front with an airbag.

☒ Child is not secured by safety seat harness and is sitting loose in safety seat.

☒ Booster seat used without a shield or a shoulder belt.

☒ Safety belt is fastened to or around wrong part of safety seat.

☒ Tether strap is not used, missing, or at wrong angle of attachment, when required.

☒ Use of incompatible safety belts.

☒ Safety belt is not used to secure safety seat in vehicle. The safety seat is loose on vehicle seat.

☒ Harness strap adjustment slides are not securely locked, permitting straps to release in a crash.

Warning: After an accident, rescue experts suggest that the entire seat be removed from the car, rather than unbuckling the child first.

CHILD SAFETY SEAT RECALLS

Manufacturers are required to put address cards in child seat packages. Mail the registration card as soon as you open the box! This is the only way you will receive notification of a seat recall. Keep a copy of the manufacturer's address and contact the manufacturer if you move. To find out if the seat you are using has ever been recalled go to http://www-odi.nhtsa.dot.gov/cars/problems/recalls/childseat.cfm. You can also contact the Auto Safety Hotline at 800-424-9393, (D.C. call 202-366-0123.)

ROLLOVER

The risk of rollover is a significant safety issue, especially with sport utility vehicles. Because of their relatively high center of gravity, they don't hug the road like smaller, lower automobiles and trucks. As a result, they are more likely to turn over on sharp turns or corners. Not only does a rollover increase the likelihood of injuries, but it also increases the risk of the occupant being thrown from the vehicle. In fact, the danger of rollover with sport utilities is so severe that manufacturers are now required to place a sticker where it can be seen by the driver every time the vehicle is used. Each year, approximately 10,000 people die in rollover-related accidents.

To understand the concept behind these vehicles' propensity to roll over, consider this: place a section of 2x4 lumber on its 2-inch side. It is easily tipped over by a force pushing against the side. But if you place it on its 4-inch side, the same force will cause it to slide rather than tip over. Similarly, in a moving vehicle, the forces generated by a turn can cause a narrow, tall vehicle to roll over. This is why SUVs are more susceptible to rolling over.

This year in the safety checklist we include a feature called roll-sensing side airbags. Roll-sensing side airbags are a special side airbag system which keeps the side airbags inflated longer in the event of a rollover. This feature is found in many SUVs and can reduce the likelihood of injury when a vehicle flips. See the car pages (81-270) for which 2013 models have this feature.

Congress required the U.S. Department of Transportation to develop a dynamic (moving) rating system to accompany the static (stationary) rating system. To date, this complex test has resulted in a simple "tip" or "no-tip" rating. Consumers are never told the speed of the tip and certain vehicles are not tested, just listed as "no tip."

Following are rollover ratings for many 2013 vehicles. We have been publishing these ratings for a number of years and recently, the National Highway Traffic Safety Administration adopted this rating system.

The rollover rating is based on the Static Stability Factor (SSF) and consists of a formula that uses the track width of the vehicle (tire to tire) and height to determine which vehicles are more or less likely to roll over when compared to each other. You can't use this information to exactly predict rollovers. However, all things being equal, if two vehicles are in the same situation where a rollover could occur, the one with a high SSF is less likely to roll over than one with a lower SSF. Because this formula doesn't consider such things as driver behavior and the weight of the vehicle, among other factors, some experts do not believe it tells the whole story. We agree, and urged the government to provide an even better rollover rating system.

In the meantime, knowing how the vehicles rate using the SSF can be a key consideration in your evaluation of the vehicle.

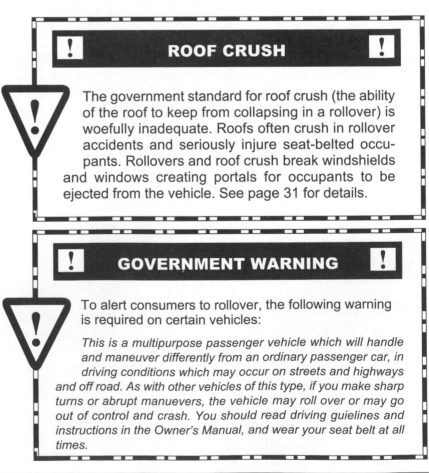

ROOF CRUSH

The government standard for roof crush (the ability of the roof to keep from collapsing in a rollover) is woefully inadequate. Roofs often crush in rollover accidents and seriously injure seat-belted occupants. Rollovers and roof crush break windshields and windows creating portals for occupants to be ejected from the vehicle. See page 31 for details.

GOVERNMENT WARNING

To alert consumers to rollover, the following warning is required on certain vehicles:

This is a multipurpose passenger vehicle which will handle and maneuver differently from an ordinary passenger car, in driving conditions which may occur on streets and highways and off road. As with other vehicles of this type, if you make sharp turns or abrupt manuevers, the vehicle may roll over or may go out of control and crash. You should read driving guielines and instructions in the Owner's Manual, and wear your seat belt at all times.

ROOF CRUSH

Since 1970, the auto industry has fought efforts by the National Highway Traffic Safety Administration to issue a dynamic roof crush standard to protect occupants in rollover crashes. From 1970 to 2007, the number of deaths to occupants in rollover crashes climbed from 1,400 to over 10,000 each year while annual occupant fatalities declined from 43,200 to 28,900. NHTSA has stuck with the outdated, static roof crush standard issued in 1971 even though it was to have been phased out by 1977 for a dynamic standard. On the other hand, NHTSA has issued effective dynamic front and side crash test standards that have significantly reduced death and serious injury.

The current standard calls for roofs to withstand 1.5 times the weight of the vehicle, applied to one side of the roof, for vehicles up to 6,000 pounds. Vehicles weighing more need not meet any standard. A new standard will be phased in for 2013 to 2017 models which will double the roof strength requirement for vehicles weighing up to 6,000 pounds. Both the driver and passenger sides of the roof will have to withstand a force equal to three times the weight of the vehicle. While an improvement, the new standard falls short of requiring a dynamic crash test that better replicates what happens in real world crashes.

Today, some vehicles have strong roofs but all too many have weak roofs. In a rollover crash, the first side of a vehicle that hits the ground generally does not crush but the second, or trailing side, that hits the ground often does crush. This failure will either break the windows and allow the occupants to eject or crush the occupants that stay in the vehicle. To identify which vehicles today have strong roofs, the Center for Auto Safety (CAS) had the Center for Injury Research (CfIR) conduct dynamic rollover roof crush tests using the Jordan Rollover System (JRS).

The table below shows the results of the CAS testing. The cumulative crush is how much the roof will crush inward after two full rolls. More than 5 inches of roof crush is unacceptable because an occupant's head is likely to be hit. The Strength to Weight Ratio (SWR) is how much weight the roof on one side will support before crushing inward 5 inches when tested in a static fashion as the government does.

The dynamic rollover test shows that good roof design can result in a vehicle with a lower static SWR outperforming a vehicle with a higher static SWR in limiting roof intrusion in a rollover, demonstrating the problem with the static government test. CAS has developed a comparative rating for the roof strength that ranges from Very Good to Very Poor.

Dynamic tests, such as the JRS, show how vehicle geometry effects safety. Vehicles with the very square roofs such as the Ridgeline are more vulnerable to roof crush. A vehicle with a more rounded roof, such as the XC90, will roll more like a barrel with less force on the corners of the roof.

The design of the roof in unison with the body of the vehicle is critical to its ability to protect occupants. If any of the critical roof structural elements buckles the roof will collapse and injure belted occupants who are seated underneath.

Good design will also keep windows in place to prevent occupants from being ejected in rollovers. Only a dynamic test can demonstrate whether seat belts, pre-tensioners and side curtains function together to protect occupants from ejection and injury in rollovers.

Center for Auto Safety Roof Crush Test Results

Vehicle*	Cumulative Crush (in.)	Dynamic SWR	Static SWR	Rating
Volvo XC90 2005-09	1.8	5.2	4.6	Very Good
VW Tiguan 2009-11	2.4	4.9	4.4	Very Good
VW Jetta 2007-09	3.4	4.4	5.1	Good
Honda CR-V 2007-10	3.6	4.3	2.6	Good
Toyota Camry Hybrid 2007-10	4.3	4.2	3.9	Good
Toyota Prius 2010	3.8	4.2	4.2	Good
Toyota Camry 2007-09	4.3	4	4.3	Good
Nissan Versa 2009-10	4.4	4	3.7	Good
Subaru Forester 2003-08	4.6	3.9	4.3	Moderate
Hyundai Sonata 2006-09	4.6	3.9	3.2	Moderate
Chevrolet Mailbu 2009-10	5	3.7	4.4	Moderate
Pontiac G6 2006-09	7	2.8	2.3	Poor
Chrysler 300 2006-09	7.4	2.6	2.5	Poor
Jeep Gr. Cherokee 2007-10	9.1	1.8	2.2	Very Poor
Scion xB 2008-10	10.4	1.2	6.8	Very Poor
Chevy Tahoe 2007-09	10.9	1	2.1	Very Poor
Honda Ridgeline 2006-09	10.9	1	2.4	Very Poor

*Year tested is first model year listed with later models having similar roof strength and design.

This work was funded by the Santos Family Foundation on sixteen vehicles donated by the State Farm Insurance Company.

STATIC STABILITY FACTOR

Vehicle	SSF (High=Better)/ Chance of Rollover		Vehicle	SSF (High=Better)/ Chance of Rollover		Vehicle	SSF (High=Better)/ Chance of Rollover	
Acura ILX	1.44*	Low	Ford Taurus	1.39	Low	Nissan Altima	1.43	Low
Acura MDX	1.3	Moderate	Honda Accord	1.45*	Low	Nissan Altima Coupe	1.46*	Low
Acura RDX	1.24*	High	Honda Accord Coupe	1.47*	Very Low	Nissan Armada	1.14*	Very High
Acura TL	1.49	Very Low	Honda Civic	1.4*	Low	Nissan Cube	1.19*	Very High
Acura TSX	1.46*	Very Low	Honda Civic Coupe	1.44*	Low	Nissan Frontier	1.14*	Very High
Audi A3	1.41*	Low	Honda CR-V	1.22	High	Nissan Juke	1.25	High
Audi A4	1.46	Very Low	Honda Fit	1.35	Moderate	Nissan Leaf	1.32*	Moderate
Audi A5	1.53*	Very Low	Honda Insight	1.38*	Moderate	Nissan Maxima	1.45	Low
Audi A6	1.47*	Very Low	Honda Odyssey	1.34	Moderate	Nissan Murano	1.21	High
Audi A7	1.54*	Very Low	Honda Pilot	1.24	High	Nissan Pathfinder	1.23*	High
Audi Allroad	1.43*	Low	Honda Ridgeline	1.24*	High	Nissan Quest	1.21*	High
Audi Q5	1.27*	High	Hyundai Accent	1.35	Moderate	Nissan Rogue	1.19*	Very High
Audi Q7	1.25*	High	Hyundai Azera	1.46*	Low	Nissan Sentra	1.36	Moderate
BMW 1 Series	1.4*	Low	Hyundai Elantra	1.41	Low	Nissan Titan	1.18*	Very High
BMW 3 Series	1.48	Very Low	Hyundai Genesis	1.46*	Low	Nissan Versa	1.29	High
BMW 5 Series	1.49	Very Low	Hyundai Santa Fe	1.29	High	Nissan Xterra	1.07*	Very High
BMW 7 Series	1.48*	Very Low	Hyundai Sonata	1.47	Very Low	Porsche Cayenne	1.27*	High
BMW X1	1.27*	High	Hyundai Tucson	1.21	High	Ram 1500	1.15	Very High
BMW X3	1.27*	High	Hyundai Veloster	1.49*	Very Low	Scion FR-S	1.59*	Very Low
BMW X5	1.22	High	Infiniti EX	1.36*	Moderate	Scion iQ	1.28	High
Buick Enclave	1.24*	High	Infiniti FX	1.27*	High	Scion tC	1.46*	Very Low
Buick Encore	1.21*	High	Infiniti G	1.4*	Low	Scion xB	1.23*	High
Buick LaCrosse	1.37	Moderate	Infiniti JX	1.26*	High	Scion xD	1.3*	Moderate
Buick Regal	1.41	Low	Infiniti M	1.39	Low	Smart ForTwo	1.15*	Very High
Buick Verano	1.39	Low	Infiniti QX	1.16*	Very High	Subaru BRZ	1.59*	Very Low
Cadillac ATS	1.44*	Low	Jaguar XF	1.43*	Low	Subaru Forester	1.21	High
Cadillac CTS	1.44	Low	Jeep Compass	1.19*	Very High	Subaru Impreza	1.37*	Moderate
Cadillac SRX	1.26*	High	Jeep Gr. Cherokee	1.17	Very High	Subaru Legacy	1.39*	Low
Cadillac XTS	1.37	Moderate	Jeep Patriot	1.19*	Very High	Subaru Outback	1.27*	High
Chevrolet Avalanche	1.15*	Very High	Jeep Wrangler	1.13*	Very High	Subaru XV Crosstrek	1.23*	High
Chevrolet Camaro	1.53	Very Low	Kia Forte	1.44	Low	Suzuki Kizashi	1.41*	Low
Chevrolet Corvette	1.67*	Very Low	Kia Optima	1.48	Very Low	Suzuki SX4	1.32	Moderate
Chevrolet Cruze	1.41	Low	Kia Rio	1.38	Low	Toyota 4Runner	1.12	Very High
Chevrolet Equinox	1.19	Very High	Kia Sorento	1.21	High	Toyota Avalon	1.45*	Low
Chevrolet Impala	1.39	Low	Kia Soul	1.27	High	Toyota Camry	1.42	Low
Chevrolet Malibu	1.4	Low	Land Rover Range Rover	1.19*	Very High	Toyota Corolla	1.36	Moderate
Chevrolet Silverado	1.2	Very High	Land Rover RR Evoque	1.32*	Moderate	Toyota FJ Cruiser	1.14*	Very High
Chevrolet Sonic	1.34	Moderate	Lexus CT	1.41*	Low	Toyota Highlander	1.22*	High
Chevrolet Suburban	1.13	Very High	Lexus ES	1.4	Low	Toyota Matrix	1.31*	Moderate
Chevrolet Tahoe	1.49	Very Low	Lexus GS	1.45	Low	Toyota Prius	1.36	Moderate
Chevrolet Traverse	1.25*	High	Lexus IS	1.44	Low	Toyota Prius C	1.36*	Moderate
Chevrolet Volt	1.45*	Low	Lexus RX	1.21	High	Toyota Prius V	1.31*	Moderate
Chrysler 200	1.4	Low	Lincoln MKS	1.39	Low	Toyota RAV4	1.2*	Very High
Chrysler 300	1.24	High	Lincoln MKZ	1.42*	Low	Toyota Sequoia	1.16*	Very High
Chrysler T&C	1.25*	High	Mazda Mazda2	1.33*	Moderate	Toyota Sienna	1.3	Moderate
Dodge Avenger	1.37	Moderate	Mazda Mazda3	1.41	Low	Toyota Tacoma	1.19	Very High
Dodge Challenger	1.47*	Very Low	Mazda Mazda5	1.23*	High	Toyota Tundra	1.18	Very High
Dodge Charger	1.45	Low	Mazda Mazda6	1.49	Very Low	Toyota Venza	1.26	High
Dodge Dart	1.42	Low	Mazda CX-5	1.23	High	Toyota Yaris	1.31	Moderate
Dodge Durango	1.16	Very High	Mazda CX-9	1.24*	High	Volkswagen Beetle	1.43	Low
Dodge Gr. Caravan	1.24	High	Mazda MX-5 Miata	1.6*	Very Low	Volkswagen CC	1.46*	Very Low
Dodge Journey	1.2	Very High	Merc.-Benz C-Class	1.42*	Low	Volkswagen Golf	1.38*	Moderate
Fiat 500	1.29	High	Merc.-Benz E-Class	1.46*	Low	Volkswagen Jetta	1.4	Low
Ford C-MAX	1.26*	High	Merc.-Benz GL-Class	1.16*	Very High	Volkswagen Passat	1.42	Low
Ford Edge	1.25	High	Merc.-Benz GLK-Class	1.19*	Very High	Volkswagen Routan	1.22*	High
Ford Escape	1.19	Very High	Merc.-Benz M-Class	1.19*	Very High	Volkswagen Tiguan	1.2	Very High
Ford Expedition	1.18	Very High	Merc.-Benz S-Class	1.45*	Low	Volkswagen Touareg	1.24*	High
Ford Explorer	1.22	High	Mini Clubman	1.37*	Moderate	Volvo C70	1.48*	Very Low
Ford F-150	1.14	Very High	Mini Cooper	1.41*	Low	Volvo S60	1.45	Low
Ford Fiesta	1.33*	Moderate	Mini Countryman	1.31*	Moderate	Volvo S80	1.41*	Low
Ford Flex	1.25*	High	Mitsubishi Lancer	1.36	Moderate	Volvo XC60	1.22	High
Ford Focus	1.38	Low	Mitsubishi Outlander	1.19	Very High	Volvo XC90	1.19*	Very High
Ford Fusion	1.44*	Low	Mitsu. Outlander Sport	1.21*	High			
Ford Mustang	1.53	Very Low	Nissan 370Z	1.59*	Very Low	*Calculated		

FUEL ECONOMY

As gas prices bounce up and down, regular driving still takes a big bite out of our pocketbooks. The good news is that higher fuel efficiency standards are forcing car companies to provide more fuel efficient vehicles. Buying right and practicing more fuel efficient driving will make a huge difference in your vehicle's operating costs.

Using the EPA ratings is the best way to incorporate fuel efficiency in selecting a new car. By comparing these ratings, even among cars of the same size, you'll find that fuel efficiency varies greatly. One compact car might get 36 miles per gallon (mpg) while another compact gets only 22 mpg. If you drive 15,000 miles a year and you pay $3.43 per gallon for fuel, the 36 mpg car will save you $909 *a year* over the "gas guzzler."

In 2008, the EPA changed the way it estimates miles per gallon to better represent today's driving conditions. Their new method adjusts for aggressive driving (high speeds and faster acceleration), air conditioning use, and cold temperature operation.

Octane Ratings: Once you've purchased your car, you'll be faced with choosing the right gasoline. Oil companies spend millions of dollars trying to get you to buy so-called higher performance or high octane fuels. Using high octane fuel can add considerably to your gas bill, and the vast majority of vehicles do not need it. Check your owner's manual and only use what's recommended, which is usually 87. Very few vehicles require "premium" gasoline.

The octane rating of a gasoline is not a measure of power or quality. It is simply a measure of the gas' resistance to engine knock, which is the pinging sound you hear when the air and fuel mixture in your engine ignites prematurely during acceleration.

Your engine may knock when accelerating a heavily loaded car uphill or when the humidity is low. This is normal and docs not call for a higher-octane gasoline.

FIVE FACTORS AFFECTING FUEL ECONOMY

1. Engine Size: The smaller the engine the better your fuel efficiency. A 10% increase in the size of your engine can increase your fuel consumption rate by 6%. Smaller engines can be cheaper to maintain as well.

2. Transmission: If used properly, manual transmissions are generally more fuel-efficient than automatics. In fact, a 5-speed manual can add up to 6.5 mpg over a 4-speed automatic transmission. Getting an automatic with an overdrive gear can improve your fuel economy by up to 9 percent.

3. Cruise Control: Using cruise control can save fuel because driving at a constant speed uses less fuel than changing speeds frequently.

4. Trim Packages and Power Options: Upgrading a car's trim level and adding options such as navigation systems or a sunroof can increase the weight of your car. Every 200 pounds of weight shaves off about 1 mile per gallon off your mileage. The weight of the average car in 1981 was 3,202 pounds, today it's around 4,000 pounds.

5. Hybrids: Most manufacturers offer hybrid vehicles that have both gasoline and electric engines. Hybrids can offer 30% better fuel economy and lower emissions. [Beware, until they are more readily available, you'll still have to pay considerably more to buy them.]

TWELVE WAYS TO SAVE MONEY AT THE PUMP

Here are a few simple things you can do that will save you a lot of money. Note: Savings are based on gas at $3.43.

1. Make Sure Your Tires are Inflated Properly: 27% of vehicles have tires that are under-inflated. Properly inflated tires can improve mileage by 3%, which is like getting 10 cents off a gallon of gas. Check the label on your door or glove box to find out what the pressure range should be for your tires. Don't use the "max pressure" written on your tire. Electronic gauges are fast, easy to use and accurate. Don't rely on the numbers on the air pump.

2. Check Your Air Filter: A dirty air filter by itself can rob a car by as much as 10% percent of its mileage. If an engine doesn't get enough air, it will burn too much gasoline. Replacing a dirty filter can knock 34 cents off a gallon of gas.

3. Get Your Alignment Checked: Not only does poor alignment cause your tires to wear out faster and cause poor handling, but it can cause your engine to work harder and reduce your fuel efficiency by 10%.

4. Don't Use High Octane Gasoline: Check your owner's manual. Very, very few cars actually need high-octane gas. Using 87-octane gas will save you over 10 cents per gallon over mid-grade and 20 cents over premium.

5. Get a Tune Up: A properly tuned engine is a fuel saver. Have a trusted mechanic tune your engine to exact factory specifications and you could save up to 13 cents a gallon.

6. Check Your Gas Cap: It is estimated that nearly 17 % of the cars on the road have broken or missing gasoline caps. This hurts your mileage and can harm the environment by allowing your gasoline to evaporate.

7. Don't Speed: A car moving at 55 mph gets better fuel economy than the same car at 65 mph. For every 5 mph you reduce your highway speed, you can reduce fuel consumption by 7%, which is like getting 24 cents off a gallon of gas.

8. Avoid Excess Idling: An idling car gets 0 mpg. Cars with larger engines typically waste more gas at idle than cars with smaller engines.

9. Drive Smoother: The smoother your accelerations and decelerations, the better your mileage. A smooth foot can save 57 cents a gallon.

10. Combine Trips: Short trips can be expensive because they usually involve a "cold" vehicle. For the first mile or two before the engine gets warmed up, a cold vehicle only gets 30 to 40% of the mileage it gets at full efficiency.

11. Empty your Roof Rack and Trunk: 50% of engine power, traveling at highway speed, is used in overcoming aerodynamic drag or wind resistance. Any protrusion on a vehicle's roof can reduce gas mileage, typical roof racks reduce fuel economy by about 6 mpg. 100 lbs. of extra weight will reduce your mileage by .5 mpg.

12. Choose Your Gas Miser: If you own more than one vehicle, choosing to drive the one with better gas mileage will save you money. If you drive 15,000 miles per year, half in a vehicle with 20 mpg and half with a 30 mpg vehicle and switch to driving 75% of your trips in the 30 mpg vehicle, you will save $214 annually with gas at $3.43.

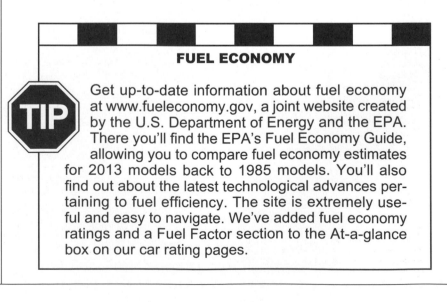

FUEL ECONOMY

TIP

Get up-to-date information about fuel economy at www.fueleconomy.gov, a joint website created by the U.S. Department of Energy and the EPA. There you'll find the EPA's Fuel Economy Guide, allowing you to compare fuel economy estimates for 2013 models back to 1985 models. You'll also find out about the latest technological advances pertaining to fuel efficiency. The site is extremely useful and easy to navigate. We've added fuel economy ratings and a Fuel Factor section to the At-a-glance box on our car rating pages.

FUEL ECONOMY MISERS AND GUZZLERS

Because the success of the EPA program depends on consumers' ability to compare the fuel economy ratings easily, we have included key mileage figures on our ratings pages. Listed below are the best and worst of this year's ratings according to annual fuel cost. The complete EPA fuel economy guide is available at www.fueleconomy.gov.

Vehicle	Specifications	MPG (city/hwy)	Annual Fuel Cost
FUEL ECONOMY MISERS AND GUZZLERS			
THE BEST			
Plug In Hybrid Electric Vehicles (PHEVs)			
Chevrolet Volt	1.4L, 4 cyl., Continuously Variable, FWD	63/61^	$829.84
Toyota Prius Plug-in Hybrid	1.8L, 4 cyl., Continuously Variable, FWD	59/56^	$887.07
Ford C-MAX PHEV	2L, 4 cyl., Continuously Variable, FWD	63/54^	$887.07
Gas			
Toyota Prius	1.8L, 4 cyl., Continuously Variable, FWD	51/48	$1,029.00
Toyota Prius c	1.5L, 4 cyl., Continuously Variable, FWD	53/46	$1,029.00
Ford C-MAX Hybrid	2L, 4 cyl., Continuously Variable, FWD	47/47	$1,094.68
Ford Fusion Hybrd	2L, 4 cyl., Continuously Variable, FWD	47/47	$1,094.68
Lincoln MKZ Hybrid	2L, 4 cyl., Continuously Variable, FWD	45/45	$1,143.33
Honda Insight	1.3L, 4 cyl., Continuously Variable, FWD	41/44	$1,225.00
Lexus CT 200h	1.8L, 4 cyl., Continuously Variable, FWD	43/40	$1,225.00
Toyota Prius v	1.8L, 4 cyl., Continuously Variable, FWD	44/40	$1,225.00
Lexus ES 300h	2.5L, 4 cyl., Selectable Continuously Variable, FWD	40/39	$1,286.25
Scion iQ	1.3L, 4 cyl., Continuously Variable, FWD	36/37	$1,390.54
Nissan Versa	1.6L, 4 cyl., Continuously Variable, FWD	31/40	$1,470.00
Acura ILX	1.5L, 4 cyl., Selectable Continuously Variable, FWD	39/38	$1,472.37#
Chevrolet Spark	1.2, 4 cyl., 5 sp. Manual, FWD	32/38	$1,513.24
Smart fortwo	1L, 3 cyl., 5 sp. Automated Manual, RWD	34/38	$1,554.17#
Chevrolet Cruze Eco	1.4L, 4 cyl., 6 sp Manual, FWD	28/42	$1,559.09
Chevrolet Sonic	1.4L, 4 cyl., 6 sp. Manual, FWD	29/40	$1,559.09
Ford Fiesta	1.4L, 4 cyl., 5 sp. Manual, FWD	29/39	$1,559.09
Mazda Mazda3	2L, 4 cyl., 6-sp Semi Automatic, FWD	28/40	$1,559.09
Toyota Yaris	1.5L, 4 cyl., 5 sp. Manual, FWD	30/37	$1,559.09
Chevrolet Spark	1.2L, 4 cyl., 4 sp. Automatic, FWD	28/37	$1,607.81
Hyundai Accent	1.6L, 4 cyl., 6 sp Manual, FWD	28/37	$1,607.81
Hyundai Elantra	1.8L, 4 cyl., 6 sp. Automatic, FWD	28/38	$1,607.81
Kia Rio	1.6L, 4 cyl., 6 sp. Manual, FWD	29/37	$1,607.81
Mazda Mazda2	1.5L, 4 cyl., 5 sp. Manual, FWD	29/35	$1,607.81
Toyota Yaris	1.5L, 4 cyl., 4 sp. Automatic, FWD	30/36	$1,607.81
THE WORST**			
Mercedes-Benz G 550	5.5L, 8 cyl., 7 sp. Automatic, 4WD	12/15	$4,303.85#
Mercedes-Benz G 63 AMG	5.5L, 8 cyl., 7 sp. Automatic, 4WD	12/14	$4,303.85#
Chevy/GMC C2500 Suburban/Yukon XL 2WD	6L, 8 cyl., 6 sp. Automatic, RWD	10/16	$4,287.50
Chevy/GMC K2500 Suburban/Yukon XL 4WD	6L, 8 cyl., 6 sp. Automatic, 4WD	10/15	$4,287.50
BMW X5 M	4.4L, 8 cyl., 6 sp. Semi-Automatic, AWD	12/17	$3,996.43#
BMW X6 M	4.4L, 8 cyl., 6 sp. Semi-Automatic, AWD	12/17	$3,996.43#
Cadillac CTS/CTS Wagon	6.2L, 8 cyl., 6 sp. Semi-Automatic, RWD	12/18	$3,996.43#
Chevrolet Camaro	6.2L, 8 cyl., 6 sp. Semi-Automatic, RWD	12/18	$3,996.43#
Jeep Grand Cherokee SRT8	6.4L, 8 cyl., 5 sp. Automatic, 4WD	12/18	$3,996.43#
Lexus LX 570	5.7L, 8 cyl., 6 sp. Semi-Automatic, 4WD	12/17	$3,996.43#
Ford F150 Pickup	6.2L, 8 cyl., 6 sp. Semi-Automatic, 4WD	12/16	$3,957.69
Ford F150 Raptor Pickup	6.2L, 8 cyl., 6 sp. Semi-Automatic, 4WD	11/16	$3,957.69
Land Rover Range Rover Sport	5L, 8 cyl., 6 sp. Semi-Automatic, 4WD	13/18	$3,730.00#
Mercedes-Benz C 63 AMG	6.2L, 8 cly., 7 sp. Automatic, RWD	13/19	$3,730.00#
Mercedes-Benz GL 550 4MATIC	4.7L, 8 cyl., 7 sp. Automatic, 4WD	13/18	$3,730.00#
Mercedes-Benz ML 63 AMG	5.5L, 8 cyl., 7 sp. Automatic, 4WD	13/17	$3,730.00#
Cadillac Escalade ESV	6.2L, 8 cyl., 6 sp. Automatic, AWD	13/18	$3,675.00
Cadillac Escalade EXT	6.2L, 8 cyl., 6 sp. Automatic, AWD	13/18	$3,675.00
Chevrolet/GMC C15 Silverado/Sierra 2WD	6.2L, 8 cyl., 6 sp. Automatic, RWD	13/18	$3,675.00
Chevrolet/GMC K15 Silverado/Sierra 4WD	6.2L, 8 cyl., 6 sp. Automatic, 4WD	12/18	$3,675.00
GMC K1500 Yukon XL	6.2L, 8 cyl., 6 sp. Automatic, AWD	13/18	$3,675.00
Nissan Armada	5.6L, 8 cyl., 5 sp. Automatic, 4WD	12/18	$3,675.00
Nissan Titan	5.6L, 8 cyl., 5 sp. Automatic, 4WD	12/17	$3,675.00
Toyota Sequoia	5.7L, 8 cyl., 6 sp. Semi-Automatic, 4WD	13/17	$3,675.00

Note: 2013 annual fuel cost is based on driving 15,000 miles per year and a projected regular gas price of $3.43. ^Combined electric/gas mpg. # Premium required at $3.73.
**Low volume exotic vehicles (over $120,000) and cargo vans were excluded.

COMPARING WARRANTIES

After buying your car, maintenance will be a significant portion of your operating costs. The strength of your warranty and the cost of repairs after the warranty expires will determine these costs. Comparing warranties and repair costs, before you buy, can save you thousands of dollars down the road.

Along with your new car comes a warranty which is a promise from the manufacturer that the car will perform as it should. Most of us never read the warranty until it is too late. In fact, because warranties are often difficult to read and understand, most of us don't really know what our warranty offers.

To keep your warranty in effect, you must operate and maintain your car according to the instructions in your owner's manual. It is important to keep a record of all maintenance performed on your car.

Be careful not to confuse a warranty with a service contract. A service contract must be purchased separately while a warranty is yours at no extra cost when you buy the car.

Warranties are difficult to compare because they contain fine print and confusing language. The following table will help you compare this year's new car warranties. Because the table does not contain all the details about each warranty, review the actual warranty to understand its fine points. You have the right to inspect a warranty before you buy—it's the law.

The table provides information on four critical items in a warranty:

The Basic Warranty covers most parts against manufacturer's defects. Tires, batteries, and items you add to the car are covered under separate warranties. The table describes coverage in terms of months and miles. For example, 48/50 means the warranty is good for 48 months or 50,000 miles, whichever comes first. This is the most important part of your warranty.

The Power Train Warranty usually lasts longer than the basic warranty. Because each manufacturer's definition of the power train is different, it is important to find out exactly what your warranty will cover. Power train coverage should include parts of the engine, transmission, and drive train. The warranty on some luxury cars will often cover additional systems such as steering, suspension, and electrical systems.

The Corrosion Warranty usually applies only to actual holes due to rust. Read this section carefully because many corrosion warranties do not apply to what the manufacturer may describe as cosmetic rust or bad paint.

The Roadside Assistance column indicates whether or not the warranty includes a program for helping with problems on the road. In addition to mechanical failures, these programs cover such things as lockouts, jump starts, flat tires, running out of gas, and towing. Most are offered for the length of the basic warranty. Some have special limitations or added features, many of which we point out. Because each one is different, check yours carefully. If it is an option that you have to pay extra for, we don't list it.

The last column, the **Warranty Rating Index**, provides an overall assessment of this year's warranties. **The higher the Index number, the better the warranty.** The Index number incorporates the important features of each warranty. In developing the Index, we gave the most weight to the basic and power train components of the warranties. The corrosion warranty was weighted somewhat less, and roadside assistance received the least weight. We also considered special features such as the manufacturer offering free scheduled maintenance or if rental cars were offered when warranty repairs were being done.

The best ratings are in ***BOLD***.

WARRANTY OFFERS THAT CAN SAVE YOU HUNDREDS

This year a few manufacturers are offering free maintainance and free wear and tear part replacement for the first three, four and even five years. These programs will save you hundreds of dollars in ownership costs.

WARRANTY COMPARISON

Manufacturer	Basic Warranty	Power Train Warranty	Corrosion Warranty	Roadside Assistance	Index	Warranty Rating
Acura	48/50	72/70	60/Unlimited	48/50	1295	Poor
Audi[1]	**48/50**	**48/50**	**144/Unlimited**	**48/Unlimited**	**1702**	**Very Good**
BMW[2]	**48/50**	**48/50**	**144/Unlimited**	**48/50**	**1772**	**Very Good**
Buick	48/50	72/70	72/100	72/70	1375	Average
Cadillac	48/50	72/70	72/Unlimited[3]	72/70	1623	Good
Chevrolet	36/36	60/100	72/100[4]	60/100	1496	Average
Chrysler	36/36	60/100	72/100[5]	60/100	1550	Good
Dodge	36/36	60/100	60/100[6]	36/36[7]	1418	Average
Fiat	48/50	48/50	144/Unlimited	48/Unlimited	1676	Good
Ford[8]	36/36	60/60	60/Unlimited	60/60	1158	Very Poor
GMC	36/36	60/100	72/100	60/100	1352	Poor
Honda	36/36	60/60	60/Unlimited	Optional	978	Very Poor
Hyundai[9]	**60/60**	**120/100**	**84/Unlimited**	**60/Unlimited**	**1890**	**Very Good**
Infiniti	48/60	72/70	84/Unlimited	48/Unlimited	1518	Average
Jaguar	48/50[10]	48/50	72/Unlimited	48/50	1229	Poor
Jeep	36/36	60/100	60/100	34/36[11]	1217	Poor
Kia	60/60	120/100[12]	60/100	60/60	1580	Good
Land Rover	48/50	48/50	72/Unlimited	48/50	1229	Poor
Lexus[13]	48/50	72/70	72/Unlimited	48/Unlimited	1420	Average
Lincoln[14]	48/50	72/70	60/Unlimited	72/70	1361	Average
Mazda	36/36	60/60	60/Unlimited	36/36	1086	Very Poor
Mercedes-Benz[15]	48/50	48/50	48/50	Lifetime	1185	Poor
Mini[16]	**48/50**	**48/50**	**144/Unlimited**	**48/Unlimited**	**1784**	**Very Good**
Mitsubishi	**60/60**	**120/100**	**84/100**	**60/Unlimited**	**1756**	**Very Good**
Nissan	36/36	60/60	60/Unlimited	36/36	1086	Very Poor
Porsche	48/50	48/50	144/Unlimited	48/50	1625	Good
Ram	36/36	60/100	60/100[6]	36/36[7]	1418	Average
Scion[17]	36/36	60/60	60/Unlimited	24/25	1084	Very Poor
Smart[18]	48/50	48/50	48/50	48/50	1035	Very Poor
Subaru[19]	36/36	60/60	60/Unlimited	36/36	1158	Very Poor
Suzuki[20]	36/36	84/100	60/Unlimited	36/36	1290	Poor
Toyota[21]	36/36	60/60	60/Unlimited	24/25	1076	Very Poor
Volkswagen[22]	36/36	60/60	144/Unlimited	36/36	1608	Good
Volvo[23]	**60/50**	**60/50**	**144/Unlimited**	**60/Unlimited**	**1974**	**Very Good**

[1] Free Maintenance 12/5
[2] Free Maintenance 48/50
[3] All Corrosion 48/50
[4] All Corrosion 36/36
[5] All Corrosion 36/Unlimited
[6] All Corrosion 36/Unlimited
[7] Roadside assistance for parts covered under powertrain warranty 50/100
[8] Hybrid components 96/100
[9] Wear Items 12/12; Battery 24/Unlimited
[10] 1st scheduled maintenance free
[11] Roadside assistance for parts covered under powertrain warranty 50/100
[12] Only transferable up to 60,000 miles

[13] Hybrid Components 96/100; Wheel Alignment and Balancing 12/20
[14] Hybrid Components 96/100
[15] Wheel Alignment and Balancing 12/12
[16] Free Maintenance 36/36
[17] Free Scheduled Maintaince 24/25; Wheel Alignment 12/20
[18] Wheel Alignment and Balancing 12/12
[19] Wear Items 36/36
[20] Battery 24/24
[21] Hybrid Components 96/100; Free Scheduled Maintaince 24/25
[22] Free Scheduled Maintenance 36/36; Wear Items 12/12
[23] Free Maintenance 60/50

SECRET WARRANTIES

If dealers report a number of complaints about a certain part and the manufacturer determines that the problem is due to faulty design or assembly, the manufacturer may permit dealers to repair the problem at no charge to the customer even though the warranty is expired. In the past, this practice was often reserved for customers who made a big fuss. The availability of the free repair was never publicized, which is why we call these "secret warranties."

Manufacturers deny the existence of secret warranties. They call these free repairs "policy adjustments" or "goodwill service." Whatever they are called, most consumers never hear about them.

Many secret warranties are disclosed in service bulletins that the manufacturers send to dealers. These bulletins outline free repair or reimbursement programs, as well as other problems and their possible causes and solutions.

Service bulletins from many manufacturers may be on file at the National Highway Traffic Safety Administration. You can visit www.nhtsa.gov to access NHTSA's Service Bulletin database.

If you find that a secret warranty is in effect and repairs are being made at no charge after the warranty has expired, contact the Center for Auto Safety, 1825 Connecticut Ave. NW, #330, Washington, DC 20009. They will publish the information so others can benefit.

Disclosure Laws: Spurred by the proliferation of secret warranties and the failure of the FTC to take action, California, Connecticut, Virginia, Wisconsin, and Maryland have passed legislation that requires consumers to be notified of secret warranties on their cars. Several other states have introduced similar warranty bills.

Typically, the laws require the following: direct notice to consumers within a specified time after the adoption of a warranty adjustment policy; notice of the disclosure law to new car buyers; reimbursement within a number of years after payment to owners who paid for covered repairs before they learned of the extended warranty service; and dealers must inform consumers who complain about a covered defect that it is eligible for repair under warranty.

If you live in a state with a secret warranty law already in effect, write your state attorney general's office (in care of your state capital) for information. To encourage passage of such a bill, contact your state representative (in care of your state capital).

Some state lemon laws require dealers and manufacturers to give you copies of Technical Service Bulletins on problems affecting your vehicle. These bulletins may alert you to a secret warranty on your vehicle or help you make the case for a free repair if there isn't a secret warranty. See page 59 for an overview of your state's lemon law. If you would like to see the complete law, go to www.auto-safety.org to view your state's lemon laws.

LITTLE SECRETS OF THE AUTO INDUSTRY

TIP

Every auto company makes mistakes building cars. When they do, they often issue technical service bulletins telling dealers how to fix the problem. Rarely do they publicize these fixes, many of which are offered for free, called secret warranties. The Center for Auto Safety has published a book called *Little Secrets of the Auto Industry*, a consumer guide to secret warranties. This book explains how to find out about secret warranties, offers tips for going to small claims court and getting federal and state assistance, and lists information on state secret warranty laws. To order a copy, send $17.50 to: Center for Auto Safety, Pub. Dept. CB, 1825 Connecticut Ave. NW, Suite 330, Washington, DC 20009.

KEEPING IT GOING

Comparing maintenance costs before you buy can help decide which car to purchase. These costs include preventive maintenance servicing—such as changing the oil and filters—as well as the cost of repairs after your warranty expires. Below we enable you to compare the costs of preventive maintenance and nine likely repairs for the 2013 models.

Preventive Maintenance: The first column in the table is the periodic servicing, specified by the manufacturer, that keeps your car running properly. For example, regularly changing the oil and oil filter. Every owner's manual specifies a schedule of recommended servicing for at least the first 60,000 miles and many now go to 100,000 miles. The tables on the following pages estimate the labor cost of following this preventive maintenance schedule for 60,000 miles, the length of a typical warranty. Service parts are not included in this total.

Repairs Costs: The tables also list the costs for nine repairs that typically occur during the first 100,000 miles. There is no precise way to predict exactly when a repair will be needed. But if you keep a car for 75,000 to 100,000 miles, it is likely that you will experience most of these repairs at least once. The last column provides a relative indication of how expensive these nine repairs are for many cars. Repair cost is rated as Very Good if the total for nine repairs is in the lower fifth of all the cars rated, and Very Poor if the total is in the highest fifth.

Most repair shops use "flat-rate manuals" to estimate repair costs. These manuals list the approximate time required for repairing many items. Each automobile manufacturer publishes its own manual and there are several independent manuals as well. For many repairs, the time varies from one manual to another. Some repair shops even use different manuals for different repairs. To determine a repair bill, a shop multiplies the time listed in its manual by its hourly labor rate and then adds the cost of parts.

Some dealers and repair shops create their own maintenance schedules which call for more frequent (and thus more expensive) servicing than the manufacturer's recommendations. If the service recommended by your dealer or repair shop doesn't match what the manufacturer recommends, make sure you understand and agree to the extra items. Our cost estimates are based on published repair times multiplied by a nationwide average labor rate of $70 per hour and include the cost of replaced parts and related adjustments.

Prices in the following tables may not predict the exact costs of these repairs. For example, labor rates for your area may be more or less than the national average. However, the prices will provide you with a relative comparison of costs for various automobiles.

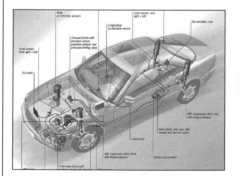

	PM Costs to 60,000 Miles	REPAIR COSTS									Relative Repair Cost*
		Front Brake Pads	Starter	Fuel Injector	Fuel Pump	Struts/ Shocks	Timing Belt/Chain	Water Pump	Muffler	Headlamps	
Subcompact											
Chevrolet Sonic	574	199	366	117	362	192	361	178	506	656	Vry. Gd.
Fiat 500	357	155	272	334	442	124	271	294	189	639	Vry. Gd.
Ford Fiesta	1,904	130	417	101	341	199	381	315	333	679	Vry. Gd.
Honda Fit	672	124	718	180	464	350	491	268	233	748	Good
Hyundai Accent	616	103	301	131	308	268	293	353	346	480	Vry. Gd.
Hyundai Veloster											
Kia Rio	630	110	345	176	301	196	303	478	383	627	Vry. Gd.
Kia Soul	742	117	366	190	327	484	289	261	421	1,110	Good
Mazda Mazda2	665	129	359	167	345	287	468	340	251	716	Vry. Gd.
Mazda MX-5 Miata	672	129	272	191	397	400	380	231	613	1,269	Good
Mini Clubman	532	184	433	178	392	327	818	358	869	800	Average
Mini Cooper	448	165	433	178	357	327	818	372	490	1,412	Average
Mini Countryman	532	191	432	177	392	331	818	358	976	837	Average
Nissan 370Z	462	174	458	284	438	480	515	510	578	2,160	Vry. Pr.
Nissan Versa	462	117	335	247	423	240	351	177	286	686	Vry. Gd.
Scion iQ											
Scion xB	546	126	451	248	408	237	652	281	251	661	Good
Scion xD	231	114	461	227	408	186	1,018	734	279	443	Good
Smart ForTwo	777	118	474	166	416	538	1,061	432	955	677	Poor
Suzuki SX4	1,344	191	684	243	918	510	667	445	512	828	Poor
Toyota Yaris	378	118	318	220	401	219	473	222	255	386	Vry. Gd.
Volkswagen Beetle	483	150	791	362	365	381	794	665	830	1,080	Poor
Compact											
Acura ILX	784	124	498	255	408	213	518	272	175	633	Vry. Gd.
Audi A3	616	157	433	348	403	320	475	622	426	778	Good
Audi A4	756	183	722	383	438	616	314	692	493	906	Poor
BMW 1 Series	224	215	570	255	392	353	733	693	868	935	Poor
BMW 3 Series	140	223	570	185	381	554	723	550	525	1,182	Poor
Buick Verano											
Cadillac ATS	994	228	279	304	551	334	610	389	1,196	1,092	Poor
Chevrolet Cruze	973	199	254	111	462	169	274	185	541	486	Vry. Gd.
Chevrolet Volt	784	144	0	99	412	102	389	172	493	820	Vry. Gd.
Dodge Dart	840	119	174	91	372	305	437	178	571	986	Vry. Gd.
Ford C-MAX	0	130	423	234	238	198	568	494	255	664	Vry. Gd.
Ford Focus	910	130	423	224	238	198	568	494	255	664	Vry. Gd.
Honda Civic	574	124	498	255	408	213	518	272	175	633	Vry. Gd.
Honda Civic Coupe	574	185	498	255	408	213	518	272	175	406	Vry. Gd.
Honda Insight	714	128	666	233	349	533	413	265	238	474	Good
Hyundai Elantra	763	129	329	142	202	332	352	225	780	733	Vry. Gd.
Kia Forte	455	138	206	172	311	429	422	259	319	432	Vry. Gd.
Lexus CT	434	116	0	382	425	268	1,317	429	572	1,983	Poor
Mazda Mazda3	714	147	206	196	571	257	384	239	398	610	Vry. Gd.
Mercedes-Benz C-Class	1,225	170	712	250	449	662	549	609	951	1,213	Vry. Pr.
Mitsubishi Lancer	392	167	857	335	560	469	460	439	383	845	Average
Nissan Altima Coupe	462	213	356	288	411	264	566	210	398	665	Good
Nissan Cube	462	135	352	266	431	258	477	207	256	694	Vry. Gd.
Nissan Leaf	518	135	0	0	0	334	0	701	0	1,973	Vry. Gd.
Nissan Sentra	546	220	426	309	460	222	331	187	317	758	Vry. Gd.
AVERAGE OF ALL VEHICLES	**$718**	**$176**	**$435**	**$251**	**$463**	**$413**	**$754**	**$407**	**$588**	**$1,016**	

	PM Costs to 60,000 Miles	REPAIR COSTS									Relative Repair Cost*
		Front Brake Pads	Starter	Fuel Injector	Fuel Pump	Struts/ Shocks	Timing Belt/Chain	Water Pump	Muffler	Headlamps	
Scion FR-S											
Scion tC	245	129	639	302	416	254	1,115	285	302	933	Average
Subaru BRZ											
Subaru Impreza	784	137	518	203	386	486	244	350	383	808	Good
Suzuki Kizashi	756	231	715	281	970	544	889	389	471	1,106	Vry. Pr.
Toyota Corolla	427	118	465	239	418	311	1,102	217	389	637	Good
Toyota Matrix	427	128	472	262	411	336	1,102	217	447	697	Average
Toyota Prius	434	116	0	382	390	293	1,340	422	269	723	Good
Toyota Prius C	434	116	0	382	390	293	1,340	422	269	723	Good
Toyota Prius V	434	116	0	382	390	293	1,340	422	269	723	Good
Volkswagen Golf	434	160	498	174	352	403	687	476	771	578	Average
Volkswagen Jetta	434	152	437	331	467	382	369	692	664	726	Average
Volvo C70	798	175	429	289	630	342	371	365	570	853	Average
Intermediate											
Acura TL	784	144	486	159	374	266	339	415	706	1,547	Average
Acura TSX	658	127	535	124	494	292	385	205	733	1,458	Average
Audi A5	756	183	638	243	438	616	306	692	611	1,006	Poor
BMW 5 Series	105	228	592	255	571	448	1,237	786	884	1,425	Vry. Pr.
Buick Regal	973	259	331	304	588	207	449	616	922	1,041	Poor
Cadillac CTS	994	228	279	304	551	334	610	389	1,196	1,092	Poor
Chevrolet Camaro	994	271	244	295	329	376	473	375	481	477	Good
Chevrolet Corvette	826	244	603	179	1,335	314	790	410	707	2,200	Vry. Pr.
Chevrolet Malibu	973	236	324	121	470	233	452	354	574	679	Good
Chrysler 200	1,043	158	174	91	583	283	437	178	475	972	Good
Dodge Avenger	1,043	119	174	91	372	305	437	178	571	986	Vry. Gd.
Ford Fusion	539	153	290	88	356	298	461	211	514	411	Vry. Gd.
Ford Mustang	1,043	133	376	150	342	173	677	262	372	624	Vry. Gd.
Honda Accord	770	201	549	103	497	338	382	217	501	637	Good
Honda Accord Coupe	770	184	528	82	444	324	410	184	491	671	Good
Hyundai Azera	756	153	267	264	373	322	1,088	374	315	1,453	Average
Hyundai Genesis	812	185	406	211	354	456	704	305	536	806	Good
Hyundai Sonata	693	137	281	200	350	260	546	299	340	587	Vry. Gd.
Infiniti G	462	146	453	333	424	495	1,066	451	555	1,968	Vry. Pr.
Infiniti M	490	156	453	319	424	746	1,066	552	653	2,261	Vry. Pr.
Kia Optima	672	148	384	239	384	549	556	312	392	810	Good
Lexus ES	672	170	444	273	388	511	1,689	253	338	857	Poor
Lexus GS	602	174	468	501	428	669	339	335	817	539	Average
Lexus IS	588	138	860	623	393	702	2,028	461	787	1,454	Vry. Pr.
Lincoln MKZ	539	244	202	102	328	248	461	204	472	850	Vry. Gd.
Mazda Mazda6	616	159	192	88	500	200	434	204	297	714	Vry. Gd.
Mercedes-Benz E-Class	1,169	177	705	208	378	1,276	424	476	1,032	1,199	Vry. Pr.
Nissan Altima	462	131	356	288	411	264	566	219	508	665	Good
Nissan Maxima	644	142	377	353	424	304	793	327	623	683	Average
Subaru Legacy	1,029	157	420	285	393	504	277	350	365	847	Good
Subaru Outback	1,029	157	420	264	393	525	247	350	365	847	Good
Toyota Avalon	434	170	486	312	428	474	1,559	326	329	877	Poor
Toyota Camry	672	146	459	290	396	505	1,531	253	365	857	Poor
Volkswagen CC	476	160	657	380	401	447	552	664	443	782	Average
Volkswagen Passat	476	170	333	348	621	441	444	568	471	810	Average
AVERAGE OF ALL VEHICLES	**$718**	**$176**	**$435**	**$251**	**$463**	**$413**	**$754**	**$407**	**$588**	**$1,016**	

REPAIR COSTS

	PM Costs to 60,000 Miles	Front Brake Pads	Starter	Fuel Injector	Fuel Pump	Struts/ Shocks	Timing Belt/ Chain	Water Pump	Muffler	Headlamps	Relative Repair Cost*
Volvo S60	707	173	432	311	709	460	532	424	598	961	Average
Large											
Audi A6	756	217	739	415	619	397	1,574	304	541	1,078	Vry. Pr.
Audi A7	959	260	875	463	694	3,276	1,870	672	671	5,036	Vry. Pr.
Audi Allroad	756	183	722	383	438	616	314	692	493	906	Poor
BMW 7 Series	126	497	793	225	452	1,182	3,172	471	914	2,913	Vry. Pr.
Buick LaCrosse	973	269	425	250	493	278	586	475	753	1,134	Poor
Cadillac XTS	994	228	279	304	551	334	610	389	1,196	1,092	Poor
Chevrolet Impala	994	228	547	273	607	368	630	390	891	672	Average
Chrysler 300	1,015	218	199	130	304	242	559	161	1,026	1,315	Average
Dodge Challenger	1,141	218	195	193	378	286	511	238	1,379	612	Poor
Dodge Charger	1,001	218	199	158	304	198	559	157	1,019	704	Good
Ford Taurus	707	130	394	168	404	294	843	888	622	1,016	Poor
Jaguar XF	1,260	214	828	239	509	544	903	231	524	1,225	Poor
Lincoln MKS	700	130	401	420	355	232	975	1,006	1,305	2,361	Vry. Pr.
Mercedes-Benz S-Class	1,505	193	670	285	494	2,850	577	612	807	3,213	Vry. Pr.
Volvo S80	707	182	418	293	726	239	427	329	582	1,029	Average
Minivan											
Chrysler Town and Country	1,120	218	346	151	495	170	581	500	541	629	Good
Dodge Grand Caravan	1,099	218	346	179	495	184	581	203	541	629	Good
Honda Odyssey	728	140	438	145	386	194	304	351	616	536	Vry. Gd.
Mazda Mazda5	714	147	206	102	374	258	434	239	433	1,191	Good
Nissan Quest	546	146	353	312	426	354	1,145	406	514	766	Average
Toyota Sienna	868	126	483	320	971	242	1,496	1,037	390	886	Vry. Pr.
Volkswagen Routan	434	220	344	178	515	191	1,102	286	535	738	Average
Small SUV											
Acura RDX	644	144	471	141	447	204	396	264	445	1,679	Average
BMW X1	231	217	545	199	392	511	705	779	1,077	1,352	Vry. Pr.
Buick Encore											
Ford Escape	602	130	329	186	343	161	634	276	250	460	Vry. Gd.
Honda CR-V	672	140	513	131	342	375	452	185	364	622	Vry. Gd.
Hyundai Tucson	756	128	304	121	318	324	426	313	541	668	Vry. Gd.
Infiniti EX	462	165	389	319	402	396	515	825	584	872	Average
Jeep Compass	1,078	157	233	105	275	262	287	189	415	721	Vry. Gd.
Jeep Patriot	1,078	157	233	91	288	220	427	189	436	442	Vry. Gd.
Jeep Wrangler	875	199	181	201	308	178	360	175	311	374	Vry. Gd.
Mazda CX-5	616	169	248	88	357	320	434	204	645	1,356	Good
Mitsubishi Outlander Sport	1,008	177	861	284	759	400	274	406	452	1,230	Poor
Nissan Juke	462	139	456	377	405	268	764	271	326	490	Good
Subaru Forester	826	153	514	189	423	396	359	351	368	1,201	Good
Subaru XV Crosstrek	791	137	518	203	386	486	244	350	383	808	Good
Toyota RAV4	476	196	487	284	735	282	1,689	225	996	642	Vry. Pr.
Volkswagen Tiguan	476	160	498	393	376	397	573	647	430	682	Average
Mid-Size SUV											
Acura MDX	644	144	485	218	462	184	314	408	636	1,641	Average
Audi Q5	756	183	704	335	575	518	2,424	692	582	1,076	Vry. Pr.
BMW X3	231	217	545	199	392	511	705	779	1,077	1,352	Vry. Pr.
BMW X5	182	265	571	412	446	680	733	705	1,274	3,466	Vry. Pr.
Cadillac SRX	973	186	343	372	568	1,617	896	361	728	927	Vry. Pr.
Chevrolet Equinox	994	280	362	404	776	217	503	497	743	899	Poor
Dodge Journey	1,099	169	346	203	495	338	725	453	719	520	Good
AVERAGE OF ALL VEHICLES	**$718**	**$176**	**$435**	**$251**	**$463**	**$413**	**$754**	**$407**	**$588**	**$1,016**	

	PM Costs to 60,000 Miles	REPAIR COSTS									
		Front Brake Pads	Starter	Fuel Injector	Fuel Pump	Struts/Shocks	Timing Belt/Chain	Water Pump	Muffler	Headlamps	Relative Repair Cost*
Ford Edge	588	147	394	164	400	202	863	1,015	428	907	Average
Ford Explorer	707	137	390	129	417	241	765	854	814	1,237	Poor
Honda Pilot	714	140	462	145	443	256	304	421	625	799	Good
Hyundai Santa Fe	756	156	320	220	441	234	1,451	424	745	1,010	Poor
Infiniti FX	546	158	403	330	425	536	1,308	552	617	3,558	Vry. Pr.
Kia Sorento	728	124	228	249	362	405	1,451	392	742	711	Poor
Lexus RX	700	129	729	358	437	226	1,608	715	723	1,112	Vry. Pr.
Mazda CX-9	602	176	311	190	382	307	854	902	558	1,048	Poor
Mercedes-Benz GLK-Class	1,365	168	1,010	250	475	562	549	609	1,190	1,101	Vry. Pr.
Mercedes-Benz M-Class	1,365	87	810	243	394	704	1,424	567	650	990	Vry. Pr.
Mitsubishi Outlander	1,036	166	280	298	686	400	506	450	417	1,345	Average
Nissan Murano	546	138	353	333	463	429	1,285	392	487	792	Poor
Nissan Pathfinder	840	260	542	323	502	250	683	260	512	716	Average
Nissan Rogue	546	139	331	315	315	217	929	275	557	1,621	Poor
Nissan Xterra	840	174	378	325	446	207	683	290	330	668	Good
Porsche Cayenne	840	355	579	324	455	1,318	1,086	433	1,757	995	Vry. Pr.
Toyota FJ Cruiser	546	146	464	290	486	167	1,552	343	342	591	Average
Toyota Highlander	560	126	511	344	765	535	1,594	491	701	748	Vry. Pr.
Toyota Venza	910	126	482	307	665	507	1,435	615	611	755	Vry. Pr.
Volkswagen Touareg	406	217	580	705	542	803	1,105	443	886	1,312	Vry. Pr.
Volvo XC60	707	182	404	311	768	543	511	333	566	1,014	Poor
Volvo XC90	812	301	407	311	578	486	522	324	925	1,043	Poor
Large SUV											
Audi Q7	840	233	690	492	351	2,663	1,935	244	981	1,076	Vry. Pr.
Buick Enclave	938	253	340	314	515	267	771	403	982	1,868	Vry. Pr.
Chevrolet Suburban	994	275	288	141	519	989	630	465	955	1,900	Vry. Pr.
Chevrolet Tahoe	994	247	288	130	593	297	679	612	1,004	671	Average
Chevrolet Traverse	938	253	340	314	515	331	771	403	900	801	Poor
Dodge Durango	1,071	198	405	210	640	142	717	189	545	545	Good
Ford Expedition	756	162	273	150	437	263	785	257	546	595	Good
Ford Flex	623	133	394	189	368	194	828	850	665	993	Average
Infiniti JX	546	158	403	330	425	536	1,308	582	617	3,558	Vry. Pr.
Infiniti QX	840	146	493	265	472	469	1,170	251	483	1,643	Poor
Jeep Grand Cherokee	1,029	319	482	204	612	258	717	149	778	735	Average
Land Rover Range Rover	756	570	685	860	473	730	1,005	660	339	2,858	Vry. Pr.
Mercedes-Benz GL-Class	1,358	421	670	248	380	814	535	675	720	1,004	Poor
Nissan Armada	840	149	497	255	478	274	1,280	279	584	891	Poor
Toyota 4Runner	546	131	506	311	546	160	1,583	437	492	765	Poor
Toyota Sequoia	637	148	837	325	806	299	1,044	445	398	719	Poor
Compact Pickup											
Nissan Frontier	840	146	402	329	505	200	683	290	371	689	Good
Toyota Tacoma	504	126	531	314	775	149	1,069	373	472	710	Average
Standard Pickup											
Chevrolet Avalanche	994	247	288	140	603	270	678	458	950	657	Average
Chevrolet Silverado	994	258	288	148	597	309	686	451	977	649	Average
Ford F-150	546	162	411	131	462	153	996	281	426	611	Good
Honda Ridgeline	700	140	462	152	442	368	304	380	452	559	Vry. Gd.
Nissan Titan	840	177	525	255	532	252	1,280	279	557	861	Poor
Ram 1500	1,638	146	246	155	419	176	572	263	298	508	Vry. Gd.
Toyota Tundra	637	148	654	323	806	195	1,182	434	506	758	Poor
AVERAGE OF ALL VEHICLES	**$718**	**$176**	**$435**	**$251**	**$463**	**$413**	**$754**	**$407**	**$588**	**$1,016**	

SERVICE CONTRACTS

Service contracts are one of the most expensive options you can buy. In fact, service contracts are a major profit source for many dealers.

A service contract is not a warranty. It is more like an insurance plan that, in theory, covers repairs that are not covered by your warranty or that occur after the warranty runs out. They are often inaccurately referred to as "extended warranties."

Service contracts are generally a poor value. The companies who sell contracts are very sure that, on average, your repairs will cost considerably less than what you pay for the contract—if not, they wouldn't be in business.

Here are some important questions to ask before buying a service contract:

How reputable is the company responsible for the contract? If the company offering the contract goes out of business, you will be out of luck. The company may be required to be insured, but find out if they actually are and by whom. Check with your Better Business Bureau or office of consumer affairs if you are not sure of a company's reputation. Service contracts from car and insurance companies are more likely to remain in effect than those from independent companies.

Exactly what does the contract cover and for how long? Service contracts vary considerably—different items are covered and different time limits are offered. This is true even among service contracts offered by the same company. For example, one company has plans that range from 4 years/36,000 miles maximum coverage to 6 years/100,000 miles maximum coverage, with other options for only power train coverage. Make sure you know what components are covered because if a breakdown occurs on a part that is not covered, you are responsible for the repairs.

If you plan to resell your car in a few years, you won't want to purchase a long-running service contract. Some service contracts automatically cancel when you resell the car, while others require a hefty transfer fee before extending privileges to the new owner.

Some automakers offer a "menu" format, which lets you pick the items you want covered in your service contract. Find out if the contract pays for preventive maintenance, towing, and rental car expenses. If not written into the contract, assume they are not covered.

Make sure the contract clearly specifies how you can reach the company. Knowing this before you purchase a service contract can save you time and aggravation in the future.

How will the repair bills be paid? It is best to have the service contractor pay bills directly. Some contracts require you to pay the repair bill, and reimburse you later.

Where can the car be serviced? Can you take the car to any mechanic if you have trouble on the road? What if you move?

What other costs can be expected? Most service contracts will have a deductible expense. Compare deductibles on various plans. Also, some companies charge the deductible for each individual repair while other companies pay per visit, regardless of the number of repairs being made.

What are your responsibilities? Make sure you know what you have to do to uphold the contract. For example if you have to follow the manufacturer's recommended maintenance, keep detailed records or the contract could be voided. You will find your specific responsibilities in the contact. Be sure to have the seller point them out.

TIP

One alternative to buying a service contract is to deposit the cost of the contract into a savings account. If the car needs a major repair not covered by your warranty, the money in your account will cover the cost. Most likely, you'll be building up a down payment for your next car!

TIPS FOR DEALING WITH A MECHANIC

Call around. Don't choose a shop simply because it's nearby. Calling a few shops may turn up estimates cheaper by half.

Don't necessarily go for the lowest price. A good rule is to eliminate the highest and lowest estimates; the mechanic with the highest estimate is probably charging too much, and the lowest may be cutting too many corners.

Check the shop's reputation. Call your local consumer affairs agency and the Better Business Bureau. They don't have records on every shop, but unfavorable reports on a shop should disqualify it.

Look for certification. Mechanics can be certified by the National Institute for Automotive Service Excellence, an industry-wide yardstick for competence. Certification is offered in eight areas of repair and shops with certified mechanics are allowed to advertise this fact. However, make sure the mechanic working on your car is certified for the repair you need.

Take a look around. A well-kept shop reflects pride in workmanship. A skilled and efficient mechanic would probably not work in a messy shop.

Don't sign a blank check. The service order you sign should have specific instructions or describe your vehicle's symptoms. Avoid signing a vague work order. Be sure you are called for final approval before the shop does extra work. Many states require a written estimate signed by you and require that the shop get your permission for repairs that exceed the estimate by 10%.

Show interest. Ask about the repair. But don't act like an expert if you don't really understand what's wrong. Express your satisfaction. If you're happy with the work, compliment the mechanic and ask for him or her the next time you come in. You will get to know each other and the mechanic will get to know your vehicle.

Take a test-drive. Before you pay for a major repair, you should take the car for a test-drive. The few extra minutes you spend checking out the repair could save you a trip back to the mechanic. If you find that the problem still exists, there will be no question that the repair wasn't properly completed.

REPAIR PROTECTION BY CREDIT CARD

Paying your auto repair bills by credit card can provide a much needed recourse if you are having problems with an auto mechanic. According to federal law, you have the right to withhold payment for sloppy or incorrect repairs. Of course, you may withhold no more than the amount of the repair in dispute.

In order to use this right, you must first try to work out the problem with the mechanic. Also, unless the credit card company owns the repair shop (this might be the case with gasoline credit cards used at gas stations), two other conditions must be met. First, the repair shop must be in your home state (or within 100 miles of your current address), and second, the cost of repairs must be over $50. Until the problem is settled or resolved in court, the credit card company cannot charge you interest or penalties on the amount in dispute.

If you decide to take action, send a letter to the credit card company and a copy to the repair shop, explaining the details of the problem and what you want as settlement. Send the letter by certified mail with a return receipt requested.

Sometimes the credit card company or repair shop will attempt to put a "bad mark" on your credit record if you use this tactic. Legally, you can't be reported as delinquent if you've given the credit card company notice of your dispute, but a creditor can report that you are disputing your bill, which goes in your record. However, you have the right to challenge any incorrect information and add your side of the story to your file.

For more information, write to the Federal Trade Commission, Credit Practices Division, 601 Pennsylvania Avenue, NW, Washington, DC 20580.

TIRE RATINGS

Buying tires has become an infrequent task because today's radial tires last much longer than the tires of the past. Surprisingly, a tire has to perform more functions simultaneously than any other part of the car (steering, bearing the load, cushioning the ride, and stopping).

Because comparing tires is difficult, many consumers mistakenly use price and brand name to determine quality. Because there are hundreds of tire lines to choose from, and only a few tire manufacturers, the difference in many tires may only be the brand name.

But there is help. The U.S. government requires tires to be rated according to their safety and expected mileage.

Treadwear, traction, and heat resistance grades are printed on the sidewall and are attached to the tire on a paper label. Ask the dealer for the grades of the tires they sell. Using this rating system, a sampling of top rated tires follows on page 48.

Treadwear: The treadwear grade gives you an idea of the mileage you can expect from a tire. It is shown in numbers–720, 700, 680, 660, and so forth. Higher numbers mean longer tire life. A tire with a grade of 600 should give you twice as much mileage as one rated 300. Use the treadwear grade as a relative basis of comparison.

Traction: Traction grades of AA, A, B, and C describe the tire's ability to stop on wet surfaces. Tires graded AA will stop on a wet road in a shorter distance than tires graded B or C. Tires rated C have poor traction.

Heat Resistance: Heat resistance is graded A, B, and C. An A rating means the tire will run cooler than one rated B or C and be less likely to fail if driven over long distances at highway speeds. Tires that run cooler tend to be more fuel-efficient. Hot-running tires can result in blow-outs or tread separation.

TIRE CARE

Pump 'em Up: An estimated one-third of us are driving on underinflated tires. Because even good tires lose air, it is important to check your tire pressure monthly. Underinflated tires can be dangerous, use more fuel and cause premature tire failure. When checking your tires, be sure to use an accurate gauge and inflate to the pressure indicated in your owner's manual, not the maximum pressure printed on your tire.

When to Replace: If any part of Lincoln's head is visible when you insert the top of a penny into a tread groove, it's time to replace the tire. While this old rule of thumb is still valid, today's tires also have a built-in wear indicator. A series of horizontal bars appear across the surface when the tread depth reaches the danger zone.

GETTING THE BEST PRICE

The price of the same tire can vary depending on where you shop so shopping around is vital to finding a good buy. Most tire ads appear in the sports section of your Wednesday and Saturday daily newspaper. You are most likely to find the best prices at independent tire dealers who carry a variety of tire brands.

The price of a tire is based on its size, and tires come in as many as nine sizes. For example, the list price of the same tire can range from $74.20 to $134.35, depending on its size.

To get the best buy:

1. Check to see which manufacturer makes the least expensive "off brand." Only a few manufacturers produce the over 1,800 types of tires sold in the U.S.

2. Don't forget to compare balancing and mounting costs. These extra charges can add up to more than $25 or be offered at no cost.

3. Never pay list price for a tire. A good rule of thumb is to pay at least 30-40 percent off the suggested list price.

4. Use the treadwear grade the same way you would the "unit price" in a supermarket. The tire with the lowest cost per grade point is the best value. For example, if tire A costs $100 and has a treadwear grade of 600, and tire B costs $80 and has a treadwear grade of 300, tire A is the better buy, even though its initial cost is more.

Tire A: $100÷600=$0.17 per point
Tire B: $80÷300=$0.27 per point

Where you live is a key factor in how long your tires will last. In addition to construction and design, tire wear is affected by the level of abrasive material in the road surface. Generally, the road surfaces of the West Coast, Great Lakes region, and northern New England are easiest on tires. The Appalachian and Rocky Mountain areas are usually hardest on tires.

HOW TO READ A TIRE

Tire Type and Size: The most important information on a tire are the letters and the numbers indicating its type and size.

1. Tire Type: The P at the beginning of the tire size indicates that the tire is a passenger vehicle tire. LT indicates light truck tire, and T indicates a temporary or spare tire.

2. Tire Width is the first part of the number and is measured in millimeters, from sidewall to sidewall.

3. Tire Height is the next number and tells you the height of the tire from the bead to the tread. This is described as a percentage of the tire width. In our example, the tire's height is 65 percent of its width. The smaller the aspect ratio, the wider the tire in relation to its height.

4. Tire Construction designates how the tire was made. R indicates radial construction which is the most common type. Older tires were made using diagonal bias D or bias belted B construction, but these tire types are no longer used on passenger vehicles.

5. Wheel Diameter identifies the wheel rim diameter (in inches-15) needed for this tire.

6. Load Index: The load rating indicates the maximum load for that tire. A higher number indicates a higher load capacity. The rating 95, for example, corresponds to a load capacity of 1521 pounds. Larger vehicles, SUVs and pickups need tires with a higher load capacity.

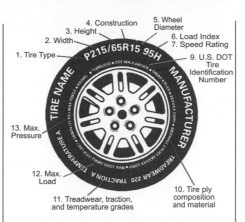

4. Construction
5. Wheel Diameter
3. Height
6. Load Index
2. Width
7. Speed Rating
1. Tire Type
P215/65R15 95H
9. U.S. DOT Tire Identification Number
13. Max. Pressure
12. Max. Load
11. Treadwear, traction, and temperature grades
10. Tire ply composition and material

7. Speed Rating indicates the maximum speed that the tire can sustain a ten minute endurance test without being in danger. All passenger car tires are rated at least S and pass the test at speeds up to 112 mph. Other ratings are as follows: T up to 118 mph, H up to 130 mph, V up to 149 mph and Z 150 mph or higher. Other types of tires, temporary spares and snow tires are lower on the rating scale.

8. Severe Conditions: M+S indicates the tire meets the Rubber Manu. Association's definition of a mud and snow tire. There are no performance tests for this standard. If the tire has an M+S and a "mountain and snowflake" symbol then the traction is at least 10% better than the regular version of the tire. These symbols are not in the above example.

9. Tire Identification Number
Example: DOT NJ HR 2AF 5212
The letters DOT certify compliance with all applicable safety standards established by the U.S. Department of Transportation. The next four characters is a code where the first two characters indicate the manufacturer and the second two characters indicate the plant where the tire was made.

Next you may see an optional string of three to four characters. Most manufacturers use these to record company specific information they use to identify their products or that can be used to identify tires in the market for recall purposes.

The last four digits determine the week and year the tire was made. The digits 5212 would signify that the tire was made during the 52nd week of 2012. Don't buy tires more than two years old. Tires naturally degrade with age, so you want the newest possible tires for the longest life (and safe operation.)

10. Tire Ply Composition and Material indicates the type of cord (polyester or steel) and number of plies in the tire, 4-ply, 6-ply, 8-ply, for both the tread and the sidewall.

11. Treadwear, Traction and Temperature Grades are three performance grades assigned to the tire and are the best way to truly evaluate the tires expected performance in these three critical areas. See page 46 for more information.

12. Max Load Limit tells you the cold inflation load limit in lbs. (pounds) and in kg (kilograms). The number corresponds to the load index.

13. Max Pressure is the maximum recommended pressure in psi (pounds per square inch) and in kPa (kilopascals). However, this is not the tire pressure for your car. You must check your owner's manual for the proper tire pressure for the tires on your car.

A Sampling of Top Rated Tires

Brand Name	Model	Description	Traction	Heat	Treadwear
Michelin	Hydroedge	ALL	A	B	760
Goodyear	Assurance Tripletred	ALL	A	B	740
Vogue	Wide Trac Touring LI	S-Rated	A	B	720
Cooper	Lifeliner STE	ALL	A	B	700
Cordovan	Grand Spirit Touring LS	ALL	A	B	700
Mastercraft	Touring LX	ALL	A	B	700
Toyo	800 Ultra	ALL	A	B	700
Michelin	X One With Durablack	ALL	A	B	700
Michelin	Cross Terrain Suv S-SP Rated	ALL	A	B	700
Big O	Legacy Tour Plus	P185,195,205 & 215/70R14 T	A	B	700
Big O	Legacy Tour Plus	P205,215/65R15 T	A	B	700
Big O	Legacy Tour Plus	P205,215,225 & 235/70R15 T	A	B	700
Big O	Legacy Tour Plus	P255 & 215/60R16 T	A	B	700
Big O	Legacy Tour Plus	P215/65R16 T	A	B	700
Big O	Legacy Tour Plus	P195/65R14 T	A	B	700
Big O	Legacy Tour Plus	P195/65R15 T	A	B	700
Mentor	Vantage Touring LE	ALL	A	B	700
Co-op	Goldenmark Luxury Touring (T)	ALL	A	B	700
Multi-Mile	Excel	ALL	A	B	700
Cordovan	Century	ALL	A	B	700
Bridgestone	Turanza LS "T"	ALL	A	B	700
Monarch	Ultra Tour LS	ALL	A	B	700
Lee	Ultra Tour LS	ALL	A	B	700
Kelly	Navigator Platinum TE	ALL Except	A	B	700
Republic	Ultra Tour LS	ALL	A	B	700
National	Ovation	P235/75R15	A	B	700
Delta	Esteem XLE	P235/75R15	A	B	700
Laramie	Grandeur Touring GT 60/65/70 Series	14-16	A	B	700
Jetzon	Grandeur Touring GT 60/65/70 Series	14-16	A	B	700
Telstar	Grandeur Touring GT 60/65/70 Series	14-16	A	B	700
Neutral	Touring LST	ALL Others	A	B	700
Goodyear	Assurance Comfortred	ALL	A	B	700
Bridgestone	Dueler HL Alenza T-Rated	ALL	A	B	700
Michelin	X Radial	ALL	A	B	680
National	Ovation	ALL 15 Except	A	B	680
Delta	Esteem XLE 70 & 75 Series	ALL 15 Except	A	B	680
Michelin	Harmony	ALL	A	B	680
Michelin	Destiny	ALL	A	B	680
Michelin	Agility	ALL	A	B	680
Big O	Legacy Tour Plus 60/65/70 Series	14-16	A	B	660
Riken	Raptor Touring Edition 70/75 Series	P205+	A	B	660
American	Gold Tour Plus 70/75 Series	P205+	A	B	660
Cavalier	Primera 70/75 Series	P205+	A	B	660
Trivant	Primera 70/75 Series	P205+	A	B	660
Co-op	Goldenmark Luxury Touring (S)	ALL	A	B	660
National	Ovation 70 & 75 Series	ALL 14	A	B	660
Delta	Esteem XLE 70 & 75 Series	ALL 14	A	B	660
Neutral	Touring LST 75 Series	ALL	A	B	660
Mastercraft	Touring LX	13 Only	A	B	640
Goodyear	Aquatred 3	ALL Others	AA	B	640
BFGoodrich	The Advantage Plus 70/75 Series	ALL	A	B	640
Hallmark	Ultra Touring GT	ALL	A	B	640
Lee	Ultra Touring GT	ALL	A	B	640
Riken	Raptor Touring Edition 70/75 Series	Thru P195	A	B	640
Cooper	Lifeliner STE	13	A	B	640
Sigma	Supreme Touring S-Series	ALL Others	A	B	640

For a complete listing of all the tires on the market, you can call the Auto Safety Hot Line toll free, at 888-327-4236 or 800-424-9153 (TTY). Or, go to www.safercar.gov

WARNING

As tires age, they naturally dry out and can become potentially dangerous. Some experts recommend getting rid of a six-year-old tire no matter what condition it is in. Recently, a national news organization went undercover and found 12 year old tires for sale, so be sure to check your tire date before purchasing. Ask for tires that are less than one year old.

INSURANCE

Insurance is a big part of ownership expenses, yet it's often forgotten in the showroom. As you shop, remember that the car's design and accident history may affect your insurance rates. Some cars cost less to insure because experience has shown that they are damaged less, less expensive to fix after a collision, or stolen less.

Shop Around: You can save hundreds of dollars by shopping around for insurance.

There are a number of factors that determine what coverage will cost you. A car's design can affect both the chances and severity of an accident. For example, a well-designed bumper may escape damage in a low-speed crash. Some cars are easier to repair than others or may have less expensive parts. Cars with four doors tend to be damaged less than cars with two doors.

Other factors that effect your insurance costs include:

Your Annual Mileage: The more you drive, the more your vehicle will be "exposed" to a potential accident. Driving less than 7,500 miles per year often gets a discount. Ask your insurer if they offer this option.

Where You Drive: If you regularly drive and park in the city, you will most likely pay more than if you drive in rural areas.

Youthful Drivers: Usually the highest premiums are paid by male drivers under the age of 25. Whether or not the under-25-year-old male is married also affects insurance rates. (Married males pay less.) As the driver gets older, rates are lowered.

Insurance discounts and surcharges depend upon the way a vehicle is traditionally driven. Sports cars, for example, are usually surcharged due, in part, to the typical driving habits of their owners. Four-door sedans and station wagons generally merit discounts.

Not all companies offer discounts or surcharges, and many cars receive neither. Some companies offer a discount or impose a surcharge on collision premiums only. Others apply discounts and surcharges on both collision and comprehensive coverage. Discounts and surcharges usually range from 10–30 percent. Remember that one company may offer a discount on a particular car while another may not.

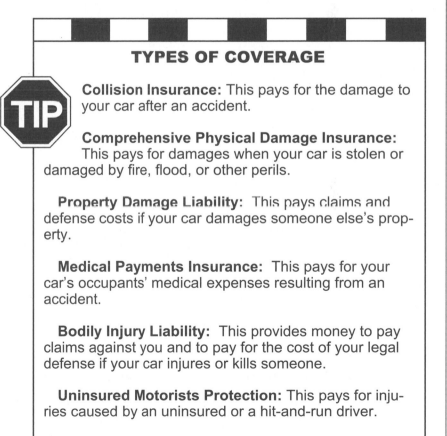

TYPES OF COVERAGE

TIP

Collision Insurance: This pays for the damage to your car after an accident.

Comprehensive Physical Damage Insurance: This pays for damages when your car is stolen or damaged by fire, flood, or other perils.

Property Damage Liability: This pays claims and defense costs if your car damages someone else's property.

Medical Payments Insurance: This pays for your car's occupants' medical expenses resulting from an accident.

Bodily Injury Liability: This provides money to pay claims against you and to pay for the cost of your legal defense if your car injures or kills someone.

Uninsured Motorists Protection: This pays for injuries caused by an uninsured or a hit-and-run driver.

REDUCING INSURANCE COSTS

Get Your Discounts: After you have shopped around and found the best deal by comparing the costs of different coverages, be sure you get all the discounts you are entitled to.

Most insurance companies offer discounts of 5-30 percent on various parts of your insurance bill. Ask your insurance company for a complete list of the discounts that it offers. These can vary by company and from state to state.

Here are some of the most common insurance discounts:

Driver Education/Defensive Driving Courses: Discounts for completing a state-approved driver education course can mean a $40 reduction in the cost of coverage. Discounts of 5–15 percent are available in some states to those who complete a defensive driving course.

Good Student Discounts of up to 25 percent for full-time high school or college students who are in the upper 20 percent of their class, on the dean's list, or have a B or better grade point average.

Good Driver Discounts are available to drivers with an accident and violation-free record, (or no incidents in 3 years).

Mature Driver Credit: Drivers ages 50 and older may qualify for up to a 10 percent discount or a lower price bracket.

Sole Female Driver: Some companies offer discounts of 10 percent for females, ages 30 to 64, who are the only driver in a household.

Non-Drinkers and Non-Smokers: A limited number of companies offer incentives ranging from 10–25 percent to those who abstain.

Farmer Discounts: Many companies offer farmers either a discount of 10–30 percent or a lower price bracket.

Car Pooling: Commuters sharing driving may qualify for discounts of 5–25 percent or a lower price bracket.

Children away at school don't drive the family car very often, so if they're on your policy and they're at school, let your company know. If you insure them separately, discounts of 10–40 percent or a lower price bracket are available.

Desirable Cars: Premiums are usually much higher for cars with high collision rates or that are the favorite target of thieves.

Anti-Theft Device Credits: Discounts of 5-15 percent are offered in some states for cars equipped with a hood lock and an alarm or a disabling device (active or passive) that prevents the car from being started.

Multipolicy and Multicar Policy Discount: Some companies offer discounts of up to 10–20 percent for insuring your home and auto with the same company, or more than one car.

First Accident Allowance: Some insurers offer a "first accident allowance," which guarantees that if a customer achieves five accident-free years, his or her rates won't go up after the first at-fault accident.

Deductibles: Opting for the largest reasonable deductible is the obvious first step in reducing premiums. Increasing your deductible to $500 from $200 could cut your collision premium

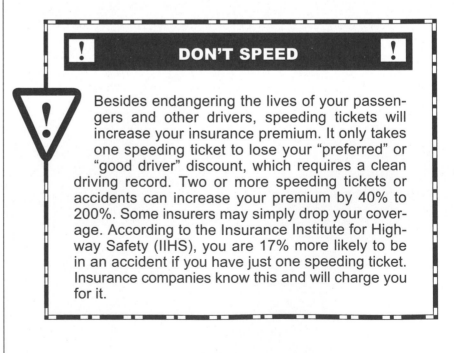

! DON'T SPEED !

Besides endangering the lives of your passengers and other drivers, speeding tickets will increase your insurance premium. It only takes one speeding ticket to lose your "preferred" or "good driver" discount, which requires a clean driving record. Two or more speeding tickets or accidents can increase your premium by 40% to 200%. Some insurers may simply drop your coverage. According to the Insurance Institute for Highway Safety (IIHS), you are 17% more likely to be in an accident if you have just one speeding ticket. Insurance companies know this and will charge you for it.

about 20 percent. Raising the deductible to $1,000 from $200 could lower your premium about 45 percent. The discounts may vary by company.

Collision Coverage: The older the car, the less the need for collision insurance. Consider dropping collision insurance entirely on an older car. Regardless of how much coverage you carry, the insurance company will only pay up to the car's "book value." For example, if your car requires $1,000 in repairs, but its "book value" is only $500, the insurance company is required to pay only $500.

Organizations: If you are a member of AARP, AAA, the military, a union, a professional group, an alumni association, or similar organization, you may be able to get a discount. Often insurance companies will enter joint ventures with organizations.

YOUNG DRIVERS

TIP

Each year, teenagers account for about 15 percent of highway deaths. According to the Insurance Institute for Highway Safety (IIHS), the highest driver death rate per 100,000 people is among 18-year-olds. Parents need to make sure their children are fully prepared to be competent, safe drivers before letting them out on the road. All states issue learner's permits. However, only 35 states and the District of Columbia require permits before getting a driver's license. It isn't difficult for teenagers to get a license and only 14 states prohibit teenagers from driving during night and early morning. Call your state's MVA for young driver laws.

AUTO THEFT

The Highway Loss Data Institute (HLDI) regularly compiles statistics on motor vehicle thefts. Using the frequency of theft claims per 1,000 insured vehicles, the HLDI lists the following as the most and least stolen vehicles among the 2008-2010 models.

Most Stolen	Claim Frequency*
Cadillac Escalade	10.8
Ford F-250 Crew 4WD	9.7
Chevrolet Silverado 1500 Crew	9.2
Ford F-450 Crew 4WD	7.9
GMC Sierra 1500 Crew	7.3
Chrysler 300	7.1
Ford F-350 Crew 4WD	7.0
Chevrolet Avalanche 1500	6.4
GMC Yukon	6.4
Chrysler 300 HEMI	6.3

Least Stolen	Claim Frequency*
Audi A6 4WD	0.5
Mercury Mariner	0.5
Chevrolet Equinox	0.6
Volkswagen CC	0.6
Chevrolet Equinox 4WD	0.6
Lexus RX 350	0.6
Saturn VUE	0.6
Chevrolet Aveo	0.6
BMW 5 Series 4WD	0.7
Mini Cooper Clubman	0.7
Average All Passenger Vehicles	**1.7**

*Claim Frequency means the number of vehicles stolen per 1000 insured vehicles, for example about 11 Cadillac Escalades are stolen or broken into for every 1,000 insured. Source: Highway Loss Data Institute (www.iihs.org)

BUMPERS

The main purpose of the bumper is to protect your car in low-speed collisions. Despite this intention, many of us have been victims of a $500-$3500 repair bill resulting from a seemingly minor impact. The federal government used to require that automakers equip cars with bumpers capable of withstanding up to 5 mph crashes with no damage. Unfortunately, in the early eighties, under pressure from car companies, the government rolled back this requirement. Now, the federal law only requires car companies to build bumpers that protect cars in 2.5 mph collisions-about the speed at which we walk. This rollback enables the car companies to sell lots of expensive parts, and has cost consumers millions of dollars in increased insurance premiums and repair costs.

The good news is that Canada has a 5 mph (8k) standard and many car companies use the same designs in models sold in the U.S. In addition, the state of California requires that companies disclose which bumpers meet the old 5 mph standard which has motivated some companies to build better bumper systems.

In order to see how well bumpers actually protect our vehicles, the Insurance Institute for Highway Safety conducts a variety of bumper tests. In their low speed (6 mph) tests, it's shocking how poorly bumpers protect vehicles. In these tests, it can easily cost $2-$3,700 after a low speed fender bender.

Unfortunately, we can't simply look at a bumper and determine how good it will be at doing its job-protecting a car from inevitable bumps. The solution to this problem is quite simple–require carmakers to tell the consumer the highest speed at which their car could be crashed with no damage.

Federal standards *do* require that car bumpers be designed to match up to each other in a collision. This is an attempt to enable the bumpers to hit each other and absorb the energy of the crash rather than other parts of the car. Unfortunately there is a big hole in this federal requirement because SUVs, pickups, and minivans don't have to meet the same bumper height rules as cars. With such a high percentage of SUVs, pickups and mini-vans on the road, huge bumper mismatches in crashes are quite common. Mismatching between cars and SUVs results in excessive damage and pricey repairs.

In order to see how well bumpers actually function in car and SUV collisions, the Insurance Institute for Highway Safety conducted two types of tests at 10 mph; one with an SUV hitting the rear of a car and one with a car traveling at 10 mph and crashing into the rear of an SUV. For more results, visit the Insurance Institute for Highway Safety at www.iihs.org. The table below shows how much this bumper mismatch problem can cost you.

DAMAGE REPAIR COSTS IN 10 MPH FRONT-INTO-

Source: Insurance Institute for Highway Safety

REAR CRASH TESTS

SUV INTO CAR	SUV Damage	Car Damage	Total Damage
Honda CR-V into Honda Civic	$1,721	$1,274	$2,995
Toyota RAV4 into Toyota Corolla	$1,434	$2,327	$3,761
Hyundai Tucson into Kia Forte	$850	$3,223	$4,073
Volkswagen Tiguan into Volkswagen Golf	$2,329	$2,058	$4,387
Jeep Patriot into Dodge Caliber	$1,415	$3,095	$4,510
Ford Escape into Ford Focus	$1,470	$3,386	$4,856
Nissan Rogue into Nissan Sentra	$2,884	$4,560	$7,444

CAR INTO SUV	Car Damage	SUV Damage	Total Damage
Kia Forte into Hyundai Tucson	$1,510	$2,091	$3,601
Dodge Caliber into Jeep Patriot	$2,559	$1,338	$3,897
Honda Civic into Honda CR-V	$4,921	$1,053	$5,974
Volkswagen Golf into Volkswagen Tiguan	$4,555	$1,872	$6,427
Nissan Sentra into Nissan Rogue	$5,114	$1,428	$6,542
Ford Focus into Ford Escape	$5,203	$2,208	$7,411
Corolla into Toyota RAV4	$3,852	$6,015	$9,867

See www.IIHS.org

Americans spend billions of dollars on vehicle repairs every year. While many of those repairs are satisfactory, there are times when getting your vehicle fixed can be a very difficult process. In fact, vehicle defects and repairs are the number one cause of consumer complaints, according to the Federal Trade Commission. This chapter is designed to help you resolve your complaint, whether it's for a new vehicle still under warranty or for one you've had for years. In addition, we offer a guide to arbitration, the names and addresses of consumer groups, federal agencies, and the manufacturers themselves. Finally, we tell you how to take the important step of registering your complaint with the U.S. Department of Transportation.

No matter what your complaint, keep accurate records. Copies of the following items are indispensable in helping to resolve your problems:

☑ your service invoices

☑ bills you have paid

☑ letters you have written to the manufacturer or the repair facility owner

☑ written repair estimates from your independent mechanic.

☑ notes on discussion with company representatives including names and dates.

RESOLVING COMPLAINTS

Here are some basic steps to help you resolve your problem:

1 First, return your vehicle to the repair facility that did the work. Bring a written list of the problems and make sure that you keep a copy of the list. Give the repair facility a reasonable opportunity to examine your vehicle and attempt to fix it. Speak directly to the service manager (not to the service writer who wrote up your repair order), and ask him or her to test drive the vehicle with you so that you can point out the problem.

2 If that doesn't resolve the problem, take the vehicle to a diagnostic center for an independent examination. This may cost $45 to $60. Get a written statement defining the problem and outlining how it may be fixed. Give your repair shop a copy. If your vehicle is under warranty, do not allow any warranty repair by an independent mechanic; you may not be reimbursed by the manufacturer.

3 If your repair shop does not respond to the independent assessment, present your problem to a mediation panel. These panels hear both sides of the story and try to come to a resolution.

If the problem is with a new vehicle dealer, or if you feel that the manufacturer is responsible, you may be able to use one of the manufacturer's mediation programs.

If the problem is solely with an independent dealer, a local Better Business Bureau (BBB) may be able to mediate your complaint. It may also offer an arbitration hearing. In any case, the BBB should enter your complaint into its files on that establishment.

When contacting any mediation program, determine how long the process takes, who makes the final decision, whether you are bound by that decision, and whether the program handles all problems or only warranty complaints.

4 If there are no mediation programs in your area, contact private consumer groups, local government agencies, or your local "action line" newspaper columnist, newspaper editor, or radio/TV broadcaster. A phone call or letter from them may persuade a repair facility to take action. Send a copy of your letter to the repair shop.

5 One of your last resorts is to bring a lawsuit against the dealer, manufacturer, or repair facility in small claims court. The fee for filing such an action is usually small, and you generally act as your own attorney, saving attorney's fees. There is a monetary limit on the amount you can claim, which varies from state to state. Your local consumer affairs office, state attorney general's office, or the clerk of the court can tell you how to file such a suit.

6 Finally, talk with an attorney. It's best to select an attorney who is familiar with handling automotive problems. Call the lawyer referral service listed in the telephone directory and ask for the names of attorneys who deal with automobile problems. If you can't afford an attorney, contact the Legal Aid Society.

WARRANTY COMPLAINTS
If your vehicle is under warranty or you are having problems with a factory-authorized dealership, here are some special guidelines:

1 Have the warranty available to show the dealer. Make sure you call the problem to the dealer's attention before the end of the warranty period.

2 If you are still dissatisfied after giving the dealer a reasonable opportunity to fix your vehicle, contact the manufacturer's representative (also called the zone representative) in your area. This person can authorize the dealer to make repairs or take other steps to resolve the dispute. Your dealer will have your zone representative's name and telephone number. Explain the problem and ask for a meeting and a personal inspection of your vehicle.

3 If you can't get satisfaction from the zone representative, call or write the manufacturer's owner relations department. Your owner's manual contains this phone number and address. In each case, as you move up the chain, indicate the steps you have already taken and keep careful records of your efforts.

4 Your next option is to present your problem to a complaint handling panel or to the arbitration program in which the manufacturer of your vehicle participates.

If you complain of a problem during the warranty period, you have a right to have the problem fixed even after the war-

ranty runs out. If your warranty has not been honored, you may be able to "revoke acceptance," which means that you return the vehicle to the dealer. If you are successful, you may be entitled to a replacement vehicle or to a full refund of the purchase price

and reimbursement of legal fees under the Magnuson-Moss Warranty Act. Or, if you are covered by one of the state lemon laws, you may be able to return the vehicle and receive a refund or replacement from the manufacturer.

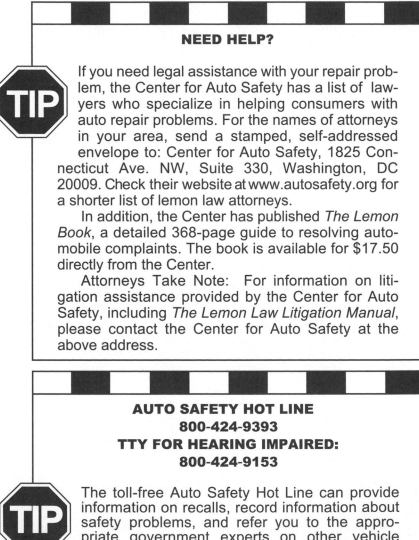

NEED HELP?

If you need legal assistance with your repair problem, the Center for Auto Safety has a list of lawyers who specialize in helping consumers with auto repair problems. For the names of attorneys in your area, send a stamped, self-addressed envelope to: Center for Auto Safety, 1825 Connecticut Ave. NW, Suite 330, Washington, DC 20009. Check their website at www.autosafety.org for a shorter list of lemon law attorneys.

In addition, the Center has published *The Lemon Book*, a detailed 368-page guide to resolving automobile complaints. The book is available for $17.50 directly from the Center.

Attorneys Take Note: For information on litigation assistance provided by the Center for Auto Safety, including *The Lemon Law Litigation Manual*, please contact the Center for Auto Safety at the above address.

AUTO SAFETY HOT LINE
800-424-9393
TTY FOR HEARING IMPAIRED:
800-424-9153

The toll-free Auto Safety Hot Line can provide information on recalls, record information about safety problems, and refer you to the appropriate government experts on other vehicle related problems. You can even have recall information mailed to you within 24 hours of your call at no charge. Most importantly, you can call the hot line to report safety problems which will become part of the National Highway Traffic Safety Administration's complaint database.

COMPLAINT INDEX

Thanks to the efforts of the Center for Auto Safety, we are able to provide you with the vehicle complaints on file with the National Highway Traffic Safety Administration (NHTSA). Each year, thousands of Americans file online or call the government in order to register complaints about their vehicles. The federal government collects this information but has never released it to the public.

The complaint index is the result of our analysis of these complaints. It is based on a ratio of the number of complaints for each vehicle to the sales of that vehicle. In order to predict the expected complaint performance of the 2013 models, we have examined the complaint history of that car's series. The term series refers to the fact that when a manufacturer introduces a new model, that vehicle remains essentially unchanged, on average, for four to six years. For example, the Cadillac Escalade was redesigned in 2002 and remains essentially the same car for 2013. As such, we have compiled the complaint experience for that series in order to give you some information to use in deciding which car to buy. For vehicles introduced or significantly changed in 2013, we do not yet have enough data to develop a complaint index.

The following table presents the projected best and worst complaint ratings for the 2013 models for which we can develop ratings. Higher index numbers mean the vehicle generated a greater number of complaints. Lower numbers indicate fewer complaints.

2013 PROJECTED COMPLAINT INDEX

THE BEST	INDEX*
Scion iQ	206
Mazda Mazda2	409
Kia Rio	455
Suzuki Kizashi	474
Volvo C70	553
Chevrolet Silverado	658
Lexus CT	834
Mazda Mazda6	872
Mercedes-Benz S-Class	911
Ford F-150	953
Mercedes-Benz M-Class	963
Nissan Cube	1005
Mercedes-Benz C-Class	1012
Mercedes-Benz E-Class	1024
Lincoln Navigator	1050
Acura MDX	1080
Audi Q5	1102
Mazda CX-9	1127
Mazda MX-5 Miata	1178
Audi A4	1188

THE WORST	INDEX*
Hyundai Veloster	17354
Toyota Prius	14817
Volkswagen Beetle	10683
Dodge Journey	10241
Infiniti M	10172
Jeep Wrangler	9473
Hyundai Sonata	8769
Volkswagen Routan	8554
Nissan Quest	8333
Nissan Leaf	8195
Ford Focus	8126
Chevrolet Volt	8035
Kia Sorento	7268
BMW 5 Series	6986
Jaguar XF	6842
Hyundai Azera	6523
Volkswagen Golf	5730
Ford Explorer	5652
Ford Fiesta	5464
Audi A3	5277

*IMPORTANT NOTE: The numbers represent relative index scores, not the number of complaints received. The complaint index score considers sales volume and years on the road. Lower index numbers are better.

CENTER FOR AUTO SAFETY

Every year automobile manufacturers spend millions of dollars making their voices heard in government decision making. For example, General Motors and Ford have large staffs in Detroit and Washington that work solely to influence government activity. But who looks out for the consumer?

For over 30 years, the nonprofit Center for Auto Safety (CAS) has told the consumer's story to government agencies, to Congress, and to the courts. Its efforts focus on all consumers rather than only those with individual complaints.

CAS was established in 1970 by Ralph Nader and Consumers Union. As consumer concerns about auto safety issues expanded, so did the work of CAS. It became independent of its founders in 1972. CAS' activities include:

Initiating Safety Recalls: CAS analyzes over 50,000 consumer complaints each year. By following problems as they develop, CAS requests government investigations and recalls of defective vehicles. CAS was responsible for the Ford Pinto faulty gas tank recall, the Firestone 500 steel-belted radial tire recall, and the record recall of over three million Evenflo One Step child seats.

Representing the Consumer in Washington: CAS follows the activities of federal agencies and Congress to ensure that they carry out their responsibilities to the American taxpayer. CAS brings a consumer's point of view to vehicle safety policies and rule-making. Since 1970, CAS has submitted more than 500 petitions and comments on federal safety standards.

One major effort on safety standards has been the successful fight to get airbags in every car. After opposing airbags for decades, the auto industry now can't get enough lifesaving airbags in cars with some models having eight airbags. With airbags to protect consumers in front and side crashes, CAS is now working to strengthen weak roofs that cannot support a vehicle's own weight and crush in rollovers that result in 27,000 deaths and serious injuries each year.

In 1992, CAS uncovered a fire defect that dwarfed the highly publicized flammability of the Ford Pinto. It had to do with the side saddle gas tanks on full size 1973–87 GM pickups and 1988–90 crew cabs that can explode on impact. Over 2,000 people have been killed in fire crashes involving these trucks. After mounting a national campaign to warn consumers to steer clear of these GM fire hazards, the U.S. Department of Transportation granted CAS' petition and conducted one of its biggest defect investigations in history. The result—GM was asked to recall its pickups. GM, sadly, denied this request.

Exposing Secret Warranties: CAS played a prominent role in the disclosure of secret warranties, "policy adjustments," as they are called by manufacturers. These occur when an automaker agrees to pay for repair of certain defects beyond the warranty period but refuses to notify consumers.

Lemon Laws: CAS' work on Lemon Laws aided in the enactment of state laws which make it easier to return a defective new automobile and get money back.

Tire Ratings: After a suspension between 1982 and 1984, consumers have reliable treadwear ratings to help them get the most miles for their dollar. CAS' lawsuit overturned DOT's revocation of this valuable tire information program.

Legal Action: When CAS has exhausted other means of obtaining relief for consumer problems, it will initiate legal action. For example, in 1978 when the Department of Energy attempted to raise the price of unleaded gasoline four cents per gallon without notice or comment, CAS succeeded in stopping this illegal move through a lawsuit, thus saving consumers $2 billion for the 3-year period that the decision was in effect.

A 1985 Center for Auto Safety lawsuit against the Environmental Protection Agency (EPA) forced the EPA to recall polluting

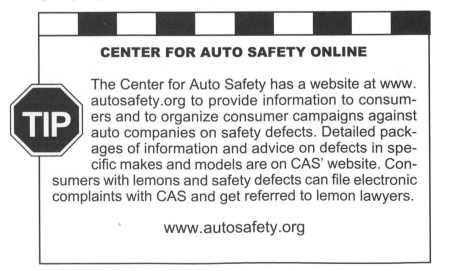

CENTER FOR AUTO SAFETY ONLINE

The Center for Auto Safety has a website at www.autosafety.org to provide information to consumers and to organize consumer campaigns against auto companies on safety defects. Detailed packages of information and advice on defects in specific makes and models are on CAS' website. Consumers with lemons and safety defects can file electronic complaints with CAS and get referred to lemon lawyers.

www.autosafety.org

cars, rather than let companies promise to make cleaner cars in the future. As part of the settlement, GM (which was responsible for the polluting cars) funded a $7 million methanol bus demonstration program in New York City.

In 2003, a CAS lawsuit forced the Department of Transportation (DOT) to require auto companies to use more accurate direct tire pressure monitors on the vehicle dash that identified which tire had low pressure versus an indirect system that only told consumers they had low tire pressure on some tire.

CAS also challenges class actions settlements that don't deliver for consumers. We have knocked off coupon settlement after coupon settlement in which consumers got useless coupons to buy a new car while trial lawyers got cold cash. In 2010 we challenged a Honda Civic Hybrid gas mileage settlement that gave consumers a DVD on how to drive better. In 2009, we challenged a Ford Explorer rollover settlement that gave consumers a restricted $500 coupon toward a new $30,000 Explorer or $300 for a different Ford model that only 148 out of 1,000,000 class members redeemed for about $50,000 total while attorneys got $25 million in fees and costs.

CAS is your safety and lemon insurance. CAS depends on public support to do all its good work. Annual membership is $25. All contributions are tax-deductible. To contribute by credit card, go to the CAS website at: www.autosafety.org/make-donation-cas.

To contribute by mail, send a check to: Center for Auto Safety, 1825 Connecticut Ave., NW #330, Washington, DC 20009-5708.

Consumer Groups and Government

Below are the names of additional consumer groups you may find helpful:

Advocates for Highway and Auto Safety
750 First St., NE, Suite 901
Washington, DC 20002
(202) 408-1711/408-1699 fax
www.saferoads.org
An alliance of consumer, health and safety groups and insurance companies.

Consumer Action
221 Main St., Suite 480
San Francisco, CA 94105
(415) 777-9635
www.consumer-action.org
Complaint handling and advocacy related to consumer rights.

Consumers for Auto Reliability and Safety
1303 J St., Suite 270
Sacramento, CA 95814
(530) 759-9440/www.carconsumers.com
Auto safety, airbags, and lemon laws.

KIDS AND CARS
7532 Wyoming St.
Kansas City, MO 64114
(816) 216-7085
www.kidsandcars.org
Safety and advocacy related to protecting children in and around motor vehicles.

Public Health Advocacy Institute
Motor Vehicle Hazard Archives Project
www.AutoHazardInfo.org
mvhap_phai@yahoo.com
The Project's mission is to preserve and broaden access to historical and current information about motor vehicle hazards and injury control. The website offers free information about vehicle safety and motor vehicle hazard control.

SafetyBelt Safe, U.S.A.
P.O. Box 553
Altadena, CA 91003
(800) 745-SAFE, stombrella@carseat.org
www.carseat.org
Excellent information and training on child safety seats and safety belt usage.

S.A.N.E., Inc.
2490 N. Park Road, #209 South
Hollywood, FL 33021
(954) 989-1251/www.saferautos.org
namrissam@bellsouth.net
Advocates and distributes information for better driving behavior and vehicle safety.

Several federal agencies conduct automobile-related programs. Following is each agency with a description of the type of work it performs and how to contact them.

National Highway Traffic Safety Administration
1200 New Jersey Ave., SE, West Bldg.
Washington, DC 20590
(888) 327-4236/www.nhtsa.dot.gov
www.safercar.gov
NHTSA issues safety and fuel economy standards for new motor vehicles; investigates safety defects and enforces recall of defective vehicles and equipment; conducts research and demonstration programs on vehicle safety, fuel economy, driver safety, and automobile inspection and repair; provides grants for state highway safety programs in areas such as police traffic services, driver education and licensing, emergency medical services, pedestrian safety, and alcohol abuse.

Environmental Protection Agency
1200 Pennsylvania Ave., NW
Washington, DC 20460
(202) 272-0167/www.epa.gov
www.fueleconomy.gov
EPA's responsibilities include setting and enforcing air and noise emission standards for motor vehicles and measuring fuel economy in new vehicles (EPA Fuel Economy Guide).

Federal Trade Commission
600 Pennsylvania Ave., NW
Washington, DC 20580
(877) FTC-HELP/www.ftc.gov
The FTC regulates advertising, credit practices, marketing abuses, and professional services and ensures that products are properly labeled (as in fuel economy ratings). The commission covers unfair or deceptive trade practices in motor vehicle sales and repairs, as well as non-safety defects.

U.S. Department of Justice
Consumer Protection Branch
950 Pennsylvania Ave., NW
Washington, DC 20503
(800) 869-4499 or 202-514-2000
www.usdoj.gov/civil.feedback@doj.gov
The DOJ enforces federal law that requires manufacturers to label new automobiles and forbids removal or alteration of labels before delivery to consumers. Labels must contain make, model, vehicle identification number, dealer's name, suggested base price, manufacturer option costs, and manufacturer's suggested retail price.

AUTOMOBILE MANUFACTURERS

Acura (Division of Honda)
John Mendel, Executive Vice President
See Honda for address
Customer Relations: 800-382-2238

Audi (See Volkswagen for address)
Scott Keosh, President
Customer Relations: 800-822-2834
E-mail: auditalk@audi.com

BMW
Ludwig Willisch, President
300 Chestnut Ridge Road
Woodcliff Lake, NJ 07677-7731
Customer Relations: 800-831-1117

Buick (Division of General Motors)
P.O. Box 33136
Detroit, MI 48232-5136
Customer Relations: 800-521-7300

Cadillac (Division of General Motors)
P.O. Box 33169
Detroit, MI 48232-5169
Customer Relations: 800-458-8006

Chevrolet (Division of General Motors)
P.O. Box 33170
Detroit, MI 48232-5170
Customer Relations: 800-222-1020
Fax: 313-556-5108

Chrysler (Chrysler, Dodge, Jeep, Ram)
Sergio Marchionne, CEO
1000 Chrysler Drive
Auburn Hills, MI 48321-8004
Customer Relations: 800-992-1997

Dodge (See Chrysler)

Ford (Ford, Lincoln)
Alan Mulally, President and CEO
P.O. Box 6248
Dearborn, MI 48121
Customer Relations: 800-392-3673
www.customersaskford.com

General Motors
(Buick, Cadillac, Chev., GMC)
Daniel Akerson, Chairman and CEO
300 Renaissance Center
Detroit, MI 48243

GMC (Division of General Motors)
P.O. Box 33172
Detroit, MI 48232
Customer Relations: 800-462-8782

Honda (Honda, Acura)
Tetsuo Iwamura, President and CEO
1919 Torrance Blvd.
Torrance, CA 90501
Customer Relations: 800-999-1009

Hyundai
John Krafcik, President and CEO
3200 Park Center Dr
Costa Mesa, CA 92626
Customer Relations: 800-633-5151
E-mail: consumeraffairs@hmausa.com

Infiniti (Division of Nissan)
See Nissan for address and executive
Customer Relations: 800-647-7261

Jaguar, Land Rover
Andy Goss, President
555 MacArthur Blvd.
Mahwah, NJ 07430
Jag Customer Relations: 800-452-4827

Jeep (See Chrysler)

Kia
Byung Mo Ahn, President and CEO
P.O. Box 52410
Irvine, CA 92619-2410
Customer Relations: 800-333-4542

Land Rover (See Jaguar)
Customer Relations: 800-637-6837
Fax: 201-760-8514

Lexus (Division of Toyota)
Mark Templin, VP and General Mgr.
P.O. Box 2991
Mail Drop L201
Torrance, CA 90501-2732
Customer Relations: 800-255-3987

Lincoln (Division of Ford)
P.O. Box 6128
Dearborn, MI 48121
Customer Relations: 800-521-4140

Mazda
Jim O' Sullivan, President and CEO
P.O. Box 19734
Irvine, CA 92623-9734
Customer Relations: 800-222-5500

Mercedes-Benz
Stephen Cannon, President and CEO
P.O. Box 350
Montvale, NJ 07645
Customer Relations: 800-367-6372

Mini (Division of BMW)
Jim McDowell, Vice President
P.O. Box 1227
Westwood, NJ 07675-1227
Customer Relations: 866-275-6464

Mitsubishi
Yoichi Yokozawa, President and CEO
P.O. Box 6014, Cypress, CA 90630-0014
Customer Relations: 888-648-7820

Nissan
Carlos Ghosn, President and CEO
P.O. Box 685003
Franklin, TN 37068-5003
Customer Relations: 800-647-7261

Porsche
Detlev von Platen, President and CEO
980 Hammond Dr.
Suite 1000
Atlanta, GA 30328
Customer Relations: 800-767-7243

Ram (See Chrysler)

Scion (Division of Toyota)
Jack Hollis, Vice President
P.O. Box 2742
Torrence, CA 90509-2742
Customer Relations: 866-707-2466

Smart (Division of Mercedes-Benz)
Tracy Matura, General Manager
See Mercedes-Benz for address
Customer Relations: 800-762-7887

Subaru
Takeshi Tachimori, President and CEO
Subaru Plaza
P.O. Box 6000
Cherry Hill, NJ 08034-6000
Customer Relations: 800-782-2783

Suzuki
Seiichi Maruyama, President
PO Box 1100
Brea, CA 92822-1100
Customer Relations: 800-934-0934

Toyota (Toyota, Lexus, Scion)
Jim Lentz, President and CEO
19001 S. Western Ave.
Torrance, CA 90501
Customer Relations: 800-331-4331

Volkswagen
Jonathan Browning, President and CEO
2200 Ferdinand Porsche Dr.
Herndon, VA 20171
Customer Relations: 800-822-8987

Volvo
John Maloney, President and CEO
One Volvo Dr.
PO Box 914
Rockleigh, NJ 07647
Customer Relations: 800-458-1552

LEMON LAWS

Sometimes, despite our best efforts, we buy a vehicle that just doesn't work right. There may be little problem after little problem, or perhaps one big problem that never seems to be fixed. Because of the "sour" taste that such vehicles leave in the mouths of consumers who buy them, these vehicles are known as "lemons."

In the past, it's been difficult to obtain a refund or replacement if a vehicle was a lemon. The burden of proof was left to the consumer. Because it is hard to define exactly what constitutes a lemon, many lemon owners were unable to win a case against a manufacturer. And when they won, consumers had to pay for their attorneys giving them less than if they had traded in their lemon.

Thanks to "Lemon Laws" passed by all states, lemon-aide is available when consumers get stuck with a lemon. Although there are some important state-to-state variations, all of the laws have similarities: They establish a period of coverage, usually two years from delivery or the written warranty period, whichever is shorter; they may require some form of noncourt arbitration; and most importantly they define a lemon. In most states a new car, truck, or van is "presumed" to be a lemon when it has been taken back to the shop 3 to 4 times for the same problem or is out of service for a total of 30 days during the covered period. This time does not mean consecutive days and can be for different problems. 15 states have safety lemon provisions which presume a vehicle is a lemon after only 1 to 2 repairs of a defect likely to cause death or serious injury. Be sure to keep careful records of your repairs since some states now require only one of the repairs to be within the specified time period. Thirty-three states provide for the award of attorney fees with the other 17 relying on the Federal lemon law for fees.

A vehicle may be covered by the lemon law even though it doesn't meet the "presumption."

Specific information about your state's law can be obtained from your state attorney general's office or at the Center for Auto Safety's website. The following table offers a general description of the Lemon Law in your state and what you need to do to set it in motion (Notification/Trigger). We indicate where state-run arbitration programs are available. State-run programs are the best type of arbitration. Be aware, a few state lemon laws are so bad consumers should only rely on the Federal lemon law and state contract law. We have marked these bad laws with a ☒ while the best laws have a ☑.

> ☑ **The Best Lemon Laws**
> ☒ **The Worst Lemon Laws**

Alabama	Qualification: 3 unsuccessful repairs or 30 calendar days within shorter of 24 months or 24,000 miles, provided 1 repair attempt or 1 day out of service is within shorter of 1 year or 12,000 miles. Notice/Trigger: Certified mail to manufacturer + opportunity for final repair attempt within 14 calendar days.
Alaska	Qualification: 3 unsuccessful repairs or 30 business days out of service within shorter of 1 year or warranty. Notice/Trigger: Certified mail to manufacturer + dealer (or repair agent) that problem has not been corrected in reasonable number of attempts + refund or replacement demanded within 60 days. Manufacturer has 30 calendar days for final repair attempt.
Arizona	Qualification: 4 unsuccessful repairs or 30 calendar days out of service within warranty period or shorter of 2 years or 24,000 miles. Notice/Trigger: Written notice + opportunity to repair to manufacturer.
Arkansas ☑ BEST	Qualification: 3 unsuccessful repairs, 5 total repairs of any nonconformity, or 1 unsuccessful repair of problem likely to cause death or serious bodily injury within longer of 24 months or 24,000 miles. Notice/Trigger: Certified or registered mail to manufacturer who has 10 days to notify consumer of repair facility. Facility has 10 days to repair.

L—Law specifically applies to leased vehicles; S-C—State has certified guidelines for arbitration; S-R—State-run arbitration mechanism available

California ☑ BEST	Qualification: 4 repair attempts or 30 calendar days out of service or 2 repair attempts for defect likely to cause death or serious bodily injury within shorter of 18 months or 18,000 miles, or "reasonable" number of attempts during entire express warranty period. Notice/Trigger: Direct written notice to manufacturer at address clearly specified in owner's manual. Covers small businesses with up to 5 vehicles under 10,000 pounds GVWR.
Colorado ☒ WORST	Qualification: 4 unsuccessful repairs or 30 business days out of service within shorter of 1 year or warranty. Notice/Trigger: Prior certified mail notice + opportunity to repair for manufacturer.
Connecticut	Qualification: 4 unsuccessful repairs or 30 calendar days out of service within shorter of 2 years or 24,000 miles, or 2 unsuccessful repairs of problem likely to cause death or serious bodily injury within warranty period or 1 year. Notice/Trigger: Report to manufacturer, agent, or dealer. Written notice to manufacturer only if required in owner's manual or warranty. S-R
Delaware	Qualification: 4 unsuccessful repairs or 30 calendar days out of service within shorter of 1 year or warranty. Notice/Trigger: Written notice + opportunity to repair to manufacturer.
D.C.	Qualification: 4 unsuccessful repairs or 30 calendar days out of service or 1 unsuccessful repair of safety-related defect, within shorter of 2 years or 18,000 miles. Notice/Trigger: Report to manufacturer, agent, or dealer.
Florida	Qualification: 3 unsuccessful repairs or 15 calendar days within 24 months from delivery. Notice/Trigger: Certified or express mail notice to manufacturer who has 10 days to notify consumer of repair facility plus 10 more calendar days for final repair attempt after delivery to designated dealer. S-R
Georgia	Qualification: 1 unsuccessful repair of serious safety defect or 3 unsuccessful repair attempts or 30 calendar days out of service within shorter of 24,000 miles or 24 months. Notification/Trigger: Overnight or certified mail notice return receipt requested. Manufacturer has 7 days to notify consumer of repair facility & consumer has 14 days from manufacturer receipt of original notice to deliver vehicle to repair facility. Facility has 28 calendar days from manufacturer receipt of original notice to repair. State-run arbitration mechanism available. Law specifically applies to leased vehicles.
Hawaii	Qualification: 3 unsuccessful repair attempts, or 1 unsuccessful repair attempt of defect likely to cause death or serious bodily injury, or out of service for total of 30 days within shorter of 2 years or 24,000 miles. Notice/Trigger: Written notice + opportunity to repair to manufacturer. S-R
Idaho	Qualification: 4 repair attempts or 30 business days out of service within shorter of 2 years or 24,000 miles, or 1 repair of complete failure of braking or steering likely to cause death or serious bodily injury. Notice/Trigger: Written notice to manufacturer or dealer + one opportunity to repair to manufacturer. S-R.
Illinois	Qualification: 4 unsuccessful repairs or 30 business days out of service within shorter of 1 year or 12,000 miles. Notice/Trigger: Written notice + opportunity to repair to manufacturer.
Indiana ☒ WORST	Qualification: 4 unsuccessful repairs or 30 business days out of service within shorter of 18 months or 18,000 miles. Notice/Trigger: Written notice to manufacturer only if required in the warranty.

L—Law specifically applies to leased vehicles; S-C—State has certified guidelines for arbitration; S-R—State-run arbitration mechanism available

Iowa	Qualification: 3 unsuccessful repairs, or 1 unsuccessful repair of nonconformity likely to cause death or serious bodily injury, or 30 calendar days out of service within shorter of 2 years or 24,000 miles. Notice/Trigger: Certified registered mail + final opportunity to repair within 10 calendar days of receipt of notice to manufacturer.
Kansas	Qualification: 4 unsuccessful repairs or 30 calendar days out of service or 10 total repairs within shorter of 1 year or warranty. Notice/Trigger: Actual notice to manufacturer.
Kentucky	Qualification: 4 unsuccessful repairs or 30 calendar days out of service within shorter of 1 year or 12,000 miles. Notice/Trigger: Written notice to manufacturer.
Louisiana	Qualification: 4 unsuccessful repairs or 90 calendar days out of service within shorter of 1 year or warranty. Notice/Trigger: Report to manufacturer or dealer.
Maine	Qualification: 3 unsuccessful repairs (or 1 unsuccessful repair of serious failure of brakes or steering) or 15 business days out of service within shorter of warranty or 3 years or 18,000 miles. Applies to vehicles within first 18,000 miles or 3 years regardless of whether claimant is original owner. Notice/Trigger: Written notice to manufacturer or dealer. Manufacturer has 7 business days after receipt for final repair attempt. S-R
Maryland	Qualification: 4 unsuccessful repairs, 30 calendar days out of service or 1 unsuccessful repair of braking or steering system within shorter of 15 months or 15,000 miles. Notice/Trigger: Certified mail return receipt requested + opportunity to repair within 30 calendar days of receipt of notice to manufacturer or factory branch.
Massachusetts	Qualification: 3 unsuccessful repairs or 10 business days out of service within shorter of 1 year or 15,000 miles. Notice/Trigger: Notice to manufacturer or dealer who has 7 business days to attempt final repair. S-R
Michigan	Qualification: 4 unsuccessful repairs within 2 years from date of first unsuccessful repair or 30 calendar days within shorter of 1 year or warranty. Notice/Trigger: Certified mail return receipt requested to manufacturer who has 5 business days to repair after delivery. Consumer may notify manufacturer after third repair attempt.
Minnesota	Qualification: 4 unsuccessful repairs or 30 business days or 1 unsuccessful repair of total braking or steering loss likely to cause death or serious bodily injury within shorter of 2 years or warranty. Notice/Trigger: Written notice + opportunity to repair to manufacturer, agent, or dealer.
Mississippi	Qualification: 3 unsuccessful repairs or 15 business days out of service within shorter of 1 year or warranty. Notice/Trigger: Written notice to manufacturer who has 10 business days to repair after delivery to designated dealer.
Missouri	Qualification: 4 unsuccessful repairs or 30 business days out of service within shorter of 1 year or warranty. Notice/Trigger: Written notice to manufacturer who has 10 calendar days to repair after delivery to designated dealer.
Montana	Qualification: 4 unsuccessful repairs or 30 business days out of service after notice within shorter of 2 years or 18,000 miles. Notice/Trigger: Written notice + opportunity to repair to manufacturer. S-R
Nebraska	Qualification: 4 unsuccessful repairs or 40 calendar days out of service within shorter of 1 year or warranty. Notice/Trigger: Certified mail + opportunity to repair to manufacturer.

L—Law specifically applies to leased vehicles; S-C—State has certified guidelines for arbitration; S-R—State-run arbitration mechanism available

Nevada	Qualification: 4 unsuccessful repairs or 30 calendar days out of service within shorter of 1 year or warranty. Notice/Trigger: Written notice to manufacturer.
New Hampshire	Qualification: 3 unsuccessful repairs by same dealer or 30 business days out of service within warranty. Notice/Trigger: Report to manufacturer, distributor, agent, or dealer (on forms provided by manufacturer) + final opportunity to repair before arbitration. S-R
New Jersey ☑ BEST	Qualification: 3 Unsuccessful repairs or 20 calendar days out of service within shorter of 2 years or 24,000 miles; or 1 unsuccessful repair of a serious safety defect likely to cause death or serious bodily injury. Notice/Trigger: Certified mail notice, return receipt requested to manufacturer who has 10 days to repair. Consumer may notify manufacturer at any time after the second repair attempt, or after the first repair attempt in the case of a serious safety defect.
New Mexico ☒ WORST	Qualification: 4 unsuccessful repairs or 30 business days out of service within shorter of 1 year or warranty. Notice/Trigger: Written notice + opportunity to repair to manufacturer, agent, or dealer.
New York	Qualification: 4 unsuccessful repairs or 30 calendar days out of service within shorter of 2 years or 18,000 miles. Notice/Trigger: Notice to manufacturer, agent, or dealer.
North Carolina	Qualification: 4 unsuccessful repairs within shorter of 24 months, 24,000 miles or warranty or 20 business days out of service during any 12 month period of warranty. Notice/Trigger: Written notice to manufacturer + opportunity to repair within 15 calendar days of receipt only if required in warranty or owner's manual.
North Dakota ☒ WORST	Qualification: 3 unsuccessful repairs or 30 business days out of service within shorter of 1 year or warranty. Notice/Trigger: Direct written notice + opportunity to repair to manufacturer. (Manufacturer's informal arbitration process serves as prerequisite to consumer refund or replacement.)
Ohio ☑ BEST	Qualification: 3 unsuccessful repairs of same nonconformity, 30 calendar days out of service, 8 total repairs of any nonconformity, or 1 unsuccessful repair of problem likely to cause death or serious bodily injury within shorter of 1 year or 18,000 miles. Notice/Trigger: Report to manufacturer, its agent, or dealer.
Oklahoma	Qualification: 4 unsuccessful repairs or 30 calendar days out of service within shorter of 1 year or warranty. Notice/Trigger: Written notice + opportunity to repair to manufacturer.
Oregon	Qualification: 4 unsuccessful repairs or 30 business days within shorter of 1 year or 12,000 miles. Notice/Trigger: Direct written notice + opportunity to repair to manufacturer.
Pennsylvania	Qualification: 3 unsuccessful repairs or 30 calendar days within shorter of 1 year, 12,000 miles, or warranty. Notice/Trigger: Delivery to authorized service + repair facility. If delivery impossible, written notice to manufacturer or its repair facility obligates them to pay for delivery.
Rhode Island	Qualification: 4 unsuccessful repairs or 30 calendar days out of service within shorter of 1 year or 15,000 miles. Notice/Trigger: Report to dealer or manufacturer who has 7 days for final repair opportunity.

L—Law specifically applies to leased vehicles; S-C—State has certified guidelines for arbitration; S-R—State-run arbitration mechanism available

South Carolina	Qualification: 3 unsuccessful repairs or 30 calendar days out of service within shorter of 1 year or 12,000 miles. Notice/Trigger: Certified mail + opportunity to repair (not more than 10 business days) to manufacturer only if manufacturer informed consumer of such at time of sale.
South Dakota	Qualification: 4 unsuccessful repairs, 1 of which occurred during shorter of 1 year or 12,000 miles, or 30 calendar days out of service during shorter of 24 months or 24,000 miles. Notice/Trigger: Certified mail to manufacturer + final opportunity to repair + 7 calendar days to notify consumer of repair facility.
Tennessee	Qualification: 4 unsuccessful repairs or 30 calendar days out of service within shorter of 1 year or warranty. Notice/Trigger: Certified mail notice to manufacturer + final opportunity to repair within 10 calendar days.
Texas	Qualification: 4 unsuccessful repairs when 2 occurred within shorter of 1 year or 12,000 miles, + other 2 occur within shorter of 1 year or 12,000 miles immediately following second repair attempt; or 2 unsuccessful repairs of serious safety defect when 1 occurred within shorter of 1 year or 12,000 miles + other occurred within shorter of 1 year or 12,000 miles immediately following first repair; or 30 calendar days out of service within shorter of 2 years or 24,000 miles + at least 2 attempts were made within shorter of 1 year or 12,000 miles. Notice/Trigger: Written notice to manufacturer. S-R
Utah	Qualification: 4 unsuccessful repairs or 30 business days out of service within shorter of 1 year or warranty. Notice/Trigger: Report to manufacturer, agent, or dealer. S-R
Vermont	Qualification: 3 unsuccessful repairs when at least first repair was within warranty, or 30 calendar days out of service within warranty. Notice/Trigger: Written notice to manufacturer (on provided forms) after third repair attempt, or 30 days. Arbitration must be held within 45 days after notice, during which time manufacturer has 1 final repair. S-R Note: Repairs must been done by same authorized agent or dealer, unless consumer shows good cause for taking vehicle to different agent or dealer.
Virginia	Qualification: 3 unsuccessful repairs, or 1 repair attempt of serious safety defect, or 30 calendar days out of service within 18 months. Notice/Trigger: Written notice to manufacturer. If 3 unsuccessful repairs or 30 days already exhausted before notice, manufacturer has 1 more repair attempt not to exceed 15 days.
Washington	Qualification: 4 unsuccessful repairs, 30 calendar days out of service (15 during warranty period), or 2 repairs of serious safety defect, first reported within shorter of warranty or 24 months or 24,000 miles. One repair attempt + 15 of 30 days must fall within manufacturer's express warranty of at least 1 year of 12,000 miles. Notice/Trigger: Written notice to manufacturer. S-R Note: Consumer should receive replacement or refund within 40 calendar days of request.
West Virginia ☑ BEST	Qualification: 3 unsuccessful repairs or 30 calendar days out of service or 1 unsuccessful repair of problem likely to cause death or serious bodily injury within shorter of 1 year or warranty. Notice/Trigger: Written notice + opportunity to repair to manufacturer.
Wisconsin	Qualification: 4 unsuccessful repairs or 30 calendar days out of service within shorter of 1 year or warranty. Notice/Trigger: Report to manufacturer or dealer. Note: Consumer should receive replacement or refund within 30 calendar days after offer to return title.
Wyoming	Qualification: 3 unsuccessful repairs or 30 business days out of service within 1 year. Notice/Trigger: Direct written notice + opportunity to repair to manufacturer. S-R State-run arbitration mechanism available.

L—Law specifically applies to leased vehicles; S-C—State has certified guidelines for arbitration; S-R—State-run arbitration mechanism available

5 BASIC STEPS TO CAR BUYING

Buying a car means matching wits with a seasoned professional. But if you know what to expect, you'll have a much better chance of getting a really good deal!

There's no question that buying a car can be an intimidating experience. But it doesn't have to be. First of all, you have in your hands all of the information you need to make an informed choice. Secondly, if you approach the purchase logically, you'll always maintain control of the decision. Start with the following basic steps:

1 Narrow your choice down to a particular class of car—sports, station wagon, minivan, sedan, large luxury, SUV, truck, or economy car. These are general classifications and some cars may fit into more than one category. In most cases, *The Car Book* presents the vehicles by size class.

2 Determine what features are really important to you. Most buyers consider safety on the top of their list, which is why the "Safety" chapter is right up front in *The Car Book*. Airbags, power options, ABS, and the number of passengers, as well as "hidden" elements such as maintenance and insurance costs, should be considered at this stage in your selection process.

3 Find three or four cars that meet the needs you outlined above and your pocketbook. It's important not to narrow your choice down to one car because then you lose all your bargaining power in the showroom. (Why? Because you might lose the psychological ability to walk away from a bad deal!) In fact, because cars today are more similar than dissimilar, it's not hard to keep three or four choices in mind. In the car rating pages in the back of the book, we suggest some competitive choices for your consideration. For example, if you are interested in the Honda Accord, you should also consider the Toyota Camry and Ford Fusion.

4 Make sure you take a good, long test drive. The biggest car buying mistake most of us make is to overlook those nagging problems that seem to surface only after we've brought the car home. Spend at least an hour driving the car without a salesperson preferably. If a dealership won't allow you to testdrive a car without a salesperson, go somewhere else. The test-drive should include time on the highway, parking, taking the car in and out of your driveway or garage, sitting in the back seat, and using the trunk or storage area.

TIP: Whatever you do, don't talk price until you're ready to buy!

5 This is the stage most of us dread—negotiating the price. While price negotiation is a car buying tradition, a few carmakers and dealers are trying to break tradition by offering so-called "no-haggle pricing." Since they're still in the minority and because it's very hard for an individual to establish true competition between dealers, we offer a great means to avoid negotiating altogether by using the non-profit CarBargains pricing service described on page 68.

THE 180-DEGREE TURN

TIP

When buying a car, remember that you have the most important weapon in the bargaining process: the 180-degree turn. Be prepared to walk away from a deal, even at the risk of losing the "very best deal" your salesperson has ever offered, and you will be in the best position to get a real "best deal." Remember: Dealerships need you, the buyer, to survive.

IN THE SHOWROOM

Being prepared is the best way to turn a potentially intimidating showroom experience into a profitable one. Here's some advice on handling what you'll find in the showroom.

Beware of silence. Silence is often used to intimidate, so be prepared for long periods of time when the salesperson is "talking with the manager." This tactic is designed to make you want to "just get the negotiation over with." Instead of becoming a victim, do something that indicates you are serious about looking elsewhere. Bring the classified section of the newspaper and begin circling other cars or review brochures from other manufacturers. By sending the message that you have other options, you increase your bargaining power and speed up the process.

Don't fall in love with a car. Never look too interested in any particular car. Advise family members who go with you against being too enthusiastic about any one car. Tip: Beat the dealers at their own game—bring along a friend who tells you that the price is "too much compared to the other deal."

Keep your wallet in your pocket. Don't leave a deposit, even if it's refundable. You'll feel pressure to rush your shopping, and you'll have to return and face the salesperson again before you are ready.

Shop at the end of the month. Salespeople anxious to meet sales goals are more willing to negotiate a lower price at this time.

Buy last year's model. The majority of new cars are the same as the previous year, with minor cosmetic changes. You can save considerably by buying in early fall when dealers are clearing space for "new" models. The important trade-off you make using this technique is that the carmaker may have added a new safety feature to an otherwise unchanged vehicle.

Buying from stock. You can often get a better deal on a car that the dealer has on the lot. However, these cars often have expensive options you may not want or need. Do not hesitate to ask the dealer to remove an option (and its accompanying charge) or sell you the car without charging for the option. The longer the car sits there, the more interest the dealer pays on the car, which increases the dealer's incentive to sell.

Ordering a car. Cars can be ordered from the manufacturer with exactly the options you want. Simply offering a fixed amount over invoice may be attractive because it's a sure sale and the dealership has not invested in the car. All the salesperson has to do is take your order.

If you do order a car, make sure when it arrives that it includes only the options you requested. Don't fall for the trick where the dealer offers you unordered options at a "special price," because it was their mistake. If you didn't order an option, don't pay for it.

⚠ BEWARE OF MANDATORY ARBITRATION AGREEMENTS

More and more dealers are adding mandatory binding arbitration agreements, which they often call "dispute resolution mechanisms," to your purchase contract. What this means is that you waive the right to sue or appeal any problem you have with the vehicle. Before you start negotiating the price, ask if the dealer requires Mandatory Binding Arbitration. If so, and they won't remove that requirement, you should buy elsewhere. Many dealers do not have this requirement.

GETTING THE BEST PRICE

One of the most difficult aspects of buying a new car is getting the best price. Most of us are at a disadvantage negotiating because we don't know how much the car actually cost the dealer. The difference between what the dealer paid and the sticker price represents the negotiable amount.

Beware, now that most savvy consumers know to check the so-called "dealer invoice," the industry has camouflaged this number. Special incentives, rebates, and kickbacks can account for $500 to $2,000 worth of extra profit to a dealer selling a car at "dealer invoice." The non-profit Center for the Study of Services recently discovered that in 37 percent of cases when dealers are forced to bid against each other for the sale, they offered the buyer a price below the "dealer invoice"—an unlikely event if the dealer was actually losing money. The bottom line is that "dealer invoice" doesn't really mean dealer cost.

You can't really negotiate with only one dealer, you need to get two or three bidding against each other. Introducing competition is the best way to get the lowest price on a new car. To do this you have to convince two or three dealers that you are, in fact, prepared to buy a car; that you have decided on the make, model, and features; and that your decision now rests solely on which dealer will give you the best price. You can try to do this by phone, but often dealers will not give you the best price, or will quote you a price over the phone that they will not honor later. Instead, you should try to do this in person. As anyone knows who

has ventured into an auto showroom simply to get the best price, the process can be lengthy as well as terribly arduous. Nevertheless, if you can convince the dealer that you are serious and are willing to take the time to go to a number of dealers, it will pay off. Other-wise, we suggest you use the CarBargains service described on page 68.

Here are some other showroom strategies:

Shop away from home. If you find a big savings at a dealership far from your home or on the Internet, call a local dealer with the price. They may very well match it. If not, pick up the car from the distant dealer, knowing your trip has saved you hundreds of dollars. You can still bring it to your local dealer for warranty work and repairs.

Beware of misleading advertising. New car ads are meant to get you into the showroom. They usually promise low prices, big rebates, high trade-in, and spotless integrity—don't be deceived. Advertised prices are rarely the true selling price. They usually exclude transportation charges, service fees, or document fees. And always look out for the asterisk, both in advertisements and on invoices. It can be a signal that the advertiser has something to hide.

Don't talk price until you're ready to buy. On your first few trips to the showroom, simply look over the cars, decide what options you want, and do your test-driving.

Shop the corporate twins. Page 75 contains a list of corporate twins—nearly identical cars that carry different name plates. Check the price and options of the twins of the car you like. A higher-priced twin may have more options, so it may be a better deal than the lower-priced car without the options you want.

Watch out for dealer preparation overcharges. Before paying the dealer to clean your car, make sure that preparation is not included in the basic price. The price sticker will state: "Manufacturer's suggested retail price of this model includes dealer preparation."

If you must negotiate . . . negotiate up from the "invoice" price rather than down from the sticker price. Simply make an offer close to or at the "invoice" price. If the salesperson says that your offer is too low to make a profit, ask to see the factory invoice.

Don't trade in. Although it is more work, you can usually do better by selling your old car yourself than by trading it in. To determine what you'll gain by selling the car yourself, check the NADA Official Used Car Guide at your credit union or library. On the web, the Kelly Blue Book website at kbb.com is a good source for invoice pricing. The difference between the trade-in price (what the dealer will give you) and the retail price (what you typically can sell it for) is your extra payment for selling the car yourself.

If you do decide to trade your car in at the dealership, keep the buying and selling separate. First, negotiate the best price for your new car, then find out how much the dealer will give you for your old car. Keeping the two deals separate ensures that you know what you're paying for your new car and simplifies the entire transaction.

Question everything the dealer writes down. Nothing is etched in stone. Because things are written down, we tend not to question them. This is wrong—always assume that anything written down is negotiable.

BUYING FOR SAFETY

So how do you buy for safety? Many consumers mistakenly believe that handling and performance are the key elements in the safety of a car. While an extremely unresponsive car could cause an accident, most new cars meet basic handling requirements. In fact, many people actually feel uncomfortable driving high performance cars because the highly responsive steering, acceleration, and suspension systems can be difficult to get used to. But the main reason handling is overrated as a safety measure is that automobile collisions are, by nature, accidents. Once they've begun, they are beyond human capacity to prevent, no matter how well your car handles. So the key to protecting yourself is to purchase a car that offers a high degree of crash protection.

AVOIDING LEMONS

One way to avoid the sour taste of a lemon after you've bought your car is to protect yourself before you sign on the dotted line. These tips will help you avoid problems down the road.

1 Avoid new models. Any new car in its very first year of production often turns out to have a lot of defects. Sometimes the manufacturer isn't able to remedy the defects until the second, third, or even fourth year of production. If the manufacturer has not worked out problems by the third model year, the car will likely be a lemon forever.

2 Avoid the first cars off the line. Most companies close down their assembly lines every year to make annual changes. In addition to adding hundreds of dollars to the price of a new car, these changes can introduce new defects. It can take a few months to iron out these bugs. Ask the dealer when the vehicle you are interested in was manufactured, or look on the metal tag found on the inside of the driver-side door frame to find the date of manufacture.

3 Avoid delicate options. Delicate options have the highest frequency-of-repair records. Power seats, power windows, and special roofs are nice conveniences—until they break down. Of all the items on the vehicles, they tend to be the most expensive to repair.

4 Inspect the dealer's checklist. Request a copy of the dealer's pre-delivery service and adjustment checklist (also called a "make-ready list") at the time your new vehicle is delivered. Write the request directly on the new vehicle order. This request informs the dealer that you are aware of the dealer's responsibility to check your new car for defects.

5 Examine the car on delivery. Most of us are very excited to take the vehicle home. A few minutes of careful inspection can save hours of misery later. Look over the body for any damage; check for the spare tire and jack equipment; make sure all electrical items work, and all the hubcaps and body molding are on. You may want to take a short test-drive. Finally, make sure you have the owner's manual, warranty forms, and all the legal documents.

CarBargains' Best Price Service

Even with the information that we provide you in this chapter of *The Car Book*, many of us still will not be comfortable negotiating for a fair price. In fact, as we indicated on the previous page, we believe it's really very difficult to negotiate the best price with a single dealer. The key to getting the best price is to get dealers to compete with each other.

CarBargains is a service of the non-profit Consumers' CHECK-BOOK, a consumer group that provides comparative price and quality information for many products and services.

CarBargains will "shop" the dealerships in your area and obtain at least five price quotes for the make and model of the car that you want to buy. The dealers who submit quotes know that they are competing with other area dealerships and have agreed to honor the prices that they submit. It is important to note that CarBargains is not an auto broker or "car buying" service; they have no affiliation with dealers.

Here's how the service works:

1. You provide CarBargains with the make, model, and style of car you wish to buy (Toyota Camry XLE, for example) by phone or mail.

2. Within two weeks, CarBargains will send you dealer quote sheets from at least five local dealers who have bid against one another to sell you that car. Each dealer's offer is actually a commitment to a dollar amount above (or below) "factory invoice cost" for that model. You get the name and phone number of the manager responsible for handling the quote.

You will also receive a print-out that enables you to figure the exact cost for each available option you might want on the vehicle.

3. Determine which dealer offers the best price using the dealer quote sheets. Add up the cost including the specific options you want. Contact the sales manager of that dealership and arrange to purchase the car.

If a car with the options you want is not available on the dealer's lot, you can, in many cases, have the dealer order the car from the factory or from another dealer at the agreed price.

When you receive your quotes, you will also get some suggestions on low-cost sources of financing and a valuation of your used car (trade-in).

The price for this service ($200) may seem expensive, but when you consider the savings that will result by having dealers bid against each other, as well as the time and effort of trying to get these bids yourself, we believe it's a great value. The dealers know they have a bona fide buyer (you've paid for the service); they know they are bidding against five to seven of their competitors; and, you have CarBargains' experts on your side.

To obtain CarBargains' competitive price quotes, call them at 800-475-7283 or visit their website at www.carbargains.org. Or, you can send a check for $200 to CarBargains, 1625 K St., NW, 8th Floor, Washington, DC 20006. Be sure to include your complete mailing address, phone number, and e-mail address (in case of questions), and the exact make, model, style, and year of the car you want to buy. You should receive your report within two weeks.

⚠ AUTO BROKERS ⚠

While CarBargains is a non-profit organization created to help you find the best price for the car you want to purchase, auto brokers are typically in the business to make money. As such, the price you end up paying for the car will include additional profit for the broker. There have been cases where the auto broker makes certain promises, takes your money, and you never hear from him again. While many brokers are legitimately trying to get their customers the best price, others have developed special relationships with certain dealers and may not do much shopping for you. As a consumer, it is difficult to tell which are which. This is why we recommend CarBargains. If CarBargains is not for you, then we suggest you consider using a buying service associated with your credit union or auto club. They can arrange for the purchase of a car at some fixed price over "dealer invoice."

FINANCING

You've done your test-drive, researched prices, studied crash tests, determined the options you want, and haggled to get the best price. Now you have to decide how to pay for the car.

If you have the cash, pay for the car right away. You avoid finance charges, you won't have a large debt haunting you, and the full value of the car is yours. You can then make the monthly payments to yourself to save up for your next car.

However, most of us cannot afford to pay cash for a car, which leaves two options: financing or leasing. While leasing may seem more affordable, financing will actually cost you less. When you finance a car, you own it after you finish your payments. At the end of a lease, you have nothing. We don't recommend leasing, but if you want more information, see page 71.

Shop around for interest rates. Most banks and credit unions will knock off at least a quarter of a percent for their customers. Have these quotes handy when you talk financing with the dealer.

The higher your down payment, the less you'll have to finance. This will not only reduce your overall interest charges, but often qualifies you for a lower interest rate.

Avoid long car loans. The monthly payments are lower, but you'll pay far more in overall interest charges. For example, a two-year, $20,000 loan at 7 percent will cost you $1,491 in interest; the same amount at five years will cost you $3,761—over twice as much!

Beware of manufacturer promotional rates—the 0 to 1 percent rates you see advertised. These low rates are usually only valid on two or three-year loans and only for the most credit-worthy customers.

Read everything you are asked to sign and ask questions about anything you don't fully understand.

Make sure that an extended warranty has not been added to the purchase price. Dealers will sometimes do this without telling you. Extended warranties are generally a bad value. See the "Warranties" chapter for more information.

Credit Unions vs. Banks: Credit unions generally charge fewer and lower fees and offer better rates than banks. In addition, credit unions offer counseling services where consumers can find pricing information on cars or compare monthly payments for financing. You can join a credit union either through your employer, an organization or club, or if you have a relative who is part of a credit union.

DON'T BE TONGUE-TIED

Beware of high-pressure phrases like "I've talked to the manager and this is really the best we can do. As it is, we're losing money on this deal." Rarely is this true. Dealers are in the business to make money and most do very well. Don't tolerate a take-it-or-leave-it attitude. Simply repeat that you will only buy when you see the deal you want and that you don't appreciate the dealer pressuring you. Threaten to leave if the dealer continues to pressure you to buy today.

Don't let the dealer answer your questions with a question. If you ask, "Can I get air conditioning with this car?" and the salesperson answers, "If I get you air conditioning in this car, will you buy today?" this response tries to force you to decide to buy before you are ready. Ask the dealer to just answer your question and say that you'll buy when you're ready. It's the dealer's job to answer questions, not yours.

If you are having a difficult time getting what you want, ask the dealer: "Why won't you let me buy a car today?" Most salespeople will be thrown off by this phrase as they are often too busy trying to use it on you. If they respond in frustration, "OK, what do you want?" then you can make straightforward answers to simple questions.

Get a price; don't settle for: "If you're shopping price, go to the other dealers first and then come back." This technique ensures that they don't have to truly negotiate. Your best response is: "I only plan to come back if your price is the lowest, so that's what I need today, your lowest price."

TYPICAL OPERATING COSTS

Here are the annual operating costs for some popular vehicles. These costs include operating expenses (fuel, oil, maintenance, and tires) and ownership expenses (insurance, financing, taxes, depreciation, and licensing) and are based on keeping the vehicle for 3 years and driving 20,000 miles per year. This information is from Runzheimer International. Runzheimer evaluated thirty 2013 model cars, vans, SUVs, and light trucks and determined the most and least expensive to operate among those vehicles. (Source: Runzheimer International, www.runzheimer.com)

Projected Ownership and Operating Costs for Selected 2013 Cars

Most Expensive

BMW 550I 8-cyl. 4.4L	$22,973
Mercedes-Benz E350 6-cyl. 3.5L	$20,565
Cadillac CTS Premium 6-cyl. 3.6L	$20,379
Chrysler 300 S 8-cyl. 5.7L	$17,465
Ford Taurus Limited 6-cyl. 3.5L	$15,560

Least Expensive

Ford Focus Titanium 4-cyl. 2L	$11,263
Nissan Altima S 4-cyl. 2.5 L	$11,041
Ford Focus SE 4-cyl. 2L	$10,001
Chevrolet Sonic LTZ 4-cyl. 1.8L	$9,800
Toyota Corolla LE 4-cyl. 1.8L	$9,743

Projected Ownership and Operating Costs for Selected 2013 Light Trucks, Vans, and SUVs

Most Expensive

Chevrolet Tahoe LS 4WD 8-cyl. 5.3L	$18,275
Ford E-150 XLT Wagon 8-cyl. 5.4L	$17,269
Chevrolet Silverado 1500 LT 2WD 8-cyl. 4.8L	$15,386
Ford Edge SEL AWD 6-cyl. 3.5L	$14,383
GMC Sierra 1500 Work 2WD 8-cyl. 4.8L	$14,094

Least Expensive

Ram 1500 Tradesman 2WD 6-cyl. 3.6L	$12,998
Toyota Sienna 6-cyl. 3.5L	$12,601
Chevrolet Equinox 2LT FWD 4-cyl. 2.4L	$12,334
Ford Escape SE FWD 4-cyl. 2L	$11,820
Toyota Tacoma 2WD 4-cyl. 2.7L	$10,556

Runzheimer International is a management consulting firm that provides workforce mobility solutions relating to business vehicles, relocation, travel management, corporate aircraft, and mobile device management programs. (Source: Runzheimer International, www.runzheimer.com)

LEASING VS. BUYING

Because the unpredictibility of the value of a vehicle at the end of a lease, more and more companies are getting out of the leasing business. That's good news because, in general, leasing costs more than buying outright or financing. When you pay cash or finance a car, you own an asset; leasing leaves you with nothing except all the headaches and responsibilities of ownership with none of the benefits. When you lease you pay a monthly fee for a predetermined time in exchange for the use of a car. However, you also pay for maintenance, insurance, and repairs as if you owned the car. Finally, when it comes time to turn in the car, it has to be in top shape—otherwise, you'll have to pay for repairs or body work.

If you are considering a lease, here are some leasing terms you need to know and some tips to get you through the process:

Capitalized Cost is the price of the car on which the lease is based. Negotiate this as if you were buying the car. Capitalized Cost Reduction is your down payment.

Know the make and model of the vehicle you want. Tell the agent exactly how you want the car equipped. You don't have to pay for options you don't request. Decide in advance how long you will keep the car.

Find out the price of the options on which the lease is based. Typically, they will be full retail price. Their cost can be negotiated (albeit with some difficulty) before you settle on the monthly payment.

Make sure options like a sunroof or stereo are added to the Capitalized Cost. When you purchase dealer-added options, be sure they add the full cost of the option to the Capitalized Cost so that you only pay for the depreciated value of the option, not the full cost.

Find out how much you are required to pay at delivery. Most leases require at least the first month's payment. Others have a security deposit, registration fees, or other "hidden costs." When shopping around, make sure price quotes include security deposit and taxes—sales tax, monthly use tax, or gross receipt tax. Ask how the length of the lease affects your monthly cost.

Find out how the lease price was determined. Lease prices are generally based on the manufacturer's suggested retail price, less the predetermined residual value. The best values are cars with a high expected residual value. To protect themselves, leasers tend to underestimate residual value, but you can do little about this estimate.

Find out the annual mileage limit. Don't accept a contract with a lower limit than you need. Most standard contracts allow 15,000 to 18,000 miles per year. If you go under the allowance one year, you can go over it the next. Watch out for Excess Mileage fees. If you go over, you'll get charged per mile.

Avoid "capitalized cost reduction" or "equity leases." Here the leaser offers to lower the monthly payment by asking you for more money up front—in other words, a down payment.

Ask about early termination. Between 30 and 40 percent of two-year leases are terminated early and 40–60 percent of four-year leases terminate early—this means expensive early termination fees. If you terminate the lease before it is up, what are the financial penalties? Typically, they are very high so watch out. Ask the dealer exactly what you would owe at the end of each year if you wanted out of the lease. Remember, if your car is stolen, the lease will typically be terminated. While your insurance should cover the value of

LEASEWISE

If you must lease, why haggle when you can let someone else do it for you? LeaseWise, a service from the non-profit Center for the Study of Services, makes dealers bid for your lease. First, they get leasing bids from dealers on the vehicles you're interested in. Next, you'll receive a detailed report with all the bids, the dealer and invoice cost of the vehicle, and a complete explanation of the various bids. Then, you can lease from the lowest bidder or use the report as leverage with another dealer. The service costs $335. For more information, call 800-475-7283, or visit www.checkbook.org.

the car, you still may owe additional amounts per your lease contract.

Avoid maintenance contracts. Getting work done privately is cheaper in the long run. And don't forget, this is a new car with a standard warranty.

Arrange for your own insurance. By shopping around, you can generally find less expensive insurance than what's offered by the leaser.

Ask how quickly you can expect delivery. If your agent can't deliver in a reasonable time, maybe he or she can't meet the price quoted.

Retain your option to buy the car at the end of the lease at a predetermined price. The price should equal the residual value; if it is more then the leaser is trying to make an additional profit. Regardless of how the end-of-lease value is determined, if you want the car, make an offer based on the current "Blue Book" value of the car at the end of the lease.

Residual Value is the value of your car at the end of the lease.

Here's what Automotive Lease Guide estimates the residual value after five years will be for a few 2012 vehicles:

Hyundai Elantra	44%
Toyota Prius	40%
Acura MDX	37%
Jeep Liberty	27%
Nissan Titan	27%

LEASING VS. BUYING

The following table compares the costs of leasing vs. buying the same car over three and six years. Your actual costs may vary, but you can use this format to compare the cars you are considering. Our example assumes the residual value to be 68 percent after three years and 43 percent after six years.

3 Years

	Lease	Finance
MSRP	$29,000.00	$29,000.00
Purchase Cost of Car	$26,100.00	$26,100.00
Down Payment	$2,436.00[5]	$2,900.00
Monthly Payment	$273.00[5]	$432.00
Total Payments	$9,828.00	$15,552.00[1]
Amount left on loan		$9,909.00
Value of vehicle at 3 yrs.		$19,720.00
Excess miles & disposition[7]	$825.00	
Overall Cost, first 3 yrs.	$13,089.00	$8,641.00
Savings over Leasing		**$4,448.00**

If you choose to keep the car you financed for six years, the savings over leasing becomes huge!

6 Years

	Lease[2]	Finance[3]
MSRP	$30,450.00	$29,000.00
Cost of Car	$27,405.00	$26,100.00
Down Payment	$2,740.50[5]	$2,900.00
Monthly Payment	$273.00[5]	$432.00
Total Payments	$9,828.00	$25,920.00
Amount Left on Loan		–
Value of vehicle at 6 yrs.[8]		$12,470.00
Excess miles & disposition[7]	$825.00	
Overall Cost, 6 yrs.	$23,742.00[4]	$16,350.00
Savings over Leasing		**$7,392.00**

[1] First 3 years of 5-year loan with 4.5 percent annual percentage rate.
[2] These are the second 3 year lease costs which assume a 5% increase for a similar vehicle.
[3] Five year loan with 4.5 percent annual percentage rate, no monthly payments in sixth year.
[4] Two 3-year leases.
[5] Initial lease and monthly payments based on lease deals for January 2013 offered by major manufacturers on US News and World Report.
[6] 68% based on average actual 36-month residual value for the top 100 selling vehicles for model year 2006, 07 and 08.
[7] Total average excess miles fee of $475 based on 12000 miles limit and 25% of consumers driving over the mile limit unexpectedly for 1500 miles with charges of $0.17/mile, 50% pre-paying for expected mile overages of 1500 miles at $0.12/mile, and 25% not exceeding the mileage limit. Disposition fee based on average of $350.
[8] 43% based on average actual 36-month residual value for the top 100 selling vehicles for model year 2003, 04 and 05.

USING THE INTERNET

The Internet is changing the way car buyers research and shop for cars. But the Internet should be used with caution. Anyone—and we mean *anyone*—can publish a website with no guarantee concerning the accuracy of the information on it. We advise that you only visit websites that have a familiar non-web counterpart. A good example is the Center for Auto Safety's website at www.autosafety.org where you can find information on auto safety, including publications and newsletters which are typically mailed out to subscribers.

Use the Internet as an information resource. Unfortunately, most automaker websites are nothing more than sophisticated ads with little comparative information.

Good information, like pricing and features, *can* be found online. We've listed some useful websites on this page.

There are also several online car shopping services that have launched. We view most of them with skepticism. Many online car shopping services are tied to a limited, often non-competitive, group of dealers. They may claim the lowest price, but you'll most likely have a dealer calling you with a price that is not much better than what you'd get if you went into a dealership to haggle.

Auto insurance and financing sites are sometimes no better. Don't rely solely on these online services; getting quotes from other sources is the only way to make sure you truly have the best deal.

Finally, clicking a mouse is no substitute for going out and test-driving a car. If you are shopping for a used car, you must check out the actual car before signing on the dotted line. Do not rely on online photos. In fact, online classifieds for cars are no more reliable than looking in a newspaper.

If you do use an online car shopping service, be sure to shop around on your own. Visit dealerships, get quotes from several car shopping services, and research the value of your used car (see www.nadaguides.com). Beware that if you give anyone online your phone number, or email address, you are opening yourself up to unwanted email, junk mail, and even sales calls.

ON THE WEB

TIP

autosafety.org
The Center for Auto Safety (CAS) provides consumers with a voice for auto safety and quality in Washington and to help lemon owners fight back across the country.

carfax.com
Used car buyers will want to visit Carfax. Carfax collects information from numerous sources to provide a vehicle history on a specific vehicle, based on the Vehicle Identification Number (VIN). Carfax can help uncover costly and potentially dangerous hidden problems or confirm the clean history of a vehicle.

checkbook.org
The Center for the Study of Services (CSS) is an independent, nonprofit consumer organization and the creator of Consumers' CHECKBOOK. One of the few car buying services worth using, CHECKBOOK's CarBargains service pits dealers against each other, keeping you from haggling, and using the power of competitive bidding to get you a great price.

nhtsa.gov
The National Highway Traffic Safety Administration (NHTSA) website contains useful information on safety standards, crash tests, recalls, technical service bulletins, child seats, and safety advisories.

fueleconomy.gov
This joint effort by the Department of Energy and the Environmental Protection Agency contains EPA fuel economy ratings for passenger cars and trucks from 1985 to the present, gas saving tips, greenhouse gas and air pollution ratings, energy impact scores, a downloadable Fuel Economy Guide, and a variety of other useful information in a very user-friendly format.

DEPRECIATION

Over the past 20 years, new vehicle depreciation costs have steadily increased. A study conducted by Runzheimer International shows that depreciation and interest now account for just over 50 percent of the costs of owning and operating a vehicle. Recently, however, the increasing cost of depreciation has slowed down. This is due to the relatively stable prices of new vehicles and to the slow increase in finance rates. The higher cost of gasoline consumes a larger percentage of the automotive dollar than ever before. Other costs, including insurance, maintenance, and tires, have remained at relatively steady shares of the automotive dollar.

While there is no foolproof method for predicting retained vehicle value, your best bet is to purchase a popular vehicle model. Chances are it will also be a popular used vehicle model, meaning that the retained value may be higher when you go to sell it.

Most new cars are traded in within four years and are then available on the used car market. The priciest used cars may not be the highest quality. Supply and demand, as well as appearance, are important factors in determining used car prices.

The following table indicates which of the top-selling 2009 cars held their value the best and which did not.

2009 VEHICLES WITH THE BEST AND WORST RESALE VALUE

THE BEST				THE WORST			
Model	2009 Price	2012 Price	Retain. Value	Model	2009 Price	2012 Price	Retain. Value
Toyota Tundra	$26,680	$26,625	99.8%	Ford Taurus	$25,170	$13,275	52.7%
Jeep Wrangler	$20,460	$19,875	97.1%	Buick LaCrosse	$25,640	$14,075	54.9%
Toyota Tacoma	$19,130	$16,925	88.5%	Merc.-Benz E-Class	$53,200	$29,375	55.2%
Toyota Yaris	$13,765	$11,725	85.2%	Buick Lucerne	$29,265	$16,425	56.1%
Honda Fit	$15,550	$13,125	84.4%	Chevrolet Impala	$23,790	$13,425	56.4%
Mini Cooper	$18,550	$15,650	84.4%	Chrysler T&C	$26,340	$15,450	58.7%
Nissan Frontier	$24,110	$19,775	82.0%	BMW 5 Series	$45,800	$26,975	58.9%
Mazda Mazda3	$15,590	$12,775	81.9%	Chrysler 300	$26,915	$15,900	59.1%
Toyota Venza	$27,425	$22,300	81.3%	Dodge Grand Caravan	$23,890	$14,250	59.6%
Nissan Versa	$11,990	$9,725	81.1%	Jeep Grand Cherokee	$32,120	$19,275	60.0%
Toyota Corolla	$16,150	$12,825	79.4%	Chrysler Sebring	$20,015	$12,025	60.1%
Chev. Silver./GMC Sierra	$32,205	$25,475	79.1%	Ford Expedition	$37,745	$23,150	61.3%
Hyundai Elantra	$15,120	$11,750	77.7%	Dodge Journey	$26,470	$16,275	61.5%
Jeep Patriot	$19,040	$14,800	77.7%	Ford Explorer	$30,790	$19,050	61.9%
Toyota Matrix	$17,100	$13,250	77.5%	Hyundai Sonata	$19,900	$12,325	61.9%
Honda Civic	$16,305	$12,600	77.3%	Subaru Legacy	$21,795	$13,500	61.9%
Hyundai Accent	$12,070	$9,325	77.3%	Dodge Avenger	$19,815	$12,300	62.1%
Toyota Highlander	$29,050	$22,375	77.0%	Dodge Charger	$24,935	$15,525	62.5%
Honda CR-V	$22,445	$16,925	75.4%	Cadillac CTS	$36,560	$23,000	62.9%
Subaru Impreza	$18,495	$13,900	75.2%	Chevrolet Malibu	$21,605	$13,600	62.9%
Merc.-Benz C-Class	$33,190	$24,875	74.9%	Honda Odyssey	$26,355	$16,575	62.9%
Subaru Forester	$21,195	$15,725	74.2%	Acura TL	$34,995	$22,275	63.7%
Nissan Rogue	$21,420	$15,875	74.1%	Kia Optima	$18,950	$12,100	63.9%
Ford Mustang	$20,995	$15,525	73.9%	Mazda Mazda6	$21,150	$13,550	64.1%
Toyota Prius	$23,375	$17,225	73.7%	Ford Flex	$34,175	$21,975	64.3%

CORPORATE TWINS

"Corporate twins" refers to vehicles that have different names but share the same mechanics, drivetrain, and chassis. In most cases the vehicles are identical. Sometimes the difference is in body style, price, or options as with the Chevrolet Tahoe and the Cadillac Escalade. Traditionally, corporate twins have been limited mainly to domestic car companies. Today, due to the many car company mergers, corporate twins include cars that were once considered European or Asian coupled with a domestic model name.

CORPORATE TWINS

Chrysler Corp.
Chrysler 200
Dodge Avenger

Chrysler 300
Dodge Charger

Chrysler Town & Country
Dodge Grand Caravan

Ford Motor Co.
Ford Edge
Lincoln MKX

Ford Expedition
Lincoln Navigator

Ford Fusion
Lincoln MKZ

General Motors
Buick Verano
Chevrolet Cruze

General Motors (cont.)
Cadillac Escalade
Chevrolet Tahoe
GMC Yukon

Cadillac Escalade ESV
Chevrolet Suburban
GMC Yukon XL

Cadillac Escalade EXT
Chevrolet Avalanche

Chevrolet Equinox
GMC Terrain

Chevrolet Silverado
GMC Sierra

Chevrolet Traverse
GMC Acadia

Hyundai-Kia
Hyundai Accent
Kia Rio

Hyundai-Kia (cont.)
Hyundai Tucson
Kia Sportage

Nissan
Nissan Pathfinder
Infiniti JX

Toyota
Scion FR-S
Subaru BRZ

Lexus GX
Toyota 4Runner

Lexus LX
Toyota Land Cruiser

Volkswagen
Porsche Cayenne
Volkswagen Touareg

Cadillac Escalade

Chevrolet Tahoe

GMC Yukon

RATINGS

This section provides an overview of the most important features of this year's new models. Nearly all the information you'll need to make a smart choice is concisely presented on one page. (The data are collected for the model expected to be the most popular.) Here's what you'll find and how to interpret the data we've provided:

The Ratings

These are the ratings in nine important categories, as well as an overall comparative rating. We have adopted the Olympic rating system with "10" being the best.

Overall Rating: This is the "bottom line." Using a combination of all of the key ratings, this tells how this vehicle stacks up against the others on a scale of 1 to 10. Due to the importance of safety, the combined crash test rating is 20 percent of the overall rating while the other eight ratings are 10 percent each. Vehicles with no front or side crash test results, as of our publication date, cannot be given an overall rating. In other categories, if information is unavailable, an "average" is included in order to develop an overall rating.

Overall Crash Test: This rating represents a combination of the front and side crash test ratings and provides a relative comparison of how this year's models did against each other. We give the best performers a 10 and the worst a 1. Remember to compare crash test results relative to other cars in the same size class. For details, see page 18.

Safety Features: This is an evaluation of how much extra safety is built into the car. We give credit for head, torso and pelvis side airbags, roll-sensing side airbags, knee bolster bag, crash imminent braking, daytime running lamps, adjustable upper seat belt anchorages, lane departure warning, dynamic brake support, and frontal collision warning. We also include dynamic head restraint and blind spot detection among other important safety features. See the "Safety Checklist" box on each page for more details.

Rollover: Many consumers are aware that vehicles with higher centers of gravity could be more likely to roll over. Comparing the tendency of a vehicle to roll over is very difficult, as there is no agreed upon comparative rating system. The U.S. government adopted the rating system that we have been using called the static stability formula (SSF). The government provides the SSF rating for some vehicles. For those vehicles not on the government list, we use the SSF formula to provide a rating. The details behind the SSF appear on page 30.

Preventive Maintenance: Each manufacturer suggests a preventive maintenance schedule designed to keep the car in good shape and to protect your rights under the warranty. Those with the lowest estimated PM costs get a 10 and the highest a 1. See pages 39-43 for the estimated costs and more information.

Repair Costs: It is virtually impossible to predict exactly what any new car will cost you in repairs. As such, we take nine typical repairs that you are likely to experience after your warranty expires and compare those costs among this year's models. Those with the lowest cost get a 10 and the highest a 1. See pages 39-43 for specific part repair cost and more information.

Warranty: This is an overall assessment of the manufacturer's basic, powertrain, corrosion, and roadside assistance warranties when compared to all other manufacturer warranties. We give the highest-rated warranties a 10 and the lowest a 1. For details, see the Warranty section.

Fuel Economy: Here we compare the EPA mileage ratings of each car. The misers get a 10 and the guzzlers get a 1. For the purposes of the overall rating we pick the fuel economy rating of what is expected to be the most popular engine and drive train configuration. See page 33 for more information.

Complaints: This is where you'll find how each vehicle stacks up against hundreds of others on the road, based on the U.S. government complaint data for that vehicle. If the car has not been around long enough to have developed a complaint history, it is given a 5 (average). The least complained about cars get a 10 and the most problematic a 1. See the "Complaints Chapter" for details.

Insurance Costs: Insurance companies rate vehicles to determine how much they plan to charge for insurance. Here, you'll find whether you can expect to pay higher or lower insurance premium for what we expect to be the most popular model. We looked at data from the insurance rating program of the largest insurer in America. Vehicles with a low rating (1 or 3) are more expensive to insure, vehicles with a high rating (8 or 10) are less expensive to insure and those receiving a 5 are typical. This rating will give you a basic idea of the cost to insure the vehicle. Because insurance companies may rate vehicles differently, it's best to compare prices between companies.

At-a-Glance

Status: Here we tell you if a vehicle is all-new, unchanged, or has received appearance change. All-new vehicles (the minority) are brand new from the ground up. Unchanged vehicles are essentially the same, but could have some different color or feature options. Vehicles with an appearance change are those whose internal workings stayed essentially the same, but have updated body panels.

Year Series Started: We generally recommend against buying a car during its first model year of production. Each year the model is made, the production usually improves and as a result there are fewer defects. Therefore, the longer a car has been made, the less likely you

are to be plagued with manufacturing and design defects. On the other hand, the newer a car is, the more likely it is to have the latest in features and safety.

Twins: These are cars with different make and model names but share the same mechanics, drive train, and chassis. In some cases the vehicles are identical, in other cases the body style, pricing or options are different.

Body Styles: This is a listing of the various body styles available such as coupe, sedan, wagon, etc. SUVs and minivans are only offered in one body style. Data on the page are for the first style listed.

Seating: This is the number of seating positions in the most popular model. When more than one number is listed (for example, 5/6) it means that different seat configurations are available.

Anti-theft Device: This lists the anti-theft devices standard for the vehicle. An immobilizer is an electronic device fitted to an automobile which prevents the engine from running unless the correct key (or other token) is present. This prevents the car from being "hot-wired" and driven away. A car alarm is an electronic device that emits high-volume sound and can sometimes flash the vehicles headlights in an attempt to discourage theft of the vehicle itself, its contents, or both. Passive devices automatically enter an armed state after the ignition is turned off and doors are closed. Active devices require the user to perform some action like pressing

a button to arm and disarm the system.

Parking Index Rating: Using the car's length, wheelbase, and turning circle, we have calculated how easy it will be to maneuver this car in tight spots. This rating of "very easy" to "very hard" is an indicator of how much difficulty you may have parking.

Where Made: Here we tell you where the car was assembled. You'll find that traditional domestic companies often build their vehicles in other countries. Also, many foreign companies build their cars in the U.S.

Fuel Factor

MPG Rating (city/hwy): This is the EPA-rated fuel economy for city and highway driving measured in miles per gallon. Most models have a variety of fuel economy ratings because of different engine and transmission options. We've selected the combination expected to be most popular.

Driving Range: Given the car's expected fuel economy and gas tank size, this value gives you an idea of the number of miles you can expect to go on one tank of gas.

Fuel: The type of fuel specified by the manufacturer: regular, premium, E85.

Annual Fuel Cost: This is an estimate based on driving 15,000 miles per year at $3.43/gallon for regular and $3.73/gallon for premium. If the vehicle takes E85 (85% ethanol and 15% gasoline) or gasoline we calculated the annual cost using gasoline.

Gas Guzzler Tax: Auto companies are required to pay a gas guzzler tax on the sale of cars with exceptionally low fuel economy.

This tax does not apply to light trucks.

Greenhouse Gas Emissions: This shows the amount (in tons) of greenhouse gases (carbon dioxide, nitrous oxide, and methane) that a vehicle emits per year along with the CO2 emitted in producing and distributing the fuel.

Barrels of Oil Used Per Year: This is the number of barrels of petroleum the vehicle will likely use each year. One barrel, once refined, makes about 19.5 gallons of gas.

Competition

Here we tell you how the car stacks up with some of its key competitors. Use this information to broaden your choice of new car possibilities. This list is only a guideline, not an all-inclusive list of every possible alternative.

Price Range

This box contains information on the MSRP. When available, we offer a variety of prices between the base and the most luxurious version of the car. The difference is often substantial. Usually the more expensive versions have fancy trim, larger engines, and lots of automatic equipment. The least expensive versions usually have manual transmissions and few extra features. In addition to the price range, we provide the estimated dealer markup. Be prepared for higher retail prices when you get to the showroom.

Manufacturers like to load their cars with factory options, and dealers like to add their own items such as fabric protection and paint sealant. Remember, prices and dealer costs can change during the year. Use these figures for general reference and comparisons, not as a precise indication of exactly how much the car you are interested in will cost. See page 68 for a buying service designed to ensure that you get the very best price.

Safety Checklist

Crash Tests

Frontal and Side Crash Test Ratings: : Here's where we tell you if the front or side crash test index was very good, good, average, poor or very poor when compared to 2013 cars tested to date. To provide this rating we use the crash test for the vehicles with the best available safety equipment among the models when multiple models were tested. In 2011, the government developed a new crash test program. Because only about half

TYPES OF AIRBAGS

Airbags were introduced over 30 years ago and have been so successful in saving lives that car makers now include a variety of types. Here's a rundown of the basic types of airbags available. Manufacturers have varying marketing names for these airbags.

Front: These deploy toward the front occupants and are now standard in all vehicles.
Side: These deploy from the side of the seat or door and protect both the front and rear passengers in a side impact. Bags mounted in seats offer protection in a wider range of seating positions.
Head: These deploy from above the doors and are often called curtain airbags. They can reduce head injuries, shield from spraying glass, and provide protection in rollovers.
Rollover Protection: These head curtain airbags remain inflated for five seconds to protect in a sustained rollover.
Knee Bolster: These fill space between the front occupant's knees and instrument panel protecting the knees and legs.

the vehicles have been tested under the new program, many will not have a rating. For details about the crash test programs, see page 18.

Airbags

Head Side Airbag: This side airbag protects the head area from impacting the roof, door, and window and can offer extra rollover protection.

Torso Side Airbag: This type of side airbag protects the chest from serious injury in a side impact crash.

Pelvis Side Airbag: Provides extra protection around the pelvis and hip area, as this portion of the body is usually closest to the vehicles interior.

Rollover Sensing Airbags: Some companies offer a special side airbag system which keeps the side airbags inflated longer in the event of a rollover. This can reduce the likelihood of injury when a vehicle flips.

Knee Bolster Airbag: The airbag is inflated to fill space between the knees of the front occupant and the instrument panel.

Crash Avoidance

Frontal Collision Warning: This feature uses radar or laser sensors to detect an imminent crash in front of the vehicle. Systems may warn the driver with a light and/or audible alert, retract the seat belts removing excess slack, and automatically apply partial or full braking to minimize the crash severity.

Blind Spot Detection: This is a blind spot monitor that uses radar or other technologies to detect objects in the driver's blind spot. When switching lanes a visible and/or audible alert warns if a vehicle has entered your blind spot.

Crash Imminent Braking (CIB): This technology is intended to mitigate crashes by automatically applying the vehicle's brakes just prior to impact. This is often coupled with Dynamic Brake Support which applies more pressure to the brakes when it senses a collision is imminent.

Lane Departure Warning: This mechanism warns a driver when the vehicle begins to move out of its lane (unless a turn signal is on in that direction). The warning may be a light, audible chime, or a vibrating steering wheel.

General

Automatic Crash Notification: Using cellular technology and global positioning systems, some vehicles have the ability to send a call for help in the event of airbag deployment or accident. You'll have to pay extra for this feature.

Daytime Running Lights: Some cars offer daytime running lights that can reduce your chances of being in a crash by up to 40 percent by increasing the visibility of your vehicle. We indicate whether daytime running lights are standard, optional, or not available.

Safety Belts/Restraints

Dynamic Head Restraints: Many people position their seat and head restraint according to their own body and comfort requirements. This may not be the best position to protect you in a crash. These adjustors, sensing a crash, will automatically move the seat and head-rest to the optimal position to help reduce injury during a rear-end crash.

Pretensioners: How snugly your seat belt fits is a critical factor in crash protection. Some manufacturers offer special devices that, sensing a potential crash, tighten up and/or lock the safety belt.

Adjustable Front Belts: Proper positioning of the safety belt across your chest is critical to obtaining the benefits of buckling up. Some systems allow you to adjust the height of the belt so it crosses your chest properly.

Specifications

Drive: This indicates the type of drive the manufacturer offers. This could be two wheel drive in the front (FWD) or rear (RWD) or all or four wheel drive (AWD/4WD).

Engine: This is the engine size (liters) and type that is expected to be the most popular. The engine types specify V6 or V8 for six or eight cylinders and I4 for four in-line.

Transmission: This is the type of transmission expected to be the most popular. Most drivers today prefer automatic transmissions. The number listed with the transmission (5-sp.) is the number of gears or speeds. Then we list whether it's automatic or manual and if the transmission is a continuously variable transmission (CVT). CVT changes smoothly and efficiently between gears. This can provide better fuel economy than other transmissions by enabling the engine to run at its most efficient speed.

Tow Rating: Ratings of very low, low, average, high, and very high indicate the vehicle's relative ability to tow trailers or other loads. Some manufacturers do not provide a tow rating.

Head/Leg Room: This tells how roomy the front seat is. The values are given in inches and rated in comparison to all other vehicles.

Interior Space: This tells how roomy the car's passenger area should feel. This value is given in cubic feet and rated in comparison to all other vehicles. Many SUVs do not provide interior space specifications.

Cargo Space: This gives you the cubic feet available for cargo. For minivans, the volume is behind the last row of seats. In cars, it's the trunk space. We rate the roominess of the cargo space compared to all SUVs and cars. For trucks we list the Truck Bed Volume and rate it, small, medium, or large, compared to other truck bed volumes available.

Wheelbase/Length: The wheelbase is the distance between the centers of the front and rear wheels and the length is the distance from front bumper to rear bumper. Wheelbase can affect the ride and length affects how big the car "feels."

DESTINATION CHARGES

TIP

Destination charges are a non-negotiable part of buying a new car, no matter where you purchase it. They are an important factor when comparing prices. You'll find the destination charges on the price sticker attached to the vehicle. According to automakers, destination charges are the cost of shipping a vehicle from its "final assembly point" to the dealership. But, the following table illustrates that there is little correlation between destination charges and where the cars are assembled:

Vehicle	Destination Charge*	Assembly Country
Chevrolet Silverado	$995	U.S.A.
Jeep Patriot	$995	U.S.A.
BMW 5 Series	$875	Germany
Kia Sorento	$800	South Korea

*Data based on 2013 model year cars.

Ratings—10 Best, 1 Worst

Combo Crash Tests	7
Safety Features	2
Rollover	8
Preventive Maintenance	5
Repair Costs	9
Warranty	4
Fuel Economy	8
Complaints	–
Insurance Costs	–
OVERALL RATING	**8**

Acura ILX

Acura ILX

At-a-Glance

Status/Year Series Started	All New/2013
Twins	-
Body Styles	Sedan
Seating	5
Anti-Theft Device	Std. Pass. Immobil. & Alarm
Parking Index Rating	Easy
Where Made	Greensburg, IN
Fuel Factor	
MPG Rating (city/hwy)	Good-24/35
Driving Range (mi.)	Short-369
Fuel Type	Premium
Annual Fuel Cost	Low-$2,002
Gas Guzzler Tax	No
Greenhouse Gas Emissions (tons/yr.)	Average-6.6
Barrels of Oil Used per year	Average-11.8

How the Competition Rates

Competitors	Rating	Pg.
Audi A3		86
BMW 1 Series		94
Cadillac ATS	9	106

Price Range

	Retail	Markup
Base 2.0L	$25,900	
Base 2.4L	$29,200	
Hybrid	$34,400	

Safety Checklist

Crash Tests:
Frontal . . . . –
Side . . . . –

Airbags:
Head . . . . Fr & Rr. Roof Curtain
Torso . . . . Front Torso from Seat
Pelvis . . . . None
Roll Sensing . . . . No
Knee Bolster . . . . None

Crash Avoidance:
Frontal Collision Warning . . . . None
Blind Spot Detection . . . . None
Crash Imminent Braking . . . . None
Lane Departure Warning . . . . None

General:
Auto. Crash Notification . . . . None
Day Running Lamps . . . . Standard

Safety Belt/Restraint:
Dynamic Head Restraints . . . . None
Adjustable Belt . . . . Standard Front
Pretensioners . . . . Standard Front

Acura ILX

Specifications

Drive	FWD
Engine	2.0-liter I4
Transmission	5-sp. Automatic
Tow Rating (lbs.)	–
Head/Leg Room (in.)	Cramped-37.9/42.3
Interior Space (cu. ft.)	Very Cramped-89
Cargo Space (cu. ft.)	Cramped-12.4
Wheelbase/Length (in.)	105.1/179.1

Ratings—10 Best, 1 Worst

Combo Crash Tests	5
Safety Features	8
Rollover	5
Preventive Maintenance	7
Repair Costs	5
Warranty	4
Fuel Economy	1
Complaints	10
Insurance Costs	10
OVERALL RATING	**8**

Acura MDX

At-a-Glance

Status/Year Series Started	Unchanged/2007
Twins	-
Body Styles	SUV
Seating	7
Anti-Theft Device	Std. Pass. Immobil. & Alarm
Parking Index Rating	Hard
Where Made	Lincoln, AL
Fuel Factor	
MPG Rating (city/hwy)	Very Poor-16/21
Driving Range (mi.)	Short-376
Fuel Type	Premium
Annual Fuel Cost	Very High-$3,122
Gas Guzzler Tax	No
Greenhouse Gas Emissions (tons/yr.)	Very High-10.2
Barrels of Oil Used per year	Very High-18.3

How the Competition Rates

Competitors	Rating	Pg.
BMW X5	6	100
Ford Explorer	6	138
Volvo XC90		270

Price Range	Retail	Markup
Base	$43,280	9%
Technology Package	$46,955	9%
Advance Package	$52,905	9%
Advance & Entertain. Package	$54,805	9%

Acura MDX

Safety Checklist

Crash Tests:
Frontal . . . . Average
Side . . . . Average

Airbags:
Head . . . . Fr. & Rr. Roof Curtain
Torso . . . . Front Pelvis/Torso from Seat
Pelvis . . . . Front Pelvis/Torso from Seat
Roll Sensing . . . . Yes
Knee Bolster . . . . None

Crash Avoidance:
Frontal Collision Warning . . . . Optional
Blind Spot Detection . . . . Optional
Crash Imminent Braking . . . . Optional
Lane Departure Warning . . . . None

General:
Auto. Crash Notification . . . . None
Day Running Lamps . . . . Standard

Safety Belt/Restraint:
Dynamic Head Restraints . . . . . . Standard Front
Adjustable Belt . . . . Standard Front
Pretensioners . . . . Standard Front

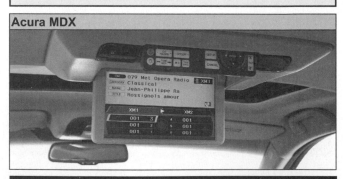

Acura MDX

Specifications

Drive	AWD
Engine	3.7-liter V6
Transmission	6-sp. Automatic
Tow Rating (lbs.)	Average-5000
Head/Leg Room (in.)	Cramped-39.2/41.2
Interior Space (cu. ft.)	Very Roomy-142.2
Cargo Space (cu. ft.)	Cramped-15
Wheelbase/Length (in.)	108.3/191.6

Ratings—10 Best, 1 Worst

Combo Crash Tests	–
Safety Features	4
Rollover	3
Preventive Maintenance	7
Repair Costs	6
Warranty	4
Fuel Economy	4
Complaints	–
Insurance Costs	10
OVERALL RATING	**–**

Acura RDX

Acura RDX

At-a-Glance

Status/Year Series Started. . . . . All New/2013
Twins . . . . -
Body Styles . . . . SUV
Seating 5
Anti-Theft Device . . . . . Std. Pass. Immobil. & Alarm
Parking Index Rating . . . . Hard
Where Made. . . . . Marysville, OH
Fuel Factor. . . . .
  MPG Rating (city/hwy) Poor-19/27
  Driving Range (mi.) . . . . Very Short-351
  Fuel Type. . . . . Premium
  Annual Fuel Cost . . . . High-$2,552
  Gas Guzzler Tax . . . . No
  Greenhouse Gas Emissions (tons/yr.). High-8.3
  Barrels of Oil Used per year High-15.0

How the Competition Rates

Competitors	Rating	Pg.
Buick Encore		102
Lexus RX	5	186
Volkswagen Tiguan		264

Price Range

Price Range	Retail	Markup
FWD	$34,320	
AWD	$35,720	
FWD w/Tech	$38,020	
AWD w/Tech	$39,420	

Safety Checklist

Crash Tests:
  Frontal. . . . . –
  Side. . . . . –
Airbags:
  Head . . . . Fr & Rr. Roof Curtain
  Torso. . . . . Front Torso from Seat
  Pelvis . . . . None
  Roll Sensing . . . . .Yes
  Knee Bolster . . . . None
Crash Avoidance:
  Frontal Collision Warning . . . . None
  Blind Spot Detection . . . . None
  Crash Imminent Braking . . . . None
  Lane Departure Warning . . . . None
General:
  Auto. Crash Notification . . . . None
  Day Running Lamps . . . . Standard
Safety Belt/Restraint:
  Dynamic Head Restraints. . . . . None
  Adjustable Belt . . . . .Standard Front
  Pretensioners . . . . .Standard Front

Acura RDX

Specifications

Drive. . . . . AWD
Engine 3.5-liter V6
Transmission . . . . .6-sp. Automatic
Tow Rating (lbs.) . . . . Very Low-1500
Head/Leg Room (in.) Cramped-38.7/42
Interior Space (cu. ft.). Average-103.5
Cargo Space (cu. ft.) Roomy-26.1
Wheelbase/Length (in.) 105.7/183.5

Ratings—10 Best, 1 Worst

Combo Crash Tests	2
Safety Features	6
Rollover	9
Preventive Maintenance	5
Repair Costs	5
Warranty	4
Fuel Economy	4
Complaints	7
Insurance Costs	8
OVERALL RATING	**5**

Acura TL

Acura TL

At-a-Glance

Status/Year Series Started	Unchanged/2009
Twins	-
Body Styles	Sedan
Seating	5
Anti-Theft Device	Std. Pass. Immobil. & Alarm
Parking Index Rating	Hard
Where Made	Marysville, OH
Fuel Factor	
MPG Rating (city/hwy)	Poor-20/29
Driving Range (mi.)	Long-430
Fuel Type	Premium
Annual Fuel Cost	High-$2,407
Gas Guzzler Tax	No
Greenhouse Gas Emissions (tons/yr.)	High-7.9
Barrels of Oil Used per year	High-14.3

How the Competition Rates

Competitors	Rating	Pg.
Cadillac CTS	9	107
Infiniti G		166
Lexus ES	8	183

Price Range	Retail	Markup
Base	$35,905	7%
SH-AWD	$39,455	8%
SH-AWD w/Tech. Pkg.	$43,185	8%
SH-AWD w/Advance Pkg.	$45,385	8%

Safety Checklist

Crash Tests:
Frontal . . . . Poor
Side . . . . Poor
Airbags:
Head . . . . .Fr & Rr. Roof Curtain
Torso . . . . .Front Pelvis/Torso from Seat
Pelvis . . . . .Front Pelvis/Torso from Seat
Roll Sensing . . . . No
Knee Bolster . . . . None
Crash Avoidance:
Frontal Collision Warning . . . . None
Blind Spot Detection . . . . Optional
Crash Imminent Braking . . . . Optional
Lane Departure Warning . . . . None
General:
Auto. Crash Notification . . . . None
Day Running Lamps . . . . Standard
Safety Belt/Restraint:
Dynamic Head Restraints . . . . . .Standard Front
Adjustable Belt . . . . .Standard Front
Pretensioners . . . . .Standard Front

Acura TL

Specifications

Drive	FWD
Engine	3.5-liter V6
Transmission	6-sp. Automatic
Tow Rating (lbs.)	–
Head/Leg Room (in.)	Cramped-38.4/42.5
Interior Space (cu. ft.)	Average-98.2
Cargo Space (cu. ft.)	Cramped-13.1
Wheelbase/Length (in.)	109.3/194

Ratings—10 Best, 1 Worst

Combo Crash Tests	–
Safety Features	4
Rollover	9
Preventive Maintenance	6
Repair Costs	6
Warranty	4
Fuel Economy	6
Complaints	7
Insurance Costs	3
OVERALL RATING	**–**

Acura TSX

Acura TSX Wagon

At-a-Glance

Status/Year Series Started. Unchanged/2009
Twins . . . . -
Body Styles . . . . Sedan, Wagon
Seating 5
Anti-Theft Device . . . . . . Std. Pass. Immobil. & Alarm
Parking Index Rating . . . . Average
Where Made. Sayama, Japan
Fuel Factor . . . .
  MPG Rating (city/hwy) Average-22/31
  Driving Range (mi.) . . . . Very Long-468
  Fuel Type . . . . .Premium
  Annual Fuel Cost . . . . Average-$2,211
  Gas Guzzler Tax . . . . .No
  Greenhouse Gas Emissions (tons/yr.). . Average-7.0
  Barrels of Oil Used per year Average-12.7

How the Competition Rates

Competitors	Rating	Pg.
Chrysler 200	3	123
Hyundai Sonata	9	161
Lexus IS	7	185

Price Range

	Retail	Markup
Base	$30,510	7%
Special Edition	$31,510	8%
Tech. Package	$33,610	7%
V6 w/Tech. Package	$39,150	8%

Safety Checklist

Crash Tests:
  Frontal . . . . –
  Side . . . . –
Airbags:
  Head . . . . .Fr & Rr. Roof Curtain
  Torso. . . . . .Front Pelvis/Torso from Seat
  Pelvis . . . . .Front Pelvis/Torso from Seat
  Roll Sensing . . . . No
  Knee Bolster . . . . None
Crash Avoidance:
  Frontal Collision Warning . . . . None
  Blind Spot Detection . . . . None
  Crash Imminent Braking . . . . None
  Lane Departure Warning . . . . None
General:
  Auto. Crash Notification . . . . None
  Day Running Lamps . . . . Standard
Safety Belt/Restraint:
  Dynamic Head Restraints . . . . .Standard Front
  Adjustable Belt . . . . .Standard Front
  Pretensioners . . . . .Standard Front

Acura TSX

Specifications

Drive . . . . FWD
Engine 2.4-liter I4
Transmission . . . . .5-sp. Automatic
Tow Rating (lbs.) . . . . –
Head/Leg Room (in.) Cramped-37.6/42.4
Interior Space (cu. ft.). Cramped-94.5
Cargo Space (cu. ft.) Cramped-14
Wheelbase/Length (in.) 106.4/185.6

Ratings—10 Best, 1 Worst

Combo Crash Tests	–
Safety Features	3
Rollover	7
Preventive Maintenance	7
Repair Costs	7
Warranty	9
Fuel Economy	4
Complaints	2
Insurance Costs	8
OVERALL RATING	**–**

Audi A3

At-a-Glance

Status/Year Series Started........ Unchanged/2006
Twins .... -
Body Styles .... Hatchback
Seating 5
Anti-Theft Device .... Std. Pass. Immobil & Alarm
Parking Index Rating .... Very Easy
Where Made.................. Ingolstadt, Germany
Fuel Factor....................
   MPG Rating (city/hwy) Poor-21/24
   Driving Range (mi.) .... Very Short-325
   Fuel Type.................... Premium
   Annual Fuel Cost .... High-$2,514
   Gas Guzzler Tax .... No
   Greenhouse Gas Emissions (tons/yr.)..... High-7.6
   Barrels of Oil Used per year High-13.7

How the Competition Rates

Competitors	Rating	Pg.
BMW 1 Series		86
Lexus CT		182
Volkswagen Golf		260

Price Range

Price Range	Retail	Markup
Premium	$27,270	8%
Premium TDI	$30,250	8%
Premium Plus	$30,750	8%
Premium Plus TDI	$32,250	8%

Audi A3

Safety Checklist

Crash Tests:
   Frontal. . . . . –
   Side. . . . . –
Airbags:
   Head . . . . Fr. & Rr. Roof Curtain
   Torso. . . . . . .Std. Fr. & Opt. Rr. Torso from Seat
   Pelvis Std. Fr. & Opt. Rr. Pelvis/Torso from Seat
   Roll Sensing . . . . No
   Knee Bolster . . . . None
Crash Avoidance:
   Frontal Collision Warning . . . . None
   Blind Spot Detection . . . . None
   Crash Imminent Braking . . . . None
   Lane Departure Warning . . . . None
General:
   Auto. Crash Notification . . . . None
   Day Running Lamps . . . . Standard
Safety Belt/Restraint:
   Dynamic Head Restraints. . . . . None
   Adjustable Belt . . . . .Standard Front
   Pretensioners . . . . Standard Front & Rear

Audi A3

Specifications

Drive. . . . . FWD
Engine 2.0-liter I4
Transmission . . . . .6-sp. Automatic
Tow Rating (lbs.) . . . . –
Head/Leg Room (in.) Cramped-39/41.2
Interior Space (cu. ft.). . . . . Very Cramped-89
Cargo Space (cu. ft.) Average-19.5
Wheelbase/Length (in.) 101.5/169

Ratings—10 Best, 1 Worst

Combo Crash Tests	8
Safety Features	6
Rollover	9
Preventive Maintenance	5
Repair Costs	4
Warranty	9
Fuel Economy	6
Complaints	9
Insurance Costs	8
OVERALL RATING	**10**

Audi A4

 Audi A4

At-a-Glance

Status/Year Series Started Appearance Change/2009
Twins . . . . -
Body Styles . . . . .Sedan
Seating 5
Anti-Theft Device . . . . . . .Std. Pass. Immobil & Alarm
Parking Index Rating . . . . Average
Where Made. . . . . . . Ingolstadt/Neckarsulm, Germany
Fuel Factor . . . .
  MPG Rating (city/hwy) Average-22/32
  Driving Range (mi.) Average-412
  Fuel Type . . . . .Premium
  Annual Fuel Cost . . . . Average-$2,186
  Gas Guzzler Tax . . . . .No
  Greenhouse Gas Emissions (tons/yr.). . Average-7.1
  Barrels of Oil Used per year Average-12.7

How the Competition Rates

Competitors	Rating	Pg.
BMW 3 Series	10	95
Cadillac ATS	9	106
Mercedes-Benz C-Class	4	196

Price Range	Retail	Markup
Premium	$32,500	8%
Premium Plus	$36,700	8%
Prestige	$42,250	8%
Prestige S-Line	$47,300	8%

Safety Checklist

Crash Tests:
  Frontal . . . . Very Good
    Side. . . . . Average
Airbags:
  Head . . . . Fr. & Rr. Roof Curtain
  Torso . . . . . . .Std. Fr. & Opt. Rr. Torso from Seat
  Pelvis Std. Fr. & Opt. Rr. Pelvis/Torso from Seat
  Roll Sensing . . . . No
  Knee Bolster . . . . None
Crash Avoidance:
  Frontal Collision Warning . . . . Standard
  Blind Spot Detection . . . . Optional
  Crash Imminent Braking . . . . Optional
General:
  Lane Departure Warning . . . . None
  Auto. Crash Notification . . . . None
  Day Running Lamps . . . . Standard
Safety Belt/Restraint:
  Dynamic Head Restraints . . . . None
  Adjustable Belt . . . . .Standard Front
  Pretensioners . . . . Standard Front & Rear

Audi A4

Specifications

Drive. . . . . FWD
Engine 2.0-liter I4
Transmission . . . . .CVT
Tow Rating (lbs.) . . . . –
Head/Leg Room (in.) Average-40/41.3
Interior Space (cu. ft.). Cramped-91
Cargo Space (cu. ft.) Cramped-12.4
Wheelbase/Length (in.) 110.6/185.1

Ratings—10 Best, 1 Worst

Combo Crash Tests	–
Safety Features	6
Rollover	9
Preventive Maintenance	5
Repair Costs	4
Warranty	9
Fuel Economy	5
Complaints	8
Insurance Costs	5
OVERALL RATING	**–**

Audi A5

At-a-Glance

Status/Year Series Started Appearance Change/2008
Twins .... -
Body Styles .... Coupe, Convertible
Seating 4
Anti-Theft Device .... Std. Pass. Immobil & Alarm
Parking Index Rating .... Average
Where Made............. Neckarsulm, Germany
Fuel Factor ....
  MPG Rating (city/hwy) Average-20/30
  Driving Range (mi.) Short-379
  Fuel Type...................... Premium
  Annual Fuel Cost .... Average-$2,378
  Gas Guzzler Tax ....No
  Greenhouse Gas Emissions (tons/yr.)..... High-7.6
  Barrels of Oil Used per year High-13.7

How the Competition Rates

Competitors	Rating	Pg.
BMW 3 Series	10	95
Cadillac CTS	9	107
Lincoln MKS	6	187

Price Range

	Retail	Markup
Premium Manual	$37,850	8%
Premium Plus	$42,600	8%
Prestige CVT FrontTrak	$52,800	8%
Prestige S-Line Tip Cabrio	$57,700	8%

Audi A5

Safety Checklist

Crash Tests:
  Frontal. . . . . –
  Side. . . . . –
Airbags:
  Head . . . . Fr. & Rr. Roof Curtain
  Torso. . . . . Front Pelvis/Torso from Seat
  Pelvis . . . . Front Pelvis/Torso from Seat
  Roll Sensing . . . . No
  Knee Bolster . . . . .Standard Front
Crash Avoidance:
  Frontal Collision Warning . . . . Standard
  Blind Spot Detection . . . . Optional
  Crash Imminent Braking . . . . Optional
  Lane Departure Warning . . . . None
General:
  Auto. Crash Notification . . . . None
  Day Running Lamps . . . . Standard
Safety Belt/Restraint:
  Dynamic Head Restraints. . . . . None
  Adjustable Belt . . . . None
  Pretensioners . . . . Standard Front & Rear

Audi A5

Specifications

Drive . . . . AWD
Engine 2.0-liter I4
Transmission . . . . .8-sp. Automatic
Tow Rating (lbs.) . . . . –
Head/Leg Room (in.) Average-40/41.3
Interior Space (cu. ft.). . . . . Very Cramped-84
Cargo Space (cu. ft.) . . . . .Very Cramped-10.2
Wheelbase/Length (in.) 108.3/182.1

Ratings—10 Best, 1 Worst

Combo Crash Tests	–
Safety Features	9
Rollover	9
Preventive Maintenance	5
Repair Costs	2
Warranty	9
Fuel Economy	8
Complaints	5
Insurance Costs	8
OVERALL RATING	**–**

Audi A6

At-a-Glance

Status/Year Series Started........ Unchanged/2012
Twins .... -
Body Styles ....Sedan
Seating 5
Anti-Theft Device ....Std. Pass. Immobil & Alarm
Parking Index Rating .... Hard
Where Made.............. Neckarsulm, Germany
Fuel Factor..........................
  MPG Rating (city/hwy) Good-25/33
  Driving Range (mi.) .... Very Long-556
  Fuel Type........................Premium
  Annual Fuel Cost .... Low-$1,994
  Gas Guzzler Tax ....No
  Greenhouse Gas Emissions (tons/yr.).. Average-6.6
  Barrels of Oil Used per year Average-11.8

How the Competition Rates

Competitors	Rating	Pg.
BMW 7 Series		97
Cadillac XTS	8	109
Volvo S80		268

Price Range	Retail	Markup
2.0T Premium	$42,200	8%
2.0T Premium Plus	$46,500	8%
3.0T Premium	$50,400	8%
3.0T Prestige	$56,950	8%

Audi A6

Safety Checklist

Crash Tests:
  Frontal. . . . .–
  Side. . . . .–
Airbags:
  Head . . . . Fr. & Rr. Roof Curtain
  Torso. . . . . . .Std. Fr. & Opt. Rr. Torso from Seat
  PelvisStd. Fr. & Opt. Rr. Pelvis/Torso from Seat
  Roll Sensing . . . . .Yes
  Knee Bolster . . . . Standard
Crash Avoidance:
  Frontal Collision Warning . . . . Standard
  Blind Spot Detection . . . . Optional
  Crash Imminent Braking . . . . Optional
  Lane Departure Warning . . . . None
General:
  Auto. Crash Notification . . . . None
  Day Running Lamps . . . . Standard
Safety Belt/Restraint:
  Dynamic Head Restraints . . . . None
  Adjustable Belt . . . . .Standard Front
  Pretensioners . . . . Standard Front & Rear

Audi A6

Specifications

Drive. . . . . FWD
Engine 2.0-liter I4
Transmission . . . . .CVT
Tow Rating (lbs.) . . . . –
Head/Leg Room (in.) . . . . .Very Cramped-37.2/41.3
Interior Space (cu. ft.). Average-98
Cargo Space (cu. ft.) Cramped-14.1
Wheelbase/Length (in.) 114.7/193.9

Ratings—10 Best, 1 Worst

Combo Crash Tests	–
Safety Features	9
Rollover	10
Preventive Maintenance	3
Repair Costs	1
Warranty	9
Fuel Economy	3
Complaints	–
Insurance Costs	5
OVERALL RATING	**–**

Audi A7

Audi A7

At-a-Glance

Status/Year Series Started Unchanged/2012
Twins . . . . -
Body Styles . . . . .Sedan
Seating 4/5
Anti-Theft Device . . . . . . .Std. Pass. Immobil & Alarm
Parking Index Rating . . . . .Very Hard
Where Made. . . . . Neckarsulm, Germany
Fuel Factor . . . .
 MPG Rating (city/hwy) Poor-18/28
 Driving Range (mi.) Long-425
 Fuel Type . . . . .Premium
 Annual Fuel Cost . . . . High-$2,609
 Gas Guzzler Tax . . . . .No
 Greenhouse Gas Emissions (tons/yr.) High-8.7
 Barrels of Oil Used per year High-15.7

How the Competition Rates

Competitors	Rating	Pg.
BMW 5 Series	9	96
Infiniti G		166
Jaguar XF		170

Price Range	Retail	Markup
Premium	$60,100	8%
Premium Plus	$63,800	8%
Prestige	$66,150	8%

Safety Checklist

Crash Tests:
 Frontal. . . . .–
 Side. . . . .–
Airbags:
 Head . . . . Fr. & Rr. Roof Curtain
 Torso . . . . .Std. Fr. & Opt. Rr. Torso from Seat
 Pelvis Std. Fr. & Opt. Rr. Pelvis/Torso from Seat
 Roll Sensing . . . . .Yes
 Knee Bolster . . . . .Standard Front
Crash Avoidance:
 Frontal Collision Warning . . . . Standard
 Blind Spot Detection . . . . Optional
 Crash Imminent Braking . . . . Optional
 Lane Departure Warning . . . . None
General:
 Auto. Crash Notification . . . . None
 Day Running Lamps . . . . Standard
Safety Belt/Restraint:
 Dynamic Head Restraints . . . . None
 Adjustable Belt . . . . .Standard Front
 Pretensioners . . . . Standard Front & Rear

Audi A7

Specifications

Drive . . . . AWD
Engine 3.0-liter V6
Transmission . . . . .8-sp. Automatic
Tow Rating (lbs.) . . . . –
Head/Leg Room (in.) . . . . .Very Cramped-36.9/41.3
Interior Space (cu. ft.). Cramped-94
Cargo Space (cu. ft.) Roomy-24.5
Wheelbase/Length (in.) 114.7/195.6

Ratings—10 Best, 1 Worst

Combo Crash Tests	8
Safety Features	8
Rollover	8
Preventive Maintenance	5
Repair Costs	4
Warranty	9
Fuel Economy	4
Complaints	–
Insurance Costs	–
OVERALL RATING	**9**

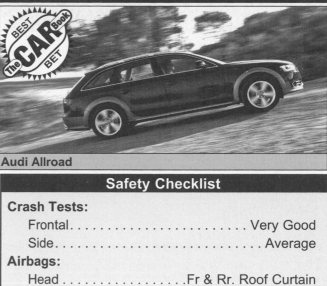

Audi Allroad

Safety Checklist

Crash Tests:
- Frontal . . . . Very Good
- Side . . . . Average

Airbags:
- Head . . . . Fr & Rr. Roof Curtain
- Torso . . . . Front Pelvis/Torso from Seat
- Pelvis . . . . Front Pelvis/Torso from Seat
- Roll Sensing . . . . Yes
- Knee Bolster . . . . None

Crash Avoidance:
- Frontal Collision Warning . . . . Standard
- Blind Spot Detection . . . . Optional
- Crash Imminent Braking . . . . Optional
- Lane Departure Warning . . . . None

General:
- Auto. Crash Notification . . . . None
- Day Running Lamps . . . . Standard

Safety Belt/Restraint:
- Dynamic Head Restraints . . . . None
- Adjustable Belt . . . . Standard Front
- Pretensioners . . . . Standard

Audi Allroad

At-a-Glance

- Status/Year Series Started . . . . All New/2013
- Twins . . . . -
- Body Styles . . . . Wagon
- Seating 5
- Anti-Theft Device . . . . . . Std. Pass. Immobil. & Alarm
- Parking Index Rating . . . . Average
- Where Made . . . . Ingolstadt, Germany
- Fuel Factor . . . .
  - MPG Rating (city/hwy) Poor-20/27
  - Driving Range (mi.) Short-383
  - Fuel Type . . . . Premium
  - Annual Fuel Cost . . . . High-$2,471
  - Gas Guzzler Tax . . . . No
  - Greenhouse Gas Emissions (tons/yr.) High-8.0
  - Barrels of Oil Used per year High-14.3

How the Competition Rates

Competitors	Rating	Pg.
BMW 5 Series	10	96
Subaru XV Crosstrek		238
Volkswagen Jetta	6	261

Price Range	Retail	Markup
Premium	$39,600	8%
Premium Plus	$42,900	8%
Prestige	$48,800	8%

Audi Allroad

Specifications

- Drive . . . . AWD
- Engine 2.0-liter I4
- Transmission . . . . 8-sp. Automatic
- Tow Rating (lbs.) . . . . –
- Head/Leg Room (in.) Cramped-38.8/41.3
- Interior Space (cu. ft.) Cramped-90
- Cargo Space (cu. ft.) Roomy-27.6
- Wheelbase/Length (in.) 110.4/185.9

Ratings—10 Best, 1 Worst

Combo Crash Tests	–
Safety Features	8
Rollover	4
Preventive Maintenance	5
Repair Costs	1
Warranty	9
Fuel Economy	4
Complaints	9
Insurance Costs	8
OVERALL RATING	**–**

Audi Q5

Audi Q5

At-a-Glance

Status/Year Series Started Appearance Change/2009
Twins . . . . -
Body Styles . . . . SUV
Seating 5
Anti-Theft Device . . . . . . Std. Pass. Immobil. & Alarm
Parking Index Rating . . . . Hard
Where Made. . . . . .Ingolstadt, Germany
Fuel Factor . . . .
  MPG Rating (city/hwy) Poor-20/28
  Driving Range (mi.) . . . . Very Long-454
  Fuel Type. . . . . .Premium
  Annual Fuel Cost . . . . High-$2,438
  Gas Guzzler Tax .No
  Greenhouse Gas Emissions (tons/yr.) High-8.0
  Barrels of Oil Used per year High-14.3

How the Competition Rates

Competitors	Rating	Pg.
Cadillac SRX	7	108
Lexus RX	5	186
Volvo XC60	9	269

Price Range	Retail	Markup
2.0T Premium	$35,900	8%
2.0T Premium Plus	$40,200	8%
3.0T Premium Plus	$43,900	8%
3.0T Prestige S-Line	$53,900	8%

Safety Checklist

Crash Tests:
  Frontal. . . . . –
  Side. . . . . –
Airbags:
  Head . . . . .Fr & Rr. Roof Curtain
  Torso. . . . . . .Std. Fr. & Opt. Rr. Torso from Seat
  Pelvis Std. Fr. & Opt. Rr. Pelvis/Torso from Seat
  Roll Sensing . . . . .Yes
  Knee Bolster . . . . None
Crash Avoidance:
  Frontal Collision Warning . . . . Standard
  Blind Spot Detection . . . . Optional
  Crash Imminent Braking . . . . None
  Lane Departure Warning . . . . None
General:
  Auto. Crash Notification . . . . None
  Day Running Lamps . . . . Standard
Safety Belt/Restraint:
  Dynamic Head Restraints. . . . . None
  Adjustable Belt . . . . .Standard Front
  Pretensioners . . . . Standard

Audi Q5

Specifications

Drive. . . . . AWD
Engine 3.0-liter I4
Transmission . . . . .8-sp. Automatic
Tow Rating (lbs.) Average-4400
Head/Leg Room (in.) Cramped-39.4/41
Interior Space (cu. ft.). Average-101.5
Cargo Space (cu. ft.) Roomy-29.1
Wheelbase/Length (in.) 110.5/182.6

Ratings—10 Best, 1 Worst

Combo Crash Tests	–
Safety Features	6
Rollover	3
Preventive Maintenance	4
Repair Costs	1
Warranty	9
Fuel Economy	2
Complaints	6
Insurance Costs	8
OVERALL RATING	**–**

Audi Q7

Audi Q7

At-a-Glance

Status/Year Series Started Unchanged/2007
Twins . . . . -
Body Styles . . . . SUV
Seating 7
Anti-Theft Device . . . . . . Std. Pass. Immobil. & Alarm
Parking Index Rating . . . . .Very Hard
Where Made. . . . . Bratislava, Slovakia
Fuel Factor
  MPG Rating (city/hwy) . . . . .Very Poor-16/22
  Driving Range (mi.) . . . . Very Long-482
  Fuel Type . . . . .Premium
  Annual Fuel Cost . . . . Very High-$3,068
  Gas Guzzler Tax . . . . .No
  Greenhouse Gas Emissions (tons/yr.)Very High-10.2
  Barrels of Oil Used per year . . . . . . .Very High-18.3

How the Competition Rates

Competitors	Rating	Pg.
BMW X5	6	100
Land Rover Range Rover		180
Toyota Sequoia		252

Price Range

	Retail	Markup
Premium	$46,800	8%
Premium Plus	$53,150	8%
Prestige TDI	$64,550	8%
Prestige S-Line TDI	$66,550	8%

Safety Checklist

Crash Tests:
  Frontal. . . . .–
  Side. . . . .–
Airbags:
  Head . . . . Fr. & Rr. Roof Curtain
  Torso. . . . . .Front Pelvis/Torso from Seat
  Pelvis . . . . .Front Pelvis/Torso from Seat
  Roll Sensing . . . . .Yes
  Knee Bolster . . . . None
Crash Avoidance:
  Frontal Collision Warning . . . . None
  Blind Spot Detection . . . . Optional
  Crash Imminent Braking. . . . . None
  Lane Departure Warning . . . . None
General:
  Auto. Crash Notification . . . . None
  Day Running Lamps . . . . Standard
Safety Belt/Restraint:
  Dynamic Head Restraints. . . . . None
  Adjustable Belt . . . . . .Standard Front and Rear
  Pretensioners . . . . Standard

Audi Q7

Specifications

Drive. . . . . AWD
Engine 3.0-liter V6
Transmission . . . . .8-sp. Automatic
Tow Rating (lbs.) High-5500
Head/Leg Room (in.) Cramped-39.5/41.3
Interior Space (cu. ft.). . . . . Very Roomy-133.2
Cargo Space (cu. ft.) . . . . .Very Cramped-10.9
Wheelbase/Length (in.) 118.2/200.3

Ratings—10 Best, 1 Worst

Combo Crash Tests	–
Safety Features	4
Rollover	7
Preventive Maintenance	10
Repair Costs	3
Warranty	9
Fuel Economy	3
Complaints	2
Insurance Costs	8
OVERALL RATING	–

BMW 1 Series Sedan

BMW 1 Series Coupe

At-a-Glance

Status/Year Series Started........ Unchanged/2008
Twins .... -
Body Styles .... Coupe, Convertible
Seating 4
Anti-Theft Device .... Std. Pass. Immobil.
Parking Index Rating .... Easy
Where Made................. Leipzig, Germany
Fuel Factor....................................
  MPG Rating (city/hwy) Poor-18/27
  Driving Range (mi.) .... Very Short-290
  Fuel Type....................... Premium
  Annual Fuel Cost .... High-$2,642
  Gas Guzzler Tax .... No
  Greenhouse Gas Emissions (tons/yr.)..... High-8.7
  Barrels of Oil Used per year High-15.7

How the Competition Rates

Competitors	Rating	Pg.
Lexus CT		282
Mercedes-Benz C-Class	4	196
Volvo C70		266

Price Range	Retail	Markup
128i	$31,200	9%
135i	$39,300	9%
135is	$43,250	9%
135is Convertible	$47,950	9%

Safety Checklist

Crash Tests:
 Frontal . . . . –
   Side. . . . . –
Airbags:
   Head . . . . Fr. & Rr. Roof Curtain
   Torso. . . . . Front Torso from Seat
   Pelvis . . . . None
   Roll Sensing . . . . No
   Knee Bolster . . . . None
Crash Avoidance:
   Frontal Collision Warning . . . . None
   Blind Spot Detection . . . . None
   Crash Imminent Braking . . . . None
   Lane Departure Warning . . . . None
General:
   Auto. Crash Notification . . . . Optional
   Day Running Lamps . . . . Standard
Safety Belt/Restraint:
   Dynamic Head Restraints . . . . . . Standard Front
   Adjustable Belt . . . . None
   Pretensioners . . . . Standard Front

BMW 1 Series Convertible

Specifications

Drive. . . . . RWD
Engine 2.0-liter I4
Transmission . . . . 8-sp. Automatic
Tow Rating (lbs.) . . . . –
Head/Leg Room (in.) . . . . . Very Cramped-37.9/41.4
Interior Space (cu. ft.). . . . . Very Cramped-86
Cargo Space (cu. ft.) . . . . Very Cramped-10
Wheelbase/Length (in.) 104.7/172.2

Ratings—10 Best, 1 Worst	
Combo Crash Tests	8
Safety Features	8
Rollover	9
Preventive Maintenance	10
Repair Costs	3
Warranty	9
Fuel Economy	6
Complaints	–
Insurance Costs	8
OVERALL RATING	**10**

BMW 3 Series Coupe

BMW 3 Series Sedan

At-a-Glance

Status/Year Series Started	All New/2013
Twins	-
Body Styles	Sedan, Coupe, Wagon
Seating	5
Anti-Theft Device	Std. Pass. Immobil.
Parking Index Rating	Easy
Where Made	Regensburg/Munich, Germany
Fuel Factor	
MPG Rating (city/hwy)	Average-22/33
Driving Range (mi.)	Average-411
Fuel Type	Premium
Annual Fuel Cost	Average-$2,161
Gas Guzzler Tax	No
Greenhouse Gas Emissions (tons/yr.)	Average-7.1
Barrels of Oil Used per year	Average-12.7

How the Competition Rates

Competitors	Rating	Pg.
Audi A4	10	87
Lexus IS	7	185
Mercedes-Benz C-Class	4	196

Price Range	Retail	Markup
328i	$36,500	9%
328xi Coupe	$40,400	9%
335i Hybrid	$49,300	9%
335is Convertible	$60,800	9%

Safety Checklist

Crash Tests:
Frontal	Good
Side	Very Good

Airbags:
Head	Fr. & Rr. Roof Curtain
Torso	Front Torso from Seat
Pelvis	None
Roll Sensing	No
Knee Bolster	Standard Front

Crash Avoidance:
Frontal Collision Warning	Optional
Blind Spot Detection	Optional
Crash Imminent Braking	Optional
Lane Departure Warning	Optional

General:
Auto. Crash Notification	Optional
Day Running Lamps	Standard

Safety Belt/Restraint:
Dynamic Head Restraints	Optional
Adjustable Belt	None
Pretensioners	Standard

BMW 3 Series Sport Wagon

Specifications

Drive	RWD
Engine	3.0-liter I4
Transmission	8-sp. Automatic
Tow Rating (lbs.)	–
Head/Leg Room (in.)	Roomy-40/42
Interior Space (cu. ft.)	Cramped-96
Cargo Space (cu. ft.)	Cramped-13
Wheelbase/Length (in.)	110.6/182

Ratings—10 Best, 1 Worst

Combo Crash Tests	6
Safety Features	9
Rollover	9
Preventive Maintenance	10
Repair Costs	1
Warranty	9
Fuel Economy	7
Complaints	1
Insurance Costs	10
OVERALL RATING	**9**

BMW 5 Series Sedan

BMW 5 Series Sport Wagon

At-a-Glance

Status/Year Series Started	Unchanged/2011
Twins	-
Body Styles	Sedan, Hatchback
Seating	5
Anti-Theft Device	Std. Pass. Immobil
Parking Index Rating	Very Hard
Where Made	Dingolfing, Germany
Fuel Factor	
MPG Rating (city/hwy)	Good-24/34
Driving Range (mi.)	Very Long-512
Fuel Type	Premium
Annual Fuel Cost	Low-$2,023
Gas Guzzler Tax	No
Greenhouse Gas Emissions (tons/yr.)	Average-6.5
Barrels of Oil Used per year	Average-11.8

How the Competition Rates

Competitors	Rating	Pg.
Infiniti G		166
Lexus GS		184
Mercedes-Benz E-Class		197

Price Range	Retail	Markup
528i	$47,500	9%
535i	$53,100	9%
550i	$62,400	9%
550xi	$64,700	9%

Safety Checklist

Crash Tests:
Frontal . . . . Poor
Side . . . . Very Good

Airbags:
Head . . . . Fr. & Rr. Roof Curtain
Torso . . . . Front Torso from Seat
Pelvis . . . . None
Roll Sensing . . . . No
Knee Bolster . . . . Standard Front

Crash Avoidance:
Frontal Collision Warning . . . . Optional
Blind Spot Detection . . . . Optional
Crash Imminent Braking . . . . Optional
Lane Departure Warning . . . . Optional

General:
Auto. Crash Notification . . . . Standard
Day Running Lamps . . . . Standard

Safety Belt/Restraint:
Dynamic Head Restraints . . . . . . Standard Front
Adjustable Belt . . . . None
Pretensioners . . . . Standard Front

BMW 5 Series

Specifications

Drive	RWD
Engine	2.0-liter I4
Transmission	8-sp. Automatic
Tow Rating (lbs.)	–
Head/Leg Room (in.)	Roomy-41/41.4
Interior Space (cu. ft.)	Average-102
Cargo Space (cu. ft.)	Cramped-14
Wheelbase/Length (in.)	116.9/193.1

Ratings—10 Best, 1 Worst

Combo Crash Tests	–
Safety Features	10
Rollover	9
Preventive Maintenance	10
Repair Costs	1
Warranty	9
Fuel Economy	2
Complaints	5
Insurance Costs	3

OVERALL RATING   –

BMW 7 Series

BMW 7 Series

At-a-Glance

Status/Year Series Started Appearance Change/2011
Twins . . . . -
Body Styles . . . . .Sedan
Seating 5
Anti-Theft Device . . . . Std. Pass. Immobil.
Parking Index Rating . . . . .Very Hard
Where Made. . . . . Dingolfing, Germany
Fuel Factor . . . .
  MPG Rating (city/hwy) . . . . .Very Poor-16/24
  Driving Range (mi.) Average-395
  Fuel Type . . . . .Premium
  Annual Fuel Cost . . . . Very High-$2,972
  Gas Guzzler Tax . . . . .No
  Greenhouse Gas Emissions (tons/yr.) Very High-9.7
  Barrels of Oil Used per year High-17.3

How the Competition Rates

Competitors	Rating	Pg.
Audi A7		90
Jaguar XF		170
Mercedes-Benz S-Class		261

Price Range

Price Range	Retail	Markup
740i	$73,300	9%
750i	$86,300	9%
750Lxi	$93,000	9%
760Li	$140,200	9%

Safety Checklist

Crash Tests:
  Frontal. . . . .–
  Side. . . . .–
Airbags:
  Head . . . . Fr. & Rr. Roof Curtain
  Torso. . . . . Front Torso from Seat
  Pelvis . . . . None
  Roll Sensing . . . . .Yes
  Knee Bolster . . . . .Standard Front
Crash Avoidance:
  Frontal Collision Warning . . . . Optional
  Blind Spot Detection . . . . Optional
  Crash Imminent Braking . . . . Optional
  Lane Departure Warning . . . . Optional
General:
  Auto. Crash Notification . . . . Standard
  Day Running Lamps . . . . Standard
Safety Belt/Restraint:
  Dynamic Head Restraints . . . . . .Standard Front
  Adjustable Belt . . . . None
  Pretensioners . . . . .Standard Front

BMW 7 Series

Specifications

Drive. . . . . RWD
Engine 4.4-liter V8
Transmission . . . . .8-sp. Automatic
Tow Rating (lbs.) . . . . –
Head/Leg Room (in.) Roomy-41/41.2
Interior Space (cu. ft.). Roomy-107
Cargo Space (cu. ft.) Cramped-14
Wheelbase/Length (in.) 120.9/200

Ratings—10 Best, 1 Worst

Combo Crash Tests	–
Safety Features	6
Rollover	4
Preventive Maintenance	10
Repair Costs	2
Warranty	9
Fuel Economy	3
Complaints	–
Insurance Costs	–
OVERALL RATING	**–**

BMW X1

At-a-Glance

Status/Year Series Started	All New/2013
Twins	-
Body Styles	SUV
Seating	5
Anti-Theft Device	Std. Pass. Immobil.
Parking Index Rating	Average
Where Made	Leipzig, Germany
Fuel Factor	
MPG Rating (city/hwy)	Poor-18/27
Driving Range (mi.)	Very Short-352
Fuel Type	Premium
Annual Fuel Cost	High-$2,642
Gas Guzzler Tax	No
Greenhouse Gas Emissions (tons/yr.)	High-8.7
Barrels of Oil Used per year	High-15.7

How the Competition Rates

Competitors	Rating	Pg.
Acura RDX		83
Buick Encore		102
Volkswagen Tiguan	4	264

Price Range	Retail	Markup
sDrive28i	$30,650	9%
xDrive28i	$32,350	9%
xDrive35i	$38,450	9%

BMW X1

Safety Checklist

Crash Tests:
Frontal . . . . –
Side . . . . –

Airbags:
Head . . . . Fr. & Rr. Roof Curtain
Torso . . . . Front Torso from Seat
Pelvis . . . . None
Roll Sensing . . . . Yes
Knee Bolster . . . . None

Crash Avoidance:
Frontal Collision Warning . . . . None
Blind Spot Detection . . . . None
Crash Imminent Braking . . . . None
Lane Departure Warning . . . . None

General:
Auto. Crash Notification . . . . Optional
Day Running Lamps . . . . Standard

Safety Belt/Restraint:
Dynamic Head Restraints . . . . . . Standard Front
Adjustable Belt . . . . None
Pretensioners . . . . Standard Front

BMW X1

Specifications

Drive	4WD
Engine	2.0-liter R4
Transmission	8-sp. Automatic
Tow Rating (lbs.)	Average-4409
Head/Leg Room (in.)	Roomy-41/41.4
Interior Space (cu. ft.)	Average-98
Cargo Space (cu. ft.)	Cramped-14.8
Wheelbase/Length (in.)	108.7/176.3

BMW X3

Ratings—10 Best, 1 Worst

Combo Crash Tests	–
Safety Features	9
Rollover	4
Preventive Maintenance	10
Repair Costs	2
Warranty	9
Fuel Economy	3
Complaints	6
Insurance Costs	8
OVERALL RATING	**–**

BMW X3

At-a-Glance

Status/Year Series Started........ Unchanged/2011
Twins .... -
Body Styles .... SUV
Seating 5
Anti-Theft Device .... Standard Pass. Immobil.
Parking Index Rating .... Hard
Where Made.................. Spartanburg, SC
Fuel Factor ....
  MPG Rating (city/hwy) Poor-19/26
  Driving Range (mi.) Short-383
  Fuel Type......................Premium
  Annual Fuel Cost .... High-$2,588
  Gas Guzzler Tax ....No
  Greenhouse Gas Emissions (tons/yr.)..... High-8.7
  Barrels of Oil Used per year High-15.7

How the Competition Rates

Competitors	Rating	Pg.
Audi Q5		92
Infiniti FX		165
Porsche Cayenne		225

Price Range	Retail	Markup
xDrive28i	$38,500	9%
xDrive35i	$43,600	9%

Safety Checklist

Crash Tests:
  Frontal............................–
  Side.............................–
Airbags:
  Head .... Fr. & Rr. Roof Curtain
  Torso .... Front Torso from Seat
  Pelvis .... None
  Roll Sensing ....Yes
  Knee Bolster .... Standard Driver
Crash Avoidance:
  Frontal Collision Warning .... Optional
  Blind Spot Detection .... None
  Crash Imminent Braking .... Optional
  Lane Departure Warning .... Optional
General:
  Auto. Crash Notification .... Optional
  Day Running Lamps .... Standard
Safety Belt/Restraint:
  Dynamic Head Restraints......Standard Front
  Adjustable Belt .... None
  Pretensioners ....Standard Front

BMW X3

Specifications

Drive................................... 4WD
Engine 2.0-liter I4
Transmission .... 8-sp. Automatic
Tow Rating (lbs.) Average-4409
Head/Leg Room (in.) Cramped-41/39.9
Interior Space (cu. ft.)..........Cramped-90.1
Cargo Space (cu. ft.) Roomy-27.6
Wheelbase/Length (in.) 110.6/183

Ratings—10 Best, 1 Worst

Combo Crash Tests	4
Safety Features	8
Rollover	3
Preventive Maintenance	10
Repair Costs	1
Warranty	9
Fuel Economy	2
Complaints	7
Insurance Costs	5
OVERALL RATING	**6**

BMW X5

BMW X5

At-a-Glance

Status/Year Series Started........	Unchanged/2007
Twins	-
Body Styles	SUV
Seating	5
Anti-Theft Device	Std. Pass. Immobil.
Parking Index Rating	Very Hard
Where Made.	Spartanburg, SC
Fuel Factor	
MPG Rating (city/hwy)	Very Poor-16/23
Driving Range (mi.)	Long-417
Fuel Type	Premium
Annual Fuel Cost	Very High-$3,018
Gas Guzzler Tax	No
Greenhouse Gas Emissions (tons/yr.)	Very High-9.6
Barrels of Oil Used per year	High-17.3

How the Competition Rates

Competitors	Rating	Pg.
Audi Q7		93
Cadillac SRX	7	108
Volvo XC90		270

Price Range

	Retail	Markup
xDrive35i	$47,500	9%
xDrive35i Premium	$55,200	9%
xDrive50i	$64,200	9%
M	$88,850	9%

Safety Checklist

Crash Tests:
- Frontal . . . . Very Poor
- Side . . . . Very Good

Airbags:
- Head . . . . Fr. & Rr. Roof Curtain
- Torso. . . . . Front Torso from Seat
- Pelvis . . . . None
- Roll Sensing . . . . Yes
- Knee Bolster . . . . None

Crash Avoidance:
- Frontal Collision Warning . . . . Optional
- Blind Spot Detection . . . . None
- Crash Imminent Braking . . . . None
- Lane Departure Warning . . . . Optional

General:
- Auto. Crash Notification . . . . Standard
- Day Running Lamps . . . . Standard

Safety Belt/Restraint:
- Dynamic Head Restraints . . . . . . Standard Front
- Adjustable Belt . . . . None
- Pretensioners . . . . Standard Front

BMW X5

Specifications

Drive.	4WD
Engine	3.0-liter V6
Transmission	8-sp. Automatic
Tow Rating (lbs.)	High-6000
Head/Leg Room (in.)	Very Cramped-39.3/40
Interior Space (cu. ft.)	Average-102.4
Cargo Space (cu. ft.)	Roomy-23.2
Wheelbase/Length (in.)	115.5/191.1

Buick Enclave

Ratings—10 Best, 1 Worst

Combo Crash Tests	9
Safety Features	8
Rollover	3
Preventive Maintenance	3
Repair Costs	2
Warranty	5
Fuel Economy	2
Complaints	6
Insurance Costs	10
OVERALL RATING	**7**

Buick Enclave

At-a-Glance

Status/Year Series Started Appearance Change/2008	
Twins	-
Body Styles	SUV
Seating	7/8
Anti-Theft Device	Std. Pass. Immobil. & Alarm
Parking Index Rating	Very Hard
Where Made	Lansing, MI
Fuel Factor	
MPG Rating (city/hwy)	Very Poor-17/24
Driving Range (mi.)	Long-431
Fuel Type	Regular
Annual Fuel Cost	High-$2,629
Gas Guzzler Tax	No
Greenhouse Gas Emissions (tons/yr.)	Very High-9.6
Barrels of Oil Used per year	High-17.3

How the Competition Rates

Competitors	Rating	Pg.
Acura MDX	8	82
Audi Q7		93
Lexus RX	5	186

Price Range

	Retail	Markup
Convenience	$38,445	5%
Leather	$42,460	5%
Premium	$45,625	5%
Premium AWD	$47,625	5%

Safety Checklist

Crash Tests:
Frontal . . . . Good
Side . . . . Very Good
Airbags:
Head . . . . Fr. & Rr. Roof Curtain
Torso . . . . Front Pelvis/Torso from Seat
Pelvis . . . . Front Pelvis/Torso from Seat
Roll Sensing . . . . Yes
Knee Bolster . . . . None
Crash Avoidance:
Frontal Collision Warning . . . . None
Blind Spot Detection . . . . Optional
Crash Imminent Braking . . . . Optional
Lane Departure Warning . . . . None
General:
Auto. Crash Notification . . . . Standard
Day Running Lamps . . . . Standard
Safety Belt/Restraint:
Dynamic Head Restraints . . . . None
Adjustable Belt . . . . Standard Front & Rear
Pretensioners . . . . Standard Front

Buick Enclave

Specifications

Drive	FWD
Engine	3.6-liter V6
Transmission	6-sp. Automatic
Tow Rating (lbs.)	Average-4500
Head/Leg Room (in.)	Average-40.4/41.3
Interior Space (cu. ft.)	Very Roomy-151.1
Cargo Space (cu. ft.)	Roomy-23.3
Wheelbase/Length (in.)	118.96/201.9

Ratings—10 Best, 1 Worst

Combo Crash Tests	–
Safety Features	10
Rollover	3
Preventive Maintenance	10
Repair Costs	–
Warranty	5
Fuel Economy	8
Complaints	–
Insurance Costs	–
OVERALL RATING	**–**

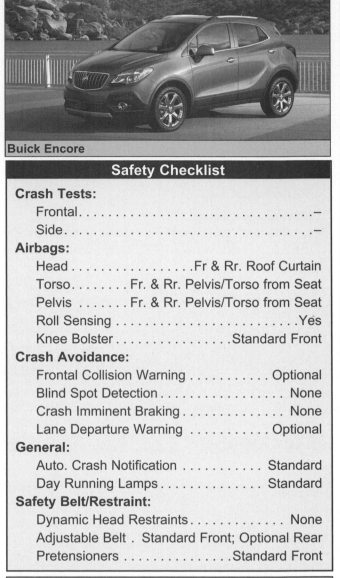

Buick Encore

Buick Encore

At-a-Glance

Status/Year Series Started	All New/2013
Twins	-
Body Styles	SUV
Seating	5
Anti-Theft Device	Std. Pass. Immobil. & Alarm
Parking Index Rating	Easy
Where Made	Bupyong, South Korea
Fuel Factor	
MPG Rating (city/hwy)	Good-25/33
Driving Range (mi.)	Short-384
Fuel Type	Regular
Annual Fuel Cost	Low-$1,833
Gas Guzzler Tax	No
Greenhouse Gas Emissions (tons/yr.)	Low-5.2
Barrels of Oil Used per year	Average-11.8

How the Competition Rates

Competitors	Rating	Pg.
Ford Escape	7	136
Honda CR-V	7	150
Mazda CX-5	6	193

Price Range	Retail	Markup
Base FWD	$24,200	4%
Convenience	$26,510	4%
Leather	$28,210	4%
Premium	$29,690	4%

Safety Checklist

Crash Tests:
Frontal . . . . –
Side . . . . –
Airbags:
Head . . . . Fr & Rr. Roof Curtain
Torso . . . . Fr. & Rr. Pelvis/Torso from Seat
Pelvis . . . . Fr. & Rr. Pelvis/Torso from Seat
Roll Sensing . . . . Yes
Knee Bolster . . . . Standard Front
Crash Avoidance:
Frontal Collision Warning . . . . Optional
Blind Spot Detection . . . . None
Crash Imminent Braking . . . . None
Lane Departure Warning . . . . Optional
General:
Auto. Crash Notification . . . . Standard
Day Running Lamps . . . . Standard
Safety Belt/Restraint:
Dynamic Head Restraints . . . . None
Adjustable Belt . Standard Front; Optional Rear
Pretensioners . . . . Standard Front

Buick Encore

Specifications

Drive	AWD
Engine	1.4-liter I4
Transmission	6-sp. Automatic
Tow Rating (lbs.)	–
Head/Leg Room (in.)	Cramped-39.6/40.8
Interior Space (cu. ft.)	Cramped-92.8
Cargo Space (cu. ft.)	Average-18.8
Wheelbase/Length (in.)	100.6/168.5

Buick LaCrosse

Ratings—10 Best, 1 Worst

Combo Crash Tests	8
Safety Features	8
Rollover	6
Preventive Maintenance	3
Repair Costs	4
Warranty	5
Fuel Economy	8
Complaints	5
Insurance Costs	8
OVERALL RATING	**8**

Buick LaCrosse

Buick LaCrosse

At-a-Glance

Status/Year Series Started........ Unchanged/2010
Twins .... -
Body Styles .... Sedan
Seating 5
Anti-Theft Device ...... Std. Pass. Immobil. & Alarm
Parking Index Rating .... Hard
Where Made.................... Kansas Clty, KS
Fuel Factor
  MPG Rating (city/hwy)............. Good-25/36
  Driving Range (mi.) .... Very Long-455
  Fuel Type........................... Regular
  Annual Fuel Cost .... Low-$1,775
  Gas Guzzler Tax .... No
  Greenhouse Gas Emissions (tons/yr.)..... High-8.7
  Barrels of Oil Used per year High-15.7

How the Competition Rates

Competitors	Rating	Pg.
Acura TL	5	84
Cadillac XTS	8	109
Volvo S80		268

Price Range	Retail	Markup
Base	$31,660	4%
Leather	$33,870	4%
Premium II	$36,705	4%
Touring	$39,240	4%

Safety Checklist

Crash Tests:
  Frontal....................... Very Good
  Side........................... Average
Airbags:
  Head .... Fr & Rr. Roof Curtain
  Torso.......... Front Pelvis/Torso from Seat
  Pelvis .... Front Pelvis/Torso from Seat
  Roll Sensing .... Yes
  Knee Bolster .... None
Crash Avoidance:
  Frontal Collision Warning .... None
  Blind Spot Detection .... Optional
  Crash Imminent Braking.............. None
  Lane Departure Warning .... None
General:
  Auto. Crash Notification .... Standard
  Day Running Lamps.............. Standard
Safety Belt/Restraint:
  Dynamic Head Restraints............. None
  Adjustable Belt ......Standard Front and Rear
  Pretensioners ....Standard Front

Buick LaCrosse

Specifications

Drive.................................. FWD
Engine 2.4-liter I4
Transmission .... 6-sp. Automatic
Tow Rating (lbs.) .... Very Low-1000
Head/Leg Room (in.) ...... Very Cramped-38/41.7
Interior Space (cu. ft.)........... Average-101.7
Cargo Space (cu. ft.) .... Very Cramped-11.4
Wheelbase/Length (in.) 111.7/197

Ratings—10 Best, 1 Worst

Combo Crash Tests	8
Safety Features	7
Rollover	7
Preventive Maintenance	3
Repair Costs	4
Warranty	5
Fuel Economy	8
Complaints	4
Insurance Costs	5
OVERALL RATING	**7**

Buick Regal

Buick Regal

At-a-Glance

```
Status/Year Series Started........ Unchanged/2011
Twins ......................................... -
Body Styles ...........................Sedan
Seating...................................5
Anti-Theft Device ...... Std. Pass. Immobil. & Alarm
Parking Index Rating ...................Easy
Where Made.................. Oshawa, Ontario
Fuel Factor ...
  MPG Rating (city/hwy) ......... Good-25/36
  Driving Range (mi.) ......... Very Long-455
  Fuel Type........................Regular/E85
  Annual Fuel Cost ............. Low-$1,775
  Gas Guzzler Tax .......................No
  Greenhouse Gas Emissions (tons/yr.).. Average-6.3
  Barrels of Oil Used per year ........ Average-11.4
```

How the Competition Rates

Competitors	Rating	Pg.
Dodge Avenger	2	126
Hyundai Azera		157
Lincoln MKZ		188

Price Range

	Retail	Markup
Base 2.4L	$29,015	4%
Premium 1 2.4L	$30,635	4%
Premium 2 Turbo	$32,045	4%
GS	$34,980	4%

Safety Checklist

Crash Tests:
```
  Frontal........................... Good
  Side................... Very Good
```
Airbags:
```
  Head ................Fr & Rr. Roof Curtain
  Torso...........Front Pelvis/Torso from Seat
  Pelvis .........Front Pelvis/Torso from Seat
  Roll Sensing .........................Yes
  Knee Bolster ..................... None
```
Crash Avoidance:
```
  Frontal Collision Warning ............. None
  Blind Spot Detection ................. None
  Crash Imminent Braking............. None
  Lane Departure Warning ............. None
```
General:
```
  Auto. Crash Notification ........... Standard
  Day Running Lamps.............. Standard
```
Safety Belt/Restraint:
```
  Dynamic Head Restraints............. None
  Adjustable Belt ......Standard Front and Rear
  Pretensioners ...............Standard Front
```

Buick Regal

Specifications

```
Drive............................... FWD
Engine ......................... 2.4-liter I4
Transmission .................6-sp. Automatic
Tow Rating (lbs.) ...................... −
Head/Leg Room (in.) ...........Cramped-38.8/42.1
Interior Space (cu. ft.)............Cramped-96.81
Cargo Space (cu. ft.) .........Very Cramped-11.1
Wheelbase/Length (in.) ............107.8/190.2
```

Ratings—10 Best, 1 Worst

Combo Crash Tests	10
Safety Features	10
Rollover	7
Preventive Maintenance	–
Repair Costs	–
Warranty	5
Fuel Economy	6
Complaints	8
Insurance Costs	8
OVERALL RATING	**10**

Buick Verano

Buick Verano

At-a-Glance

Status/Year Series Started. Unchanged/2012
Twins . . . . Chevrolet Cruze
Body Styles . . . . Sedan
Seating 5
Anti-Theft Device . . . . . . Std. Pass. Immobil. & Alarm
Parking Index Rating . . . . Easy
Where Made. . . . . Orion Township, MI
Fuel Factor . . . .
  MPG Rating (city/hwy) Average-21/32
  Driving Range (mi.) Short-388
  Fuel Type Regular/E85
  Annual Fuel Cost . . . . Average-$2,071
  Gas Guzzler Tax . . . . No
  Greenhouse Gas Emissions (tons/yr.) . . Average-7.3
  Barrels of Oil Used per year Average-13.2

How the Competition Rates

Competitors	Rating	Pg.
Audi A3		86
Dodge Dart		129
Lexus IS	7	185

Price Range	Retail	Markup
Base	$23,080	4%
Convenience	$24,375	4%
Leather	$26,755	4%

Safety Checklist

Crash Tests:
  Frontal. . . . . Very Good
  Side. . . . . Very Good
Airbags:
  Head . . . . .Fr & Rr. Roof Curtain
  Torso. . . . . Fr. & Rr. Pelvis/Torso from Seat
  Pelvis . . . . Fr. & Rr. Pelvis/Torso from Seat
  Roll Sensing . . . . .Yes
  Knee Bolster . . . . .Standard Front
Crash Avoidance:
  Frontal Collision Warning . . . . None
  Blind Spot Detection . . . . Optional
  Crash Imminent Braking . . . . None
  Lane Departure Warning . . . . None
General:
  Auto. Crash Notification . . . . Standard
  Day Running Lamps . . . . Standard
Safety Belt/Restraint:
  Dynamic Head Restraints . . . . None
  Adjustable Belt . . . . . .Standard Front and Rear
  Pretensioners . . . . .Standard Front

Buick Verano

Specifications

Drive. . . . . FWD
Engine 2.4-liter I4
Transmission . . . . .6-sp. Automatic
Tow Rating (lbs.) . . . . Very Low-1000
Head/Leg Room (in.) Cramped-38.3/42
Interior Space (cu. ft.). Cramped-95
Cargo Space (cu. ft.) Cramped-14.3
Wheelbase/Length (in.) 105.7/183.9

Ratings—10 Best, 1 Worst

Combo Crash Tests	10
Safety Features	10
Rollover	8
Preventive Maintenance	3
Repair Costs	3
Warranty	8
Fuel Economy	6
Complaints	–
Insurance Costs	5
OVERALL RATING	**9**

Cadillac ATS

Cadillac ATS

At-a-Glance

Status/Year Series Started	All New/2013
Twins	-
Body Styles	Sedan
Seating	5
Anti-Theft Device	Std. Pass. Immobil. & Alarm
Parking Index Rating	Average
Where Made	Lansing, MI
Fuel Factor	
MPG Rating (city/hwy)	Average-22/32
Driving Range (mi.)	Average-410
Fuel Type	Regular
Annual Fuel Cost	Low-$2,010
Gas Guzzler Tax	No
Greenhouse Gas Emissions (tons/yr.)	Average-7.1
Barrels of Oil Used per year	Average-12.7

How the Competition Rates

Competitors	Rating	Pg.
Acura ILX	8	81
Mercedes-Benz C-Class	4	196
Volvo C70		266

Price Range	Retail	Markup
Base 2.5L	$33,095	6%
Luxury 2.0T	$39,395	6%
Performance 2.0T	$41,895	6%
Premium 3.6L AWD	$47,795	6%

Safety Checklist

Crash Tests:
- Frontal . . . . Very Good
- Side . . . . Very Good

Airbags:
- Head . . . . Fr & Rr. Roof Curtain
- Torso . . . . Front Pelvis/Torso from Seat
- Pelvis . . . . Front Pelvis/Torso from Seat
- Roll Sensing . . . . Yes
- Knee Bolster . . . . Standard Front

Crash Avoidance:
- Frontal Collision Warning . . . . Optional
- Blind Spot Detection . . . . Optional
- Crash Imminent Braking . . . . Optional
- Lane Departure Warning . . . . Optional

General:
- Auto. Crash Notification . . . . Standard
- Day Running Lamps . . . . Standard

Safety Belt/Restraint:
- Dynamic Head Restraints . . . . None
- Adjustable Belt . . . . Standard Rear
- Pretensioners . . . . Standard Front

Cadillac ATS

Specifications

Drive	RWD
Engine	2.5-liter I4
Transmission	6-sp. Automatic
Tow Rating (lbs.)	Very Low-1000
Head/Leg Room (in.)	Average-38.6/42.5
Interior Space (cu. ft.)	Cramped-90.9
Cargo Space (cu. ft.)	Very Cramped-10.2
Wheelbase/Length (in.)	109.3/182.8

Ratings—10 Best, 1 Worst

Combo Crash Tests	9
Safety Features	8
Rollover	8
Preventive Maintenance	3
Repair Costs	3
Warranty	8
Fuel Economy	3
Complaints	5
Insurance Costs	8
OVERALL RATING	**9**

Cadillac CTS Coupe

Cadillac CTS Sedan

At-a-Glance

Status/Year Series Started	Unchanged/2003
Twins	-
Body Styles	Sedan, Coupe, Wagon
Seating	4
Anti-Theft Device	Std. Pass. Immobil. & Opt. Pass. Alarm
Parking Index Rating	Easy
Where Made	Lansing, MI
Fuel Factor	
MPG Rating (city/hwy)	Poor-18/27
Driving Range (mi.)	Short-381
Fuel Type	Regular
Annual Fuel Cost	High-$2,430
Gas Guzzler Tax	No
Greenhouse Gas Emissions (tons/yr.)	High-8.7
Barrels of Oil Used per year	High-15.7

How the Competition Rates

Competitors	Rating	Pg.
Acura TL	5	84
Infiniti G		166
Lexus ES	8	183

Price Range	Retail	Markup
Base	$38,905	6%
Performance	$43,340	6%
Premium	$48,290	6%
V	$63,215	7%

Safety Checklist

Crash Tests:
- Frontal . . . . Very Good
- Side . . . . Good

Airbags:
- Head . . . . .Fr & Rr. Roof Curtain
- Torso . . . . .Front Pelvis/Torso from Seat
- Pelvis . . . . .Front Pelvis/Torso from Seat
- Roll Sensing . . . . .Yes
- Knee Bolster . . . . None

Crash Avoidance:
- Frontal Collision Warning . . . . None
- Blind Spot Detection . . . . None
- Crash Imminent Braking . . . . None
- Lane Departure Warning . . . . None

General:
- Auto. Crash Notification . . . . Standard
- Day Running Lamps . . . . Standard

Safety Belt/Restraint:
- Dynamic Head Restraints . . . . . .Standard Front
- Adjustable Belt . . . . .Standard Front
- Pretensioners . . . . .Standard Front

Cadillac CTS Wagon

Specifications

Drive	RWD
Engine	3.6-liter V6
Transmission	6-sp. Automatic
Tow Rating (lbs.)	–
Head/Leg Room (in.)	Very Cramped-36.9/42.4
Interior Space (cu. ft.)	Average-99
Cargo Space (cu. ft.)	Cramped-15
Wheelbase/Length (in.)	113.4/188.5

Ratings—10 Best, 1 Worst

Combo Crash Tests	9
Safety Features	9
Rollover	3
Preventive Maintenance	3
Repair Costs	2
Warranty	8
Fuel Economy	2
Complaints	6
Insurance Costs	8
OVERALL RATING	**7**

Cadillac SRX

Cadillac SRX

At-a-Glance

Status/Year Series Started Appearance Change/2010
Twins . . . . -
Body Styles . . . . SUV
Seating 5
Anti-Theft Device . . . . . . Std. Pass. Immobil. & Alarm
Parking Index Rating . . . . .Very Hard
Where Made. . . . . .Ramos Arizpe, Mexico
Fuel Factor . . . .
  MPG Rating (city/hwy) . . . . .Very Poor-17/24
  Driving Range (mi.) Average-411
  Fuel Type. . . . . .Regular
  Annual Fuel Cost . . . . High-$2,629
  Gas Guzzler Tax . . . . .No
  Greenhouse Gas Emissions (tons/yr.) Very High-9.6
  Barrels of Oil Used per year High-17.3

How the Competition Rates

Competitors	Rating	Pg.
Acura MDX	8	82
Lexus RX	5	186
Volvo XC90		270

Price Range	Retail	Markup
Base	$37,155	6%
Luxury	$45,025	6%
Performance	$47,715	6%
Premium	$50,555	6%

Safety Checklist

Crash Tests:
  Frontal . . . . Very Good
  Side. . . . . Good
Airbags:
  Head . . . . .Fr & Rr. Roof Curtain
  Torso. . . . . .Front Pelvis/Torso from Seat
  Pelvis . . . . .Front Pelvis/Torso from Seat
  Roll Sensing . . . . .Yes
  Knee Bolster . . . . None
Crash Avoidance:
  Frontal Collision Warning . . . . Optional
  Blind Spot Detection . . . . Optional
  Crash Imminent Braking . . . . Optional
  Lane Departure Warning . . . . Optional
General:
  Auto. Crash Notification . . . . Standard
  Day Running Lamps . . . . Standard
Safety Belt/Restraint:
  Dynamic Head Restraints . . . . None
  Adjustable Belt . . . . . .Standard Front and Rear
  Pretensioners . . . . .Standard Front

Cadillac SRX

Specifications

Drive. . . . . AWD
Engine 3.6-liter V6
Transmission . . . . .6-sp. Automatic
Tow Rating (lbs.) Low-3500
Head/Leg Room (in.) Cramped-39.7/41.2
Interior Space (cu. ft.). Average-100.6
Cargo Space (cu. ft.) Roomy-29.9
Wheelbase/Length (in.) 110.5/190.3

Ratings—10 Best, 1 Worst

Combo Crash Tests	10
Safety Features	10
Rollover	6
Preventive Maintenance	3
Repair Costs	3
Warranty	8
Fuel Economy	3
Complaints	–
Insurance Costs	–
OVERALL RATING	**8**

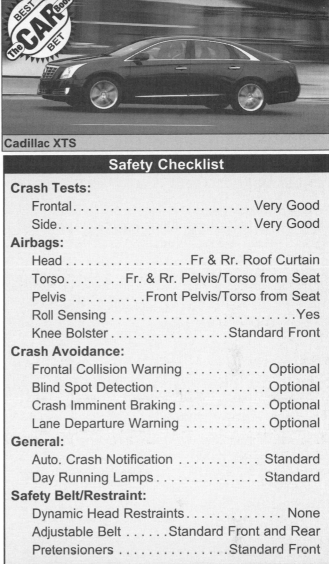
Cadillac XTS

Cadillac XTS

Cadillac XTS

At-a-Glance

Status/Year Series Started . . . . All New/2013
Twins . . . . -
Body Styles . . . . Sedan
Seating 5
Anti-Theft Device . . . . . . Std. Pass. Immobil. & Alarm
Parking Index Rating . . . . Very Hard
Where Made. . . . . Oshawa, Ontario
Fuel Factor . . . .
   MPG Rating (city/hwy) Poor-17/28
   Driving Range (mi.) Average-392
   Fuel Type . . . . .Regular
   Annual Fuel Cost . . . . High-$2,491
   Gas Guzzler Tax . . . . .No
   Greenhouse Gas Emissions (tons/yr.) High-8.7
   Barrels of Oil Used per year High-15.7

How the Competition Rates

Competitors	Rating	Pg.
Audi A7		90
BMW 7 Series		97
Lincoln MKS	6	187

Price Range

	Retail	Markup
Base	$44,075	6%
Luxury	$48,690	6%
Premium	$53,585	6%
Platinum AWD	$60,385	6%

Safety Checklist

Crash Tests:
   Frontal . . . . Very Good
   Side . . . . Very Good
Airbags:
   Head . . . . .Fr & Rr. Roof Curtain
   Torso . . . . Fr. & Rr. Pelvis/Torso from Seat
   Pelvis . . . . .Front Pelvis/Torso from Seat
   Roll Sensing . . . . .Yes
   Knee Bolster . . . . .Standard Front
Crash Avoidance:
   Frontal Collision Warning . . . . Optional
   Blind Spot Detection . . . . Optional
   Crash Imminent Braking . . . . Optional
   Lane Departure Warning . . . . Optional
General:
   Auto. Crash Notification . . . . Standard
   Day Running Lamps . . . . Standard
Safety Belt/Restraint:
   Dynamic Head Restraints . . . . None
   Adjustable Belt . . . . . .Standard Front and Rear
   Pretensioners . . . . .Standard Front

Cadillac XTS

Specifications

Drive. . . . . FWD
Engine 3.6-liter V6
Transmission . . . . .6-sp. Automatic
Tow Rating (lbs.) . . . . Very Low-1000
Head/Leg Room (in.) . . . . . . Very Roomy-40.1/45.8
Interior Space (cu. ft.). Roomy-104.2
Cargo Space (cu. ft.) Average-18
Wheelbase/Length (in.) 111.7/202

Ratings—10 Best, 1 Worst	Avalanche	Escalade EXT
Combo Crash Tests	–	–
Safety Features	8	8
Rollover	1	2
Preventive Maintenance	3	3
Repair Costs	6	2
Warranty	6	8
Fuel Economy	1	1
Complaints	6	6
Insurance Costs	8	5
OVERALL RATING	–	

Chevrolet Avalanche

Cadillac Escalade EXT

At-a-Glance

Status/Year Series Started	Unchanged/2002
Twins	Cadillac Escalade EXT
Body Styles	SUV, Crew Cab Pickup
Seating	6
Anti-Theft Device	Std. Pass. Immobil. & Alarm
Parking Index Rating	Very Hard
Where Made	Silao, Mexico
Fuel Factor	
MPG Rating (city/hwy)	Very Poor-14/20
Driving Range (mi.)	Very Long-510
Fuel Type	Regular
Annual Fuel Cost	Very High-$3,179
Gas Guzzler Tax	No
Greenhouse Gas Emissions (tons/yr.)	Very High-10.7
Barrels of Oil Used per year	Very High-19.4

How the Competition Rates

Competitors	Rating	Pg.
Ford F-150	5	139
Honda Ridgeline		155
Ram 1500	2	226

Price Range	Retail	Markup
LS 2WD	$35,980	8%
LS 4WD	$39,030	8%
LT 4WD	$41,675	8%
LTZ 4WD	$47,885	8%

Safety Checklist

Crash Tests:
Frontal .... –
Side .... –

Airbags:
Head .... Fr & Rr. Roof Curtain
Torso .... Front Pelvis/Torso from Seat
Pelvis .... Front Pelvis/Torso from Seat
Roll Sensing .... Yes
Knee Bolster .... None

Crash Avoidance:
Frontal Collision Warning .... None
Blind Spot Detection .... Optional
Crash Imminent Braking .... None
Lane Departure Warning .... None

General:
Auto. Crash Notification .... Standard
Day Running Lamps .... Standard

Safety Belt/Restraint:
Dynamic Head Restraints .... None
Adjustable Belt ...... Standard Front and Rear
Pretensioners .... Standard Front

Chevrolet Avalanche

Specifications

Drive	4WD
Engine	5.3-liter V8
Transmission	6-sp. Automatic
Tow Rating (lbs.)	Very High-8000
Head/Leg Room (in.)	Roomy-41.1/41.3
Interior Space (cu. ft.)	Roomy-120.2
Cargo Space (cu. ft.)	Very Roomy-45.5
Wheelbase/Length (in.)	130/221.3

Ratings—10 Best, 1 Worst	
Combo Crash Tests	10
Safety Features	3
Rollover	10
Preventive Maintenance	3
Repair Costs	8
Warranty	6
Fuel Economy	3
Complaints	5
Insurance Costs	3
OVERALL RATING	**8**

Chevrolet Camaro

Safety Checklist

Crash Tests:
Frontal . . . . Very Good
Side . . . . Very Good
Airbags:
Head . . . . Front Head/Torso from Seat
Torso . . . . Front Head/Torso from Seat
Pelvis . . . . None
Roll Sensing . . . . No
Knee Bolster . . . . None
Crash Avoidance:
Frontal Collision Warning . . . . None
Blind Spot Detection . . . . None
Crash Imminent Braking . . . . None
Lane Departure Warning . . . . None
General:
Auto. Crash Notification . . . . Standard
Day Running Lamps . . . . Standard
Safety Belt/Restraint:
Dynamic Head Restraints . . . . None
Adjustable Belt . . . . Standard Rear
Pretensioners . . . . Standard Front

Chevrolet Camaro Convertible

At-a-Glance

Status/Year Series Started	Unchanged/2010
Twins	-
Body Styles	Coupe
Seating	4
Anti-Theft Device	Std. Pass. Immobil. & Alarm
Parking Index Rating	Hard
Where Made	Oshawa, Ontario
Fuel Factor	
MPG Rating (city/hwy)	Poor-18/27
Driving Range (mi.)	Average-402
Fuel Type	Regular
Annual Fuel Cost	High-$2,430
Gas Guzzler Tax	No
Greenhouse Gas Emissions (tons/yr.)	High-8.7
Barrels of Oil Used per year	High-15.7

How the Competition Rates

Competitors	Rating	Pg.
Dodge Challenger	3	127
Ford Mustang	2	144
Nissan 370Z		208

Chevrolet Camaro

Specifications

Drive	RWD
Engine	3.6-liter V6
Transmission	6-sp. Automatic
Tow Rating (lbs.)	–
Head/Leg Room (in.) . . . . . Very Cramped-37.4/42.4
Interior Space (cu. ft.)	Cramped-93
Cargo Space (cu. ft.) . . . . Very Cramped-11.3
Wheelbase/Length (in.)	112.3/190.4

Price Range

Price Range	Retail	Markup
LS	$24,545	4%
LT	$25,760	4%
SS	$32,635	4%
ZL 1 Convertible	$59,545	4%

Ratings—10 Best, 1 Worst

Combo Crash Tests	–
Safety Features	2
Rollover	10
Preventive Maintenance	4
Repair Costs	1
Warranty	6
Fuel Economy	1
Complaints	4
Insurance Costs	10
OVERALL RATING	**–**

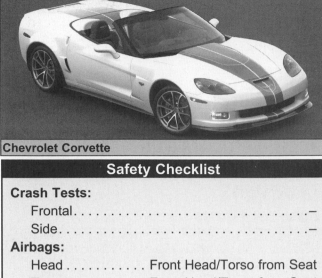

Chevrolet Corvette

Chevrolet Corvette

At-a-Glance

Status/Year Series Started. Unchanged/2005
Twins . . . . -
Body Styles . . . . Coupe, Convertible
Seating 2
Anti-Theft Device . . . . . . Std. Pass. Immobil. & Alarm
Parking Index Rating . . . . Average
Where Made. . . . . .Bowling Green, KY
Fuel Factor . . . .
  MPG Rating (city/hwy) . . . . .Very Poor-14/21
  Driving Range (mi.) . . . . .Very Short-297
  Fuel Type . . . . .Regular
  Annual Fuel Cost . . . . .Very High-$3,124
  Gas Guzzler Tax . . . . .No
  Greenhouse Gas Emissions (tons/yr.)Very High-10.7
  Barrels of Oil Used per year . . . . . . .Very High-19.4

How the Competition Rates

Competitors	Rating	Pg.
Dodge Challenger		127
Ford Mustang	2	144
Nissan 370z		208

Price Range

Price Range	Retail	Markup
Base Coupe	$49,600	10%
GS Convertible	$59,600	10%
Z06 Coupe	$75,600	10%
ZR1 Coupe	$111,600	7%

Safety Checklist

Crash Tests:
  Frontal. . . . .–
  Side. . . . .–
Airbags:
  Head . . . . Front Head/Torso from Seat
  Torso. . . . . Front Head/Torso from Seat
  Pelvis . . . . None
  Roll Sensing . . . . No
  Knee Bolster . . . . None
Crash Avoidance:
  Frontal Collision Warning . . . . None
  Blind Spot Detection . . . . None
  Crash Imminent Braking . . . . None
  Lane Departure Warning . . . . None
General:
  Auto. Crash Notification . . . . Standard
  Day Running Lamps . . . . Standard
Safety Belt/Restraint:
  Dynamic Head Restraints . . . . None
  Adjustable Belt . . . . None
  Pretensioners . . . . .Standard Front

Chevrolet Corvette

Specifications

Drive. . . . . RWD
Engine 6.2-liter V8
Transmission . . . . .6-sp. Manual
Tow Rating (lbs.) . . . . –
Head/Leg Room (in.) Average-38/43
Interior Space (cu. ft.) . . . . Very Cramped-52
Cargo Space (cu. ft.) . . . . Very Cramped-11
Wheelbase/Length (in.) 105.7/174.6

Ratings—10 Best, 1 Worst

Combo Crash Tests	10
Safety Features	10
Rollover	7
Preventive Maintenance	3
Repair Costs	10
Warranty	6
Fuel Economy	7
Complaints	4
Insurance Costs	1
OVERALL RATING	**9**

Chevrolet Cruze

Chevrolet Cruze

At-a-Glance

Status/Year Series Started	Unchanged/2010
Twins	Buick Verano
Body Styles	Sedan
Seating	5
Anti-Theft Device	Std. Pass. Immobil. & Alarm
Parking Index Rating	Easy
Where Made	Lordstown, OH
Fuel Factor	
MPG Rating (city/hwy)	Good-22/35
Driving Range (mi.)	Average-412
Fuel Type	Regular
Annual Fuel Cost	Low-$1,948
Gas Guzzler Tax	No
Greenhouse Gas Emissions (tons/yr.)	Average-6.7
Barrels of Oil Used per year	Average-12.2

How the Competition Rates

Competitors	Rating	Pg.
Ford Focus	6	142
Honda Civic		148
Toyota Corolla	4	244

Price Range

	Retail	Markup
2LS Manual	$17,130	4%
1LT	$19,655	4%
2LT	$22,325	4%
LTZ	$23,550	5%

Safety Checklist

Crash Tests:
Frontal . . . . Very Good
Side . . . . Good

Airbags:
Head . . . . .Fr & Rr. Roof Curtain
Torso . . . . Fr. & Rr. Pelvis/Torso from Seat
Pelvis . . . . Fr. & Rr. Pelvis/Torso from Seat
Roll Sensing . . . . .Yes
Knee Bolster . . . . .Standard Front

Crash Avoidance:
Frontal Collision Warning . . . . None
Blind Spot Detection . . . . Optional
Crash Imminent Braking . . . . None
Lane Departure Warning . . . . None

General:
Auto. Crash Notification . . . . Standard
Day Running Lamps . . . . Standard

Safety Belt/Restraint:
Dynamic Head Restraints . . . . None
Adjustable Belt . . . . . .Standard Front and Rear
Pretensioners . . . . .Standard Front

Chevrolet Cruze

Specifications

Drive	FWD
Engine	1.8-liter I4
Transmission	6-sp. Automatic
Tow Rating (lbs.)	Very Low-1000
Head/Leg Room (in.)	Average-39.3/42.3
Interior Space (cu. ft.)	Cramped-95
Cargo Space (cu. ft.)	Cramped-15
Wheelbase/Length (in.)	105.7/181

Ratings—10 Best, 1 Worst	Equinox	Terrain
Combo Crash Tests	4	4
Safety Features	8	8
Rollover	2	3
Preventive Maintenance	3	3
Repair Costs	4	3
Warranty	6	4
Fuel Economy	6	6
Complaints	4	6
Insurance Costs	8	5
OVERALL RATING	**5**	**4**

Chevrolet Equinox

GMC Terrain

At-a-Glance

Status/Year Series Started	Unchanged/2005
Twins	GMC Terrain
Body Styles	SUV
Seating	5
Anti-Theft Device	Std. Pass. Immobil. & Alarm
Parking Index Rating	Very Hard
Where Made	Ontario, Canada / Spring Hill, TN
Fuel Factor	
MPG Rating (city/hwy)	Average-22/32
Driving Range (mi.)	Very Long-481
Fuel Type	Regular/E85
Annual Fuel Cost	Low-$2,010
Gas Guzzler Tax	No
Greenhouse Gas Emissions (tons/yr.)	Average-7.1
Barrels of Oil Used per year	Average-12.7

How the Competition Rates

Competitors	Rating	Pg.
Dodge Journey	1	132
Ford Explorer	7	138
Hyundai Santa Fe	9	160

Price Range

Price Range	Retail	Markup
LS 2WD	$23,755	5%
LT AWD	$27,150	5%
2LT AWD	$29,020	5%
LTZ AWD	$32,265	5%

Safety Checklist

Crash Tests:
Frontal	Average
Side	Poor

Airbags:
Head	Fr & Rr. Roof Curtain
Torso	Front Pelvis/Torso from Seat
Pelvis	Front Pelvis/Torso from Seat
Roll Sensing	Yes
Knee Bolster	None

Crash Avoidance:
Frontal Collision Warning	Optional
Blind Spot Detection	None
Crash Imminent Braking	None
Lane Departure Warning	Optional

General:
Auto. Crash Notification	Standard
Day Running Lamps	Standard

Safety Belt/Restraint:
Dynamic Head Restraints	None
Adjustable Belt	Standard Front and Rear
Pretensioners	Standard Front

Chevrolet Equinox

Specifications

Drive	AWD
Engine	2.4-liter I4
Transmission	6-sp. Automatic
Tow Rating (lbs.)	Very Low-1500
Head/Leg Room (in.)	Roomy-40.9/41.2
Interior Space (cu. ft.)	Average-99.7
Cargo Space (cu. ft.)	Roomy-31.4
Wheelbase/Length (in.)	112.5/187.8

Chevrolet Impala Large

Ratings—10 Best, 1 Worst

Combo Crash Tests	5
Safety Features	4
Rollover	7
Preventive Maintenance	3
Repair Costs	5
Warranty	6
Fuel Economy	4
Complaints	7
Insurance Costs	8
OVERALL RATING	**6**

Chevrolet Impala

Chevrolet Impala

At-a-Glance

Status/Year Series Started	Unchanged/2006
Twins	-
Body Styles	Sedan
Seating	5/6
Anti-Theft Device	Std. Pass. Immobil. & Opt. Pass. Alarm
Parking Index Rating	Hard
Where Made	Oshawa, Ontario
Fuel Factor	
MPG Rating (city/hwy)	Poor-18/29
Driving Range (mi.)	Short-380
Fuel Type	Regular/E85
Annual Fuel Cost	Average-$2,370
Gas Guzzler Tax	No
Greenhouse Gas Emissions (tons/yr.)	High-8.3
Barrels of Oil Used per year	High-15.0

How the Competition Rates

Competitors	Rating	Pg.
Dodge Charger	7	128
Ford Taurus	5	145
Toyota Avalon		242

Price Range	Retail	Markup
LS	$25,860	4%
LT	$27,385	4%
LTZ	$30,400	4%

Safety Checklist

Crash Tests:
- Frontal . . . . Very Good
- Side . . . . Poor

Airbags:
- Head . . . . Fr & Rr. Roof Curtain
- Torso . . . . Front Torso from Seat
- Pelvis . . . . None
- Roll Sensing . . . . No
- Knee Bolster . . . . None

Crash Avoidance:
- Frontal Collision Warning . . . . None
- Blind Spot Detection . . . . None
- Crash Imminent Braking . . . . None
- Lane Departure Warning . . . . None

General:
- Auto. Crash Notification . . . . Standard
- Day Running Lamps . . . . Standard

Safety Belt/Restraint:
- Dynamic Head Restraints . . . . None
- Adjustable Belt . . . . . . Standard Front and Rear
- Pretensioners . . . . Standard Front

Chevrolet Impala

Specifications

Drive	FWD
Engine	3.6-liter V6
Transmission	6-sp. Automatic
Tow Rating (lbs.)	Very Low-1000
Head/Leg Room (in.)	Average-39.4/42.3
Interior Space (cu. ft.)	Roomy-104.5
Cargo Space (cu. ft.)	Average-18.6
Wheelbase/Length (in.)	110.5/200.4

Ratings—10 Best, 1 Worst

Combo Crash Tests	8
Safety Features	10
Rollover	7
Preventive Maintenance	3
Repair Costs	8
Warranty	6
Fuel Economy	6
Complaints	–
Insurance Costs	3
OVERALL RATING	**9**

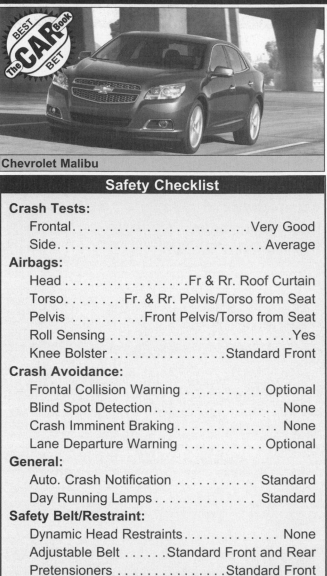

Chevrolet Malibu

Chevrolet Malibu

At-a-Glance

Status/Year Series Started	All New/2013
Twins	-
Body Styles	Sedan
Seating	5
Anti-Theft Device	Std. Pass. Immobil. & Alarm
Parking Index Rating	Average
Where Made	Fairfax, KS / Hamtramck, MI
Fuel Factor	
MPG Rating (city/hwy)	Average-22/34
Driving Range (mi.)	Long-413
Fuel Type	Regular
Annual Fuel Cost	Low-$1,967
Gas Guzzler Tax	No
Greenhouse Gas Emissions (tons/yr.)	Average-7.1
Barrels of Oil Used per year	Average-12.7

How the Competition Rates

Competitors	Rating	Pg.
Ford Fusion		143
Honda Accord	9	146
Toyota Camry	4	243

Price Range	Retail	Markup
LS	$22,390	4%
LT	$24,005	5%
2LT	$25,240	5%
LTZ	$27,830	6%

Safety Checklist

Crash Tests:
- Frontal . . . . Very Good
- Side . . . . Average

Airbags:
- Head . . . . .Fr & Rr. Roof Curtain
- Torso . . . . Fr. & Rr. Pelvis/Torso from Seat
- Pelvis . . . . .Front Pelvis/Torso from Seat
- Roll Sensing . . . . .Yes
- Knee Bolster . . . . .Standard Front

Crash Avoidance:
- Frontal Collision Warning . . . . Optional
- Blind Spot Detection . . . . None
- Crash Imminent Braking . . . . None
- Lane Departure Warning . . . . Optional

General:
- Auto. Crash Notification . . . . Standard
- Day Running Lamps . . . . Standard

Safety Belt/Restraint:
- Dynamic Head Restraints . . . . None
- Adjustable Belt . . . . . .Standard Front and Rear
- Pretensioners . . . . .Standard Front

Chevrolet Malibu

Specifications

Drive	FWD
Engine	2.4-liter I4
Transmission	6-sp. Automatic
Tow Rating (lbs.)	–
Head/Leg Room (in.)	Average-39/42.1
Interior Space (cu. ft.)	Average-100.3
Cargo Space (cu. ft.)	Average-16.3
Wheelbase/Length (in.)	107.8/191.5

Ratings—10 Best, 1 Worst	Silverado	Sierra
Combo Crash Tests*	8	8
Safety Features	6	6
Rollover	2	2
Preventive Maintenance	3	3
Repair Costs	6	6
Warranty	6	4
Fuel Economy	1	1
Complaints	10	10
Insurance Costs	8	8
OVERALL RATING	**7**	**6**

Chevrolet Silverado

Safety Checklist

Crash Tests:
- Frontal........................Average
- Side.......................Very Good

Airbags:
- Head .... Fr. & Rr. Roof Curtain
- Torso..........Front Pelvis/Torso from Seat
- Pelvis ....Front Pelvis/Torso from Seat
- Roll Sensing ....Yes
- Knee Bolster .... None

Crash Avoidance:
- Frontal Collision Warning .... None
- Blind Spot Detection .... None
- Crash Imminent Braking .... None
- Lane Departure Warning .... None

General:
- Auto. Crash Notification .... Standard
- Day Running Lamps .... Standard

Safety Belt/Restraint:
- Dynamic Head Restraints............. None
- Adjustable Belt .... Standard Front & Rear
- Pretensioners ....Standard Front

GMC Sierra

At-a-Glance

Status/Year Series Started........	Unchanged/2007
Twins	GMC Sierra
Body Styles	Pickup
Seating	5/6
Anti-Theft Device	Std. Pass. Immobil.
Parking Index Rating...............	Very Hard
Where Made.......	Fort Wayne, IN / Sllao, Mexico
Fuel Factor.......................	
MPG Rating (city/hwy)......	Very Poor-15/21
Driving Range (mi.)	Very Long-448
Fuel Type	Regular/E85
Annual Fuel Cost	Very High-$2,989
Gas Guzzler Tax	No
Greenhouse Gas Emissions (tons/yr.)	Very High-10.7
Barrels of Oil Used per year	Very High-19.4

How the Competition Rates

Competitors	Rating	Pg.
Ford F-150	5	139
Ram 1500	2	226
Toyota Tundra	2	255

Price Range	Retail	Markup
W/T 2WD	$22,595	4%
LS EXT Cab 4WD	$33,775	8%
LT Crew Cab 4WD	$36,395	8%
Hybrid 4WD	$43,265	6%

Chevrolet Silverado

Specifications

Drive.................................	4WD
Engine	5.3-liter V8
Transmission	6-sp. Automatic
Tow Rating (lbs.)	Very High-9500
Head/Leg Room (in.)	Roomy-41.2/41.3
Interior Space (cu. ft.).........	—
Cargo Space (cu. ft.)	Very Roomy-60.7
Wheelbase/Length (in.)	143.5/230

*Crash test scores are for Silverado/Sierra 1500 only.

Ratings—10 Best, 1 Worst

Combo Crash Tests	10
Safety Features	9
Rollover	6
Preventive Maintenance	7
Repair Costs	10
Warranty	6
Fuel Economy	8
Complaints	2
Insurance Costs	8
OVERALL RATING	**10**

Chevrolet Sonic Sedan

Chevrolet Sonic Hatchback

At-a-Glance

Status/Year Series Started. Unchanged/2012
Twins . . . . -
Body Styles . . . . Sedan, Hatchback
Seating 5
Anti-Theft Device . . . . . . Std. Pass. Immobil. & Alarm
Parking Index Rating . . . . Very Easy
Where Made. . . . . Orion Township, MI
Fuel Factor . . . .
  MPG Rating (city/hwy) Good-25/35
  Driving Range (mi.) . . . . .Very Short-350
  Fuel Type . . . . Regular
  Annual Fuel Cost . . . . Low-$1,793
  Gas Guzzler Tax . . . . .No
  Greenhouse Gas Emissions (tons/yr.) . . Average-6.5
  Barrels of Oil Used per year Average-11.8

How the Competition Rates

Competitors	Rating	Pg.
Ford Fiesta	4	140
Honda Fit	4	151
Mazda Mazda2		189

Price Range

	Retail	Markup
LS	$14,200	3%
LT	$15,985	3%
LTZ	$17,245	5%
2RS	$21,485	5%

Safety Checklist

Crash Tests:
  Frontal. . . . . Very Good
  Side. . . . . Good
Airbags:
  Head . . . . .Fr & Rr. Roof Curtain
  Torso. . . . . Fr. & Rr. Pelvis/Torso from Seat
  Pelvis . . . . Fr. & Rr. Pelvis/Torso from Seat
  Roll Sensing . . . . .Yes
  Knee Bolster . . . . .Standard Front
Crash Avoidance:
  Frontal Collision Warning . . . . None
  Blind Spot Detection . . . . None
  Crash Imminent Braking . . . . None
  Lane Departure Warning . . . . None
General:
  Auto. Crash Notification . . . . Standard
  Day Running Lamps . . . . Standard
Safety Belt/Restraint:
  Dynamic Head Restraints. . . . . None
  Adjustable Belt . . . . .Standard Front
  Pretensioners . . . . .Standard Front

Chevrolet Sonic

Specifications

Drive. . . . . FWD
Engine 1.8-liter I4
Transmission . . . . .5-sp. Manual
Tow Rating (lbs.) . . . . —
Head/Leg Room (in.) Cramped-38.7/41.8
Interior Space (cu. ft.). Roomy-105.2
Cargo Space (cu. ft.) Cramped-14.9
Wheelbase/Length (in.) 99.4/159

Ratings—10 Best, 1 Worst	Suburban	Escalade ESV	Yukon XL
Combo Crash Tests	10	10	10
Safety Features	7	8	7
Rollover	1	1	1
Preventive Maintenance	3	3	5
Repair Costs	2	2	4
Warranty	6	8	4
Fuel Economy	1	1	1
Complaints	8	9	8
Insurance Costs	10	5	10
OVERALL RATING	7	7	6

Chevrolet Suburban

Safety Checklist

Crash Tests:
- Frontal . . . . Very Good
- Side . . . . Very Good

Airbags:
- Head . . . . Fr. & Rr. Roof Curtain
- Torso . . . . Front Pelvis/Torso from Seat
- Pelvis . . . . Front Pelvis/Torso from Seat
- Roll Sensing . . . . Yes
- Knee Bolster . . . . None

Crash Avoidance:
- Frontal Collision Warning . . . . None
- Blind Spot Detection . . . . Optional
- Crash Imminent Braking . . . . None
- Lane Departure Warning . . . . None

General:
- Auto. Crash Notification . . . . Standard
- Day Running Lamps . . . . Standard

Safety Belt/Restraint:
- Dynamic Head Restraints . . . . None
- Adjustable Belt . . . . Standard Front & Rear
- Pretensioners . . . . Standard Front

Cadillac Escalade ESV

At-a-Glance

Status/Year Series Started	Unchanged/2007
Twins . . . . . . Cadillac Escalade ESV, GMC Yukon XL	
Body Styles	SUV
Seating	6/9
Anti-Theft Device . . . . . . Std. Pass. Immobil. & Alarm	
Parking Index Rating	Very Hard
Where Made	Arlington, TX
Fuel Factor	
MPG Rating (city/hwy)	Very Poor-15/21
Driving Range (mi.)	Very Long-542
Fuel Type	Regular/E85
Annual Fuel Cost	Very High-$2,989
Gas Guzzler Tax	No
Greenhouse Gas Emissions (tons/yr.)	Very High-10.7
Barrels of Oil Used per year	Very High-19.4

How the Competition Rates

Competitors	Rating	Pg.
Dodge Durango	5	130
Ford Expedition	4	137
Nissan Armada		211

Price Range	Retail	Markup
1500 LS 2WD	$42,545	8%
1500 LT	$49,150	8%
2500 LT	$50,740	8%
1500 LTZ	$58,440	8%

GMC Yukon XL

Specifications

Drive	4WD
Engine	5.3-liter V8
Transmission	6-sp. Automatic
Tow Rating (lbs.)	Very High-8100
Head/Leg Room (in.)	Roomy-41.1/41.3
Interior Space (cu. ft.)	Very Roomy-137.4
Cargo Space (cu. ft.)	Very Roomy-48.5
Wheelbase/Length (in.)	130/222.4

Ratings—10 Best, 1 Worst

	Tahoe	Escalade	Yukon
Combo Crash Tests	9	9	9
Safety Features	8	8	8
Rollover	1	1	1
Preventive Maintenance	3	3	3
Repair Costs	5	2	4
Warranty	6	8	4
Fuel Economy	1	1	1
Complaints	8	9	8
Insurance Costs	10	3	10
OVERALL RATING	**8**	**6**	**5**

Chevrolet Tahoe

Cadillac Escalade

At-a-Glance

Status/Year Series Started. Unchanged/2007
Twins . . . . .Cadillac Escalade, GMC Yukon
Body Styles . . . . SUV
Seating 6/9
Anti-Theft Device . . . . . . Std. Pass. Immobil. & Alarm
Parking Index Rating . . . . .Very Hard
Where Made. Arlington, TX
Fuel Factor . . . .
  MPG Rating (city/hwy) . . . . .Very Poor-15/21
  Driving Range (mi.) . . . . Very Long-448
  Fuel Type. Regular/E85
  Annual Fuel Cost . . . . Very High-$2,989
  Gas Guzzler Tax . . . . .No
  Greenhouse Gas Emissions (tons/yr.)Very High-10.7
  Barrels of Oil Used per year . . . . . . .Very High-19.4

How the Competition Rates

Competitors	Rating	Pg.
Ford Expedition	4	137
Nissan Armada		211
Toyota Sequoia		252

Price Range

Price Range	Retail	Markup
LS 2WD	$39,080	8%
LT	$47,080	8%
Hybrid	$55,100	6%
LTZ	$56,400	8%

Safety Checklist

Crash Tests:
  Frontal. . . . . .Average
  Side. . . . . .Very Poor
Airbags:
  Head . . . . Fr. & Rr. Roof Curtain
  Torso. . . . . .Front Pelvis/Torso from Seat
  Pelvis . . . . .Front Pelvis/Torso from Seat
  Roll Sensing . . . . .Yes
  Knee Bolster . . . . None
Crash Avoidance:
  Frontal Collision Warning . . . . None
  Blind Spot Detection . . . . .Optional
  Crash Imminent Braking . . . . None
  Lane Departure Warning . . . . None
General:
  Auto. Crash Notification . . . . Standard
  Day Running Lamps . . . . Standard
Safety Belt/Restraint:
  Dynamic Head Restraints . . . . None
  Adjustable Belt . . . . . .Standard Front and Rear
  Pretensioners . . . . .Standard Front

GMC Yukon

Specifications

Drive. 4WD
Engine 5.3-liter V8
Transmission . . . . .6-sp. Automatic
Tow Rating (lbs.) . . . . .Very High-8500
Head/Leg Room (in.) Roomy-41.1/41.3
Interior Space (cu. ft.). Roomy-108.9
Cargo Space (cu. ft.) Average-16.9
Wheelbase/Length (in.) 116/202

Ratings—10 Best, 1 Worst	Traverse	Acadia
Combo Crash Tests	9	9
Safety Features	8	7
Rollover	3	3
Preventive Maintenance	3	3
Repair Costs	4	4
Warranty	6	4
Fuel Economy	2	2
Complaints	9	5
Insurance Costs	10	10
OVERALL RATING	**8**	**5**

Chevrolet Traverse

GMC Acadia

At-a-Glance

Status/Year Series Started Appearance Change/2009
Twins . . . . .GMC Acadia
Body Styles . . . . SUV
Seating. 7/8
Anti-Theft Device . . . . . . Std. Pass. Immobil. & Alarm
Parking Index Rating . . . . .Very Hard
Where Made. .Lansing, MI
Fuel Factor
  MPG Rating (city/hwy) . . . . .Very Poor-17/24
  Driving Range (mi.) Long-431
  Fuel Type. . . . . .Regular
  Annual Fuel Cost . . . . High-$2,629
  Gas Guzzler Tax .No
  Greenhouse Gas Emissions (tons/yr.) Very High-9.6
  Barrels of Oil Used per year High-17.3

How the Competition Rates

Competitors	Rating	Pg.
Ford Flex		141
Honda Pilot	4	154
Toyota Highlander	2	246

Price Range	Retail	Markup
LS	$30,510	4%
LT	$33,725	5%
2LT	$36,580	5%
LTZ AWD	$42,425	6%

Safety Checklist

Crash Tests:
  Frontal. . . . . Good
  Side. . . . . Very Good
Airbags:
  Head . . . . Fr. & Rr. Roof Curtain
  Torso. . . . . .Front Pelvis/Torso from Seat
  Pelvis . . . . .Front Pelvis/Torso from Seat
  Roll Sensing . . . . .Yes
  Knee Bolster . . . . None
Crash Avoidance:
  Frontal Collision Warning . . . . None
  Blind Spot Detection . . . . Optional
  Crash Imminent Braking. . . . . None
  Lane Departure Warning . . . . None
General:
  Auto. Crash Notification . . . . Standard
  Day Running Lamps . . . . Standard
Safety Belt/Restraint:
  Dynamic Head Restraints . . . . None
  Adjustable Belt . . . . . .Standard Front and Rear
  Pretensioners . . . . .Standard Front

Chevrolet Traverse

Specifications

Drive. . . . . FWD
Engine 3.6-liter V6
Transmission . . . . .6-sp. Automatic
Tow Rating (lbs.) Average-5200
Head/Leg Room (in.) Average-40.4/41.3
Interior Space (cu. ft.). . . . . Very Roomy-150.8
Cargo Space (cu. ft.) Roomy-24.4
Wheelbase/Length (in.) 118.9/203.7

Ratings—10 Best, 1 Worst	
Combo Crash Tests	6
Safety Features	9
Rollover	9
Preventive Maintenance	5
Repair Costs	10
Warranty	6
Fuel Economy	10
Complaints	1
Insurance Costs	5
OVERALL RATING	**9**

Chevrolet Volt

Chevrolet Volt

At-a-Glance

Status/Year Series Started	Unchanged/2011
Twins	-
Body Styles	Sedan, Hatchback
Seating	4
Anti-Theft Device	Std. Pass. Immobil. & Alarm
Parking Index Rating	Easy
Where Made	Hamtramck, MI
Fuel Factor	
MPG Rating (city/hwy)	Very Good-35/40
Driving Range (mi.)	Very Short-345
Fuel Type	Premium
Annual Fuel Cost	Very Low-$1,509
Gas Guzzler Tax	No
Greenhouse Gas Emissions (tons/yr.)	Very Low-1.3
Barrels of Oil Used per year	Very Low-3.1

How the Competition Rates

Competitors	Rating	Pg.
Nissan Leaf	7	215
Toyota Prius	7	248
Ford C-Max	6	134

Price Range	Retail	Markup
4D Hatchback	$39,145	4%

Safety Checklist

Crash Tests:
Frontal . . . . Average
Side . . . . Average

Airbags:
Head . . . . Fr & Rr. Roof Curtain
Torso . . . . Front Pelvis/Torso from Seat
Pelvis . . . . Front Pelvis/Torso from Seat
Roll Sensing . . . . Yes
Knee Bolster . . . . Standard Front

Crash Avoidance:
Frontal Collision Warning . . . . Optional
Blind Spot Detection . . . . None
Crash Imminent Braking . . . . None
Lane Departure Warning . . . . Optional

General:
Auto. Crash Notification . . . . Standard
Day Running Lamps . . . . Standard

Safety Belt/Restraint:
Dynamic Head Restraints . . . . None
Adjustable Belt . . . . Optional Rear
Pretensioners . . . . Standard Front

Chevrolet Volt

Specifications

Drive	FWD
Engine	1.4-liter I4
Transmission	1-sp. Automatic
Tow Rating (lbs.)	–
Head/Leg Room (in.)	Very Cramped-37.8/42
Interior Space (cu. ft.)	Cramped-90
Cargo Space (cu. ft.)	Very Cramped-10.6
Wheelbase/Length (in.)	105.7/177.1

Ratings—10 Best, 1 Worst	
Combo Crash Tests	2
Safety Features	3
Rollover	7
Preventive Maintenance	2
Repair Costs	8
Warranty	7
Fuel Economy	5
Complaints	2
Insurance Costs	5
OVERALL RATING	**3**

Chrysler 200

Chrysler 200 Convertible

At-a-Glance

Status/Year Series Started	Unchanged/2011
Twins	Dodge Avenger
Body Styles	Sedan
Seating	5
Anti-Theft Device	Std. Pass. Immobil. & Alarm
Parking Index Rating	Average
Where Made	Sterling Heights, MI
Fuel Factor	
MPG Rating (city/hwy)	Average-21/30
Driving Range (mi.)	Average-410
Fuel Type	Regular
Annual Fuel Cost	Average-$2,119
Gas Guzzler Tax	No
Greenhouse Gas Emissions (tons/yr.)	High-7.6
Barrels of Oil Used per year	High-13.7

How the Competition Rates

Competitors	Rating	Pg.
Chevrolet Malibu	9	116
Ford Fusion		143
Nissan Maxima	4	216

Price Range	Retail	Markup
LX	$18,995	1%
Limited	$24,895	5%
Touring Convertible	$27,100	4%
Limited Convertible	$32,595	5%

Safety Checklist

Crash Tests:
Frontal............................Poor
Side.............................Very Poor

Airbags:
Head..................Fr & Rr. Roof Curtain
Torso...............Front Torso from Seat
Pelvis............................None
Roll Sensing.........................No
Knee Bolster.......................None

Crash Avoidance:
Frontal Collision Warning.............None
Blind Spot Detection..................None
Crash Imminent Braking...............None
Lane Departure Warning..............None

General:
Auto. Crash Notification..............None
Day Running Lamps...............Optional

Safety Belt/Restraint:
Dynamic Head Restraints......Standard Front
Adjustable Belt...............Standard Front
Pretensioners................Standard Front

Chrysler 200

Specifications

Drive	FWD
Engine	2.4-liter I4
Transmission	4-sp. Auto. w/Overdrive
Tow Rating (lbs.)	Very Low-1000
Head/Leg Room (in.)	Roomy-40.1/42.4
Interior Space (cu. ft.)	Average-100.3
Cargo Space (cu. ft.)	Very Roomy-45
Wheelbase/Length (in.)	108.9/191.7

Ratings—10 Best, 1 Worst

Combo Crash Tests	5
Safety Features	6
Rollover	3
Preventive Maintenance	3
Repair Costs	6
Warranty	7
Fuel Economy	4
Complaints	5
Insurance Costs	8
OVERALL RATING	**5**

Chrysler 300

Chrysler 300

At-a-Glance

Status/Year Series Started. Unchanged/2011
Twins . . . . .Dodge Charger
Body Styles . . . . .Sedan
Seating 5
Anti-Theft Device . . . . . . Std. Pass. Immobil. & Alarm
Parking Index Rating . . . . .Very Hard
Where Made. . . . . Brampton, Ontario
Fuel Factor. . . . .
  MPG Rating (city/hwy) Poor-19/31
  Driving Range (mi.) Long-439
  Fuel Type. . . . . .Regular
  Annual Fuel Cost . . . . Average-$2,236
  Gas Guzzler Tax . . . . .No
  Greenhouse Gas Emissions (tons/yr.) High-8.0
  Barrels of Oil Used per year High-14.3

How the Competition Rates

Competitors	Rating	Pg.
Buick LaCrosse	8	103
Chevrolet Impala	6	115
Lincoln MKS	6	187

Price Range	Retail	Markup
Base	$29,845	4%
S	$32,995	4%
C	$35,995	5%
SRT8	$47,820	4%

Safety Checklist

Crash Tests:
  Frontal. . . . . Average
  Side. . . . . Average
Airbags:
  Head . . . . .Fr & Rr. Roof Curtain
  Torso. . . . . .Front Pelvis/Torso from Seat
  Pelvis . . . . .Front Pelvis/Torso from Seat
  Roll Sensing . . . . No
  Knee Bolster . . . . Standard Driver
Crash Avoidance:
  Frontal Collision Warning . . . . Optional
  Blind Spot Detection . . . . Optional
  Crash Imminent Braking . . . . None
  Lane Departure Warning . . . . None
General:
  Auto. Crash Notification . . . . None
  Day Running Lamps . . . . Optional
Safety Belt/Restraint:
  Dynamic Head Restraints . . . . . .Standard Front
  Adjustable Belt . . . . .Standard Front
  Pretensioners . . . . .Standard Front

Chrysler 300

Specifications

Drive. . . . . RWD
Engine 3.6-liter V6
Transmission . . . . .8-sp. Automatic
Tow Rating (lbs.) . . . . Very Low-1000
Head/Leg Room (in.) Cramped-38.6/41.8
Interior Space (cu. ft.). Roomy-106.3
Cargo Space (cu. ft.) Average-16.3
Wheelbase/Length (in.) 120.2/198.6

Ratings—10 Best, 1 Worst

Combo Crash Tests	5
Safety Features	8
Rollover	3
Preventive Maintenance	2
Repair Costs	7
Warranty	7
Fuel Economy	2
Complaints	2
Insurance Costs	8
OVERALL RATING	**5**

Chrysler Town and Country

At-a-Glance

Status/Year Series Started	Unchanged/2008
Twins	Dodge Grand Caravan
Body Styles	Minivan
Seating	7
Anti-Theft Device	Std. Pass. Immobil. & Alarm
Parking Index Rating	Very Hard
Where Made	Windsor, Ontario
Fuel Factor	
MPG Rating (city/hwy)	Very Poor-17/25
Driving Range (mi.)	Average-397
Fuel Type	Regular
Annual Fuel Cost	High-$2,591
Gas Guzzler Tax	No
Greenhouse Gas Emissions (tons/yr.)	High-9.1
Barrels of Oil Used per year	High-16.5

How the Competition Rates

Competitors	Rating	Pg.
Honda Odyssey	7	153
Nissan Quest		219
Volkswagen Routan		263

Price Range	Retail	Markup
Touring	$29,995	4%
Touring L	$33,295	5%
Limited	$39,995	5%

Chrysler Town and Country

Safety Checklist

Crash Tests:
Frontal . . . . Average
Side . . . . Poor

Airbags:
Head . . . . Fr. & Rr. Roof Curtain
Torso . . . . Front Pelvis/Torso from Seat
Pelvis . . . . Front Pelvis/Torso from Seat
Roll Sensing . . . . Standard
Knee Bolster . . . . Standard Driver

Crash Avoidance:
Frontal Collision Warning . . . . None
Blind Spot Detection . . . . Optional
Crash Imminent Braking . . . . None
Lane Departure Warning . . . . None

General:
Auto. Crash Notification . . . . Standard
Day Running Lamps . . . . Optional

Safety Belt/Restraint:
Dynamic Head Restraints . . . . . . Standard Front
Adjustable Belt . . . . . . Standard Front and Rear
Pretensioners . . . . Standard Front

Chrysler Town and Country

Specifications

Drive	FWD
Engine	3.6-liter V6
Transmission	6-sp. Auto. w/Overdrive
Tow Rating (lbs.)	Average-3600
Head/Leg Room (in.)	Very Cramped-39.3/36.5
Interior Space (cu. ft.)	Very Roomy-163.5
Cargo Space (cu. ft.)	Roomy-33
Wheelbase/Length (in.)	121.2/202.8

Dodge Avenger

Ratings—10 Best, 1 Worst	
Combo Crash Tests	2
Safety Features	3
Rollover	6
Preventive Maintenance	2
Repair Costs	9
Warranty	5
Fuel Economy	5
Complaints	3
Insurance Costs	3
OVERALL RATING	**2**

Dodge Avenger

At-a-Glance

Status/Year Series Started	Unchanged/2008
Twins	Chrysler 200
Body Styles	Sedan
Seating	5
Anti-Theft Device	Std. Pass. Immobil. & Alarm
Parking Index Rating	Average
Where Made	Sterling Heights, MI
Fuel Factor	
MPG Rating (city/hwy)	Average-21/30
Driving Range (mi.)	Average-410
Fuel Type	Regular
Annual Fuel Cost	Average-$2,119
Gas Guzzler Tax	No
Greenhouse Gas Emissions (tons/yr.)	High-7.6
Barrels of Oil Used per year	High-13.7

How the Competition Rates

Competitors	Rating	Pg.
Chevrolet Impala	6	115
Ford Fusion		143
Nissan Maxima	4	216

Price Range	Retail	Markup
SE	$18,995	1%
SXT	$21,495	4%
R/T	$25,495	5%

Dodge Avenger

Safety Checklist

Crash Tests:
  Frontal . . . . Poor
  Side . . . . Very Poor
Airbags:
  Head . . . . Fr & Rr. Roof Curtain
  Torso . . . . Front Torso from Seat
  Pelvis . . . . None
  Roll Sensing . . . . No
  Knee Bolster . . . . None
Crash Avoidance:
  Frontal Collision Warning . . . . None
  Blind Spot Detection . . . . None
  Crash Imminent Braking . . . . None
  Lane Departure Warning . . . . None
General:
  Auto. Crash Notification . . . . None
  Day Running Lamps . . . . Optional
Safety Belt/Restraint:
  Dynamic Head Restraints . . . . . . Standard Front
  Adjustable Belt . . . . Standard Front
  Pretensioners . . . . Standard Front

Dodge Avenger

Specifications

Drive	FWD
Engine	2.4-liter I4
Transmission	4-sp. Auto. w/ Overdrive
Tow Rating (lbs.)	Very Low-1000
Head/Leg Room (in.)	Roomy-40/42.4
Interior Space (cu. ft.)	Average-100.2
Cargo Space (cu. ft.)	Cramped-13.5
Wheelbase/Length (in.)	108.9/192.6

Ratings—10 Best, 1 Worst

Combo Crash Tests	8
Safety Features	4
Rollover	7
Preventive Maintenance	1
Repair Costs	6
Warranty	5
Fuel Economy	3
Complaints	3
Insurance Costs	1
OVERALL RATING	**4**

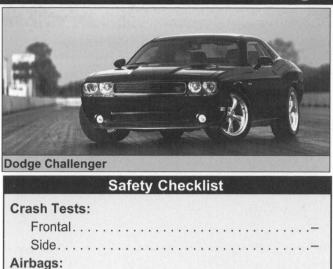

Dodge Challenger

Dodge Challenger

At-a-Glance

Status/Year Series Started	Unchanged/2009
Twins	-
Body Styles	Coupe
Seating	5
Anti-Theft Device	Std. Pass. Immobil. & Alarm
Parking Index Rating	Hard
Where Made	Brampton, Ontario
Fuel Factor	
MPG Rating (city/hwy)	Poor-18/27
Driving Range (mi.)	Average-405
Fuel Type	Regular
Annual Fuel Cost	High-$2,430
Gas Guzzler Tax	No
Greenhouse Gas Emissions (tons/yr.)	High-8.7
Barrels of Oil Used per year	High-15.7

How the Competition Rates

Competitors	Rating	Pg.
Chevrolet Camaro	8	111
Ford Mustang	2	144

Price Range	Retail	Markup
SXT	$25,495	4%
R/T	$29,995	4%
SRT8	$43,425	3%

Safety Checklist

Crash Tests:
Frontal	−
Side	−

Airbags:
Head	Fr & Rr. Roof Curtain
Torso	Front Pelvis/Torso from Seat
Pelvis	Front Pelvis/Torso from Seat
Roll Sensing	No
Knee Bolster	None

Crash Avoidance:
Frontal Collision Warning	None
Blind Spot Detection	None
Crash Imminent Braking	None
Lane Departure Warning	None

General:
Auto. Crash Notification	None
Day Running Lamps	Optional

Safety Belt/Restraint:
Dynamic Head Restraints	Standard Front
Adjustable Belt	None
Pretensioners	Standard Front

Dodge Challenger

Specifications

Drive	RWD
Engine	3.6-liter V6
Transmission	5-sp. Auto. w/Overdrive
Tow Rating (lbs.)	Very Low-1000
Head/Leg Room (in.)	Average-39.3/42
Interior Space (cu. ft.)	Cramped-91.5
Cargo Space (cu. ft.)	Average-16.2
Wheelbase/Length (in.)	116/197.7

Dodge Charger

Large

Ratings—10 Best, 1 Worst

Combo Crash Tests	8
Safety Features	6
Rollover	8
Preventive Maintenance	3
Repair Costs	8
Warranty	5
Fuel Economy	3
Complaints	6
Insurance Costs	1
OVERALL RATING	**7**

Dodge Charger

Dodge Charger

At-a-Glance

Status/Year Series Started........ Unchanged/2006
Twins ....Chrysler 300
Body Styles ....Sedan
Seating 5
Anti-Theft Device ...... Std. Pass. Immobil. & Alarm
Parking Index Rating .... Hard
Where Made................. Brampton, Ontario
Fuel Factor.............................
  MPG Rating (city/hwy)............ Poor-18/27
  Driving Range (mi.) Average-405
  Fuel Type.........................Regular
  Annual Fuel Cost .... High-$2,430
  Gas Guzzler Tax ....No
  Greenhouse Gas Emissions (tons/yr.)..... High-8.7
  Barrels of Oil Used per year High-15.7

How the Competition Rates

Competitors	Rating	Pg.
Chrysler 300	5	124
Ford Taurus	5	145
Lincoln MKS	6	187

Price Range

Price Range	Retail	Markup
SE	$25,795	4%
SXT	$28,495	4%
R/T	$29,995	5%
SRT8	$44,995	4%

Safety Checklist

Crash Tests:
  Frontal............................. Good
  Side............................... Good
Airbags:
  Head ....Fr & Rr. Roof Curtain
  Torso...........Front Pelvis/Torso from Seat
  Pelvis ....Front Pelvis/Torso from Seat
  Roll Sensing .... No
  Knee Bolster .... Standard Driver
Crash Avoidance:
  Frontal Collision Warning .... Optional
  Blind Spot Detection .... Optional
  Crash Imminent Braking.............. None
  Lane Departure Warning .... None
General:
  Auto. Crash Notification .... None
  Day Running Lamps.............. Optional
Safety Belt/Restraint:
  Dynamic Head Restraints......Standard Front
  Adjustable Belt ....Standard Front
  Pretensioners ....Standard Front

Dodge Charger

Specifications

Drive.............................. RWD
Engine 3.6-liter V6
Transmission .... 5-sp. Auto. w/ Overdrive
Tow Rating (lbs.) .... Very Low-1000
Head/Leg Room (in.) Cramped-38.6/41.8
Interior Space (cu. ft.)...........Roomy-104.7
Cargo Space (cu. ft.) Average-16.5
Wheelbase/Length (in.) 120.2/199.9

Ratings—10 Best, 1 Worst

Combo Crash Tests	9
Safety Features	7
Rollover	8
Preventive Maintenance	4
Repair Costs	9
Warranty	5
Fuel Economy	7
Complaints	–
Insurance Costs	–
OVERALL RATING	**9**

Dodge Dart

Dodge Dart

At-a-Glance

Status/Year Series Started	All New/2013
Twins	-
Body Styles	Sedan
Seating	5
Anti-Theft Device	Std. Pass. Immobil. & Alarm
Parking Index Rating	Easy
Where Made	Belvidere, IL
Fuel Factor	
MPG Rating (city/hwy)	Good-24/34
Driving Range (mi.)	Long-437
Fuel Type	Regular
Annual Fuel Cost	Low-$1,860
Gas Guzzler Tax	No
Greenhouse Gas Emissions (tons/yr.)	Average-6.7
Barrels of Oil Used per year	Average-12.2

How the Competition Rates

Competitors	Rating	Pg.
Chevrolet Cruze	9	113
Ford Focus	6	142
Volkswagen Jetta	6	261

Price Range

	Retail	Markup
SE	$15,995	0%
SXT	$17,995	2%
Rallye	$18,995	2%
Limited	$19,995	2%

Safety Checklist

Crash Tests:
Frontal	Good
Side	Very Good

Airbags:
Head	Fr & Rr. Roof Curtain
Torso	Front Pelvis/Torso from Seat
Pelvis	Fr. & Rr. Pelvis/Torso from Seat
Roll Sensing	No
Knee Bolster	Standard Front

Crash Avoidance:
Frontal Collision Warning	None
Blind Spot Detection	Optional
Crash Imminent Braking	None
Lane Departure Warning	None

General:
Auto. Crash Notification	None
Day Running Lamps	Optional

Safety Belt/Restraint:
Dynamic Head Restraints	Standard Front
Adjustable Belt	Standard Front
Pretensioners	Standard Front

Dodge Dart

Specifications

Drive	FWD
Engine	2.0-liter I4
Transmission	6-sp. Manual
Tow Rating (lbs.)	Very Low-1000
Head/Leg Room (in.)	Cramped-38.6/42.2
Interior Space (cu. ft.)	Average-97.2
Cargo Space (cu. ft.)	Cramped-13.1
Wheelbase/Length (in.)	106.4/183.9

Ratings—10 Best, 1 Worst

Combo Crash Tests	4
Safety Features	8
Rollover	2
Preventive Maintenance	2
Repair Costs	7
Warranty	5
Fuel Economy	2
Complaints	7
Insurance Costs	8
OVERALL RATING	**5**

Dodge Durango

Safety Checklist

Crash Tests:
Frontal . . . . .Very Poor
Side . . . . Good

Airbags:
Head . . . . Fr. & Rr. Roof Curtain
Torso . . . . .Front Pelvis/Torso from Seat
Pelvis . . . . .Front Pelvis/Torso from Seat
Roll Sensing . . . . .Yes
Knee Bolster . . . . None

Crash Avoidance:
Frontal Collision Warning . . . . Optional
Blind Spot Detection . . . . Optional
Crash Imminent Braking . . . . Optional
Lane Departure Warning . . . . None

General:
Auto. Crash Notification . . . . None
Day Running Lamps . . . . Optional

Safety Belt/Restraint:
Dynamic Head Restraints . . . . . .Standard Front
Adjustable Belt . . . . .Standard Front
Pretensioners . . . . .Standard Front

Dodge Durango

At-a-Glance

Status/Year Series Started Unchanged/2011
Twins . . . . -
Body Styles . . . . SUV
Seating 7
Anti-Theft Device . . . . . . Std. Pass. Immobil. & Alarm
Parking Index Rating . . . . Hard
Where Made .Detroit, MI
Fuel Factor . . . .
  MPG Rating (city/hwy) . . . . Very Poor-16/23
  Driving Range (mi.) . . . . Very Long-456
  Fuel Type . . . . .Regular
  Annual Fuel Cost . . . . Very High-$2,775
  Gas Guzzler Tax . . . . .No
  Greenhouse Gas Emissions (tons/yr.) Very High-9.6
  Barrels of Oil Used per year High-17.3

How the Competition Rates

Competitors	Rating	Pg.
Chevrolet Tahoe	8	130
Ford Expedition	4	137
Toyota 4Runner	4	241

Price Range	Retail	Markup
SXT 2WD	$28,995	5%
Crew	$36,795	6%
R/T	$38,595	6%
Citadel	$42,195	6%

Dodge Durango

Specifications

Drive . . . . AWD
Engine 3.6-liter V6
Transmission . . . . 5-sp. Auto. w/Overdrive
Tow Rating (lbs.) High-6200
Head/Leg Room (in.) Cramped-39.9/40.3
Interior Space (cu. ft.) . . . . .Very Roomy-141
Cargo Space (cu. ft.) Average-17.2
Wheelbase/Length (in.) 119.8/199.8

Dodge Grand Caravan

Minivan

Ratings—10 Best, 1 Worst

Combo Crash Tests	5
Safety Features	8
Rollover	3
Preventive Maintenance	2
Repair Costs	8
Warranty	5
Fuel Economy	2
Complaints	3
Insurance Costs	8
OVERALL RATING	**5**

Dodge Grand Caravan

Dodge Grand Caravan

At-a-Glance

Status/Year Series Started Unchanged/2008
Twins . . . . Chrysler Town and Country
Body Styles . . . . Minivan
Seating 7
Anti-Theft Device . . . . Std. Pass. Immobil.
Parking Index Rating . . . . .Very Hard
Where Made. . . . . Windsor, Ontario
Fuel Factor . . . .
  MPG Rating (city/hwy) . . . . .Very Poor-17/25
  Driving Range (mi.) Average-397
  Fuel Type . . . . .Regular
  Annual Fuel Cost . . . . High-$2,591
  Gas Guzzler Tax . . . . .No
  Greenhouse Gas Emissions (tons/yr.) High-9.1
  Barrels of Oil Used per year High-16.5

How the Competition Rates

Competitors	Rating	Pg.
Honda Odyssey	7	153
Toyota Sienna	3	253
Volkswagen Routan		263

Price Range

	Retail	Markup
SE	$19,995	1%
SXT	$26,495	5%
Crew	$28,495	5%
R/T	$29,995	5%

Safety Checklist

Crash Tests:
  Frontal . . . . Average
  Side. . . . . .Poor
Airbags:
  Head . . . . Fr. & Rr. Roof Curtain
  Torso. . . . . .Front Pelvis/Torso from Seat
  Pelvis . . . . .Front Pelvis/Torso from Seat
  Roll Sensing . . . . .Yes
  Knee Bolster . . . . Standard Driver
Crash Avoidance:
  Frontal Collision Warning . . . . None
  Blind Spot Detection . . . . Optional
  Crash Imminent Braking . . . . None
  Lane Departure Warning . . . . None
General:
  Auto. Crash Notification . . . . None
  Day Running Lamps . . . . Optional
Safety Belt/Restraint:
  Dynamic Head Restraints . . . . . .Standard Front
  Adjustable Belt . . . . . .Standard Front and Rear
  Pretensioners . . . . .Standard Front

Dodge Grand Caravan

Specifications

Drive. . . . . FWD
Engine 3.6-liter V6
Transmission . . . . .6-sp. Automatic
Tow Rating (lbs.) Average-3600
Head/Leg Room (in.) Cramped-39.8/40.7
Interior Space (cu. ft.). . . . . Very Roomy-162.8
Cargo Space (cu. ft.) Roomy-33
Wheelbase/Length (in.) 121.2/202.8

Ratings—10 Best, 1 Worst

Combo Crash Tests	3
Safety Features	6
Rollover	2
Preventive Maintenance	2
Repair Costs	7
Warranty	5
Fuel Economy	2
Complaints	1
Insurance Costs	5
OVERALL RATING	**1**

Dodge Journey

At-a-Glance

Status/Year Series Started. Unchanged/2009
Twins . . . . -
Body Styles . . . . SUV
Seating 5/7
Anti-Theft Device . . . . . . Std. Pass. Immobil. & Alarm
Parking Index Rating . . . . Hard
Where Made. . . . . Toluca, Mexico
Fuel Factor. . . . .
  MPG Rating (city/hwy) . . . . Very Poor-16/24
  Driving Range (mi.) Average-397
  Fuel Type . . . . Regular
  Annual Fuel Cost . . . . High-$2,733
  Gas Guzzler Tax . . . . No
  Greenhouse Gas Emissions (tons/yr.) High-9.1
  Barrels of Oil Used per year High-16.5

How the Competition Rates

Competitors	Rating	Pg.
Chevrolet Equinox	5	114
Ford Edge	4	135
Nissan Murano	3	217

Price Range	Retail	Markup
SE	$18,995	1%
SXT	$26,395	5%
Crew	$29,795	5%
R/T	$30,795	5%

Dodge Journey

Safety Checklist

Crash Tests:
  Frontal. . . . . Average
  Side. . . . . .Very Poor
Airbags:
  Head . . . . Fr. & Rr. Roof Curtain
  Torso. . . . . Front Torso from Seat
  Pelvis . . . . None
  Roll Sensing . . . . .Yes
  Knee Bolster . . . . Standard Driver
Crash Avoidance:
  Frontal Collision Warning . . . . None
  Blind Spot Detection . . . . None
  Crash Imminent Braking . . . . None
  Lane Departure Warning . . . . None
General:
  Auto. Crash Notification . . . . None
  Day Running Lamps . . . . Optional
Safety Belt/Restraint:
  Dynamic Head Restraints . . . . . . Standard Front
  Adjustable Belt . . . . .Standard Front
  Pretensioners . . . . .Standard Front

Dodge Journey

Specifications

Drive. . . . . AWD
Engine 3.6-liter V6
Transmission . . . . 6-sp. Automatic w/ Overdrive
Tow Rating (lbs.) Low-2500
Head/Leg Room (in.) Average-40.8/40.8
Interior Space (cu. ft.). Roomy-123.7
Cargo Space (cu. ft.) . . . . Very Cramped-10.7
Wheelbase/Length (in.) 113.8/192.4

Ratings—10 Best, 1 Worst	
Combo Crash Tests	4
Safety Features	5
Rollover	4
Preventive Maintenance	10
Repair Costs	10
Warranty	8
Fuel Economy	9
Complaints	3
Insurance Costs	3
OVERALL RATING	8

Fiat 500

At-a-Glance

Status/Year Series Started	Unchanged/2012
Twins	-
Body Styles	Hatchback
Seating	4
Anti-Theft Device	Std. Pass. Immobil. & Alarm
Parking Index Rating	Very Easy
Where Made	Toluca, Mexico
Fuel Factor	
MPG Rating (city/hwy)	Very Good-30/38
Driving Range (mi.)	Very Short-348
Fuel Type	Regular
Annual Fuel Cost	Very Low-$1,553
Gas Guzzler Tax	No
Greenhouse Gas Emissions (tons/yr.)	Low-6.1
Barrels of Oil Used per year	Average-11.0

How the Competition Rates

Competitors	Rating	Pg.
Ford Fiesta	4	140
Mazda Mazda2		189
Mini Cooper		203

Price Range	Retail	Markup
Pop	$15,500	3%
Sport	$17,500	3%
Lounge	$18,500	3%
Abarth	$22,000	4%

Fiat 500

Safety Checklist

Crash Tests:
Frontal	Poor
Side	Average

Airbags:
Head	Fr & Rr. Roof Curtain
Torso	Front Pelvis/Torso from Seat
Pelvis	Front Pelvis/Torso from Seat
Roll Sensing	No
Knee Bolster	Standard Driver

Crash Avoidance:
Frontal Collision Warning	None
Blind Spot Detection	None
Crash Imminent Braking	None
Lane Departure Warning	None

General:
Auto. Crash Notification	None
Day Running Lamps	Optional

Safety Belt/Restraint:
Dynamic Head Restraints	Standard Front
Adjustable Belt	Standard
Pretensioners	Standard Front

Fiat 500

Specifications

Drive	FWD
Engine	1.4-liter I4
Transmission	6-sp. Automatic
Tow Rating (lbs.)	–
Head/Leg Room (in.)	Very Cramped-38.9/40.7
Interior Space (cu. ft.)	Very Cramped-85.1
Cargo Space (cu. ft.)	Very Cramped-9.5
Wheelbase/Length (in.)	90.6/139.6

Ford C-MAX   Compact

Ratings—10 Best, 1 Worst

Combo Crash Tests	–
Safety Features	6
Rollover	4
Preventive Maintenance	10
Repair Costs	9
Warranty	2
Fuel Economy	10
Complaints	–
Insurance Costs	–
OVERALL RATING	–

Ford C-MAX

At-a-Glance

Status/Year Series Started . . . . All New/2013
Twins . . . . -
Body Styles . . . . Hatchback
Seating 5
Anti-Theft Device . . . . . . Std. Pass. Immobil. & Alarm
Parking Index Rating . . . . Average
Where Made. . . . . Wayne, MI
Fuel Factor . . . .
  MPG Rating (city/hwy) . . . . . . Very Good-47/47
  Driving Range (mi.) . . . . .Very Long-634.5
  Fuel Type . . . . .Regular
  Annual Fuel Cost . . . . .Very Low-$1,094.68
  Gas Guzzler Tax . . . . .No
  Greenhouse Gas Emissions (tons/yr.). Very Low-3.9
  Barrels of Oil Used per year . . . . Very Low-7.0

How the Competition Rates

Competitors	Rating	Pg.
Chevrolet Volt	9	122
Nissan Leaf	7	215
Toyota Prius	7	248

Price Range	Retail	Markup
SE Hybrid	$25,200	7%
SEL Hybrid	$28,200	7%

Ford C-MAX

Safety Checklist

Crash Tests:
  Frontal. . . . .–
  Side . . . .–
Airbags:
  Head . . . . Fr. & Rr. Roof Curtain
  Torso . . . . .Front Pelvis/Torso from Seat
  Pelvis . . . . .Front Pelvis/Torso from Seat
  Roll Sensing . . . . .Yes
  Knee Bolster . . . . Standard Driver
Crash Avoidance:
  Frontal Collision Warning . . . . None
  Blind Spot Detection . . . . None
  Crash Imminent Braking . . . . None
  Lane Departure Warning . . . . None
General:
  Auto. Crash Notification . . . . Optional
  Day Running Lamps . . . . None
Safety Belt/Restraint:
  Dynamic Head Restraints. . . . . None
  Adjustable Belt . . . . .Standard Front
  Pretensioners . . . . .Standard Front

Ford C-MAX

Specifications

Drive. . . . . FWD
Engine 2.0-liter I4
Transmission . . . . .CVT
Tow Rating (lbs.) . . . . –
Head/Leg Room (in.) Average-41/40.4
Interior Space (cu. ft.). Average-99.7
Cargo Space (cu. ft.) Roomy-24.5
Wheelbase/Length (in.) 104.3/173.6

Ratings—10 Best, 1 Worst

Ratings—10 Best, 1 Worst	Edge	MKX
Combo Crash Tests	2	–
Safety Features	5	6
Rollover	4	4
Preventive Maintenance	7	7
Repair Costs	5	7
Warranty	2	5
Fuel Economy	4	2
Complaints	7	8
Insurance Costs	10	10
OVERALL RATING	**4**	

Ford Edge

Lincoln MKX

At-a-Glance

Status/Year Series Started........ Unchanged/2007
Twins . . . . .Lincoln MKX
Body Styles . . . . SUV
Seating 5
Anti-Theft Device . . . . . . .Std. Pass. Immobil & Alarm
Parking Index Rating . . . . Hard
Where Made. . . . . .Oakville, Ontario
Fuel Factor . . . .
  MPG Rating (city/hwy) Poor-19/27
  Driving Range (mi.) Average-395
  Fuel Type . . . . .Regular
  Annual Fuel Cost . . . . Average-$2,347
  Gas Guzzler Tax .No
  Greenhouse Gas Emissions (tons/yr.) High-8.3
  Barrels of Oil Used per year High-15.0

How the Competition Rates

Competitors	Rating	Pg.
Chevrolet Equinox	5	114
Dodge Journey	1	132
Nissan Murano	3	217

Price Range

Price Range	Retail	Markup
SE	$27,525	6%
SEL	$31,080	7%
Limited	$34,940	7%
Sport AWD	$39,060	7%

Safety Checklist

Crash Tests:
  Frontal. . . . . .Very Poor
  Side. . . . . Average
Airbags:
  Head . . . . .Fr & Rr. Roof Curtain
  Torso. . . . . Front Torso from Seat
  Pelvis . . . . None
  Roll Sensing . . . . .Yes
  Knee Bolster . . . . None
Crash Avoidance:
  Frontal Collision Warning . . . . Optional
  Blind Spot Detection . . . . Optional
  Crash Imminent Braking . . . . None
  Lane Departure Warning . . . . None
General:
  Auto. Crash Notification . . . . Optional
  Day Running Lamps . . . . None
Safety Belt/Restraint:
  Dynamic Head Restraints. . . . . None
  Adjustable Belt . . . . .Standard Front
  Pretensioners . . . . .Standard Front

Ford Edge

Specifications

Drive. . . . . FWD
Engine 3.5-liter V6
Transmission . . . . .6-sp. Automatic
Tow Rating (lbs.) Low-3500
Head/Leg Room (in.) Cramped-40/40.7
Interior Space (cu. ft.). Roomy-108.4
Cargo Space (cu. ft.) Roomy-32.2
Wheelbase/Length (in.) 111.2/184.2

Ratings—10 Best, 1 Worst

Combo Crash Tests	6
Safety Features	6
Rollover	2
Preventive Maintenance	7
Repair Costs	10
Warranty	2
Fuel Economy	6
Complaints	–
Insurance Costs	8
OVERALL RATING	**7**

Ford Escape

Ford Escape

At-a-Glance

Status/Year Series Started . . . . All New/2013
Twins . . . . -
Body Styles . . . . SUV
Seating 5
Anti-Theft Device . . . . Std. Pass. Immobil & Alarm
Parking Index Rating . . . . Average
Where Made. . . . . Louisville, KY
Fuel Factor . . . .
  MPG Rating (city/hwy) Average-22/31
  Driving Range (mi.) Short-382
  Fuel Type . . . . .Regular
  Annual Fuel Cost . . . . Average-$2,033
  Gas Guzzler Tax . . . . .No
  Greenhouse Gas Emissions (tons/yr.) . . Average-7.3
  Barrels of Oil Used per year Average-13.2

How the Competition Rates

Competitors	Rating	Pg.
Honda CR-V	7	150
Jeep Compass	1	171
Toyota RAV4		251

Price Range	Retail	Markup
S	$22,470	6%
SE	$25,070	7%
SEL	$27,870	7%
Titanium AWD	$32,120	7%

Safety Checklist

Crash Tests:
  Frontal. . . . . Poor
  Side. . . . . Very Good
Airbags:
  Head . . . . .Fr & Rr. Roof Curtain
  Torso. . . . . .Front Pelvis/Torso from Seat
  Pelvis . . . . .Front Pelvis/Torso from Seat
  Roll Sensing . . . . .Yes
  Knee Bolster . . . . Standard Driver
Crash Avoidance:
  Frontal Collision Warning . . . . None
  Blind Spot Detection . . . . None
  Crash Imminent Braking . . . . None
  Lane Departure Warning . . . . None
General:
  Auto. Crash Notification . . . . Optional
  Day Running Lamps . . . . None
Safety Belt/Restraint:
  Dynamic Head Restraints . . . . None
  Adjustable Belt . . . . .Standard Front
  Pretensioners . . . . .Standard Front

Ford Escape

Specifications

Drive . . . . FWD
Engine 2.5-liter I4
Transmission . . . . 6-sp. Automatic
Tow Rating (lbs.) . . . . Very Low-1500
Head/Leg Room (in.) Cramped-39.9/40.4
Interior Space (cu. ft.). Average-98.1
Cargo Space (cu. ft.) . . . . Very Roomy-34.3
Wheelbase/Length (in.) 105.9/178.1

Ratings—10 Best, 1 Worst

	Expedition	Navigator
Combo Crash Tests	4	4
Safety Features	6	6
Rollover	2	2
Preventive Maintenance	5	5
Repair Costs	8	5
Warranty	2	5
Fuel Economy	1	1
Complaints	6	10
Insurance Costs	8	5
OVERALL RATING	**4**	**5**

Ford Expedition

Lincoln Navigator

At-a-Glance

Status/Year Series Started........ Unchanged/2003
Twins . . . . .Lincoln Navigator
Body Styles . . . . SUV
Seating 7/8
Anti-Theft Device . . . . . . .Std. Pass. Immobil & Alarm
Parking Index Rating . . . . .Very Hard
Where Made. . . . . .Louisville, KY
Fuel Factor . . . .
  MPG Rating (city/hwy) . . . . . .Very Poor-13/18
  Driving Range (mi.) Long-416
  Fuel Type . . . . .Regular
  Annual Fuel Cost . . . . Very High-$3,463
  Gas Guzzler Tax . . . . .No
  Greenhouse Gas Emissions (tons/yr.)Very High-10.1
  Barrels of Oil Used per year . . . . . . .Very High-22.0

How the Competition Rates

Competitors	Rating	Pg.
Chevrolet Suburban	7	119
Nissan Armada		211
Toyota Sequoia		252

Price Range

	Retail	Markup
XL 2WD	$36,930	7%
XLT	$42,930	7%
Limited	$49,205	7%
King Ranch	$50,780	7%

Safety Checklist

Crash Tests:
  Frontal. . . . . .Poor
  Side. . . . . Good
Airbags:
  Head . . . . Fr. & Rr. Roof Curtain
  Torso. . . . . Front Torso from Seat
  Pelvis . . . . None
  Roll Sensing . . . . .Yes
  Knee Bolster . . . . None
Crash Avoidance:
  Frontal Collision Warning . . . . None
  Blind Spot Detection . . . . None
  Crash Imminent Braking . . . . None
  Lane Departure Warning . . . . None
General:
  Auto. Crash Notification . . . . Optional
  Day Running Lamps . . . . None
Safety Belt/Restraint:
  Dynamic Head Restraints . . . . . .Standard Front
  Adjustable Belt . . . . .Standard Front
  Pretensioners . . . . .Standard Front

Ford Expedition

Specifications

Drive. 4WD
Engine 5.4-liter V8
Transmission . . . . .6-sp. Automatic
Tow Rating (lbs.) . . . . .Very High-9200
Head/Leg Room (in.) Cramped-39.6/41.1
Interior Space (cu. ft.). . . . . . . Very Roomy-160.3
Cargo Space (cu. ft.) Average-18.6
Wheelbase/Length (in.) 119/206.5

Ratings—10 Best, 1 Worst	
Combo Crash Tests	9
Safety Features	8
Rollover	3
Preventive Maintenance	6
Repair Costs	3
Warranty	2
Fuel Economy	2
Complaints	2
Insurance Costs	10
OVERALL RATING	**6**

Ford Explorer

Ford Explorer

At-a-Glance

Status/Year Series Started	Unchanged/2011
Twins	-
Body Styles	SUV
Seating	7/8
Anti-Theft Device	Std. Pass. Immobil & Alarm
Parking Index Rating	Hard
Where Made	Chicago, IL
Fuel Factor	
MPG Rating (city/hwy)	Very Poor-17/23
Driving Range (mi.)	Very Short-358
Fuel Type	Regular
Annual Fuel Cost	High-$2,671
Gas Guzzler Tax	No
Greenhouse Gas Emissions (tons/yr.)	Very High-9.6
Barrels of Oil Used per year	High-17.3

How the Competition Rates

Competitors	Rating	Pg.
Dodge Journey	1	132
Nissan Pathfinder	5	218
Toyota Highlander	4	246

Price Range	Retail	Markup
Base 2WD	$28,870	6%
XLT	$34,345	7%
Limited	$39,855	7%
Sport	$40,720	7%

Safety Checklist

Crash Tests:
Frontal . . . . Very Good
Side . . . . Good
Airbags:
Head . . . . Fr. & Rr. Roof Curtain
Torso . . . . Front Pelvis/Torso from Seat
Pelvis . . . . Front Pelvis/Torso from Seat
Roll Sensing . . . . Yes
Knee Bolster . . . . Standard Passenger
Crash Avoidance:
Frontal Collision Warning . . . . Optional
Blind Spot Detection . . . . Optional
Crash Imminent Braking . . . . None
Lane Departure Warning . . . . Optional
General:
Auto. Crash Notification . . . . Optional
Day Running Lamps . . . . None
Safety Belt/Restraint:
Dynamic Head Restraints . . . . None
Adjustable Belt . . . . Standard Front
Pretensioners . . . . Standard Front

Ford Explorer

Specifications

Drive	AWD
Engine	3.5-liter V6
Transmission	6-sp. Automatic
Tow Rating (lbs.)	Average-5000
Head/Leg Room (in.)	Roomy-41.4/40.6
Interior Space (cu. ft.)	Very Roomy-151.7
Cargo Space (cu. ft.)	Average-21
Wheelbase/Length (in.)	112.6/197.1

Ratings—10 Best, 1 Worst

Combo Crash Tests	4
Safety Features	4
Rollover	1
Preventive Maintenance	8
Repair Costs	7
Warranty	2
Fuel Economy	1
Complaints	10
Insurance Costs	10
OVERALL RATING	**5**

Ford F-150

Ford F-150

At-a-Glance

Status/Year Series Started........ Unchanged/2009
Twins .... -
Body Styles .... Pickup
Seating 5/6
Anti-Theft Device .... Std. Pass. Immobil & Alarm
Parking Index Rating ....Very Hard
Where Made...................... Dearborn, MI
Fuel Factor ....
  MPG Rating (city/hwy)...........Very Poor-14/19
  Driving Range (mi.) Average-413
  Fuel Type...........................Regular
  Annual Fuel Cost .... Very High-$3,240
  Gas Guzzler Tax ....No
  Greenhouse Gas Emissions (tons/yr.)..... High-9.2
  Barrels of Oil Used per year .... Very High-20.6

How the Competition Rates

Competitors	Rating	Pg.
Chevrolet Silverado	7	117
Nissan Titan		222
Toyota Tundra	2	255

Price Range

	Retail	Markup
XL Reg. cab 126 2WD	$23,670	8%
STX Supercab 145 4WD	$33,395	10%
SVT Raptor Supercab 133 4WD	$43,340	10%
Limited Supercrew 145 4WD	$52,455	10%

Safety Checklist

Crash Tests:
  Frontal.........................Very Poor
  Side........................... Very Good
Airbags:
  Head ....Front Roof Curtain
  Torso...........Front Pelvis/Torso from Seat
  Pelvis ....Front Pelvis/Torso from Seat
  Roll Sensing ....Yes
  Knee Bolster .... None
Crash Avoidance:
  Frontal Collision Warning .... None
  Blind Spot Detection .... None
  Crash Imminent Braking............... None
  Lane Departure Warning .... None
General:
  Auto. Crash Notification .... Optional
  Day Running Lamps .... None
Safety Belt/Restraint:
  Dynamic Head Restraints............. None
  Adjustable Belt ....Standard Front
  Pretensioners ....Standard Front

Ford F-150

Specifications

Drive................................. 4WD
Engine 5.0-liter V8
Transmission .... 6-sp. Automatic
Tow Rating (lbs.) .... Very High-7700
Head/Leg Room (in.) Roomy-41/41.4
Interior Space (cu. ft.)......... Very Roomy-130.9
Cargo Space (cu. ft.) .... Very Roomy-65.5
Wheelbase/Length (in.) 144.5/231.9

Ratings—10 Best, 1 Worst

Combo Crash Tests	7
Safety Features	4
Rollover	4
Preventive Maintenance	1
Repair Costs	10
Warranty	2
Fuel Economy	9
Complaints	2
Insurance Costs	1
OVERALL RATING	**4**

Ford Fiesta

Ford Fiesta

Ford Fiesta

At-a-Glance

Status/Year Series Started........ Unchanged/2011
Twins . . . . -
Body Styles . . . . Sedan, Hatchback
Seating 5
Anti-Theft Device . . . . Std. Pass. Immobil & Alarm
Parking Index Rating . . . . .Very Easy
Where Made. . . . . Cuautitlán, Mexico
Fuel Factor. . . . .
  MPG Rating (city/hwy) . . . . . Very Good-29/39
  Driving Range (mi.) Average-407
  Fuel Type. . . . . .Regular
  Annual Fuel Cost . . . . Very Low-$1,569
  Gas Guzzler Tax . . . . .No
  Greenhouse Gas Emissions (tons/yr.). Low-5.6
  Barrels of Oil Used per year Low-10.0

How the Competition Rates

Competitors	Rating	Pg.
Honda Fit	4	151
Hyundai Accent	8	156
Toyota Yaris	5	257

Price Range

Price Range	Retail	Markup
S	$13,200	4%
SE	$15,200	4%
Titanium	$17,200	4%
Titanium Hatchback	$18,200	4%

Safety Checklist

Crash Tests:
  Frontal. . . . . Good
  Side. . . . . .Good*
Airbags:
  Head . . . . .Fr & Rr. Roof Curtain
  Torso. . . . . .Front Pelvis/Torso from Seat
  Pelvis . . . . .Front Pelvis/Torso from Seat
  Roll Sensing . . . . No
  Knee Bolster . . . . Standard Driver
Crash Avoidance:
  Frontal Collision Warning . . . . None
  Blind Spot Detection . . . . None
  Crash Imminent Braking . . . . None
  Lane Departure Warning . . . . None
General:
  Auto. Crash Notification . . . . Optional
  Day Running Lamps. . . . . None
Safety Belt/Restraint:
  Dynamic Head Restraints. . . . . None
  Adjustable Belt . . . . .Standard Front
  Pretensioners . . . . .Standard Front

Ford Fiesta

Specifications

Drive . . . . FWD
Engine 1.6-liter I4
Transmission . . . . .5-sp. Manual
Tow Rating (lbs.) . . . . –
Head/Leg Room (in.) Average-39.1/42.2
Interior Space (cu. ft.). . . . . .Very Cramped-85.1
Cargo Space (cu. ft.) Cramped-12.8
Wheelbase/Length (in.) 98/173.6

*Additional injury potential in side test. See footnote 1 on page 19.

Ratings—10 Best, 1 Worst

Combo Crash Tests	–
Safety Features	5
Rollover	3
Preventive Maintenance	7
Repair Costs	5
Warranty	2
Fuel Economy	3
Complaints	4
Insurance Costs	5

OVERALL RATING   –

Ford Flex

Ford Flex

At-a-Glance

Status/Year Series Started   Appearance Change/2009
Twins . . . . -
Body Styles . . . . SUV
Seating 6/7
Anti-Theft Device . . . . Std. Pass. Immobil & Alarm
Parking Index Rating . . . . Very Hard
Where Made . . . . Oakville, Ontario
Fuel Factor . . . .
  MPG Rating (city/hwy) Poor-18/25
  Driving Range (mi.) Short-383
  Fuel Type . . . . Regular
  Annual Fuel Cost . . . . High-$2,498
  Gas Guzzler Tax . . . . No
  Greenhouse Gas Emissions (tons/yr.) . . Average-7.2
  Barrels of Oil Used per year High-16.5

How the Competition Rates

Competitors	Rating	Pg.
Chevrolet Traverse	8	121
Dodge Durango	5	130
Honda Pilot	4	154

Price Range

	Retail	Markup
SE	$30,885	6%
SEL	$33,325	8%
Limited	$39,230	7%
Limited Ecoboost AWD	$43,850	7%

Safety Checklist

Crash Tests:
  Frontal . . . . –
  Side . . . . –
Airbags:
  Head . . . . Fr. & Rr. Roof Curtain
  Torso . . . . Front Torso from Seat
  Pelvis . . . . None
  Roll Sensing . . . . Yes
  Knee Bolster . . . . None
Crash Avoidance:
  Frontal Collision Warning . . . . Optional
  Blind Spot Detection . . . . None
  Crash Imminent Braking . . . . None
  Lane Departure Warning . . . . None
General:
  Auto. Crash Notification . . . . Optional
  Day Running Lamps . . . . None
Safety Belt/Restraint:
  Dynamic Head Restraints . . . . None
  Adjustable Belt . . . . Standard Front
  Pretensioners . . . . Standard Front

Ford Flex

Specifications

Drive . . . . FWD
Engine 3.5-liter V6
Transmission . . . . 6-sp. Automatic
Tow Rating (lbs.) Average-4500
Head/Leg Room (in.) Roomy-41.8/40.8
Interior Space (cu. ft.) . . . . Very Roomy-155.8
Cargo Space (cu. ft.) Average-20
Wheelbase/Length (in.) 117.9/201.8

Ratings—10 Best, 1 Worst

Combo Crash Tests	8
Safety Features	4
Rollover	7
Preventive Maintenance	4
Repair Costs	9
Warranty	2
Fuel Economy	9
Complaints	1
Insurance Costs	3
OVERALL RATING	**6**

Ford Focus

At-a-Glance

Status/Year Series Started	Unchanged/2012
Twins	-
Body Styles	Sedan, Hatchback
Seating	5
Anti-Theft Device	Std. Pass. Immobil & Alarm
Parking Index Rating	Easy
Where Made	Wayne, MI
Fuel Factor	
MPG Rating (city/hwy)	Very Good-27/38
Driving Range (mi.)	Short-385
Fuel Type	Regular/E85
Annual Fuel Cost	Very Low-$1,657
Gas Guzzler Tax	No
Greenhouse Gas Emissions (tons/yr.)	Low-5.9
Barrels of Oil Used per year	Low-10.6

How the Competition Rates

Competitors	Rating	Pg.
Honda Civic		148
Kia Forte	7	175
Toyota Corolla	4	244

Price Range	Retail	Markup
S	$17,295	13%
SE	$19,295	14%
Titanium	$23,200	7%
Electric	$39,200	7%

Ford Focus

Safety Checklist

Crash Tests:
- Frontal . . . . Good
- Side . . . . Good

Airbags:
- Head . . . . .Fr & Rr. Roof Curtain
- Torso . . . . .Front Pelvis/Torso from Seat
- Pelvis . . . . .Front Pelvis/Torso from Seat
- Roll Sensing . . . . No
- Knee Bolster . . . . Standard Driver

Crash Avoidance:
- Frontal Collision Warning . . . . None
- Blind Spot Detection . . . . None
- Crash Imminent Braking . . . . None
- Lane Departure Warning . . . . None

General:
- Auto. Crash Notification . . . . Optional
- Day Running Lamps . . . . None

Safety Belt/Restraint:
- Dynamic Head Restraints . . . . None
- Adjustable Belt . . . . .Standard Front
- Pretensioners . . . . .Standard Front

Ford Focus

Specifications

Drive	FWD
Engine	2.0-liter I4
Transmission	5-sp. Manual
Tow Rating (lbs.)	–
Head/Leg Room (in.)	Cramped-38.3/41.9
Interior Space (cu. ft.)	Cramped-90
Cargo Space (cu. ft.)	Cramped-13.2
Wheelbase/Length (in.)	104.3/178.5

Ratings—10 Best, 1 Worst

Combo Crash Tests	–
Safety Features	6
Rollover	8
Preventive Maintenance	8
Repair Costs	10
Warranty	2
Fuel Economy	6
Complaints	–
Insurance Costs	3
OVERALL RATING	**–**

Ford Fusion

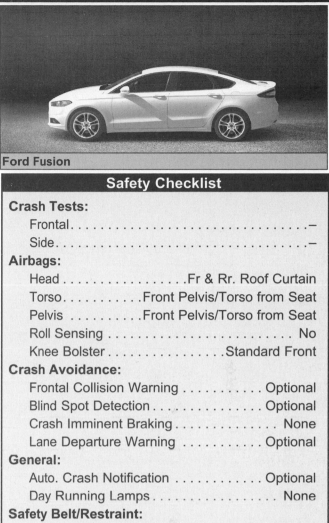

Ford Fusion

Ford Fusion

At-a-Glance

Status/Year Series Started	All New/2013
Twins	Lincoln MKZ
Body Styles	Sedan
Seating	5
Anti-Theft Device	Std. Pass. Immobil & Alarm
Parking Index Rating	Hard
Where Made	Hermosillo, Mexico / Flat Rock, MI
Fuel Factor	
MPG Rating (city/hwy)	Average-22/34
Driving Range (mi.)	Long-432
Fuel Type	Regular
Annual Fuel Cost	Low-$1,967
Gas Guzzler Tax	No
Greenhouse Gas Emissions (tons/yr.)	Average-7.1
Barrels of Oil Used per year	Average-12.7

How the Competition Rates

Competitors	Rating	Pg.
Chevrolet Malibu	9	116
Hyundai Sonata	9	161
Toyota Camry	4	243

Price Range

	Retail	Markup
S	$21,700	7%
SE	$23,700	8%
SE Hybrid	$27,200	8%
Titanium AWD	$32,200	8%

Safety Checklist

Crash Tests:
Frontal . . . . –
Side . . . . –

Airbags:
Head . . . . .Fr & Rr. Roof Curtain
Torso . . . . .Front Pelvis/Torso from Seat
Pelvis . . . . .Front Pelvis/Torso from Seat
Roll Sensing . . . . No
Knee Bolster . . . . .Standard Front

Crash Avoidance:
Frontal Collision Warning . . . . Optional
Blind Spot Detection . . . . Optional
Crash Imminent Braking . . . . None
Lane Departure Warning . . . . Optional

General:
Auto. Crash Notification . . . . Optional
Day Running Lamps . . . . None

Safety Belt/Restraint:
Dynamic Head Restraints . . . . None
Adjustable Belt . . . . .Standard Front
Pretensioners . . . . .Standard Front

Specifications

Drive	FWD
Engine	2.5-liter I4
Transmission	6-sp. Automatic
Tow Rating (lbs.)	–
Head/Leg Room (in.)	Very Roomy-39.2/44.3
Interior Space (cu. ft.)	Roomy-118.8
Cargo Space (cu. ft.)	Average-16
Wheelbase/Length (in.)	112.2/191.7

Ratings—10 Best, 1 Worst	
Combo Crash Tests	4
Safety Features	1
Rollover	10
Preventive Maintenance	2
Repair Costs	9
Warranty	2
Fuel Economy	4
Complaints	2
Insurance Costs	3
OVERALL RATING	**2**

Ford Mustang

Ford Mustang

At-a-Glance

Status/Year Series Started Appearance Change/2005
Twins . . . . -
Body Styles . . . . Coupe, Convertible
Seating 4
Anti-Theft Device . . . . Std. Pass. Immobil & Alarm
Parking Index Rating . . . . Easy
Where Made. . . . . Flat Rock, MI
Fuel Factor . . . .
  MPG Rating (city/hwy) Poor-19/31
  Driving Range (mi.) Short-368
  Fuel Type . . . . Regular
  Annual Fuel Cost . . . . Average-$2,236
  Gas Guzzler Tax . . . . No
  Greenhouse Gas Emissions (tons/yr.) High-8.0
  Barrels of Oil Used per year High-14.3

How the Competition Rates

Competitors	Rating	Pg.
Chevrolet Camaro	7	111
Chevrolet Corvette		112
Dodge Challenger		127

Price Range	Retail	Markup
Base	$22,200	6%
GT	$30,300	8%
Boss 302	$42,200	8%
Shelby GT500 Convertible	$59,200	10%

Safety Checklist

Crash Tests:
  Frontal . . . . Average
  Side . . . . Very Poor*
Airbags:
  Head . . . . Front Head/Torso from Seat
  Torso . . . . Front Head/Torso from Seat
  Pelvis . . . . None
  Roll Sensing . . . . No
  Knee Bolster . . . . None
Crash Avoidance:
  Frontal Collision Warning . . . . None
  Blind Spot Detection . . . . None
  Crash Imminent Braking . . . . None
  Lane Departure Warning . . . . None
General:
  Auto. Crash Notification . . . . Optional
  Day Running Lamps . . . . None
Safety Belt/Restraint:
  Dynamic Head Restraints . . . . None
  Adjustable Belt . . . . None
  Pretensioners . . . . Standard Front

Ford Mustang

Specifications

Drive . . . . RWD
Engine 3.7-liter V6
Transmission . . . . .6-sp. Automatic
Tow Rating (lbs.) . . . . Very Low-1000
Head/Leg Room (in.) Cramped-38.5/42.4
Interior Space (cu. ft.) . . . . Very Cramped-81
Cargo Space (cu. ft.) Cramped-13.4
Wheelbase/Length (in.) 107.1/188.5

*In side test, head of rear dummy struck convertible roof linkage resulting in a higher likelihood of serious injury.

Ratings—10 Best, 1 Worst

Combo Crash Tests	8
Safety Features	5
Rollover	7
Preventive Maintenance	6
Repair Costs	4
Warranty	2
Fuel Economy	4
Complaints	5
Insurance Costs	3
OVERALL RATING	**5**

Ford Taurus

At-a-Glance

Status/Year Series Started Appearance Change/2010
Twins . . . . -
Body Styles . . . . .Sedan
Seating 5
Anti-Theft Device . . . . . . .Std. Pass. Immobil & Alarm
Parking Index Rating . . . . .Very Hard
Where Made. .Chicago, IL
Fuel Factor. . . . .
  MPG Rating (city/hwy) Poor-19/29
  Driving Range (mi.) Long-427
  Fuel Type. . . . . .Regular
  Annual Fuel Cost . . . . Average-$2,288
  Gas Guzzler Tax . . . . .No
  Greenhouse Gas Emissions (tons/yr.). High-8.0
  Barrels of Oil Used per year High-14.3

How the Competition Rates

Competitors	Rating	Pg.
Chevrolet Malibu	9	116
Dodge Charger	7	128
Lincoln MKS	6	187

Price Range

	Retail	Markup
SE	$26,600	8%
SEL	$28,800	8%
Limited	$33,000	8%
SHO	$39,200	8%

Ford Taurus

Safety Checklist

Crash Tests:
  Frontal. . . . . Very Good
  Side. . . . . .Average
Airbags:
  Head . . . . .Fr & Rr. Roof Curtain
  Torso. . . . . .Front Torso from Seat
  Pelvis . . . . None
  Roll Sensing . . . . .Yes
  Knee Bolster . . . . None
Crash Avoidance:
  Frontal Collision Warning . . . . .Optional
  Blind Spot Detection . . . . .Optional
  Crash Imminent Braking . . . . None
  Lane Departure Warning . . . . None
General:
  Auto. Crash Notification . . . . .Optional
  Day Running Lamps . . . . None
Safety Belt/Restraint:
  Dynamic Head Restraints. . . . . None
  Adjustable Belt . . . . .Standard Front
  Pretensioners . . . . .Standard Front

Ford Taurus

Specifications

Drive. . . . . FWD
Engine 3.5-liter V6
Transmission . . . . .6-sp. Automatic
Tow Rating (lbs.) . . . . Very Low-1000
Head/Leg Room (in.) Cramped-39/41.9
Interior Space (cu. ft.). Average-102.2
Cargo Space (cu. ft.) Average-20.1
Wheelbase/Length (in.) 112/202.9

Ratings—10 Best, 1 Worst

Combo Crash Tests	8
Safety Features	4
Rollover	9
Preventive Maintenance	5
Repair Costs	8
Warranty	1
Fuel Economy	9
Complaints	–
Insurance Costs	8
OVERALL RATING	**9**

Honda Accord Sedan

Honda Accord Sedan

At-a-Glance

Status/Year Series Started . . . . All New/2013
Twins . . . . -
Body Styles . . . . Sedan
Seating 5
Anti-Theft Device . . . . . Std. Pass. Immobil. & Alarm
Parking Index Rating . . . . Hard
Where Made . . . . Marysville, OH
Fuel Factor . . . .
  MPG Rating (city/hwy) . . . . Very Good-27/36
  Driving Range (mi.) . . . . Very Long-523
  Fuel Type . . . . Regular
  Annual Fuel Cost . . . . Very Low-$1,691
  Gas Guzzler Tax . . . . No
  Greenhouse Gas Emissions (tons/yr.) . . Average-6.3
  Barrels of Oil Used per year Average-11.4

How the Competition Rates

Competitors	Rating	Pg.
Ford Fusion		143
Nissan Altima	7	209
Toyota Camry	4	243

Price Range

Price Range	Retail	Markup
LX Manual	$21,680	9%
Sport	$24,190	9%
EX-L V6	$30,070	9%
Touring	$33,430	9%

Safety Checklist

Crash Tests:
  Frontal . . . . Average
  Side . . . . Very Good
Airbags:
  Head . . . . Fr. & Rr. Roof Curtain
  Torso . . . . Front Pelvis/Torso from Seat
  Pelvis . . . . Front Pelvis/Torso from Seat
  Roll Sensing . . . . No
  Knee Bolster . . . . None
Crash Avoidance:
  Frontal Collision Warning . . . . Optional
  Blind Spot Detection . . . . None
  Crash Imminent Braking . . . . None
  Lane Departure Warning . . . . Optional
General:
  Auto. Crash Notification . . . . None
  Day Running Lamps . . . . Standard
Safety Belt/Restraint:
  Dynamic Head Restraints . . . . None
  Adjustable Belt . . . . Standard Front
  Pretensioners . . . . Standard Front

Honda Accord Sedan

Specifications

Drive . . . . FWD
Engine 2.4-liter I4
Transmission . . . . CVT
Tow Rating (lbs.) . . . . –
Head/Leg Room (in.) Average-39.1/42.5
Interior Space (cu. ft.) Average-103.2
Cargo Space (cu. ft.) Cramped-15.8
Wheelbase/Length (in.) 109.3/191.4

Ratings—10 Best, 1 Worst

Combo Crash Tests	–
Safety Features	3
Rollover	9
Preventive Maintenance	5
Repair Costs	8
Warranty	1
Fuel Economy	8
Complaints	–
Insurance Costs	5
OVERALL RATING	–

Honda Accord Coupe

Honda Accord Coupe

At-a-Glance

Status/Year Series Started	All New/2013
Twins	-
Body Styles	Coupe
Seating	5
Anti-Theft Device	Std. Pass. Immobil. & Alarm
Parking Index Rating	Average
Where Made	Marysville, OH
Fuel Factor	
MPG Rating (city/hwy)	Good-26/35
Driving Range (mi.)	Very Long-506
Fuel Type	Regular
Annual Fuel Cost	Very Low-$1,750
Gas Guzzler Tax	No
Greenhouse Gas Emissions (tons/yr.)	Average-6.3
Barrels of Oil Used per year	Average-11.4

How the Competition Rates

Competitors	Rating	Pg.
Hyundai Genesis		159
Infiniti G		166
Volkswagen CC		259

Price Range	Retail	Markup
LX-S	$24,200	10%
EX	$25,875	10%
EX-L V6	$30,350	10%
EX-L V6 w/Nav	$32,350	10%

Safety Checklist

Crash Tests:
Frontal . . . . –
Side . . . . –
Airbags:
Head . . . . .Fr & Rr. Roof Curtain
Torso . . . . .Front Pelvis/Torso from Seat
Pelvis . . . . .Front Pelvis/Torso from Seat
Roll Sensing . . . . No
Knee Bolster . . . . None
Crash Avoidance:
Frontal Collision Warning . . . . Optional
Blind Spot Detection . . . . None
Crash Imminent Braking . . . . None
Lane Departure Warning . . . . Optional
General:
Auto. Crash Notification . . . . None
Day Running Lamps . . . . Standard
Safety Belt/Restraint:
Dynamic Head Restraints . . . . None
Adjustable Belt . . . . None
Pretensioners . . . . .Standard Front

Honda Accord Coupe

Specifications

Drive	FWD
Engine	2.4-liter I4
Transmission	CVT
Tow Rating (lbs.)	–
Head/Leg Room (in.)	Average-39/42.2
Interior Space (cu. ft.)	Cramped-95.6
Cargo Space (cu. ft.)	Cramped-13.7
Wheelbase/Length (in.)	107.3/189.3

Honda Civic

Ratings—10 Best, 1 Worst

Combo Crash Tests	–
Safety Features	2
Rollover	7
Preventive Maintenance	7
Repair Costs	9
Warranty	1
Fuel Economy	9
Complaints	5
Insurance Costs	3
OVERALL RATING	**–**

Honda Civic Sedan

At-a-Glance

Status/Year Series Started Unchanged/2012
Twins . . . . -
Body Styles . . . . .Sedan
Seating 5
Anti-Theft Device Std. Pass. Immobil. & Opt. Pass. Alarm
Parking Index Rating . . . . Easy
Where Made . . . . Greensburg, IN/Alliston, Ontario
Fuel Factor . . . .
  MPG Rating (city/hwy) . . . . Very Good-28/39
  Driving Range (mi.) Long-423
  Fuel Type . . . . .Regular
  Annual Fuel Cost . . . . Very Low-$1,604
  Gas Guzzler Tax . . . . .No
  Greenhouse Gas Emissions (tons/yr.) Low-5.7
  Barrels of Oil Used per year Low-10.3

How the Competition Rates

Competitors	Rating	Pg.
Nissan Sentra		221
Suzuki Kizashi		239
Volkswagen Jetta	6	261

Price Range	Retail	Markup
DX Manual	$15,955	7%
LX	$18,805	8%
EX	$20,655	8%
Hybrid-L w/Nav	$26,900	8%

Honda Civic Sedan

Safety Checklist

Crash Tests:
  Frontal . . . .–
  Side . . . .–
Airbags:
  Head . . . . .Fr & Rr. Roof Curtain
  Torso . . . . Front Torso from Seat
  Pelvis . . . . None
  Roll Sensing . . . . No
  Knee Bolster . . . . None
Crash Avoidance:
  Frontal Collision Warning . . . . None
  Blind Spot Detection . . . . None
  Crash Imminent Braking . . . . None
  Lane Departure Warning . . . . None
General:
  Auto. Crash Notification . . . . None
  Day Running Lamps . . . . Standard
Safety Belt/Restraint:
  Dynamic Head Restraints . . . . None
  Adjustable Belt . . . . .Standard Front
  Pretensioners . . . . .Standard Front

Honda Civic Sedan

Specifications

Drive . . . . FWD
Engine 1.8-liter I4
Transmission . . . . .5-sp. Automatic
Tow Rating (lbs.) . . . . –
Head/Leg Room (in.) Average-39/42
Interior Space (cu. ft.) Cramped-94.6
Cargo Space (cu. ft.) Cramped-12.5
Wheelbase/Length (in.) 105.1/177.3

Honda Civic Coupe

Compact

Ratings—10 Best, 1 Worst	
Combo Crash Tests	–
Safety Features	2
Rollover	8
Preventive Maintenance	7
Repair Costs	10
Warranty	1
Fuel Economy	9
Complaints	–
Insurance Costs	3
OVERALL RATING	**–**

Honda Civic Coupe

At-a-Glance

Status/Year Series Started........ Unchanged/2012
Twins .... -
Body Styles ....Coupe
Seating.....................................5
Anti-Theft Device Std. Pass. Immobil. & Opt. Pass. Alarm
Parking Index Rating . . . . Easy
Where Made................... Alliston, Ontario
Fuel Factor . . . .
  MPG Rating (city/hwy) .... Very Good-28/39
  Driving Range (mi.) Long-423
  Fuel Type.......................Regular
  Annual Fuel Cost .... Very Low-$1,604
  Gas Guzzler Tax ....No
  Greenhouse Gas Emissions (tons/yr.)..... Low-5.7
  Barrels of Oil Used per year Low-10.3

How the Competition Rates

Competitors	Rating	Pg.
Ford Focus	6	142
Mazda Mazda3	5	190
Scion tC	8	229

Price Range

Price Range	Retail	Markup
DX Manual	$15,755	7%
LX	$18,605	8%
EX-L	$22,105	8%
Si w/Nav	$23,855	8%

Honda Civic Coupe

Safety Checklist

Crash Tests:
  Frontal................................ –
  Side.................................. –
Airbags:
  Head .... Fr. & Rr. Roof Curtain
  Torso.............. Front Torso from Seat
  Pelvis .... None
  Roll Sensing .... No
  Knee Bolster .... None
Crash Avoidance:
  Frontal Collision Warning .... None
  Blind Spot Detection .... None
  Crash Imminent Braking............. None
  Lane Departure Warning .... None
General:
  Auto. Crash Notification .... None
  Day Running Lamps .... Standard
Safety Belt/Restraint:
  Dynamic Head Restraints............. None
  Adjustable Belt .... Standard Front
  Pretensioners .... Standard Front

Honda Civic Coupe

Specifications

Drive.................................... FWD
Engine 1.8-liter I4
Transmission ....5-sp. Automatic
Tow Rating (lbs.) .... –
Head/Leg Room (in.) Cramped-38.1/42.2
Interior Space (cu. ft.)........Very Cramped-83.2
Cargo Space (cu. ft.) ......Very Cramped-11.7
Wheelbase/Length (in.) 103.2/176

Honda CR-V

Ratings—10 Best, 1 Worst

Combo Crash Tests	7
Safety Features	4
Rollover	3
Preventive Maintenance	6
Repair Costs	9
Warranty	1
Fuel Economy	6
Complaints	8
Insurance Costs	8
OVERALL RATING	**7**

Honda CR-V

Honda CR-V

At-a-Glance

Status/Year Series Started........ Unchanged/2012
Twins .... -
Body Styles .... SUV
Seating 5
Anti-Theft Device .Std. Pass. Immobil. & Opt. Pass. Alarm
Parking Index Rating .... Easy
Where Made............... East Liberty, OH
Fuel Factor ....
  MPG Rating (city/hwy) ... Average-22/30
  Driving Range (mi.) Short-383
  Fuel Type .... Regular
  Annual Fuel Cost ...... Average-$2,058
  Gas Guzzler Tax .... No
  Greenhouse Gas Emissions (tons/yr.).. Average-7.1
  Barrels of Oil Used per year Average-12.7

How the Competition Rates

Competitors	Rating	Pg.
Ford Escape	7	136
Hyundai Tucson	7	162
Toyota RAV4		251

Price Range

Price Range	Retail	Markup
LX	$22,695	6%
EX	$24,795	6%
EX-L	$27,445	7%
EX-L AWD w/Nav	$30,195	7%

Safety Checklist

Crash Tests:
  Frontal............................ Good
  Side............................... Poor
Airbags:
  Head .... Fr & Rr. Roof Curtain
  Torso............ Front Torso from Seat
  Pelvis .... None
  Roll Sensing .... Yes
  Knee Bolster .... None
Crash Avoidance:
  Frontal Collision Warning .... None
  Blind Spot Detection .... None
  Crash Imminent Braking .... None
  Lane Departure Warning .... None
General:
  Auto. Crash Notification .... None
  Day Running Lamps .... Standard
Safety Belt/Restraint:
  Dynamic Head Restraints........... None
  Adjustable Belt .... Standard Front
  Pretensioners .... Standard Front

Honda CR-V

Specifications

Drive................................ FWD
Engine 2.4-liter I4
Transmission .... 5-sp. Automatic
Tow Rating (lbs.) .... Very Low-1500
Head/Leg Room (in.) ... Average-39.9/41.3
Interior Space (cu. ft.)...... Roomy-104.1
Cargo Space (cu. ft.) ..... Very Roomy-37.2
Wheelbase/Length (in.) 103.1/178.3

Ratings—10 Best, 1 Worst

Combo Crash Tests	4
Safety Features	3
Rollover	6
Preventive Maintenance	6
Repair Costs	7
Warranty	1
Fuel Economy	8
Complaints	7
Insurance Costs	1
OVERALL RATING	**4**

Honda Fit

At-a-Glance

Status/Year Series Started	Unchanged/2009
Twins	-
Body Styles	Hatchback
Seating	5
Anti-Theft Device	Std. Pass. Immob. & Opt. Pass. Alarm
Parking Index Rating	Very Easy
Where Made	Suzuka, Japan
Fuel Factor	
MPG Rating (city/hwy)	Good-27/33
Driving Range (mi.)	Very Short-312
Fuel Type	Regular
Annual Fuel Cost	Very Low-$1,750
Gas Guzzler Tax	No
Greenhouse Gas Emissions (tons/yr.)	Low-5.9
Barrels of Oil Used per year	Low-10.6

How the Competition Rates

Competitors	Rating	Pg.
Hyundai Accent	8	156
Nissan Versa	4	223
Toyota Yaris	5	257

Price Range

	Retail	Markup
Base Manual	$15,325	3%
Sport	$17,910	3%
Sport w/Nav	$19,690	3%

Honda Fit

Safety Checklist

Crash Tests:
Frontal . . . . Good
Side . . . . Poor
Airbags:
Head . . . . .Fr & Rr. Roof Curtain
Torso . . . . Front Torso from Seat
Pelvis . . . . None
Roll Sensing . . . . No
Knee Bolster . . . . None
Crash Avoidance:
Frontal Collision Warning . . . . None
Blind Spot Detection . . . . None
Crash Imminent Braking . . . . None
Lane Departure Warning . . . . None
General:
Auto. Crash Notification . . . . None
Day Running Lamps . . . . Standard
Safety Belt/Restraint:
Dynamic Head Restraints . . . . . .Standard Front
Adjustable Belt . . . . .Standard Front
Pretensioners . . . . .Standard Front

Honda Fit

Specifications

Drive	FWD
Engine	1.5-liter I4
Transmission	5-sp. Automatic
Tow Rating (lbs.)	—
Head/Leg Room (in.)	Average-40.4/41.3
Interior Space (cu. ft.)	Cramped-90.8
Cargo Space (cu. ft.)	Average-20.6
Wheelbase/Length (in.)	98.4/161.6

Ratings—10 Best, 1 Worst

Combo Crash Tests	–
Safety Features	3
Rollover	6
Preventive Maintenance	6
Repair Costs	8
Warranty	1
Fuel Economy	10
Complaints	4
Insurance Costs	3
OVERALL RATING	**–**

Honda Insight

Honda Insight

At-a-Glance

Status/Year Series Started........ Unchanged/2010
Twins .... -
Body Styles .... Hatchback
Seating 5
Anti-Theft Device . Std. Pass. Immobil. & Active Alarm
Parking Index Rating .... Easy
Where Made.................. Suzuka, Japan
Fuel Factor
  MPG Rating (city/hwy) .... Very Good-41/44
  Driving Range (mi.) .... Very Long-448
  Fuel Type....................... Regular
  Annual Fuel Cost .... Very Low-$1,216
  Gas Guzzler Tax .... No
  Greenhouse Gas Emissions (tons/yr.) . Very Low-4.4
  Barrels of Oil Used per year .... Very Low-7.8

How the Competition Rates

Competitors	Rating	Pg.
Kia Soul	6	179
Scion xD		231
Toyota Prius	7	248

Price Range

Price Range	Retail	Markup
Base	$18,500	6%
LX	$20,275	6%
EX	$21,965	6%
EX w/Nav	$23,690	6%

Safety Checklist

Crash Tests:
  Frontal................................. –
  Side.................................. –
Airbags:
  Head .... Fr & Rr. Roof Curtain
  Torso............... Front Torso from Seat
  Pelvis .... None
  Roll Sensing .... No
  Knee Bolster .... None
Crash Avoidance:
  Frontal Collision Warning .... None
  Blind Spot Detection .... None
  Crash Imminent Braking .... None
  Lane Departure Warning .... None
General:
  Auto. Crash Notification .... None
  Day Running Lamps............. Standard
Safety Belt/Restraint:
  Dynamic Head Restraints...... Standard Front
  Adjustable Belt .... Standard Front
  Pretensioners .... Standard Front

Honda Insight

Specifications

Drive................................. FWD
Engine 1.3-liter I4
Transmission .... CVT
Tow Rating (lbs.) .... –
Head/Leg Room (in.) Cramped-38/42.3
Interior Space (cu. ft.).......... Very Cramped-85
Cargo Space (cu. ft.) Cramped-15.9
Wheelbase/Length (in.) 100.4/172.3

Ratings—10 Best, 1 Worst

Combo Crash Tests	7
Safety Features	7
Rollover	6
Preventive Maintenance	5
Repair Costs	9
Warranty	1
Fuel Economy	3
Complaints	4
Insurance Costs	10
OVERALL RATING	**7**

Honda Odyssey

Honda Odyssey

At-a-Glance

Status/Year Series Started........ Unchanged/2005
Twins . . . . -
Body Styles . . . . Minivan
Seating 7/8
Anti-Theft Device Std. Pass. Immobil. & Opt. Pass. Alarm
Parking Index Rating . . . . Hard
Where Made. . . . . Lincoln, AL
Fuel Factor . . . .
  MPG Rating (city/hwy). Poor-18/27
  Driving Range (mi.) . . . . Very Long-445
  Fuel Type . . . . .Regular
  Annual Fuel Cost . . . . High-$2,430
  Gas Guzzler Tax . . . . .No
  Greenhouse Gas Emissions (tons/yr.). High-8.7
  Barrels of Oil Used per year High-15.7

How the Competition Rates

Competitors	Rating	Pg.
Chrysler Town and Country	5	125
Nissan Quest		219
Toyota Sienna	3	253

Price Range

	Retail	Markup
LX	$28,575	9%
EX	$31,725	9%
Touring	$41,430	9%
Touring Elite	$43,925	9%

Safety Checklist

Crash Tests:
  Frontal. . . . . Very Good
  Side. . . . . Average

  Head . . . . Fr. & Rr. Roof Curtain
  Torso. . . . . Front Pelvis/Torso from Seat
  Pelvis . . . . .Front Pelvis/Torso from Seat
  Roll Sensing . . . . .Yes
  Knee Bolster . . . . None
Crash Avoidance:
  Frontal Collision Warning . . . . None
  Blind Spot Detection . . . . Optional
  Crash Imminent Braking . . . . None
  Lane Departure Warning . . . . None
General:
  Auto. Crash Notification . . . . None
  Day Running Lamps . . . . Standard
Safety Belt/Restraint:
  Dynamic Head Restraints. . . . . .Standard Front
  Adjustable Belt . . . . . .Standard Front and Rear
  Pretensioners . . . . .Standard Front

Honda Odyssey

Specifications

Drive. . . . . FWD
Engine 3.5-liter V6
Transmission . . . . .5-sp. Automatic
Tow Rating (lbs.) Low-3500
Head/Leg Room (in.) Cramped-39.7/40.9
Interior Space (cu. ft.). . . . . Very Roomy-172.5
Cargo Space (cu. ft.) . . . . Very Roomy-38.4
Wheelbase/Length (in.) 118.1/202.9

Ratings—10 Best, 1 Worst

Combo Crash Tests	3
Safety Features	6
Rollover	3
Preventive Maintenance	6
Repair Costs	7
Warranty	1
Fuel Economy	2
Complaints	8
Insurance Costs	8
OVERALL RATING	**4**

Honda Pilot

Honda Pilot

At-a-Glance

Status/Year Series Started........ Unchanged/2009
Twins . . . . -
Body Styles . . . . SUV
Seating 8
Anti-Theft Device Std. Pass. Immobil. & Opt. Pass. Alarm
Parking Index Rating . . . . Hard
Where Made. . . . . Lincoln, AL
Fuel Factor. . . . .
  MPG Rating (city/hwy) . . . . Very Poor-17/24
  Driving Range (mi.) Average-411
  Fuel Type. . . . . .Regular
  Annual Fuel Cost . . . . High-$2,629
  Gas Guzzler Tax . . . . .No
  Greenhouse Gas Emissions (tons/yr.) High-9.2
  Barrels of Oil Used per year High-16.5

How the Competition Rates

Competitors	Rating	Pg.
Ford Explorer	6	138
Nissan Pathfinder	5	218
Toyota 4Runner	4	241

Price Range

	Retail	Markup
LX 2WD	$29,420	9%
EX	$33,270	9%
EX-L	$36,520	9%
Touring	$41,170	9%

Safety Checklist

Crash Tests:
  Frontal. . . . . Average
  Side. . . . . .Very Poor
Airbags:
  Head . . . . Fr. & Rr. Roof Curtain
  Torso. . . . . .Front Pelvis/Torso from Seat
  Pelvis . . . . .Front Pelvis/Torso from Seat
  Roll Sensing . . . . .Yes
  Knee Bolster . . . . None
Crash Avoidance:
  Frontal Collision Warning . . . . None
  Blind Spot Detection . . . . None
  Crash Imminent Braking . . . . None
  Lane Departure Warning . . . . None
General:
  Auto. Crash Notification . . . . None
  Day Running Lamps . . . . Standard
Safety Belt/Restraint:
  Dynamic Head Restraints. . . . . .Standard Front
  Adjustable Belt . . . . . .Standard Front and Rear
  Pretensioners . . . . .Standard Front

Honda Pilot

Specifications

Drive. 4WD
Engine 3.5-liter V6
Transmission . . . . .5-sp. Automatic
Tow Rating (lbs.) Average-4500
Head/Leg Room (in.) Average-40/41.4
Interior Space (cu. ft.). . . . . Very Roomy-153.7
Cargo Space (cu. ft.) Average-18
Wheelbase/Length (in.) 109.2/191.4

Ratings—10 Best, 1 Worst

Combo Crash Tests	–
Safety Features	5
Rollover	3
Preventive Maintenance	6
Repair Costs	9
Warranty	1
Fuel Economy	1
Complaints	7
Insurance Costs	5
OVERALL RATING	**–**

Honda Ridgeline

Honda Ridgeline

At-a-Glance

Status/Year Series Started Unchanged/2006
Twins . . . . -
Body Styles . . . . Pickup
Seating 5
Anti-Theft Device .Std. Pass. Immobil. & Opt. Pass. Alarm
Parking Index Rating . . . . Very Hard
Where Made . . . . Lincoln, AL
Fuel Factor . . . .
  MPG Rating (city/hwy) . . . . . Very Poor-15/21
  Driving Range (mi.) Short-379
  Fuel Type . . . . Regular
  Annual Fuel Cost . . . . Very High-$2,989
  Gas Guzzler Tax . . . . No
  Greenhouse Gas Emissions (tons/yr.)Very High-10.8
  Barrels of Oil Used per year . . . . Very High-19.4

How the Competition Rates

Competitors	Rating	Pg.
Chevrolet Avalanche		110
Nissan Titan		222
Toyota Tacoma	1	255

Price Range	Retail	Markup
RT	$29,350	10%
RTS	$32,055	10%
RTL	$34,930	10%
RTL w/Nav	$37,280	10%

Safety Checklist

Crash Tests:
  Frontal . . . . –
  Side . . . . –
Airbags:
  Head . . . . .Fr & Rr. Roof Curtain
  Torso . . . . Front Torso from Seat
  Pelvis . . . . None
  Roll Sensing . . . . Yes
  Knee Bolster . . . . None
Crash Avoidance:
  Frontal Collision Warning . . . . None
  Blind Spot Detection . . . . None
  Crash Imminent Braking . . . . None
  Lane Departure Warning . . . . None
General:
  Auto. Crash Notification . . . . None
  Day Running Lamps . . . . Standard
Safety Belt/Restraint:
  Dynamic Head Restraints . . . . . .Standard Front
  Adjustable Belt . . . . .Standard Front
  Pretensloners . . . . .Standard Front

Honda Ridgeline

Specifications

Drive 4WD
Engine 3.5-liter V6
Transmission . . . . .5-sp. Automatic
Tow Rating (lbs.) Average-5000
Head/Leg Room (in.) Average-40.7/40.8
Interior Space (cu. ft.) Roomy-112
Cargo Space (cu. ft.) . . . . . . Very Roomy-37.6
Wheelbase/Length (in.) 122/206.9

Hyundai Accent

Ratings—10 Best, 1 Worst

Combo Crash Tests	4
Safety Features	4
Rollover	6
Preventive Maintenance	7
Repair Costs	10
Warranty	10
Fuel Economy	9
Complaints	7
Insurance Costs	1
OVERALL RATING	**8**

Hyundai Accent

Hyundai Accent

At-a-Glance

Status/Year Series Started	Unchanged/2012
Twins	Kia Rio
Body Styles	Sedan, Hatchback
Seating	5
Anti-Theft Device	None
Parking Index Rating	Very Easy
Where Made	Ulsan, South Korea
Fuel Factor	
MPG Rating (city/hwy)	Very Good-28/37
Driving Range (mi.)	Very Short-358
Fuel Type	Regular
Annual Fuel Cost	Very Low-$1,636
Gas Guzzler Tax	No
Greenhouse Gas Emissions (tons/yr.)	Low-5.9
Barrels of Oil Used per year	Low-10.6

How the Competition Rates

Competitors	Rating	Pg.
Ford Fiesta	4	140
Nissan Versa	4	223
Suzuki SX4	1	240

Price Range	Retail	Markup
GLS Manual	$14,545	3%
GS	$15,995	3%
SE	$17,095	3%

Safety Checklist

Crash Tests:
Frontal . . . . Average
Side . . . . Very Poor

Airbags:
Head . . . . Fr. & Rr. Roof Curtain
Torso . . . . Front Pelvis/Torso from Seat
Pelvis . . . . Front Pelvis/Torso from Seat
Roll Sensing . . . . No
Knee Bolster . . . . None

Crash Avoidance:
Frontal Collision Warning . . . . None
Blind Spot Detection . . . . None
Crash Imminent Braking . . . . None
Lane Departure Warning . . . . None

General:
Auto. Crash Notification . . . . None
Day Running Lamps . . . . None

Safety Belt/Restraint:
Dynamic Head Restraints . . . . . . Standard Front
Adjustable Belt . . . . Standard Front
Pretensioners . . . . Standard Front

Hyundai Accent

Specifications

Drive	FWD
Engine	1.6-liter I4
Transmission	6-sp. Automatic
Tow Rating (lbs.)	–
Head/Leg Room (in.)	Average-39.9/41.8
Interior Space (cu. ft.)	Cramped-90.1
Cargo Space (cu. ft.)	Average-21.2
Wheelbase/Length (in.)	101.2/162

Hyundai Azera

Ratings—10 Best, 1 Worst

Combo Crash Tests	–
Safety Features	5
Rollover	8
Preventive Maintenance	5
Repair Costs	5
Warranty	10
Fuel Economy	4
Complaints	1
Insurance Costs	3
OVERALL RATING	**–**

Hyundai Azera

At-a-Glance

Status/Year Series Started Unchanged/2012
Twins . . . . -
Body Styles . . . . Sedan
Seating 5
Anti-Theft Device . Std. Pass. Immobil. & Active Alarm
Parking Index Rating . . . . Average
Where Made . . . . Asan, South Korea
Fuel Factor . . . .
  MPG Rating (city/hwy) Poor-20/29
  Driving Range (mi.) Long-430
  Fuel Type . . . . Regular
  Annual Fuel Cost . . . . Average-$2,213.
  Gas Guzzler Tax . . . . No
  Greenhouse Gas Emissions (tons/yr.) High-7.9
  Barrels of Oil Used per year High-14.3

How the Competition Rates

Competitors	Rating	Pg.
Lexus ES	8	183
Nissan Maxima	4	216
Toyota Avalon		242

Price Range

	Retail	Markup
4D Sedan	$32,250	7%

Hyundai Azera

Safety Checklist

Crash Tests:
  Frontal . . . . –
  Side . . . . –
Airbags:
  Head . . . . Fr. & Rr. Roof Curtain
  Torso . . . . Fr. & Rr. Pelvis/Torso from Seat
  Pelvis . . . . Front Pelvis/Torso from Seat
  Roll Sensing . . . . No
  Knee Bolster . . . . Standard Driver
Crash Avoidance:
  Frontal Collision Warning . . . . None
  Blind Spot Detection . . . . None
  Crash Imminent Braking . . . . None
  Lane Departure Warning . . . . None
General:
  Auto. Crash Notification . . . . Optional
  Day Running Lamps . . . . Standard
Safety Belt/Restraint:
  Dynamic Head Restraints . . . . None
  Adjustable Belt . . . . Standard Front
  Pretensioners . . . . Standard Front

Specifications

Drive . . . . FWD
Engine 3.3-liter V6
Transmission . . . . .6-sp. Automatic
Tow Rating (lbs.) . . . . –
Head/Leg Room (in.) . . . . . . Very Roomy-40.3/45.5
Interior Space (cu. ft.) Roomy-107
Cargo Space (cu. ft.) Average-16.3
Wheelbase/Length (in.) 112/193.3

Ratings—10 Best, 1 Worst	
Combo Crash Tests	7
Safety Features	2
Rollover	7
Preventive Maintenance	5
Repair Costs	9
Warranty	10
Fuel Economy	9
Complaints	7
Insurance Costs	1
OVERALL RATING	**9**

Hyundai Elantra Sedan

Hyundai Elantra Coupe

At-a-Glance

Status/Year Series Started........ Unchanged/2011
Twins .... -
Body Styles .... Sedan, Coupe, Hatchback
Seating 5
Anti-Theft Device ..... Opt. Pass. Immbobil. & Alarm
Parking Index Rating .... Easy
Where Made................ Ulsan, South Korea
Fuel Factor...
  MPG Rating (city/hwy) .... Very Good-28/38
  Driving Range (mi.) Average-407
  Fuel Type................................Regular
  Annual Fuel Cost .... Very Low-$1,620
  Gas Guzzler Tax ....No
  Greenhouse Gas Emissions (tons/yr.)..... Low-5.7
  Barrels of Oil Used per year Low-10.3

How the Competition Rates

Competitors	Rating	Pg.
Honda Civic		148
Nissan Sentra		221
Toyota Corolla	4	244

Price Range	Retail	Markup
GLS Manual	$16,815	3%
GS	$18,445	3%
GT	$19,395	4%
Limited	$20,965	4%

Safety Checklist

Crash Tests:
  Frontal............................. Good
  Side............................. Average
  Head .... Fr. & Rr. Roof Curtain

Airbags:
  Torso..........Front Pelvis/Torso from Seat
  Pelvis ....Front Pelvis/Torso from Seat
  Roll Sensing .... No
  Knee Bolster....................... None

Crash Avoidance:
  Frontal Collision Warning .... None
  Blind Spot Detection .... None
  Crash Imminent Braking.............. None
  Lane Departure Warning .... None

General:
  Auto. Crash Notification .... None
  Day Running Lamps.............. Optional

Safety Belt/Restraint:
  Dynamic Head Restraints............ None
  Adjustable Belt ....Standard Front
  Pretensioners ....Standard Front

Hyundai Elantra Coupe

Specifications

Drive................................. FWD
Engine 1.8-liter I4
Transmission ....6-sp. Automatic
Tow Rating (lbs.) .... –
Head/Leg Room (in.) ....Very Roomy-40/43.6
Interior Space (cu. ft.)............. Cramped-96
Cargo Space (cu. ft.) Cramped-14.8
Wheelbase/Length (in.) 106.3/178.3

Ratings—10 Best, 1 Worst

Combo Crash Tests	–
Safety Features	6
Rollover	8
Preventive Maintenance	4
Repair Costs	7
Warranty	10
Fuel Economy	3
Complaints	3
Insurance Costs	5
OVERALL RATING	**–**

Hyundai Genesis Coupe

Hyundai Genesis Sedan

At-a-Glance

Status/Year Series Started........ Unchanged/2009
Twins . . . . -
Body Styles . . . . Sedan, Coupe
Seating 5
Anti-Theft Device . Std. Pass. Immobil. & Active Alarm
Parking Index Rating . . . . Average
Where Made. . . . . Ulsan, South Korea
Fuel Factor . . . .
  MPG Rating (city/hwy) Poor-18/28
  Driving Range (mi.) Long-414
  Fuel Type. . . . . .Regular
  Annual Fuel Cost . . . . High-$2,399
  Gas Guzzler Tax . . . . .No
  Greenhouse Gas Emissions (tons/yr.) High-8.3
  Barrels of Oil Used per year High-15.0

How the Competition Rates

Competitors	Rating	Pg.
Acura TL	5	84
Lexus ES	8	183
Volkswagen CC		259

Price Range

	Retail	Markup
V6	$34,200	7%
R-Spec	$46,800	8%

Safety Checklist

Crash Tests:
  Frontal . . . . –
  Side . . . . –
Airbags:
  Head . . . . Fr. & Rr. Roof Curtain
  Torso. . . . . Fr. & Rr. Pelvis/Torso from Seat
  Pelvis . . . . .Front Pelvis/Torso from Seat
  Roll Sensing . . . . No
  Knee Bolster . . . . None
Crash Avoidance:
  Frontal Collision Warning . . . . None
  Blind Spot Detection . . . . None
  Crash Imminent Braking . . . . None
  Lane Departure Warning . . . . Optional
General:
  Auto. Crash Notification . . . . Optional
  Day Running Lamps . . . . Optional
Safety Belt/Restraint:
  Dynamic Head Restraints . . . . . . Optional Front
  Adjustable Belt . . . . Standard Front
  Pretensioners . . . . .Standard Front

Hyundai Genesis Coupe

Specifications

Drive. . . . . FWD
Engine 3.8-liter V6
Transmission . . . . .8-sp. Automatic
Tow Rating (lbs.) . . . . –
Head/Leg Room (in.) . . . . . . Very Roomy-40.4/44.3
Interior Space (cu. ft.). Roomy-109.4
Cargo Space (cu. ft.) Cramped-15.9
Wheelbase/Length (in.) 115.6/196.3

Ratings—10 Best, 1 Worst

Combo Crash Tests	9
Safety Features	7
Rollover	4
Preventive Maintenance	5
Repair Costs	3
Warranty	10
Fuel Economy	5
Complaints	–
Insurance Costs	8
OVERALL RATING	**9**

Hyundai Santa Fe

At-a-Glance

Status/Year Series Started . . . . All New/2013
Twins . . . . -
Body Styles . . . . SUV
Seating 5
Anti-Theft Device . Std. Pass. Immobil. & Active Alarm
Parking Index Rating . . . . Average
Where Made . . . . Montgomery, AL
Fuel Factor . . . .
  MPG Rating (city/hwy) Average-21/29
  Driving Range (mi.) Long-432
  Fuel Type . . . . .Regular
  Annual Fuel Cost . . . . Average-$2,146
  Gas Guzzler Tax . . . . .No
  Greenhouse Gas Emissions (tons/yr.) High-8.7
  Barrels of Oil Used per year High-15.7

How the Competition Rates

Competitors	Rating	Pg.
Acura MDX	8	82
Nissan Rogue	5	220
Toyota RAV4		251

Price Range	Retail	Markup
Sport 2.4L	$24,450	4%
Sport 2.0L	$27,700	5%
Sport 2.0L AWD	$29,450	5%

Hyundai Santa Fe

Safety Checklist

Crash Tests:
  Frontal . . . . Very Good
  Side . . . . Good
Airbags:
  Head . . . . Fr. & Rr. Roof Curtain
  Torso . . . . .Front Pelvis/Torso from Seat
  Pelvis . . . . .Front Pelvis/Torso from Seat
  Roll Sensing . . . . .Yes
  Knee Bolster . . . . Standard Driver
Crash Avoidance:
  Frontal Collision Warning . . . . None
  Blind Spot Detection . . . . Optional
  Crash Imminent Braking . . . . None
  Lane Departure Warning . . . . None
General:
  Auto. Crash Notification . . . . Optional
  Day Running Lamps . . . . None
Safety Belt/Restraint:
  Dynamic Head Restraints . . . . None
  Adjustable Belt . . . . .Standard Front
  Pretensioners . . . . .Standard Front

Hyundai Santa Fe

Specifications

Drive . . . . FWD
Engine 2.4-liter I4
Transmission . . . . .6-sp. Automatic
Tow Rating (lbs.) . . . . Very Low-2000
Head/Leg Room (in.) Cramped-39.6/41.3
Interior Space (cu. ft.) . . . . Very Roomy-146.6
Cargo Space (cu. ft.) . . . . Very Roomy-34.2
Wheelbase/Length (in.) 110.2/193.1

Hyundai Sonata

Hyundai Sonata

Ratings—10 Best, 1 Worst

Combo Crash Tests	8
Safety Features	5
Rollover	9
Preventive Maintenance	6
Repair Costs	9
Warranty	10
Fuel Economy	8
Complaints	1
Insurance Costs	1
OVERALL RATING	**9**

Hyundai Sonata

At-a-Glance

Status/Year Series Started	Unchanged/2011
Twins	-
Body Styles	Sedan
Seating	5
Anti-Theft Device	Std. Pass. Immobil. & Active Alarm
Parking Index Rating	Average
Where Made	Montgomery, AL
Fuel Factor	
MPG Rating (city/hwy)	Good-24/35
Driving Range (mi.)	Very Long-517
Fuel Type	Regular
Annual Fuel Cost	Low-$1,841
Gas Guzzler Tax	No
Greenhouse Gas Emissions (tons/yr.)	Average-6.5
Barrels of Oil Used per year	Average-11.8

How the Competition Rates

Competitors	Rating	Pg.
Mazda Mazda6	4	192
Toyota Camry	4	243
Volkswagen Passat	9	262

Price Range	Retail	Markup
GLS	$20,995	4%
SE	$23,345	6%
Limited	$25,845	7%
Limited Turbo	$27,595	7%

Safety Checklist

Crash Tests:
Frontal . . . . Good
Side . . . . Very Good
Airbags:
Head . . . . Fr. & Rr. Roof Curtain
Torso . . . . Front Pelvis/Torso from Seat
Pelvis . . . . Front Pelvis/Torso from Seat
Roll Sensing . . . . No
Knee Bolster . . . . None
Crash Avoidance:
Frontal Collision Warning . . . . None
Blind Spot Detection . . . . None
Crash Imminent Braking . . . . None
Lane Departure Warning . . . . None
General:
Auto. Crash Notification . . . . Optional
Day Running Lamps . . . . Standard
Safety Belt/Restraint:
Dynamic Head Restraints . . . . . . Standard Front
Adjustable Belt . . . . Standard Front
Pretensioners . . . . Standard Front

Hyundai Sonata

Specifications

Drive	FWD
Engine	2.4-liter I4
Transmission	6-sp. Automatic
Tow Rating (lbs.)	–
Head/Leg Room (in.)	Very Roomy-40/45.5
Interior Space (cu. ft.)	Roomy-103.8
Cargo Space (cu. ft.)	Average-16.4
Wheelbase/Length (in.)	110/189.8

Ratings—10 Best, 1 Worst	Tucson	Sportage
Combo Crash Tests	4	6
Safety Features	6	5
Rollover	3	4
Preventive Maintenance	5	5
Repair Costs	9	8
Warranty	10	7
Fuel Economy	5	5
Complaints	6	5
Insurance Costs	5	5
OVERALL RATING	**7**	**7**

Hyundai Tucson

Kia Sportage

At-a-Glance

Status/Year Series Started. Unchanged/2010
Twins . . . . Kia Sportage
Body Styles . . . . SUV
Seating 5
Anti-Theft Device . . . . Opt. Active Alarm
Parking Index Rating . . . . .Very Easy
Where Made. . . . . Ulsan, South Korea
Fuel Factor. . . . .
  MPG Rating (city/hwy) Average-22/29
  Driving Range (mi.) Short-378
  Fuel Type. . . . . .Regular
  Annual Fuel Cost . . . . Average-$2,085
  Gas Guzzler Tax . . . . .No
  Greenhouse Gas Emissions (tons/yr.). . Average-7.3
  Barrels of Oil Used per year Average-13.2

How the Competition Rates

Competitors	Rating	Pg.
Ford Escape	7	136
Honda CR-V	7	150
Toyota RAV4		251

Price Range	Retail	Markup
GL	$20,245	4%
GLS	$22,595	4%
Limited AWD	$26,945	5%

Safety Checklist

Crash Tests:
  Frontal. . . . . Poor
  Side. . . . . Poor

Airbags:
  Head . . . . Fr. & Rr. Roof Curtain
  Torso. . . . . .Front Pelvis/Torso from Seat
  Pelvis . . . . .Front Pelvis/Torso from Seat
  Roll Sensing . . . . .Yes
  Knee Bolster . . . . None

Crash Avoidance:
  Frontal Collision Warning . . . . None
  Blind Spot Detection . . . . None
  Crash Imminent Braking . . . . None
  Lane Departure Warning . . . . None

General:
  Auto. Crash Notification . . . . None
  Day Running Lamps . . . . None

Safety Belt/Restraint:
  Dynamic Head Restraints. . . . . .Standard Front
  Adjustable Belt . . . . .Standard Front
  Pretensioners . . . . .Standard Front

Hyundai Tucson

Specifications

Drive. . . . . FWD
Engine 2.4-liter I4
Transmission . . . . .6-sp. Automatic
Tow Rating (lbs.) . . . . Very Low-2000
Head/Leg Room (in.) Average-39.4/42.1
Interior Space (cu. ft.). Average-101.9
Cargo Space (cu. ft.) Roomy-25.7
Wheelbase/Length (in.) 103.9/173.2

Hyundai Veloster

Ratings—10 Best, 1 Worst

Combo Crash Tests	–
Safety Features	3
Rollover	9
Preventive Maintenance	–
Repair Costs	–
Warranty	10
Fuel Economy	9
Complaints	1
Insurance Costs	1
OVERALL RATING	**–**

Hyundai Veloster

At-a-Glance

Status/Year Series Started........ Unchanged/2012
Twins . . . . -
Body Styles . . . . Hatchback
Seating 4
Anti-Theft Device . Std. Pass. Immobil. & Active Alarm
Parking Index Rating . . . . .Very Easy
Where Made. . . . . Ulsan, South Korea
Fuel Factor . . . .
  MPG Rating (city/hwy) . . . . Very Good-28/37
  Driving Range (mi.) Long-415
  Fuel Type. . . . . .Regular
  Annual Fuel Cost . . . . Very Low-$1,636
  Gas Guzzler Tax . . . . .No
  Greenhouse Gas Emissions (tons/yr.). Low-5.9
  Barrels of Oil Used per year Low-10.6

How the Competition Rates

Competitors	Rating	Pg.
Chevrolet Sonic	10	118
Mini Cooper		203
Scion tC	8	229

Price Range

	Retail	Markup
Base Manual	$17,450	4%
Base Automatic	$18,700	4%
Turbo Manual	$21,950	5%
Turbo Automatic	$22,950	5%

Safety Checklist

Crash Tests:
  Frontal. . . . .–
  Side. . . . .–
Airbags:
  Head . . . . Fr. & Rr. Roof Curtain
  Torso. . . . . .Front Pelvis/Torso from Seat
  Pelvis . . . . .Front Pelvis/Torso from Seat
  Roll Sensing . . . . No
  Knee Bolster . . . . None
Crash Avoidance:
  Frontal Collision Warning . . . . None
  Blind Spot Detection . . . . None
  Crash Imminent Braking. . . . . None
  Lane Departure Warning . . . . None
General:
  Auto. Crash Notification . . . . Optional
  Day Running Lamps . . . . None
Safety Belt/Restraint:
  Dynamic Head Restraints. . . . . None
  Adjustable Belt . . . . None
  Pretensioners . . . . .Standard Front

Hyundai Veloster

Specifications

Drive. . . . . FWD
Engine 1.6-liter I4
Transmission 6-sp.Manual
Tow Rating (lbs.) . . . . –
Head/Leg Room (in.) Roomy-39/43.9
Interior Space (cu. ft.). . . . . .Very Cramped-89.8
Cargo Space (cu. ft.) Cramped-15.5
Wheelbase/Length (in.) 104.3/166.2

Infiniti EX

Ratings—10 Best, 1 Worst

Combo Crash Tests	–
Safety Features	6
Rollover	6
Preventive Maintenance	9
Repair Costs	5
Warranty	6
Fuel Economy	2
Complaints	5
Insurance Costs	8
OVERALL RATING	–

Infiniti EX

Infiniti EX

At-a-Glance

```
Status/Year Series Started........ Unchanged/2008
Twins . . . . . . . . . . . . . . . . . . . . . . . . . . . . . . . . . -
Body Styles . . . . . . . . . . . . . . . . . . . . . . . . . . SUV
Seating . . . . . . . . . . . . . . . . . . . . . . . . . . . . . . . 5
Anti-Theft Device . . . . . . Std. Pass. Immobil. & Alarm
Parking Index Rating . . . . . . . . . . . . . . . . . . . Easy
Where Made. . . . . . . . . . . . . . . . . . . Tochigi, Japan
Fuel Factor . . . . . . . . . . . . . . . . . . . . . . . . . . . . .
  MPG Rating (city/hwy) . . . . . . . . . Very Poor-17/25
  Driving Range (mi.) . . . . . . . . . . . . .Average-409
  Fuel Type. . . . . . . . . . . . . . . . . . . . . .Premium
  Annual Fuel Cost . . . . . . . . . . . . Very High-$2,817
  Gas Guzzler Tax . . . . . . . . . . . . . . . . . . . . . .No
  Greenhouse Gas Emissions (tons/yr.) . . . . . High-9.2
  Barrels of Oil Used per year . . . . . . . . . . High-16.5
```

How the Competition Rates

Competitors	Rating	Pg.
Audi Q5		92
Subaru Legacy	3	236
Volkswagen Passat	9	262

Price Range

	Retail	Markup
Base RWD	$36,350	8%
Base AWD	$37,750	8%
Journey RWD	$38,650	8%
Journey AWD	$40,050	8%

Safety Checklist

```
Crash Tests:
  Frontal. . . . . . . . . . . . . . . . . . . . . . . . . . . .–
  Side. . . . . . . . . . . . . . . . . . . . . . . . . . . . . .–
Airbags:
  Head . . . . . . . . . . . . . . . Fr. & Rr. Roof Curtain
  Torso. . . . . . . . . . .Front Pelvis/Torso from Seat
  Pelvis . . . . . . . . .Front Pelvis/Torso from Seat
  Roll Sensing . . . . . . . . . . . . . . . . . . . . . . . No
  Knee Bolster . . . . . . . . . . . . . . . . . . . . . None
Crash Avoidance:
  Frontal Collision Warning . . . . . . . . . . Optional
  Blind Spot Detection . . . . . . . . . . . . . . Optional
  Crash Imminent Braking . . . . . . . . . . . Optional
  Lane Departure Warning . . . . . . . . . . Optional
General:
  Auto. Crash Notification . . . . . . . . . . . . . None
  Day Running Lamps . . . . . . . . . . . . . . . . None
Safety Belt/Restraint:
  Dynamic Head Restraints . . . . . Standard Front
  Adjustable Belt . . . . . . . . . . . . Standard Front
  Pretensioners . . . . . . . . . . . . . . Standard Front
```

Infiniti EX

Specifications

```
Drive. . . . . . . . . . . . . . . . . . . . . . . . . . . . . . AWD
Engine . . . . . . . . . . . . . . . . . . . . . . . .3.7-liter V6
Transmission . . . . . . . . . . . . . . . .7-sp. Automatic
Tow Rating (lbs.) . . . . . . . . . . . . . . . . . . . . . . . –
Head/Leg Room (in.) . . . . . Very Roomy-40.5/44.3
Interior Space (cu. ft.). . . . . . . . . . . Roomy-107.1
Cargo Space (cu. ft.) . . . . . . . . . . . . Average-18.6
Wheelbase/Length (in.) . . . . . . . . . . .110.2/182.3
```

164

Ratings—10 Best, 1 Worst

Combo Crash Tests	–
Safety Features	8
Rollover	4
Preventive Maintenance	8
Repair Costs	1
Warranty	6
Fuel Economy	2
Complaints	9
Insurance Costs	8
OVERALL RATING	–

Infiniti FX

Infiniti FX

At-a-Glance

Status/Year Series Started	Unchanged/2009
Twins	-
Body Styles	SUV
Seating	5
Anti-Theft Device	Std. Pass. Immobil. & Alarm
Parking Index Rating	Average
Where Made	Tochigi, Japan
Fuel Factor	
MPG Rating (city/hwy)	Very Poor-16/22
Driving Range (mi.)	Long-434
Fuel Type	Premium
Annual Fuel Cost	Very High-$3,068
Gas Guzzler Tax	No
Greenhouse Gas Emissions (tons/yr.)	Very High-10.2
Barrels of Oil Used per year	Very High-18.3

How the Competition Rates

Competitors	Rating	Pg.
BMW X5	6	100
Mercedes-Benz M-Class		200
Volkswagen Touareg		265

Price Range	Retail	Markup
35 Base RWD	$44,300	8%
35 Base AWD	$45,750	8%
35 Limited Edition AWD	$52,750	8%
50 AWD	$60,650	8%

Safety Checklist

Crash Tests:
Frontal . . . . –
Side . . . . –

Airbags:
Head . . . . Fr. & Rr. Roof Curtain
Torso . . . . Front Pelvis/Torso from Seat
Pelvis . . . . Front Pelvis/Torso from Seat
Roll Sensing . . . . Yes
Knee Bolster . . . . None

Crash Avoidance:
Frontal Collision Warning . . . . Optional
Blind Spot Detection . . . . None
Crash Imminent Braking . . . . Optional
Lane Departure Warning . . . . Optional

General:
Auto. Crash Notification . . . . None
Day Running Lamps . . . . None

Safety Belt/Restraint:
Dynamic Head Restraints . . . . . Standard Front
Adjustable Belt . . . . Standard Front
Pretensioners . . . . Standard Front

Infiniti FX

Specifications

Drive	AWD
Engine	3.7-liter V6
Transmission	7-sp. Automatic
Tow Rating (lbs.)	Very Low-2000
Head/Leg Room (in.)	Very Roomy-39.3/44.7
Interior Space (cu. ft.)	Average-102.5
Cargo Space (cu. ft.)	Roomy-24.8
Wheelbase/Length (in.)	113.6/191.3

Ratings—10 Best, 1 Worst

Combo Crash Tests	–
Safety Features	4
Rollover	7
Preventive Maintenance	9
Repair Costs	2
Warranty	6
Fuel Economy	4
Complaints	9
Insurance Costs	8
OVERALL RATING	**–**

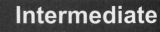
Infiniti G

Infiniti G

At-a-Glance

Status/Year Series Started	Unchanged/2007
Twins	-
Body Styles	Sedan, Coupe, Convertible
Seating	5
Anti-Theft Device	Std. Pass. Immobil. & Alarm
Parking Index Rating	Easy
Where Made	Tochigi, Japan
Fuel Factor	
MPG Rating (city/hwy)	Poor-19/27
Driving Range (mi.)	Long-439
Fuel Type	Premium
Annual Fuel Cost	High-$2,552
Gas Guzzler Tax	No
Greenhouse Gas Emissions (tons/yr.)	High-9.1
Barrels of Oil Used per year	High-16.5

How the Competition Rates

Competitors	Rating	Pg.
Acura TL	5	84
Cadillac CTS	9	107
Lexus GS		184

Price Range	Retail	Markup
25	$32,400	8%
37 Journey	$36,900	8%
37x AWD	$38,500	8%
37 Sport Convertible	$52,000	8%

Safety Checklist

Crash Tests:
Frontal	–
Side	–

Airbags:
Head	Fr. & Rr. Roof Curtain
Torso	Front Pelvis/Torso from Seat
Pelvis	Front Pelvis/Torso from Seat
Roll Sensing	No
Knee Bolster	None

Crash Avoidance:
Frontal Collision Warning	No
Blind Spot Detection	None
Crash Imminent Braking	None
Lane Departure Warning	None

General:
Auto. Crash Notification	None
Day Running Lamps	None

Safety Belt/Restraint:
Dynamic Head Restraints	Standard Front
Adjustable Belt	Standard Front
Pretensioners	Standard Front

Infiniti G

Specifications

Drive	RWD
Engine	3.7-liter V6
Transmission	7-sp. Automatic
Tow Rating (lbs.)	–
Head/Leg Room (in.)	Very Roomy-40.5/43.9
Interior Space (cu. ft.)	Average-99
Cargo Space (cu. ft.)	Cramped-13.5
Wheelbase/Length (in.)	112.2/187.9

Ratings—10 Best, 1 Worst

Combo Crash Tests	5
Safety Features	8
Rollover	3
Preventive Maintenance	8
Repair Costs	1
Warranty	6
Fuel Economy	3
Complaints	–
Insurance Costs	5
OVERALL RATING	**5**

Infiniti JX

Infiniti JX

At-a-Glance

Status/Year Series Started . . . . All New/2013
Twins . . . . .Nissan Pathfinder
Body Styles . . . . SUV
Seating 7
Anti-Theft Device . . . . . . Std. Pass. Immobil. & Alarm
Parking Index Rating . . . . Hard
Where Made. . . . . Smyrna, TN
Fuel Factor . . . .
 MPG Rating (city/hwy) Poor-18/23
 Driving Range (mi.) Average-389
 Fuel Type . . . . .Premium
 Annual Fuel Cost . . . . .Very High-$2,804
 Gas Guzzler Tax . . . . .No
 Greenhouse Gas Emissions (tons/yr.) High-9.1
 Barrels of Oil Used per year High-16.5

How the Competition Rates

Competitors	Rating	Pg.
Acura MDX	8	82
Ford Explorer	6	138
Volkswagen Touareg		265

Price Range

Price Range	Retail	Markup
FWD	$40,450	8%
AWD	$41,550	8%

Safety Checklist

Crash Tests:
 Frontal. . . . . .Poor
 Side. . . . . Good
Airbags:
 Head . . . . Fr. & Rr. Roof Curtain
 Torso. . . . . .Front Pelvis/Torso from Seat
 Pelvis . . . . .Front Pelvis/Torso from Seat
 Roll Sensing . . . . .Yes
 Knee Bolster . . . . None
Crash Avoidance:
 Frontal Collision Warning . . . . Optional
 Blind Spot Detection . . . . Optional
 Crash Imminent Braking . . . . Optional
 Lane Departure Warning . . . . Optional
General:
 Auto. Crash Notification . . . . Optional
 Day Running Lamps . . . . None
Safety Belt/Restraint:
 Dynamic Head Restraints . . . . None
 Adjustable Belt . . . . . .Standard Front and Rear
 Pretensioners . . . .

Infiniti JX

Specifications

Drive. . . . . AWD
Engine 3.5-liter V6
Transmission . . . . .CVT
Tow Rating (lbs.) Low-3500
Head/Leg Room (in.) Roomy-40.7/42.3
Interior Space (cu. ft.). . . . . Very Roomy-149.8
Cargo Space (cu. ft.) Cramped-15.8
Wheelbase/Length (in.) 114.2/196.4

Infiniti M

Ratings—10 Best, 1 Worst

Combo Crash Tests	6
Safety Features	8
Rollover	7
Preventive Maintenance	8
Repair Costs	1
Warranty	6
Fuel Economy	3
Complaints	1
Insurance Costs	8
OVERALL RATING	**6**

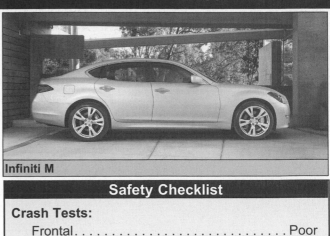

Infiniti M

Infiniti M

Infiniti M

At-a-Glance

Status/Year Series Started Unchanged/2011
Twins . . . . -
Body Styles . . . . .Sedan
Seating 5
Anti-Theft Device . . . . . . Std. Pass. Immobil. & Alarm
Parking Index Rating . . . . Average
Where Made . . . . Tochigi, Japan
Fuel Factor . . . .
  MPG Rating (city/hwy) Poor-18/26
  Driving Range (mi.) Long-418
  Fuel Type . . . . .Premium
  Annual Fuel Cost . . . . High-$2,678
  Gas Guzzler Tax . . . . .No
  Greenhouse Gas Emissions (tons/yr.) High-8.7
  Barrels of Oil Used per year High-15.7

How the Competition Rates

Competitors	Rating	Pg.
BMW 7 Series		97
Jaguar XF		170
Volvo S80		268

Price Range	Retail	Markup
M37	$48,200	8%
M35H	$54,200	8%
M56	$60,600	8%
M56x AWD	$63,100	8%

Safety Checklist

Crash Tests:
  Frontal . . . . .Poor
  Side . . . . Very Good
Airbags:
  Head . . . . Fr. & Rr. Roof Curtain
  Torso . . . . .Front Pelvis/Torso from Seat
  Pelvis . . . . .Front Pelvis/Torso from Seat
  Roll Sensing . . . . No
  Knee Bolster . . . . None
Crash Avoidance:
  Frontal Collision Warning . . . . Optional
  Blind Spot Detection . . . . Optional
  Crash Imminent Braking . . . . Optional
  Lane Departure Warning . . . . Optional
General:
  Auto. Crash Notification . . . . Optional
  Day Running Lamps . . . . None
Safety Belt/Restraint:
  Dynamic Head Restraints . . . . . .Standard Front
  Adjustable Belt . . . . .Standard Front
  Pretensioners . . . . .Standard Front

Infiniti M

Specifications

Drive . . . . RWD
Engine 3.7-liter V6
Transmission . . . . .7-sp. Automatic
Tow Rating (lbs.) . . . . –
Head/Leg Room (in.) . . . . .Very Roomy-39.1/44
Interior Space (cu. ft.) Roomy-103.6
Cargo Space (cu. ft.) Cramped-14.9
Wheelbase/Length (in.) 114.2/194.7

Ratings—10 Best, 1 Worst	
Combo Crash Tests	–
Safety Features	8
Rollover	1
Preventive Maintenance	4
Repair Costs	3
Warranty	6
Fuel Economy	1
Complaints	6
Insurance Costs	10
OVERALL RATING	**–**

Infiniti QX56

Infiniti QX56

At-a-Glance

Status/Year Series Started	Unchanged/2011
Twins	-
Body Styles	SUV
Seating	7/8
Anti-Theft Device	Std. Pass. Immobil. & Alarm
Parking Index Rating	Very Hard
Where Made	Kyushu, Japan
Fuel Factor	
MPG Rating (city/hwy)	Very Poor-14/20
Driving Range (mi.)	Long-421
Fuel Type	Premium
Annual Fuel Cost	Very High-$3,457
Gas Guzzler Tax	No
Greenhouse Gas Emissions (tons/yr.)	Very High-11.5
Barrels of Oil Used per year	Very High-20.6

How the Competition Rates

Competitors	Rating	Pg.
Audi Q7		93
Land Rover Range Rover		180
Mercedes-Benz GL-Class		198

Price Range	Retail	Markup
2WD	$58,700	8%
4WD	$61,800	8%

Safety Checklist

Crash Tests:
Frontal . . . . –
Side . . . . –

Airbags:
Head . . . . Fr. & Rr. Roof Curtain
Torso . . . . Front Pelvis/Torso from Seat
Pelvis . . . . Front Pelvis/Torso from Seat
Roll Sensing . . . . Yes
Knee Bolster . . . . None

Crash Avoidance:
Frontal Collision Warning . . . . Optional
Blind Spot Detection . . . . Optional
Crash Imminent Braking . . . . Optional
Lane Departure Warning . . . . Optional

General:
Auto. Crash Notification . . . . None
Day Running Lamps . . . . None

Safety Belt/Restraint:
Dynamic Head Restraints . . . . . . Standard Front
Adjustable Belt . . . . Standard Front & Rear
Pretensioners . . . . Standard Front

Infiniti QX56

Specifications

Drive	4WD
Engine	5.6-liter V8
Transmission	7-sp. Automatic
Tow Rating (lbs.)	Very High-8500
Head/Leg Room (in.)	Very Cramped-39.9/39.6
Interior Space (cu. ft.)	Very Roomy-151.3
Cargo Space (cu. ft.)	Average-16.6
Wheelbase/Length (in.)	121.1/208.3

Ratings—10 Best, 1 Worst

Combo Crash Tests	–
Safety Features	6
Rollover	8
Preventive Maintenance	1
Repair Costs	3
Warranty	3
Fuel Economy	3
Complaints	1
Insurance Costs	8
OVERALL RATING	**–**

Jaguar XF

Jaguar XF

At-a-Glance

Status/Year Series Started	Unchanged/2009
Twins	-
Body Styles	Sedan
Seating	5
Anti-Theft Device	Std. Pass. Immobil. & Alarm
Parking Index Rating	Hard
Where Made	Castle Bromwich, UK
Fuel Factor	
MPG Rating (city/hwy)	Poor-18/28
Driving Range (mi.)	Average-395
Fuel Type	Premium
Annual Fuel Cost	High-$2,609
Gas Guzzler Tax	No
Greenhouse Gas Emissions (tons/yr.)	High-8.7
Barrels of Oil Used per year	High-15.7

How the Competition Rates

Competitors	Rating	Pg.
Audi A7		90
BMW 7 Series		97
Mercedes-Benz S-Class		201

Price Range	Retail	Markup
2.0L I4T	$46,975	9%
3.0L SC	$50,000	9%
Supercharged	$68,100	9%
XFR	$83,200	9%

Safety Checklist

Crash Tests:
Frontal	–
Side	–

Airbags:
Head	Fr & Rr. Roof Curtain
Torso	Front Pelvis/Torso from Seat
Pelvis	Front Pelvis/Torso from Seat
Roll Sensing	No
Knee Bolster	None

Crash Avoidance:
Frontal Collision Warning	None
Blind Spot Detection	Optional
Crash Imminent Braking	Optional
Lane Departure Warning	None

General:
Auto. Crash Notification	None
Day Running Lamps	Standard

Safety Belt/Restraint:
Dynamic Head Restraints	Standard Front
Adjustable Belt	Standard Front
Pretensioners	Standard Front

Jaguar XF

Specifications

Drive	RWD
Engine	3.0-liter V6
Transmission	8-sp. Automatic
Tow Rating (lbs.)	–
Head/Leg Room (in.)	Very Cramped-37.1/41.5
Interior Space (cu. ft.)	Cramped-95
Cargo Space (cu. ft.)	Average-17.7
Wheelbase/Length (in.)	114.5/195.3

Ratings—10 Best, 1 Worst	
Combo Crash Tests	1
Safety Features	4
Rollover	2
Preventive Maintenance	2
Repair Costs	10
Warranty	3
Fuel Economy	5
Complaints	3
Insurance Costs	5
OVERALL RATING	**1**

Jeep Compass

At-a-Glance

Status/Year Series Started	Unchanged/2007
Twins	-
Body Styles	SUV
Seating	5
Anti-Theft Device	Std. Pass. Immobil.
Parking Index Rating	Easy
Where Made	Belvidere, IL
Fuel Factor	
MPG Rating (city/hwy)	Average-21/27
Driving Range (mi.)	Very Short-317
Fuel Type	Regular
Annual Fuel Cost	Average-$2,205
Gas Guzzler Tax	No
Greenhouse Gas Emissions (tons/yr.)	High-7.6
Barrels of Oil Used per year	High-13.7

How the Competition Rates

Competitors	Rating	Pg.
Acura RDX		83
Honda CR-V	7	150
Subaru Forester	3	234

Price Range	Retail	Markup
Sport FWD	$19,395	1%
Sport 4WD	$21,245	2%
Latitude FWD	$21,595	3%
Limited 4WD	$26,145	4%

Jeep Compass

Safety Checklist

Crash Tests:
Frontal .... Very Poor
Side .... Very Poor

Airbags:
Head .... Fr & Rr. Roof Curtain
Torso .... Opt. Front Torso from Seat
Pelvis .... None
Roll Sensing .... Yes
Knee Bolster .... None

Crash Avoidance:
Frontal Collision Warning .... None
Blind Spot Detection .... None
Crash Imminent Braking .... None
Lane Departure Warning .... None

General:
Auto. Crash Notification .... None
Day Running Lamps .... Optional

Safety Belt/Restraint:
Dynamic Head Restraints ...... Standard Front
Adjustable Belt .... Standard Front
Pretensioners .... Standard Front

Jeep Compass

Specifications

Drive	FWD
Engine	2.4-liter I4
Transmission	CVT2
Tow Rating (lbs.)	Very Low-1000
Head/Leg Room (in.)	Average-40.7/40.6
Interior Space (cu. ft.)	Average-101.3
Cargo Space (cu. ft.)	Roomy-22.7
Wheelbase/Length (in.)	103.7/175.1

Ratings—10 Best, 1 Worst

Combo Crash Tests	6
Safety Features	8
Rollover	2
Preventive Maintenance	2
Repair Costs	6
Warranty	3
Fuel Economy	2
Complaints	7
Insurance Costs	8
OVERALL RATING	**5**

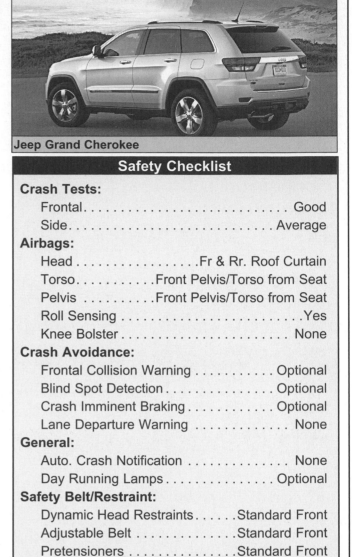

Jeep Grand Cherokee

Jeep Grand Cherokee

At-a-Glance

Status/Year Series Started........ Unchanged/2011
Twins .... -
Body Styles .... SUV
Seating 5
Anti-Theft Device ...... Std. Pass. Immobil. & Alarm
Parking Index Rating .... Average
Where Made........................ Detroit, MI
Fuel Factor..
  MPG Rating (city/hwy) .... Very Poor-17/23
  Driving Range (mi.) .... Very Long-474
  Fuel Type............................... Regular
  Annual Fuel Cost .... High-$2,671
  Gas Guzzler Tax ....No
  Greenhouse Gas Emissions (tons/yr.) Very High-9.6
  Barrels of Oil Used per year High-17.3

How the Competition Rates

Competitors	Rating	Pg.
Chevrolet Tahoe	8	120
Ford Expedition	4	137
Toyota Sequoia		252

Price Range	Retail	Markup
Laredo 2WD	$27,494	2%
Limited	$39,295	6%
Overland	$43,595	7%
SRT8	$59,995	5%

Safety Checklist

Crash Tests:
  Frontal........................... Good
  Side................................ Average
Airbags:
  Head .... Fr & Rr. Roof Curtain
  Torso.......... Front Pelvis/Torso from Seat
  Pelvis .... Front Pelvis/Torso from Seat
  Roll Sensing ....Yes
  Knee Bolster .... None
Crash Avoidance:
  Frontal Collision Warning .... Optional
  Blind Spot Detection .... Optional
  Crash Imminent Braking .... Optional
  Lane Departure Warning .... None
General:
  Auto. Crash Notification .... None
  Day Running Lamps............... Optional
Safety Belt/Restraint:
  Dynamic Head Restraints...... Standard Front
  Adjustable Belt .... Standard Front
  Pretensioners .... Standard Front

Jeep Grand Cherokee

Specifications

Drive................................. FWD
Engine 3.6-liter V6
Transmission .... 5-sp. Auto. w/ Overdrive
Tow Rating (lbs.) Average-5000
Head/Leg Room (in.) Cramped-39.9/40.3
Interior Space (cu. ft.)............ Roomy-105.4
Cargo Space (cu. ft.) .... Very Roomy-35.1
Wheelbase/Length (in.) 114.8/189.9

Ratings—10 Best, 1 Worst

Combo Crash Tests	1
Safety Features	4
Rollover	1
Preventive Maintenance	2
Repair Costs	10
Warranty	3
Fuel Economy	4
Complaints	2
Insurance Costs	5
OVERALL RATING	**1**

Jeep Patriot

Jeep Patriot

Jeep Patriot

At-a-Glance

Status/Year Series Started	Unchanged/2007
Twins	-
Body Styles	SUV
Seating	5
Anti-Theft Device	Std. Pass. Immobil.
Parking Index Rating	Easy
Where Made	Belvidere, IL
Fuel Factor	
MPG Rating (city/hwy)	Poor-21/26
Driving Range (mi.)	Very Short-310
Fuel Type	Regular
Annual Fuel Cost	Average-$2,238
Gas Guzzler Tax	No
Greenhouse Gas Emissions (tons/yr.)	High-8.0
Barrels of Oil Used per year	High-14.3

How the Competition Rates

Competitors	Rating	Pg.
Ford Escape	7	136
Mitsubishi Outlander Sport	4	207
Nissan Juke	5	214

Price Range

Price Range	Retail	Markup
Sport 2WD	$15,995	1%
Sport 4WD	$17,845	1%
Latitude 4WD	$22,800	3%
Limited 4WD	$25,430	4%

Safety Checklist

Crash Tests:
Frontal	Very Poor
Side	Poor

Airbags:
Head	Fr & Rr. Roof Curtain
Torso	Opt. Front Torso from Seat
Pelvis	None
Roll Sensing	Yes
Knee Bolster	None

Crash Avoidance:
Frontal Collision Warning	None
Blind Spot Detection	None
Crash Imminent Braking	None
Lane Departure Warning	None

General:
Auto. Crash Notification	None
Day Running Lamps	Optional

Safety Belt/Restraint:
Dynamic Head Restraints	Standard Front
Adjustable Belt	Standard Front
Pretensioners	Standard Front

Jeep Patriot

Specifications

Drive	4WD
Engine	2.4-liter I4
Transmission	CVT2
Tow Rating (lbs.)	Very Low-1000
Head/Leg Room (in.)	Average-41/40.6
Interior Space (cu. ft.)	Roomy-104.4
Cargo Space (cu. ft.)	Roomy-23
Wheelbase/Length (in.)	103.7/173.8

Ratings—10 Best, 1 Worst

Rating	
Combo Crash Tests	–
Safety Features	1
Rollover	1
Preventive Maintenance	4
Repair Costs	10
Warranty	3
Fuel Economy	2
Complaints	1
Insurance Costs	8

OVERALL RATING —

Jeep Wrangler

Jeep Wrangler Unlimited

Safety Checklist

Crash Tests:
Frontal . . . . . . –
Side . . . . . . –
Airbags:
Head . . . . . Opt. Head/Torso from Seat
Torso . . . . Opt. Front Head/Torso from Seat
Pelvis . . . . . None
Roll Sensing . . . . . No
Knee Bolster . . . . . None
Crash Avoidance:
Frontal Collision Warning . . . . None
Blind Spot Detection . . . . None
Crash Imminent Braking . . . . None
Lane Departure Warning . . . . None
General:
Auto. Crash Notification . . . . None
Day Running Lamps . . . . Optional
Safety Belt/Restraint:
Dynamic Head Restraints . . . . None
Adjustable Belt . . . . Standard Front
Pretensioners . . . . Standard Front

At-a-Glance

Status/Year Series Started Unchanged/2007
Twins . . . . . -
Body Styles . . . . SUV
Seating 4
Anti-Theft Device . . . . Std. Pass. Immobil. & Alarm
Parking Index Rating . . . . Easy
Where Made . . . . Toledo, OH
Fuel Factor . . . . .
MPG Rating (city/hwy) . . . . Very Poor-17/21
Driving Range (mi.) . . . . Very Short-346
Fuel Type . . . . Regular
Annual Fuel Cost . . . . Very High-$2,767
Gas Guzzler Tax . . . . No
Greenhouse Gas Emissions (tons/yr.) Very High-10.2
Barrels of Oil Used per year . . . . Very High-18.3

How the Competition Rates

Competitors	Rating	Pg.
Nissan Xterra		224
Subaru Forester	3	234
Toyota FJ Cruiser		245

Price Range

Price Range	Retail	Markup
Sport	$22,195	3%
Unlimited Sport	$25,695	3%
Rubicon	$30,495	6%
Unlimited Rubicon	$33,995	6%

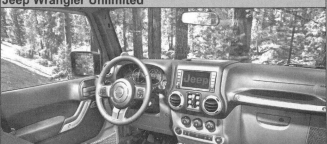
Jeep Wrangler Unlimited

Specifications

Drive 4WD
Engine 3.6-liter V6
Transmission . . . . 6-sp. Manual w/ Overdrive
Tow Rating (lbs.) . . . . Very Low-2000
Head/Leg Room (in.) Roomy-41.3/41
Interior Space (cu. ft.) . . . . Very Cramped-88.4
Cargo Space (cu. ft.) Cramped-12.8
Wheelbase/Length (in.) 95.4/152.8

Ratings—10 Best, 1 Worst

Combo Crash Tests	2
Safety Features	4
Rollover	8
Preventive Maintenance	9
Repair Costs	10
Warranty	7
Fuel Economy	9
Complaints	7
Insurance Costs	1
OVERALL RATING	**7**

Kia Forte

Kia Forte

Kia Forte

At-a-Glance

```
Status/Year Series Started........ Unchanged/2010
Twins . . . . . . . . . . . . . . . . . . . . . . . . . . . . . . . . -
Body Styles . . . . . . . . . . . . Sedan, Coupe, Hatchback
Seating . . . . . . . . . . . . . . . . . . . . . . . . . . . . . . . 5
Anti-Theft Device . . . . . . . . . . . . . . . . . . . . . . . None
Parking Index Rating . . . . . . . . . . . . . . . . . Very Easy
Where Made. . . . . . . . . . . . Hwasung, South Korea
Fuel Factor . . . . . . . . . . . . . . . . . . . . . . . . . . . .
  MPG Rating (city/hwy) . . . . . . . . . Very Good-26/36
  Driving Range (mi.) . . . . . . . . . . .Average-407
  Fuel Type . . . . . . . . . . . . . . . . . . . . . .Regular
  Annual Fuel Cost . . . . . . . . . . . . Very Low-$1,731
  Gas Guzzler Tax . . . . . . . . . . . . . . . . . . . . .No
  Greenhouse Gas Emissions (tons/yr.) . . Average-6.4
  Barrels of Oil Used per year . . . . . . . Average-11.4
```

How the Competition Rates

Competitors	Rating	Pg.
Chevrolet Cruze	9	113
Honda Civic		148
Subaru Impreza	4	235

Price Range

Price Range	Retail	Markup
LX Manual	$15,400	2%
LX Automatic	$16,400	2%
EX Automatic	$17,800	5%
SX Automatic Hatchback	$19,800	5%

Safety Checklist

```
Crash Tests:
  Frontal. . . . . . . . . . . . . . . . . . . . . . . . . . . . .Poor
  Side. . . . . . . . . . . . . . . . . . . . . . . .Very Poor*
Airbags:
  Head . . . . . . . . . . . . . . . Fr. & Rr. Roof Curtain
  Torso. . . . . . . . . .Front Pelvis/Torso from Seat
  Pelvis . . . . . . . . .Front Pelvis/Torso from Seat
  Roll Sensing . . . . . . . . . . . . . . . . . . . . . . . No
  Knee Bolster . . . . . . . . . . . . . . . . . . . . . None
Crash Avoidance:
  Frontal Collision Warning . . . . . . . . . . . . None
  Blind Spot Detection . . . . . . . . . . . . . . . None
  Crash Imminent Braking . . . . . . . . . . . . . None
  Lane Departure Warning . . . . . . . . . . . . None
General:
  Auto. Crash Notification . . . . . . . . . . . . None
  Day Running Lamps . . . . . . . . . . . . . . Optional
Safety Belt/Restraint:
  Dynamic Head Restraints . . . . . .Standard Front
  Adjustable Belt . . . . . . . . . . . . .Standard Front
  Pretensioners . . . . . . . . . . . . . .Standard Front
```

Kia Forte

Specifications

```
Drive. . . . . . . . . . . . . . . . . . . . . . . . . . . . . . . FWD
Engine . . . . . . . . . . . . . . . . . . . . . 2.0-liter I4
Transmission . . . . . . . . . . . . . . . .6-sp. Manual
Tow Rating (lbs.) . . . . . . . . . . . . . . . . . . . . . . . –
Head/Leg Room (in.) . . . . . . . .Very Roomy-40/43.3
Interior Space (cu. ft.). . . . . . . . . . . .Cramped-96.8
Cargo Space (cu. ft.) . . . . . . . . . . .Cramped-14.7
Wheelbase/Length (in.) . . . . . . . . .104.3/178.3
```

*Additional injury potential in side test. See footnote 2 on page 20.

Ratings—10 Best, 1 Worst

Combo Crash Tests	7
Safety Features	2
Rollover	9
Preventive Maintenance	6
Repair Costs	7
Warranty	7
Fuel Economy	8
Complaints	3
Insurance Costs	3
OVERALL RATING	**7**

Kia Optima

At-a-Glance

Status/Year Series Started	Unchanged/2011
Twins	-
Body Styles	Sedan
Seating	5
Anti-Theft Device	Std. Pass. Immobil. & Active Alarm
Parking Index Rating	Average
Where Made	West Point, GA
Fuel Factor	
MPG Rating (city/hwy)	Good-24/35
Driving Range (mi.)	Very Long-517
Fuel Type	Regular
Annual Fuel Cost	Low-$1,841
Gas Guzzler Tax	No
Greenhouse Gas Emissions (tons/yr.)	Average-6.5
Barrels of Oil Used per year	Average-11.8

How the Competition Rates

Competitors	Rating	Pg.
Honda Accord	9	146
Nissan Altima	7	209
Toyota Camry	4	243

Price Range	Retail	Markup
LX	$21,200	5%
EX	$23,500	7%
SX	$26,800	7%
SX Limited	$30,150	7%

Kia Optima

Safety Checklist

Crash Tests:
Frontal	Very Good
Side	Poor

Airbags:
Head	Fr. & Rr. Roof Curtain
Torso	Front Pelvis/Torso from Seat
Pelvis	Front Pelvis/Torso from Seat
Roll Sensing	No
Knee Bolster	None

Crash Avoidance:
Frontal Collision Warning	None
Blind Spot Detection	None
Crash Imminent Braking	None
Lane Departure Warning	None

General:
Auto. Crash Notification	None
Day Running Lamps	None

Safety Belt/Restraint:
Dynamic Head Restraints	None
Adjustable Belt	Standard Front
Pretensioners	Standard Front

Kia Optima

Specifications

Drive	FWD
Engine	2.4-liter I4
Transmission	6-sp. Automatic
Tow Rating (lbs.)	–
Head/Leg Room (in.)	Very Roomy-40/45.5
Interior Space (cu. ft.)	Roomy-117.6
Cargo Space (cu. ft.)	Cramped-15.4
Wheelbase/Length (in.)	110/190.7

Ratings—10 Best, 1 Worst

Combo Crash Tests	4
Safety Features	2
Rollover	7
Preventive Maintenance	7
Repair Costs	10
Warranty	7
Fuel Economy	9
Complaints	10
Insurance Costs	1
OVERALL RATING	**8**

Kia Rio

Kia Rio

At-a-Glance

Status/Year Series Started. Unchanged/2012
Twins . . . . Hyundai Accent
Body Styles . . . . Sedan, Hatchback
Seating 5
Anti-Theft Device .Opt. Pass. Immobil. & Active Alarm
Parking Index Rating . . . . .Very Easy
Where Made. . . . . Hwasung, South Korea
Fuel Factor. . . . .
  MPG Rating (city/hwy) . . . . Very Good-28/36
  Driving Range (mi.) . . . . .Very Short-355
  Fuel Type. . . . . .Regular
  Annual Fuel Cost . . . . Very Low-$1,654
  Gas Guzzler Tax . . . . .No
  Greenhouse Gas Emissions (tons/yr.). Low-5.9
  Barrels of Oil Used per year Low-10.6

How the Competition Rates

Competitors	Rating	Pg.
Chevrolet Sonic	10	118
Hyundai Accent	8	156
Suzuki SX4	1	240

Price Range

Price Range	Retail	Markup
LX Manual	$13,600	2%
LX Automatic	$14,700	4%
EX Automatic	$16,500	5%
SX Automatic	$17,700	5%

Safety Checklist

Crash Tests:
  Frontal. . . . . .Poor
  Side. . . . . .Poor
Airbags:
  Head . . . . Fr. & Rr. Roof Curtain
  Torso. . . . . .Front Pelvis/Torso from Seat
  Pelvis . . . . .Front Pelvis/Torso from Seat
  Roll Sensing . . . . No
  Knee Bolster . . . . None
Crash Avoidance:
  Frontal Collision Warning . . . . None
  Blind Spot Detection . . . . None
  Crash Imminent Braking . . . . None
  Lane Departure Warning . . . . None

  Auto. Crash Notification . . . . None
  Day Running Lamps . . . . None
Safety Belt/Restraint:
  Dynamic Head Restraints . . . . None
  Adjustable Belt . . . . .Standard Front
  Pretensioners . . . . .Standard Front

Kia Rio

Specifications

Drive. . . . . FWD
Engine 1.6-liter I4
Transmission . . . . .6-sp. Automatic
Tow Rating (lbs.) . . . . –
Head/Leg Room (in.) . . . . .Very Roomy-40/43.8
Interior Space (cu. ft.). . . . . .Very Cramped-88.6
Cargo Space (cu. ft.) Cramped-13.7
Wheelbase/Length (in.) 101.2/171.9

Ratings—10 Best, 1 Worst

Combo Crash Tests	4
Safety Features	5
Rollover	3
Preventive Maintenance	5
Repair Costs	4
Warranty	7
Fuel Economy	5
Complaints	1
Insurance Costs	5
OVERALL RATING	**3**

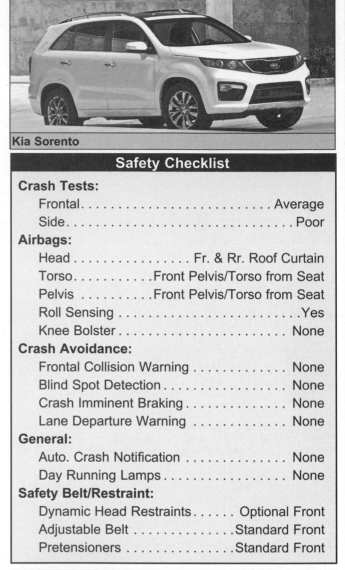
Kia Sorento

Kia Sorento

Kia Sorento

At-a-Glance

Status/Year Series Started	Unchanged/2011
Twins	-
Body Styles	SUV
Seating	5/7
Anti-Theft Device	Opt. Pass. Immobil. & Active Alarm
Parking Index Rating	Easy
Where Made	West Point, GA
Fuel Factor	
MPG Rating (city/hwy)	Average-21/29
Driving Range (mi.)	Long-432
Fuel Type	Regular
Annual Fuel Cost	Average-$2,146
Gas Guzzler Tax	No
Greenhouse Gas Emissions (tons/yr.)	High-8.3
Barrels of Oil Used per year	High-15.0

How the Competition Rates

Competitors	Rating	Pg.
Ford Edge	4	135
Nissan Rogue	5	220
Toyota Venza	3	256

Price Range

Price Range	Retail	Markup
LX I4 2WD	$23,150	3%
EX V6 2WD	$27,950	6%
EX V6 4WD	$29,650	6%
SX V6 4WD	$33,400	7%

Safety Checklist

Crash Tests:
Frontal . . . . Average
Side . . . . Poor

Airbags:
Head . . . . Fr. & Rr. Roof Curtain
Torso . . . . Front Pelvis/Torso from Seat
Pelvis . . . . Front Pelvis/Torso from Seat
Roll Sensing . . . . Yes
Knee Bolster . . . . None

Crash Avoidance:
Frontal Collision Warning . . . . None
Blind Spot Detection . . . . None
Crash Imminent Braking . . . . None
Lane Departure Warning . . . . None

General:
Auto. Crash Notification . . . . None
Day Running Lamps . . . . None

Safety Belt/Restraint:
Dynamic Head Restraints . . . . . . Optional Front
Adjustable Belt . . . . .Standard Front
Pretensioners . . . . .Standard Front

Kia Sorento

Specifications

Drive	FWD
Engine	3.5-liter V6
Transmission	6-sp. Auto. w/Overdrive
Tow Rating (lbs.)	Low-3500
Head/Leg Room (in.)	Cramped-39.2/41.3
Interior Space (cu. ft.)	Very Roomy-149.4
Cargo Space (cu. ft.)	Very Cramped-9.1
Wheelbase/Length (in.)	106.3/183.9

Ratings—10 Best, 1 Worst	
Combo Crash Tests	6
Safety Features	4
Rollover	4
Preventive Maintenance	5
Repair Costs	8
Warranty	7
Fuel Economy	7
Complaints	4
Insurance Costs	3
OVERALL RATING	**6**

Kia Soul

Kia Soul

At-a-Glance

Status/Year Series Started	Unchanged/2010
Twins	-
Body Styles	Station Wagon
Seating	5
Anti-Theft Device	None
Parking Index Rating	Very Easy
Where Made	Hwasung, South Korea
Fuel Factor	
MPG Rating (city/hwy)	Good-25/30
Driving Range (mi.)	Very Short-343
Fuel Type	Regular
Annual Fuel Cost	Low-$1,904
Gas Guzzler Tax	No
Greenhouse Gas Emissions (tons/yr.)	Average-7.3
Barrels of Oil Used per year	Average-13.2

How the Competition Rates

Competitors	Rating	Pg.
Honda Fit	4	151
Nissan Cube		212
Scion xB		230

Price Range

	Retail	Markup
Base Manual	$14,400	2%
Base Automatic	$16,200	4%
+ Automatic	$17,700	4%
Club	$19,900	5%

Safety Checklist

Crash Tests:
Frontal . . . . Average
Side . . . . Good
Airbags:
Head . . . . Fr. & Rr. Roof Curtain
Torso . . . . Front Pelvis/Torso from Seat
Pelvis . . . . Front Pelvis/Torso from Seat
Roll Sensing . . . . No
Knee Bolster . . . . None
Crash Avoidance:
Frontal Collision Warning . . . . None
Blind Spot Detection . . . . None
Crash Imminent Braking . . . . None
Lane Departure Warning . . . . None
General:
Auto. Crash Notification . . . . None
Day Running Lamps . . . . None
Safety Belt/Restraint:
Dynamic Head Restraints . . . . . . Standard Front
Adjustable Belt . . . . Standard Front
Pretensioners . . . . Standard Front

Kia Soul

Specifications

Drive	FWD
Engine	2.0-liter I4
Transmission	6-sp. Auto. w/ Overdrive
Tow Rating (lbs.)	–
Head/Leg Room (in.)	Roomy-40.2/42.1
Interior Space (cu. ft.)	Average-102.3
Cargo Space (cu. ft.)	Average-19.3
Wheelbase/Length (in.)	100.4/162.2

Ratings—10 Best, 1 Worst

Combo Crash Tests	–
Safety Features	6
Rollover	2
Preventive Maintenance	5
Repair Costs	1
Warranty	3
Fuel Economy	1
Complaints	–
Insurance Costs	10
OVERALL RATING	**–**

Land Rover Range Rover

At-a-Glance

Status/Year Series Started	All New/2013
Twins	-
Body Styles	SUV
Seating	5
Anti-Theft Device	Std. Pass. Immobil. & Alarm
Parking Index Rating	Very Hard
Where Made	Solihull, UK
Fuel Factor	
MPG Rating (city/hwy)	Very Poor-12/17
Driving Range (mi.)	Short-383
Fuel Type	Premium
Annual Fuel Cost	Very High-$4,045
Gas Guzzler Tax	No
Greenhouse Gas Emissions (tons/yr.)	Very High-12.2
Barrels of Oil Used per year	Very High-22.0

How the Competition Rates

Competitors	Rating	Pg.
Audi Q7		93
Infiniti JX	5	167
Mercedes-Benz GL-Class		198

Price Range

	Retail	Markup
HSE	$80,275	10%
HSE Lux	$84,645	10%
Supercharged	$95,670	10%
Autobiography	$126,665	10%

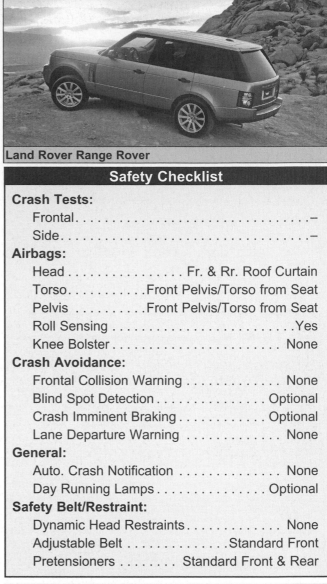

Land Rover Range Rover

Safety Checklist

Crash Tests:
- Frontal .... –
- Side .... –

Airbags:
- Head .... Fr. & Rr. Roof Curtain
- Torso .... Front Pelvis/Torso from Seat
- Pelvis .... Front Pelvis/Torso from Seat
- Roll Sensing .... Yes
- Knee Bolster .... None

Crash Avoidance:
- Frontal Collision Warning .... None
- Blind Spot Detection .... Optional
- Crash Imminent Braking .... Optional
- Lane Departure Warning .... None

General:
- Auto. Crash Notification .... None
- Day Running Lamps .... Optional

Safety Belt/Restraint:
- Dynamic Head Restraints .... None
- Adjustable Belt .... Standard Front
- Pretensioners .... Standard Front & Rear

Land Rover Range Rover

Specifications

Drive	4WD
Engine	5.0-liter V8
Transmission	8-sp. Automatic
Tow Rating (lbs.)	Very High-7716
Head/Leg Room (in.)	–
Interior Space (cu. ft.)	–
Cargo Space (cu. ft.)	Roomy-32.1
Wheelbase/Length (in.)	115/196.8

Ratings—10 Best, 1 Worst

Combo Crash Tests	–
Safety Features	8
Rollover	5
Preventive Maintenance	–
Repair Costs	–
Warranty	3
Fuel Economy	3
Complaints	–
Insurance Costs	8
OVERALL RATING	**–**

Land Rover Range Rover Evoque

At-a-Glance

Status/Year Series Started....... Unchanged/20121
Twins .... -
Body Styles .... SUV
Seating 5
Anti-Theft Device ...... Std. Pass. Immobil. & Alarm
Parking Index Rating .... Easy
Where Made................... Halewood, UK
Fuel Factor ....
  MPG Rating (city/hwy)............Poor-18/28
  Driving Range (mi.) Average-397
  Fuel Type.........................Premium
  Annual Fuel Cost .... High-$2,609
  Gas Guzzler Tax ....No
  Greenhouse Gas Emissions (tons/yr.)..... High-7.9
  Barrels of Oil Used per year High-14.3

How the Competition Rates

Competitors	Rating	Pg.
Audi Q5		92
BMW X3		99
Volkswagen Tiguan	4	264

Price Range

Price Range	Retail	Markup
Pure Plus 4 Door	$43,145	9%
Pure Premium 2 Door	$49,395	9%
Prestige Premium	$51,545	9%
Dynamic Premium 2 Door	$52,045	9%

Land Rover Range Rover Evoque

Safety Checklist

Crash Tests:
  Frontal................................–
  Side...................................–
Airbags:
  Head .... Fr. & Rr. Roof Curtain
  Torso..........Front Pelvis/Torso from Seat
  Pelvis ...... Fr. & Rr. Pelvis/Torso from Seat
  Roll Sensing ....Yes
  Knee Bolster .... Standard Driver
Crash Avoidance:
  Frontal Collision Warning .... None
  Blind Spot Detection .... Optional
  Crash Imminent Braking............. None
  Lane Departure Warning .... None
General:
  Auto. Crash Notification .... Optional
  Day Running Lamps............... Standard
Safety Belt/Restraint:
  Dynamic Head Restraints............. None
  Adjustable Belt ....Standard Front
  Pretensioners ....Standard Front

Land Rover Range Rover Evoque

Specifications

Drive.................................. AWD
Engine 2.0-liter I4
Transmission .... 6-sp. Auto. w/Overdrive
Tow Rating (lbs.) .... Very Low-1650
Head/Leg Room (in.) .... –
Interior Space (cu. ft.)................... –
Cargo Space (cu. ft.) Average-19.4
Wheelbase/Length (in.) 104.8/171.5

Ratings—10 Best, 1 Worst

Combo Crash Tests	–
Safety Features	8
Rollover	7
Preventive Maintenance	9
Repair Costs	3
Warranty	6
Fuel Economy	10
Complaints	10
Insurance Costs	5
OVERALL RATING	**–**

Lexus CT

At-a-Glance

Status/Year Series Started. Unchanged/2011
Twins . . . . -
Body Styles . . . . Hatchback
Seating 5
Anti-Theft Device Std. Pass. Immobil. & Opt. Pass. Alarm
Parking Index Rating . . . . .Very Easy
Where Made. . . . . Kyushu, Japan
Fuel Factor. . . . .
  MPG Rating (city/hwy) . . . . Very Good-43/40
  Driving Range (mi.) . . . . Very Long-495
  Fuel Type. . . . . .Regular
  Annual Fuel Cost . . . . Very Low-$1,237
  Gas Guzzler Tax . . . . .No
  Greenhouse Gas Emissions (tons/yr.). Very Low-4.4
  Barrels of Oil Used per year . . . . Very Low-7.8

How the Competition Rates

Competitors	Rating	Pg.
Audi A3		86
BMW 1 Series		94
Volkswagen Golf		260

Price Range	Retail	Markup
Base	$31,850	5%
Premium Sedan	$32,975	5%

Lexus CT

Safety Checklist

Crash Tests:
  Frontal. . . . . –
  Side. . . . . –
Airbags:
  Head . . . . Fr. & Rr. Roof Curtain
  Torso. . . . . .Front Pelvis/Torso from Seat
  Pelvis . . . . .Front Pelvis/Torso from Seat
  Roll Sensing . . . . No
  Knee Bolster . . . . .Standard Front
Crash Avoidance:
  Frontal Collision Warning . . . . None
  Blind Spot Detection . . . . None
  Crash Imminent Braking . . . . Optional
  Lane Departure Warning . . . . None
General:
  Auto. Crash Notification . . . . Standard
  Day Running Lamps . . . . Standard
Safety Belt/Restraint:
  Dynamic Head Restraints. . . . . None
  Adjustable Belt . . . . .Standard Front
  Pretensioners . . . . .Standard Front

Lexus CT

Specifications

Drive. . . . . FWD
Engine 1.8-liter I4
Transmission . . . . ECVT
Tow Rating (lbs.) . . . . –
Head/Leg Room (in.) Average-38.9/42.1
Interior Space (cu. ft.). . . . . .Very Cramped-86.1
Cargo Space (cu. ft.) Cramped-14.3
Wheelbase/Length (in.) 102.4/170.1

Ratings—10 Best, 1 Worst

Combo Crash Tests	8
Safety Features	10
Rollover	7
Preventive Maintenance	6
Repair Costs	3
Warranty	6
Fuel Economy	5
Complaints	–
Insurance Costs	5
OVERALL RATING	**8**

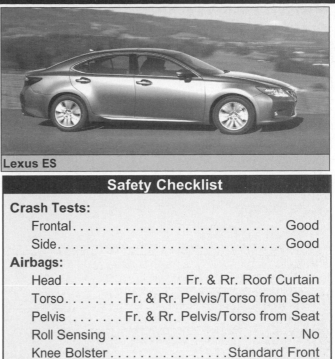

Lexus ES

Lexus ES

At-a-Glance

Status/Year Series Started	All New/2013
Twins	-
Body Styles	Sedan
Seating	5
Anti-Theft Device	Std. Pass. Immobil. & Alarm
Parking Index Rating	Very Easy
Where Made	Kyushu, Japan
Fuel Factor	
MPG Rating (city/hwy)	Average-21/31
Driving Range (mi.)	Long-423
Fuel Type	Regular
Annual Fuel Cost	Average-$2,094
Gas Guzzler Tax	No
Greenhouse Gas Emissions (tons/yr.)	High-7.6
Barrels of Oil Used per year	High-13.7

How the Competition Rates

Competitors	Rating	Pg.
Acura TL	5	84
Hyundai Sonata	9	161
Infiniti EX		164

Price Range	Retail	Markup
350	$36,100	7%
300H	$38,850	7%

Safety Checklist

Crash Tests:
Frontal . . . . Good
Side . . . . Good

Airbags:
Head . . . . Fr. & Rr. Roof Curtain
Torso . . . . Fr. & Rr. Pelvis/Torso from Seat
Pelvis . . . . Fr. & Rr. Pelvis/Torso from Seat
Roll Sensing . . . . No
Knee Bolster . . . . Standard Front

Crash Avoidance:
Frontal Collision Warning . . . . Optional
Blind Spot Detection . . . . Optional
Crash Imminent Braking . . . . Optional
Lane Departure Warning . . . . Optional

General:
Auto. Crash Notification . . . . Standard
Day Running Lamps . . . . Standard

Safety Belt/Restraint:
Dynamic Head Restraints . . . . None
Adjustable Belt . . . . Standard Front
Pretensioners . . . . Standard Front & Rear

Lexus ES

Specifications

Drive	FWD
Engine	3.5-liter V6
Transmission	6-sp. Automatic
Tow Rating (lbs.)	–
Head/Leg Room (in.)	Very Cramped-37.5/41.9
Interior Space (cu. ft.)	Average-100.1
Cargo Space (cu. ft.)	Cramped-15.2
Wheelbase/Length (in.)	111/192.7

Ratings—10 Best, 1 Worst

Combo Crash Tests	–
Safety Features	10
Rollover	8
Preventive Maintenance	7
Repair Costs	6
Warranty	6
Fuel Economy	4
Complaints	–
Insurance Costs	5
OVERALL RATING	**–**

Lexus GS350

Lexus GS450h

At-a-Glance

Status/Year Series Started . . . . All New/2013
Twins . . . . -
Body Styles . . . . Sedan
Seating 5
Anti-Theft Device . . . . . . Std. Pass. Immobil. & Alarm
Parking Index Rating . . . . Hard
Where Made. . . . . Tahara, Japan
Fuel Factor . . . .
  MPG Rating (city/hwy) Poor-19/28
  Driving Range (mi.) Short-387
  Fuel Type . . . . Premium
  Annual Fuel Cost . . . . High-$2,519
  Gas Guzzler Tax . . . . No
  Greenhouse Gas Emissions (tons/yr.) High-8.0
  Barrels of Oil Used per year High-14.3

How the Competition Rates

Competitors	Rating	Pg.
BMW 5 Series	9	96
Hyundai Genesis		159
Mercedes-Benz E-Class		197

Price Range	Retail	Markup
350 RWD	$46,900	8%
350 AWD	$49,450	8%
450H	$58,950	8%

Safety Checklist

Crash Tests:
  Frontal . . . . –
  Side . . . . –
Airbags:
  Head . . . . Fr. & Rr. Roof Curtain
  Torso . . . . Fr. & Rr. Pelvis/Torso from Seat
  Pelvis . . . . Fr. & Rr. Pelvis/Torso from Seat
  Roll Sensing . . . . No
  Knee Bolster . . . . Standard Front
Crash Avoidance:
  Frontal Collision Warning . . . . Optional
  Blind Spot Detection . . . . Optional
  Crash Imminent Braking . . . . Optional
  Lane Departure Warning . . . . Optional
General:
  Auto. Crash Notification . . . . Standard
  Day Running Lamps . . . . Standard
Safety Belt/Restraint:
  Dynamic Head Restraints . . . . None
  Adjustable Belt . . . . Standard Front
  Pretensioners . . . . Standard Front & Rear

Lexus GS450h

Specifications

Drive . . . . RWD
Engine 3.5-liter V6
Transmission . . . . 6-sp. Manual
Tow Rating (lbs.) . . . . –
Head/Leg Room (in.) Cramped-38/42.3
Interior Space (cu. ft.) Average-99
Cargo Space (cu. ft.) Cramped-14.3
Wheelbase/Length (in.) 112.2/190.7

Ratings—10 Best, 1 Worst

Combo Crash Tests	5
Safety Features	6
Rollover	8
Preventive Maintenance	7
Repair Costs	1
Warranty	6
Fuel Economy	5
Complaints	8
Insurance Costs	5
OVERALL RATING	**7**

Lexus IS350

Lexus IS350

At-a-Glance

Status/Year Series Started	Unchanged/2006
Twins	-
Body Styles	Sedan, Convertible
Seating	5
Anti-Theft Device	Std. Pass. Immobil. & Alarm
Parking Index Rating	Very Easy
Where Made	Tahara/Kyushu, Japan
Fuel Factor	
MPG Rating (city/hwy)	Average-21/30
Driving Range (mi.)	Long-415
Fuel Type	Premium
Annual Fuel Cost	Average-$2,305
Gas Guzzler Tax	No
Greenhouse Gas Emissions (tons/yr.)	High-7.7
Barrels of Oil Used per year	High-13.7

How the Competition Rates

Competitors	Rating	Pg.
Acura TSX		85
BMW 3 Series	10	95
Infiniti G		166

Price Range	Retail	Markup
250	$35,065	8%
250 AWD	$37,525	8%
350 AWD	$42,780	8%
350 Convertible	$46,790	8%

Safety Checklist

Crash Tests:
Frontal . . . . Average
Side . . . . Average
Airbags:
Head . . . . Fr. & Rr. Roof Curtain
Torso . . . . Front Pelvis/Torso from Seat
Pelvis . . . . Front Pelvis/Torso from Seat
Roll Sensing . . . . No
Knee Bolster . . . . Standard Front
Crash Avoidance:
Frontal Collision Warning . . . . None
Blind Spot Detection . . . . None
Crash Imminent Braking . . . . None
Lane Departure Warning . . . . None
General:
Auto. Crash Notification . . . . Standard
Day Running Lamps . . . . Standard
Safety Belt/Restraint:
Dynamic Head Restraints . . . . None
Adjustable Belt . . . . Standard Front
Pretensioners . . . . Standard Front & Rear

Lexus IS350

Specifications

Drive	RWD
Engine	2.5-liter V6
Transmission	6-sp. Automatic
Tow Rating (lbs.)	–
Head/Leg Room (in.)	Average-37.2/43.9
Interior Space (cu. ft.)	Very Cramped-85.7
Cargo Space (cu. ft.)	Cramped-13
Wheelbase/Length (in.)	107.5/180.3

Ratings—10 Best, 1 Worst

Combo Crash Tests	3
Safety Features	10
Rollover	3
Preventive Maintenance	6
Repair Costs	2
Warranty	6
Fuel Economy	3
Complaints	8
Insurance Costs	8
OVERALL RATING	**5**

Lexus RX350

Lexus RX350

At-a-Glance

Status/Year Series Started Appearance Change/2010
Twins . . . . -
Body Styles . . . . SUV
Seating 5
Anti-Theft Device . . . . . . Std. Pass. Immobil. & Alarm
Parking Index Rating . . . . Hard
Where Made . . . . Cambridge, Ontario
Fuel Factor . . . .
  MPG Rating (city/hwy) Poor-18/24
  Driving Range (mi.) Average-389
  Fuel Type . . . . Regular
  Annual Fuel Cost . . . . High-$2,537
  Gas Guzzler Tax . . . . No
  Greenhouse Gas Emissions (tons/yr.) High-9.1
  Barrels of Oil Used per year High-16.5

How the Competition Rates

Competitors	Rating	Pg.
Audi Q5		92
Mercedes-Benz GLK-Class		199
Volvo XC90		270

Price Range	Retail	Markup
350 FWD	$39,310	7%
350 AWD	$40,710	7%
450H FWD	$45,910	6%
450H AWD	$47,310	6%

Safety Checklist

Crash Tests:
  Frontal . . . . Poor
  Side . . . . Poor
Airbags:
  Head . . . . Fr. & Rr. Head/Torso from Seat
  Torso . . . . Rear Torso from Seat
  Pelvis . . . . Front Pelvis/Torso from Seat
  Roll Sensing . . . . Yes
  Knee Bolster . . . . Standard Front
Crash Avoidance:
  Frontal Collision Warning . . . . None
  Blind Spot Detection . . . . Optional
  Crash Imminent Braking . . . . Optional
  Lane Departure Warning . . . . None
General:
  Auto. Crash Notification . . . . Standard
  Day Running Lamps . . . . Standard
Safety Belt/Restraint:
  Dynamic Head Restraints . . . . . . Standard Front
  Adjustable Belt . . . . Standard Front
  Pretensioners . . . . Standard Front & Rear

Lexus RX350

Specifications

Drive . . . . AWD
Engine 3.5-liter V6
Transmission . . . . 6-sp. Automatic
Tow Rating (lbs.) Low-3500
Head/Leg Room (in.) Roomy-39.1/43.1
Interior Space (cu. ft.) Average-99.7
Cargo Space (cu. ft.) . . . . Very Roomy-40
Wheelbase/Length (in.) 107.9/187.8

Ratings—10 Best, 1 Worst

Combo Crash Tests	8
Safety Features	7
Rollover	7
Preventive Maintenance	6
Repair Costs	1
Warranty	5
Fuel Economy	3
Complaints	5
Insurance Costs	5
OVERALL RATING	**6**

Lincoln MKS

Lincoln MKS

At-a-Glance

Status/Year Series Started Appearance Change/2009
Twins . . . . -
Body Styles . . . . .Sedan
Seating 5
Anti-Theft Device . . . . . . .Std. Pass. Immobil & Alarm
Parking Index Rating . . . . .Very Hard
Where Made. . . . . .Chicago, IL
Fuel Factor . . . .
  MPG Rating (city/hwy) Poor-18/27
  Driving Range (mi.) Average-402
  Fuel Type. . . . . .Regular
  Annual Fuel Cost . . . . High-$2,430
  Gas Guzzler Tax . . . . .No
  Greenhouse Gas Emissions (tons/yr.). High-8.7
  Barrels of Oil Used per year High-15.7

How the Competition Rates

Competitors	Rating	Pg.
Chrysler 300	5	124
Infiniti G		166
Lexus ES	8	183

Price Range	Retail	Markup
FWD	$42,810	6%
AWD	$44,805	6%
EcoBoost AWD	$49,800	6%

Lincoln MKS

Safety Checklist

Crash Tests:
  Frontal . . . . Very Good
  Side . . . . Average
Airbags:
  Head . . . . .Fr & Rr. Roof Curtain
  Torso. . . . . Front Torso from Seat
  Pelvis . . . . None
  Roll Sensing .Yes
  Knee Bolster . . . . None
Crash Avoidance:
  Frontal Collision Warning . . . . Optional
  Blind Spot Detection . . . . Optional
  Crash Imminent Braking . . . . None
  Lane Departure Warning . . . . Optional
General:
  Auto. Crash Notification . . . . Standard
  Day Running Lamps . . . . None
Safety Belt/Restraint:
  Dynamic Head Restraints . . . . None
  Adjustable Belt . . . . .Standard Front
  Pretensioners . . . . .Standard Front

Lincoln MKS

Specifications

Drive. . . . . FWD
Engine 3.7-liter V6
Transmission . . . . .9-sp. Automatic
Tow Rating (lbs.) . . . . —
Head/Leg Room (in.) Average-39.7/41.9
Interior Space (cu. ft.). Roomy-105.8
Cargo Space (cu. ft.) Average-19.2
Wheelbase/Length (in.) 112.9/205.6

Lincoln MKZ

Ratings—10 Best, 1 Worst

Combo Crash Tests	–
Safety Features	8
Rollover	8
Preventive Maintenance	8
Repair Costs	9
Warranty	5
Fuel Economy	4
Complaints	–
Insurance Costs	8

OVERALL RATING

Lincoln MKZ

At-a-Glance

Status/Year Series Started. . . . . All New/2013
Twins . . . . Ford Fusion
Body Styles . . . . .Sedan
Seating 5
Anti-Theft Device . . . . . . .Std. Pass. Immobil & Alarm
Parking Index Rating . . . . Hard
Where Made. . . . . .Hermosillo, Mexico
Fuel Factor. . . . .
  MPG Rating (city/hwy) Poor-19/28
  Driving Range (mi.) Short-389
  Fuel Type. . . . . .Regular
  Annual Fuel Cost . . . . Average-$2,316
  Gas Guzzler Tax . . . . .No
  Greenhouse Gas Emissions (tons/yr.). High-8.3
  Barrels of Oil Used per year High-15.0

How the Competition Rates

Competitors	Rating	Pg.
Buick LaCrosse	8	103
Cadillac CTS	9	107
Lexus ES	8	183

Price Range

Price Range	Retail	Markup
Hybrid	$34,645	6%
Base	$34,645	6%
Base AWD	$36,535	6%

Safety Checklist

Crash Tests:
  Frontal. . . . . –
  Side. . . . . –
Airbags:
  Head . . . . .Fr & Rr. Roof Curtain
  Torso. . . . . .Front Pelvis/Torso from Seat
  Pelvis . . . . .Front Pelvis/Torso from Seat
  Roll Sensing . . . . No
  Knee Bolster . . . . .Standard Front
Crash Avoidance:
  Frontal Collision Warning . . . . Optional
  Blind Spot Detection . . . . Optional
  Crash Imminent Braking . . . . None
  Lane Departure Warning . . . . Optional
General:
  Auto. Crash Notification . . . . Standard
  Day Running Lamps . . . . None
Safety Belt/Restraint:
  Dynamic Head Restraints . . . . None
  Adjustable Belt . . . . .Standard Front
  Pretensioners . . . . .Standard Front

Lincoln MKZ

Specifications

Drive. . . . . FWD
Engine 3.7-liter V6
Transmission . . . . .6-sp. Automatic
Tow Rating (lbs.) . . . . –
Head/Leg Room (in.) Roomy-37.9/44.3
Interior Space (cu. ft.). Cramped-96.5
Cargo Space (cu. ft.) Cramped-15.4
Wheelbase/Length (in.) 112.2/194.1

Ratings—10 Best, 1 Worst

Combo Crash Tests	–
Safety Features	1
Rollover	5
Preventive Maintenance	6
Repair Costs	9
Warranty	2
Fuel Economy	9
Complaints	10
Insurance Costs	1
OVERALL RATING	**–**

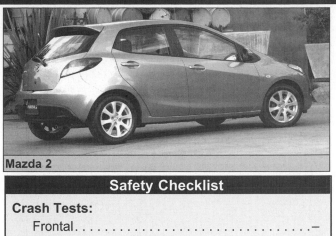

Mazda 2

Mazda 2

At-a-Glance

Status/Year Series Started........ Unchanged/2011
Twins . . . . -
Body Styles . . . . Hatchback
Seating 5
Anti-Theft Device . . . . Std. Pass. Immobil.
Parking Index Rating . . . . .Very Easy
Where Made. . . . . .Hiroshima, Japan
Fuel Factor . . . .
  MPG Rating (city/hwy) . . . . Very Good-28/34
  Driving Range (mi.) . . . . .Very Short-344
  Fuel Type . . . . .Regular
  Annual Fuel Cost . . . . Very Low-$1,692
  Gas Guzzler Tax . . . . .No
  Greenhouse Gas Emissions (tons/yr.) Low-6.1
  Barrels of Oil Used per year Average-11.0

How the Competition Rates

Competitors	Rating	Pg.
Chevrolet Sonic	10	118
Nissan Versa	4	223
Toyota Yaris	5	257

Price Range

Price Range	Retail	Markup
Sport Manual	$14,720	1%
Sport Automatic	$15,560	1%
Touring Manual	$16,210	1%
Touring Automatic	$17,050	1%

Mazda 2

Safety Checklist

Crash Tests:
  Frontal . . . . –
  Side. . . . . –
Airbags:
  Head . . . . Fr. & Rr. Roof Curtain
  Torso. . . . . Front Torso from Seat
  Pelvis . . . . None
  Roll Sensing . . . . No
  Knee Bolster . . . . None
Crash Avoidance:
  Frontal Collision Warning . . . . None
  Blind Spot Detection . . . . None
  Crash Imminent Braking . . . . None
  Lane Departure Warning . . . . None
General:
  Auto. Crash Notification . . . . None
  Day Running Lamps . . . . Nonc
Safety Belt/Restraint:
  Dynamic Head Restraints . . . . None
  Adjustable Belt . . . . .Standard Front
  Pretensioners . . . . .Standard Front

Specifications

Drive . . . . FWD
Engine 1.5-liter I4
Transmission . . . . .4-sp. Automatic
Tow Rating (lbs.) . . . . –
Head/Leg Room (in.) Average-39.1/42.6
Interior Space (cu. ft.). . . . . .Very Cramped-87.1
Cargo Space (cu. ft.) Cramped-13.3
Wheelbase/Length (in.) 98/155.5

Mazda Mazda3   Compact

Ratings—10 Best, 1 Worst

Combo Crash Tests	5
Safety Features	5
Rollover	7
Preventive Maintenance	6
Repair Costs	9
Warranty	2
Fuel Economy	7
Complaints	9
Insurance Costs	1
OVERALL RATING	**6**

Mazda 3

Mazda 3

At-a-Glance

Status/Year Series Started Unchanged/2010
Twins . . . . -
Body Styles . . . . Sedan, Hatchback
Seating 5
Anti-Theft Device Std. Pass. Immobil. & Opt. Pass. Alarm
Parking Index Rating . . . . Easy
Where Made . . . . Hiroshima, Japan
Fuel Factor
  MPG Rating (city/hwy) Good-24/33
  Driving Range (mi.) Average-397
  Fuel Type . . . . Regular
  Annual Fuel Cost . . . . Low-$1,881
  Gas Guzzler Tax . . . . No
  Greenhouse Gas Emissions (tons/yr.) . . Average-6.8
  Barrels of Oil Used per year Average-12.2

How the Competition Rates

Competitors	Rating	Pg.
Mitsubishi Lancer	6	205
Scion tC	8	229
Subaru Impreza	4	235

Price Range

Price Range	Retail	Markup
I Manual	$16,700	3%
i Touring	$20,350	5%
Mazdaspeed3	$24,200	5%
s Grand Touring Hatchback	$25,650	5%

Safety Checklist

Crash Tests:
  Frontal . . . . Good
  Side . . . . Very Poor
Airbags:
  Head . . . . Fr. & Rr. Roof Curtain
  Torso . . . . Front Pelvis/Torso from Seat
  Pelvis . . . . Front Pelvis/Torso from Seat
  Roll Sensing . . . . No
  Knee Bolster . . . . None
Crash Avoidance:
  Frontal Collision Warning . . . . None
  Blind Spot Detection . . . . Optional
  Crash Imminent Braking . . . . None
  Lane Departure Warning . . . . None
General:
  Auto. Crash Notification . . . . Optional
  Day Running Lamps . . . . None
Safety Belt/Restraint:
  Dynamic Head Restraints . . . . . . Standard Front
  Adjustable Belt . . . . Standard Front
  Pretensioners . . . . Standard Front

Mazda 3

Specifications

Drive . . . . FWD
Engine 2.0-liter I4
Transmission . . . . 5-sp. Automatic
Tow Rating (lbs.) . . . . —
Head/Leg Room (in.) Cramped-38.9/42
Interior Space (cu. ft.) Cramped-94.1
Cargo Space (cu. ft.) . . . . Very Cramped-11.8
Wheelbase/Length (in.) 103.9/180.9

Mazda Mazda5

Ratings—10 Best, 1 Worst

Combo Crash Tests	–
Safety Features	2
Rollover	3
Preventive Maintenance	6
Repair Costs	8
Warranty	2
Fuel Economy	5
Complaints	5
Insurance Costs	5
OVERALL RATING	**–**

Mazda 5

Mazda 5

At-a-Glance

Status/Year Series Started	Unchanged/2006
Twins	-
Body Styles	Minivan
Seating	7
Anti-Theft Device	Std. Pass. Immobil. & Opt. Pass. Alarm
Parking Index Rating	Average
Where Made	Hiroshima, Japan
Fuel Factor	
MPG Rating (city/hwy)	Average-22/27
Driving Range (mi.)	Short-382
Fuel Type	Regular
Annual Fuel Cost	Average-$2,144
Gas Guzzler Tax	No
Greenhouse Gas Emissions (tons/yr.)	High-7.6
Barrels of Oil Used per year	High-13.7

How the Competition Rates

Competitors	Rating	Pg.
Honda Odyssey	7	153
Toyota Prius V	5	250
Subaru Forester	3	234

Price Range	Retail	Markup
Sport Manual	$19,345	7%
Sport Automatic	$20,345	7%
Touring	$21,345	7%
Grand Touring	$24,025	7%

Safety Checklist

Crash Tests:
Frontal . . . . –
Side . . . . –
Airbags:
Head . . . . Fr. & Rr. Roof Curtain
Torso . . . . Front Pelvis/Torso from Seat
Pelvis . . . . Front Pelvis/Torso from Seat
Roll Sensing . . . . No
Knee Bolster . . . . No
Crash Avoidance:
Frontal Collision Warning . . . . None
Blind Spot Detection . . . . None
Crash Imminent Braking . . . . None
Lane Departure Warning . . . . None
General:
Auto. Crash Notification . . . . None
Day Running Lamps . . . . None
Safety Belt/Restraint:
Dynamic Head Restraints . . . . None
Adjustable Belt . . . . Standard Front
Pretensioners . . . . Standard Front

Mazda 5

Specifications

Drive	FWD
Engine	2.5-liter I4
Transmission	5-sp. Auto. w/Overdrive
Tow Rating (lbs.)	–
Head/Leg Room (in.)	Average-40.7/40.7
Interior Space (cu. ft.)	Average-97.7
Cargo Space (cu. ft.)	Roomy-27.5
Wheelbase/Length (in.)	108.3/180.5

Ratings—10 Best, 1 Worst

Combo Crash Tests	2
Safety Features	3
Rollover	9
Preventive Maintenance	7
Repair Costs	10
Warranty	2
Fuel Economy	5
Complaints	10
Insurance Costs	3
OVERALL RATING	**5**

Mazda 6

Mazda 6

At-a-Glance

Status/Year Series Started..... All New (2014)/2009
Twins . . . . -
Body Styles . . . . .Sedan
Seating 5
Anti-Theft Device .Std. Pass. Immobil. & Opt. Pass. Alarm
Parking Index Rating . . . . Easy
Where Made. . . . . Flat Rock, MI
Fuel Factor. . . . .
 MPG Rating (city/hwy) Average-21/30
 Driving Range (mi.) . . . . Very Long-449
 Fuel Type. .Regular
 Annual Fuel Cost . . . . Average-$2,119
 Gas Guzzler Tax .No
 Greenhouse Gas Emissions (tons/yr.). . Average-7.4
 Barrels of Oil Used per year Average-13.2

How the Competition Rates

Competitors	Rating	Pg.
Nissan Altima	7	209
Dodge Avenger	2	126
Toyota Camry	4	243

Price Range

Price Range	Retail	Markup
i Sport Manual	$20,725	6%
i Touring Plus	$25,170	6%
i Grand Touring	$27,750	6%
s Grand Touring	$29,990	6%

Safety Checklist

Crash Tests:
 Frontal. . . . . .Very Poor
 Side. . . . . Poor
Airbags:
 Head . . . . Fr. & Rr. Roof Curtain
 Torso. . . . . .Front Pelvis/Torso from Seat
 Pelvis . . . . .Front Pelvis/Torso from Seat
 Roll Sensing . . . . No
 Knee Bolster . . . . None
Crash Avoidance:
 Frontal Collision Warning . . . . None
 Blind Spot Detection . . . . Optional
 Crash Imminent Braking . . . . None
 Lane Departure Warning . . . . None
General:
 Auto. Crash Notification . . . . None
 Day Running Lamps . . . . None
Safety Belt/Restraint:
 Dynamic Head Restraints . . . . None
 Adjustable Belt . . . . .Standard Front
 Pretensioners . . . . .Standard Front

Mazda 6

Specifications

Drive. . . . . FWD
Engine 2.5-liter I4
Transmission . . . . .5-sp. Automatic
Tow Rating (lbs.) . . . . –
Head/Leg Room (in.) Roomy-39.4/42.5
Interior Space (cu. ft.). Average-101.9
Cargo Space (cu. ft.) Average-16.6
Wheelbase/Length (in.) 109.8/193.7

Mazda CX-5

Ratings—10 Best, 1 Worst

Combo Crash Tests	7
Safety Features	5
Rollover	3
Preventive Maintenance	7
Repair Costs	7
Warranty	2
Fuel Economy	7
Complaints	–
Insurance Costs	0
OVERALL RATING	**6**

Mazda CX-5

At-a-Glance

Status/Year Series Started. . . . . All New/2013
Twins . . . . -
Body Styles . . . . SUV
Seating 5
Anti-Theft Device .Std. Pass. Immobil. & Opt. Pass. Alarm
Parking Index Rating . . . . Easy
Where Made. . . . . .Hiroshima, Japan
Fuel Factor
　MPG Rating (city/hwy) Good-25/31
　Driving Range (mi.) Average-405
　Fuel Type. .Regular
　Annual Fuel Cost . . . . Low-$1,879
　Gas Guzzler Tax .No
　Greenhouse Gas Emissions (tons/yr.). . Average-6.5
　Barrels of Oil Used per year Average-11.8

How the Competition Rates

Competitors	Rating	Pg.
Buick Encore		102
Ford Escape	7	136
Honda CR-V	7	150

Price Range

	Retail	Markup
Sport Manual	$20,995	3%
Sport Automatic	$22,395	3%
Touring	$24,195	3%
Grand Touring AWD	$28,595	3%

Safety Checklist

Crash Tests:
　Frontal. . . . . Average
　Side. . . . . Good
Airbags:
　Head . . . . .Fr & Rr. Roof Curtain
　Torso. . . . . .Front Pelvis/Torso from Seat
　Pelvis . . . . .Front Pelvis/Torso from Seat
　Roll Sensing . . . . .Yes
　Knee Bolster . . . . None
Crash Avoidance:
　Frontal Collision Warning . . . . None
　Blind Spot Detection . . . . .Optional
　Crash Imminent Braking . . . . None
　Lane Departure Warning . . . . None
General:
　Auto. Crash Notification . . . . None
　Day Running Lamps . . . . Standard
Safety Belt/Restraint:
　Dynamic Head Restraints . . . . None
　Adjustable Belt . . . . .Standard Front
　Pretensioners . . . . .Standard Front

Mazda CX-5

Specifications

Drive. . . . . FWD
Engine 2.0-liter I4
Transmission . . . . .6-sp. Manual
Tow Rating (lbs.) . . . . Very Low-2000
Head/Leg Room (in.) Average-40.1/41
Interior Space (cu. ft.). Roomy-103.8
Cargo Space (cu. ft.) . . . . Very Roomy-34.1
Wheelbase/Length (in.) 106.3/178.7

Ratings—10 Best, 1 Worst

Combo Crash Tests	–
Safety Features	8
Rollover	3
Preventive Maintenance	7
Repair Costs	4
Warranty	2
Fuel Economy	7
Complaints	9
Insurance Costs	8
OVERALL RATING	**–**

Mazda CX-9

Mazda CX-9

At-a-Glance

Status/Year Series Started Appearance Change/2007
Twins . . . . -
Body Styles . . . . SUV
Seating 7
Anti-Theft Device .Std. Pass. Immobil. & Opt. Pass. Alarm
Parking Index Rating . . . . Hard
Where Made. . . . . Hiroshima, Japan
Fuel Factor. . . . .
  MPG Rating (city/hwy) Good-25/31
  Driving Range (mi.) . . . . Very Long-550
  Fuel Type. . . . . Regular
  Annual Fuel Cost . . . . Low-$1,879
  Gas Guzzler Tax . . . . .No
  Greenhouse Gas Emissions (tons/yr.) Very High-9.7
  Barrels of Oil Used per year High-17.3

How the Competition Rates

Competitors	Rating	Pg.
Acura MDX	8	82
Chevrolet Equinox	5	114
Nissan Murano	3	217

Price Range	Retail	Markup
Sport FWD	$29,725	8%
Sport AWD	$31,115	8%
Touring FWD	$31,645	8%
Grand Touring AWD	$35,125	8%

Safety Checklist

Crash Tests:
  Frontal. . . . .–
  Side. . . . .–
Airbags:
  Head . . . . Fr. & Rr. Roof Curtain
  Torso. . . . . Front Torso from Seat
  Pelvis . . . . None
  Roll Sensing . . . . .Yes
  Knee Bolster . . . . None
Crash Avoidance:
  Frontal Collision Warning . . . . None
  Blind Spot Detection . . . . Optional
  Crash Imminent Braking . . . . None
  Lane Departure Warning . . . . None
General:
  Auto. Crash Notification . . . . Standard
  Day Running Lamps . . . . Optional
Safety Belt/Restraint:
  Dynamic Head Restraints . . . . . .Standard Front
  Adjustable Belt . . . . .Standard Front
  Pretensioners . . . . .Standard Front

Mazda CX-9

Specifications

Drive. . . . . FWD
Engine 3.7-liter V6
Transmission . . . . 6-sp. Auto. w/Overdrive
Tow Rating (lbs.) . . . . Very Low-2000
Head/Leg Room (in.) Cramped-40/40.9
Interior Space (cu. ft.). . . . . Very Roomy-139.4
Cargo Space (cu. ft.) Average-17.2
Wheelbase/Length (in.) 113.2/200.2

Mazda MX-5 Miata

Ratings—10 Best, 1 Worst

Combo Crash Tests	–
Safety Features	1
Rollover	10
Preventive Maintenance	6
Repair Costs	7
Warranty	2
Fuel Economy	5
Complaints	9
Insurance Costs	10
OVERALL RATING	**–**

Mazda MX-5 Miata

At-a-Glance

Status/Year Series Started Appearance Change/2006
Twins . . . . -
Body Styles . . . . Coupe, Convertible
Seating 2
Anti-Theft Device .Std. Pass. Immobil. & Opt. Pass. Alarm
Parking Index Rating . . . . .Very Easy
Where Made. . . . . Hiroshima, Japan
Fuel Factor . . . .
  MPG Rating (city/hwy) Average-21/28
  Driving Range (mi.) . . . . .Very Short-301
  Fuel Type. . . . . .Regular
  Annual Fuel Cost . . . . Average-$2,174
  Gas Guzzler Tax . . . . .No
  Greenhouse Gas Emissions (tons/yr.). High-8.0
  Barrels of Oil Used per year High-14.3

How the Competition Rates

Competitors	Rating	Pg.
Scion FR-S		227
Subaru BRZ		233
Nissan 370Z		208

Price Range

	Retail	Markup
Sport Manual	$23,720	6%
Sport Automatic	$25,980	6%
Club Convertible Auto.	$27,305	6%
Grand Touring Hardtop Auto.	$30,350	6%

Mazda MX-5 Miata

Safety Checklist

Crash Tests:
  Frontal. . . . .–
  Side. . . . .–
Airbags:
  Head . . . . Front Head/Torso from Seat
  Torso. . . . . Front Head/Torso from Seat
  Pelvis . . . . None
  Roll Sensing . . . . No
  Knee Bolster . . . . None
Crash Avoidance:
  Frontal Collision Warning . . . . None
  Blind Spot Detection . . . . None
  Crash Imminent Braking . . . . None
  Lane Departure Warning . . . . None
General:
  Auto. Crash Notification . . . . None
  Day Running Lamps . . . . None
Safety Belt/Restraint:
  Dynamic Head Restraints . . . . None
  Adjustable Belt . . . . None
  Pretensioners . . . . Standard

Mazda MX-5 Miata

Specifications

Drive. . . . . .RWD
Engine 2.0-liter I4
Transmission . . . . .6-sp. Automatic
Tow Rating (lbs.) . . . . –
Head/Leg Room (in.) Cramped-37/43.1
Interior Space (cu. ft.). . . . . –
Cargo Space (cu. ft.) . . . . .Very Cramped-5.3
Wheelbase/Length (in.) 91.7/157.3

Ratings—10 Best, 1 Worst

Combo Crash Tests	2
Safety Features	9
Rollover	8
Preventive Maintenance	1
Repair Costs	2
Warranty	3
Fuel Economy	3
Complaints	10
Insurance Costs	8
OVERALL RATING	**4**

Mercedes-Benz C-Class Coupe

Mercedes-Benz C-Class Sedan

Safety Checklist

Crash Tests:
Frontal . . . . .Very Poor
Side . . . . Poor
Airbags:
Head . . . . .Fr & Rr. Roof Curtain
Torso . . . . Fr. & Rr. Torso from Seat
Pelvis . . . . .Front Pelvis/Torso from Seat
Roll Sensing . . . . No
Knee Bolster . . . . Standard Driver
Crash Avoidance:
Frontal Collision Warning . . . . Optional
Blind Spot Detection . . . . Optional
Crash Imminent Braking . . . . Optional
Lane Departure Warning . . . . Optional
General:
Auto. Crash Notification . . . . Optional
Day Running Lamps . . . . Optional
Safety Belt/Restraint:
Dynamic Head Restraints . . . . . .Standard Front
Adjustable Belt . . . . .Standard Front
Pretensioners . . . . Standard

At-a-Glance

Status/Year Series Started Unchanged/2008
Twins . . . . -
Body Styles . . . . Sedan, Coupe
Seating 5
Anti-Theft Device . Std. Active Immobil. & Pass. Alarm
Parking Index Rating . . . . Easy
Where Made . . . . Bremen, Germany
Fuel Factor . . . .
  MPG Rating (city/hwy) Poor-18/25
  Driving Range (mi.) Average-402
  Fuel Type . . . . .Premium
  Annual Fuel Cost . . . . High-$2,717
  Gas Guzzler Tax . . . . .No
  Greenhouse Gas Emissions (tons/yr.) High-8.3
  Barrels of Oil Used per year High-15.0

How the Competition Rates

Competitors	Rating	Pg.
Audi A4	10	87
BMW 3 Series	10	95
Lexus IS	7	185

Price Range	Retail	Markup
C250 Sport	$35,350	8%
C300 4Matic	$38,950	8%
C350	$41,400	8%
C63 AMG Coupe	$62,330	8%

Mercedes-Benz C-Class Coupe

Specifications

Drive . . . . RWD
Engine 3.0-liter V6
Transmission . . . . .7-sp. Automatic
Tow Rating (lbs.) . . . . –
Head/Leg Room (in.) . . . . .Very Cramped-37.1/41.7
Interior Space (cu. ft.) . . . . .Very Cramped-88.2
Cargo Space (cu. ft.) Cramped-12.4
Wheelbase/Length (in.) 108.7/180.8

Ratings—10 Best, 1 Worst	
Combo Crash Tests	–
Safety Features	9
Rollover	8
Preventive Maintenance	1
Repair Costs	2
Warranty	3
Fuel Economy	5
Complaints	10
Insurance Costs	5
OVERALL RATING	**–**

Mercedes-Benz E-Class Sedan

At-a-Glance

Status/Year Series Started........ Unchanged/2010
Twins .... -
Body Styles .... Sedan, Coupe, Wagon, Convertible
Seating 5
Anti-Theft Device . Std. Active Immobil. & Pass. Alarm
Parking Index Rating .... Average
Where Made.................... Bremen, Germany
Fuel Factor ....
  MPG Rating (city/hwy) Average-20/30
  Driving Range (mi.) .... Very Long-497
  Fuel Type.........................Premium
  Annual Fuel Cost .... Average-$2,378
  Gas Guzzler Tax ....No
  Greenhouse Gas Emissions (tons/yr.)..... High-8.0
  Barrels of Oil Used per year High-14.3

Mercedes-Benz E-Class Coupe

How the Competition Rates

Competitors	Rating	Pg.
BMW 5 Series	9	96
Infiniti G		166
Lexus GS		184

Price Range	Retail	Markup
350 Coupe	$51,120	8%
350 Luxury Sedan 4Matic	$53,500	8%
550 Cabriolet	$66,220	8%
63 AMG Wagon	$92,400	8%

Mercedes-Benz E-Class Sedan

Safety Checklist

Crash Tests:
  Frontal . . . . –
  Side . . . . –
Airbags:
  Head . . . . Fr. & Rr. Roof Curtain
  Torso . . . . . . .Std. Fr. & Opt. Rr. Torso from Seat
  Pelvis .Pelvis from Seat
  Roll Sensing . . . . .Yes
  Knee Bolster . . . . Standard Driver
Crash Avoidance:
  Frontal Collision Warning . . . . Optional
  Blind Spot Detection . . . . Optional
  Crash Imminent Braking . . . . Optional
  Lane Departure Warning . . . . Optional
General:
  Auto. Crash Notification . . . . Optional
  Day Running Lamps . . . . Optional
Safety Belt/Restraint:
  Dynamic Head Restraints . . . . . .Standard Front
  Adjustable Belt . . . . Standard Front & Rear
  Pretensioners . . . . Standard Front & Rear

Specifications

Drive. . . . . RWD
Engine 3.5-liter V6
Transmission . . . . .7-sp. Automatic
Tow Rating (lbs.) . . . . Very Low-1655
Head/Leg Room (in.) . . . . .Very Cramped-37.9/41.3
Interior Space (cu. ft.). . . . . Very Cramped-81
Cargo Space (cu. ft.) Cramped-15.9
Wheelbase/Length (in.) 113.2/191.7

Mercedes-Benz GL-Class

Ratings—10 Best, 1 Worst

Combo Crash Tests	–
Safety Features	10
Rollover	2
Preventive Maintenance	1
Repair Costs	3
Warranty	3
Fuel Economy	1
Complaints	7
Insurance Costs	10
OVERALL RATING	**–**

Mercedes-Benz GL-Class

Mercedes-Benz GL-Class

At-a-Glance

Status/Year Series Started. . . . . All New/2007
Twins . . . . -
Body Styles . . . . SUV
Seating 7
Anti-Theft Device .Std. Active Immobil. & Pass. Alarm
Parking Index Rating . . . . .Very Hard
Where Made. . . . . Tuscaloosa, AL
Fuel Factor . . . .
  MPG Rating (city/hwy) . . . . .Very Poor-14/19
  Driving Range (mi.) Long-419
  Fuel Type. . . . . .Premium
  Annual Fuel Cost . . . . Very High-$3,523
  Gas Guzzler Tax . . . . .No
  Greenhouse Gas Emissions (tons/yr.) Very High-9.4
  Barrels of Oil Used per year . . . . . . .Very High-20.6

How the Competition Rates

Competitors	Rating	Pg.
Audi Q7		93
Ford Expedition	4	137
Toyota Sequoia		252

Price Range

	Retail	Markup
GL350 CDI	$62,400	8%
GL450	$63,900	8%
GL550	$86,900	8%

Safety Checklist

Crash Tests:
  Frontal. . . . .–
  Side. . . . .–
Airbags:
  Head . . . . Fr. & Rr. Roof Curtain
  Torso. . . . . Fr. & Rr. Torso from Seat
  Pelvis . . . . None
  Roll Sensing . . . . .Yes
  Knee Bolster . . . . Standard Driver
Crash Avoidance:
  Frontal Collision Warning . . . . Optional
  Blind Spot Detection . . . . Optional
  Crash Imminent Braking . . . . Optional
  Lane Departure Warning . . . . Optional
General:
  Auto. Crash Notification . . . . Optional
  Day Running Lamps . . . . Optional
Safety Belt/Restraint:
  Dynamic Head Restraints. . . . . .Standard Front
  Adjustable Belt . . . . .Standard Front
  Pretensioners . . . . Standard

Mercedes-Benz GL-Class

Specifications

Drive. 4WD
Engine 4.6-liter V8
Transmission . . . . .7-sp. Automatic
Tow Rating (lbs.) . . . . .Very High-7500
Head/Leg Room (in.) Average-41.2/40.3
Interior Space (cu. ft.). Roomy-127.6
Cargo Space (cu. ft.) Average-16
Wheelbase/Length (in.) 121.1/201.6

Mercedes-Benz GLK-Class

Ratings—10 Best, 1 Worst	
Combo Crash Tests	–
Safety Features	10
Rollover	2
Preventive Maintenance	1
Repair Costs	2
Warranty	3
Fuel Economy	3
Complaints	2
Insurance Costs	8
OVERALL RATING	**–**

Mercedes-Benz GLK-Class

Mercedes-Benz GLK-Class

At-a-Glance

Status/Year Series Started........ Unchanged/2010
Twins .... -
Body Styles .... SUV
Seating..5
Anti-Theft Device . Std. Active Immobil. & Pass. Alarm
Parking Index Rating .... Average
Where Made...................... Bremen, Germany
Fuel Factor ....
  MPG Rating (city/hwy)...........Poor-19/24
  Driving Range (mi.) Short-365
  Fuel Type........................Premium
  Annual Fuel Cost .... High-$2,669
  Gas Guzzler Tax ....No
  Greenhouse Gas Emissions (tons/yr.)..... High-8.7
  Barrels of Oil Used per year High-15.7

How the Competition Rates

Competitors	Rating	Pg.
Audi Q5		92
Cadillac SRX	7	108
Lexus RX	5	186

Price Range	Retail	Markup
GLK350	$37,090	8%
Glk350 4Matic	$39,090	8%

Safety Checklist

Crash Tests:
  Frontal.....................................–
  Side...–
Airbags:
  Head ....Fr & Rr. Roof Curtain
  Torso............. Fr. & Rr. Torso from Seat
  Pelvis ....Front Pelvis/Torso from Seat
  Roll Sensing ....Yes
  Knee Bolster .... Standard Driver
Crash Avoidance:
  Frontal Collision Warning .... Optional
  Blind Spot Detection .... Optional
  Crash Imminent Braking .... Optional
  Lane Departure Warning .... Optional
General:
  Auto. Crash Notification .... Optional
  Day Running Lamps .... Optional
Safety Belt/Restraint:
  Dynamic Head Restraints......Standard Front
  Adjustable Belt ....Standard Front
  Pretensioners ....Standard Front

Mercedes-Benz GLK-Class

Specifications

Drive.................................. 4WD
Engine 3.5-liter V6
Transmission ....7-sp. Automatic
Tow Rating (lbs.) Low-3500
Head/Leg Room (in.) Cramped-39.02/41.4
Interior Space (cu. ft.)......Very Cramped-79.6
Cargo Space (cu. ft.) Roomy-23.3
Wheelbase/Length (in.) 108.5/178.3

Mercedes-Benz M-Class

Mid-Size SUV

Mercedes-Benz M-Class

Ratings—10 Best, 1 Worst

Combo Crash Tests	–
Safety Features	9
Rollover	2
Preventive Maintenance	1
Repair Costs	2
Warranty	3
Fuel Economy	3
Complaints	10
Insurance Costs	10
OVERALL RATING	**–**

Mercedes-Benz M-Class

Safety Checklist

Crash Tests:
Frontal. . . . . –
Side. . . . . –

Airbags:
Head . . . . Fr. & Rr. Roof Curtain
Torso. . . . . Fr. & Rr. Torso from Seat
Pelvis . . . . None
Roll Sensing . . . . Yes
Knee Bolster . . . . Standard Driver

Crash Avoidance:
Frontal Collision Warning . . . . Optional
Blind Spot Detection . . . . Optional
Crash Imminent Braking . . . . Optional
Lane Departure Warning . . . . Optional

General:
Auto. Crash Notification . . . . Optional
Day Running Lamps . . . . Optional

Safety Belt/Restraint:
Dynamic Head Restraints . . . . . . Standard Front
Adjustable Belt . . . . Standard Front
Pretensioners . . . . Standard Front & Rear

At-a-Glance

Status/Year Series Started. Unchanged/2012
Twins . . . . -
Body Styles . . . . SUV
Seating 5
Anti-Theft Device . Std. Active Immobil. & Pass. Alarm
Parking Index Rating . . . . Hard
Where Made. . . . . Tuscaloosa, AL
Fuel Factor. . . . .
  MPG Rating (city/hwy) Poor-18/23
  Driving Range (mi.) . . . . Very Long-553
  Fuel Type. . . . . Premium
  Annual Fuel Cost . . . . Very High-$2,804
  Gas Guzzler Tax . . . . No
  Greenhouse Gas Emissions (tons/yr.). High-9.2
  Barrels of Oil Used per year High-16.5

How the Competition Rates

Competitors	Rating	Pg.
BMW X5	6	100
Infiniti FX		165
Volvo XC90		270

Price Range	Retail	Markup
ML350	$47,270	8%
ML350 4Matic	$49,770	8%
ML550 4Matic	$58,800	8%
ML63 AMG	$96,100	8%

Mercedes-Benz M-Class

Specifications

Drive. . . . . AWD
Engine 3.5-liter V6
Transmission . . . . .7-sp. Automatic
Tow Rating (lbs.) High-7200
Head/Leg Room (in.) Cramped-40.3/40.3
Interior Space (cu. ft.). . . . . .Very Roomy-162
Cargo Space (cu. ft.) . . . . Very Roomy-38.2
Wheelbase/Length (in.) 114.8/189.1

Mercedes-Benz M-Class

Ratings—10 Best, 1 Worst

Combo Crash Tests	–
Safety Features	9
Rollover	8
Preventive Maintenance	1
Repair Costs	1
Warranty	3
Fuel Economy	2
Complaints	10
Insurance Costs	5
OVERALL RATING	**–**

Mercedes-Benz S-Class

At-a-Glance

Status/Year Series Started........ Unchanged/2007
Twins .... -
Body Styles .... Sedan
Seating 5
Anti-Theft Device . Std. Active Immobil. & Pass. Alarm
Parking Index Rating .... Very Hard
Where Made................ Sindelfingen, Germany
Fuel Factor ....
  MPG Rating (city/hwy) .... Very Poor-15/25
  Driving Range (mi.) Long-435
  Fuel Type.......................... Premium
  Annual Fuel Cost .... Very High-$3,059
  Gas Guzzler Tax .... No
  Greenhouse Gas Emissions (tons/yr.) Very High-9.6
  Barrels of Oil Used per year High-17.3

How the Competition Rates

Competitors	Rating	Pg.
BMW 7 Series		97
Cadillac XTS	8	109
Jaguar XF		170

Price Range	Retail	Markup
S400 Hybrid	$92,350	8%
S550 4Matic	$98,000	8%
S63 AMG	$140,000	8%
S65 AMG	$212,000	8%

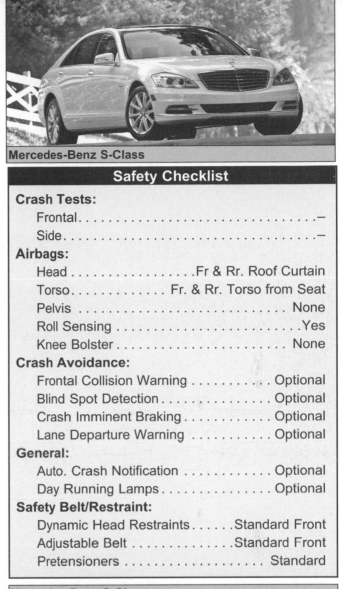

Mercedes-Benz S-Class

Safety Checklist

Crash Tests:
  Frontal.. –
  Side... –
Airbags:
  Head .... Fr & Rr. Roof Curtain
  Torso............. Fr. & Rr. Torso from Seat
  Pelvis .... None
  Roll Sensing .... Yes
  Knee Bolster .... None
Crash Avoidance:
  Frontal Collision Warning .... Optional
  Blind Spot Detection .... Optional
  Crash Imminent Braking .... Optional
  Lane Departure Warning .... Optional
General:
  Auto. Crash Notification .... Optional
  Day Running Lamps .... Optional
Safety Belt/Restraint:
  Dynamic Head Restraints...... Standard Front
  Adjustable Belt .... Standard Front
  Pretensioners .... Standard

Mercedes-Benz S-Class

Specifications

Drive................................... RWD
Engine 4.7-liter V8
Transmission .... 7-sp. Automatic
Tow Rating (lbs.) .... –
Head/Leg Room (in.) ..... Very Cramped-37.8/41.9
Interior Space (cu. ft.)............. Roomy-125
Cargo Space (cu. ft.) Average-16.4
Wheelbase/Length (in.) 124.6/206.5

Ratings—10 Best, 1 Worst

Combo Crash Tests	–
Safety Features	2
Rollover	6
Preventive Maintenance	8
Repair Costs	6
Warranty	10
Fuel Economy	9
Complaints	–
Insurance Costs	3
OVERALL RATING	**–**

Mini Clubman

Mini Clubman

At-a-Glance

Status/Year Series Started	Unchanged/2008
Twins	-
Body Styles	Hatchback
Seating	4
Anti-Theft Device	Std. Pass. Immobil.
Parking Index Rating	Very Easy
Where Made	Oxford, UK
Fuel Factor	
MPG Rating (city/hwy)	Very Good-27/35
Driving Range (mi.)	Average-397
Fuel Type	Premium
Annual Fuel Cost	Low-$1,859
Gas Guzzler Tax	No
Greenhouse Gas Emissions (tons/yr.)	Low-6.1
Barrels of Oil Used per year	Average-11.0

How the Competition Rates

Competitors	Rating	Pg.
Kia Soul	6	179
Scion xD		231
Suzuki SX4	1	240

Price Range	Retail	Markup
Clubman	$21,400	11%
Clubman S	$25,100	11%
John Cooper Clubman	$32,300	11%

Safety Checklist

Crash Tests:
Frontal.................................–
Side....................................–
Airbags:
Head .... Fr. & Rr. Roof Curtain
Torso............... Front Torso from Seat
Pelvis .... None
Roll Sensing .... No
Knee Bolster .... None
Crash Avoidance:
Frontal Collision Warning .... None
Blind Spot Detection .... None
Crash Imminent Braking .... None
Lane Departure Warning .... None
General:
Auto. Crash Notification .... None
Day Running Lamps .... None
Safety Belt/Restraint:
Dynamic Head Restraints ......Standard Front
Adjustable Belt .... None
Pretensioners ....Standard Front

Specifications

Drive	FWD
Engine	1.6-liter I4
Transmission	6-sp. Automatic
Tow Rating (lbs.)	–
Head/Leg Room (in.)	Cramped-39/41.4
Interior Space (cu. ft.)	Very Cramped-80
Cargo Space (cu. ft.)	Very Cramped-9.2
Wheelbase/Length (in.)	100.3/155.9

Ratings—10 Best, 1 Worst

Combo Crash Tests	–
Safety Features	3
Rollover	7
Preventive Maintenance	9
Repair Costs	5
Warranty	10
Fuel Economy	9
Complaints	4
Insurance Costs	5
OVERALL RATING	**–**

Mini Cooper Convertible

At-a-Glance

Status/Year Series Started	Unchanged/2007
Twins	-
Body Styles	Hatchback
Seating	4
Anti-Theft Device	Standard Pass. Immobil.
Parking Index Rating	Very Easy
Where Made	Oxford, UK
Fuel Factor	
MPG Rating (city/hwy)	Very Good-28/36
Driving Range (mi.)	Average-411
Fuel Type	Premium
Annual Fuel Cost	Low-$1,798
Gas Guzzler Tax	No
Greenhouse Gas Emissions (tons/yr.)	Low-5.7
Barrels of Oil Used per year	Low-10.3

How the Competition Rates

Competitors	Rating	Pg.
Kia Soul	6	179
Nissan Cube		212
Scion xD		231

Price Range	Retail	Markup
Base	$19,700	11%
S	$23,300	11%
John Cooper	$30,100	11%
John Cooper Roadster	$35,700	11%

Mini Cooper

Safety Checklist

Crash Tests:
Frontal . . . . –
Side . . . . –

Airbags:
Head . . . . Fr. & Rr. Roof Curtain
Torso . . . . Front Torso from Seat
Pelvis . . . . None
Roll Sensing . . . . No
Knee Bolster . . . . None

Crash Avoidance:
Frontal Collision Warning . . . . None
Blind Spot Detection . . . . None
Crash Imminent Braking . . . . None
Lane Departure Warning . . . . None

General:
Auto. Crash Notification . . . . None
Day Running Lamps . . . . Standard

Safety Belt/Restraint:
Dynamic Head Restraints . . . . . . Standard Front
Adjustable Belt . . . . None
Pretensioners . . . . Standard Front

Mini Cooper

Specifications

Drive	FWD
Engine	1.6-liter I4
Transmission	6-sp. Automatic
Tow Rating (lbs.)	–
Head/Leg Room (in.)	Cramped-38.8/41.4
Interior Space (cu. ft.)	Very Cramped-76
Cargo Space (cu. ft.)	Very Cramped-5.7
Wheelbase/Length (in.)	97.1/145.2

Ratings—10 Best, 1 Worst

Combo Crash Tests	–
Safety Features	1
Rollover	5
Preventive Maintenance	8
Repair Costs	5
Warranty	10
Fuel Economy	7
Complaints	5
Insurance Costs	3
OVERALL RATING	**–**

Mini Countryman

Mini Countryman

At-a-Glance

Status/Year Series Started	Unchanged/2012
Twins	-
Body Styles	Hatchback
Seating	5
Anti-Theft Device	Std. Pass. Immobil.
Parking Index Rating	Very Easy
Where Made	Graz, Austria
Fuel Factor	
MPG Rating (city/hwy)	Good-25/30
Driving Range (mi.)	Very Short-327
Fuel Type	Premium
Annual Fuel Cost	Average-$2,070
Gas Guzzler Tax	No
Greenhouse Gas Emissions (tons/yr.)	Average-6.7
Barrels of Oil Used per year	Average-12.2

How the Competition Rates

Competitors	Rating	Pg.
Nissan Juke	5	214
Hyundai Veloster		163
Kia Soul		179

Price Range

Price Range	Retail	Markup
Base	$22,700	
John Cooper Works	$35,550	

Safety Checklist

Crash Tests:
Frontal . . . . –
Side . . . . –
Airbags:
Head . . . . Front Head/Torso from Seat
Torso . . . . Front Head/Torso from Seat
Pelvis . . . . None
Roll Sensing . . . . No
Knee Bolster . . . . None
Crash Avoidance:
Frontal Collision Warning . . . . None
Blind Spot Detection . . . . None
Crash Imminent Braking . . . . None
Lane Departure Warning . . . . None
General:
Auto. Crash Notification . . . . None
Day Running Lamps . . . . None
Safety Belt/Restraint:
Dynamic Head Restraints . . . . None
Adjustable Belt . . . . None
Pretensioners . . . . Standard Front

Mini Countryman

Specifications

Drive	AWD
Engine	1.6-liter I4
Transmission	6-sp. Automatic
Tow Rating (lbs.)	–
Head/Leg Room (in.)	Cramped-39.9/40.4
Interior Space (cu. ft.)	Very Cramped-87
Cargo Space (cu. ft.)	Very Cramped-12.2
Wheelbase/Length (in.)	102.2/161.8

Ratings—10 Best, 1 Worst

Combo Crash Tests	4
Safety Features	3
Rollover	6
Preventive Maintenance	9
Repair Costs	5
Warranty	9
Fuel Economy	8
Complaints	5
Insurance Costs	1
OVERALL RATING	**6**

Mitsubishi Lancer Evolution

At-a-Glance

Status/Year Series Started	Unchanged/2008
Twins	-
Body Styles	Sedan, Hatchback
Seating	5
Anti-Theft Device	Std. Pass. Immobil. & Alarm
Parking Index Rating	Very Easy
Where Made	Mizushima, Japan
Fuel Factor	
MPG Rating (city/hwy)	Good-25/34
Driving Range (mi.)	Long-425
Fuel Type	Regular
Annual Fuel Cost	Low-$1,813
Gas Guzzler Tax	No
Greenhouse Gas Emissions (tons/yr.)	Average-6.3
Barrels of Oil Used per year	Average-11.4

How the Competition Rates

Competitors	Rating	Pg.
Honda Civic		148
Mazda Mazda3	5	190
Subaru Impreza	4	235

Price Range

	Retail	Markup
DE	$15,995	4%
GT	$20,995	4%
Ralliart	$28,095	4%
Evolution MR Touring	$40,045	5%

Mitsubishi Lancer GT

Safety Checklist

Crash Tests:
Frontal	Average
Side	Poor

Airbags:
Head	Fr. & Rr. Roof Curtain
Torso	Front Pelvis/Torso from Seat
Pelvis	Front Pelvis/Torso from Seat
Roll Sensing	No
Knee Bolster	Standard Driver

Crash Avoidance:
Frontal Collision Warning	None
Blind Spot Detection	None
Crash Imminent Braking	None
Lane Departure Warning	None

General:
Auto. Crash Notification	None
Day Running Lamps	Optional

Safety Belt/Restraint:
Dynamic Head Restraints	None
Adjustable Belt	Standard Front
Pretensioners	Standard Front

Mitsubishi Lancer Sportback

Specifications

Drive	FWD
Engine	2.0-liter I4
Transmission	CVT
Tow Rating (lbs.)	—
Head/Leg Room (in.)	Roomy-39.6/42.3
Interior Space (cu. ft.)	Cramped-93.5
Cargo Space (cu. ft.)	Very Cramped-12.3
Wheelbase/Length (in.)	103.7/180

Ratings—10 Best, 1 Worst	
Combo Crash Tests	1
Safety Features	4
Rollover	2
Preventive Maintenance	2
Repair Costs	5
Warranty	9
Fuel Economy	6
Complaints	5
Insurance Costs	5
OVERALL RATING	**2**

Mitsubishi Outlander

Mitsubishi Outlander

At-a-Glance

Status/Year Series Started	Unchanged/2007
Twins	-
Body Styles	SUV
Seating	5/7
Anti-Theft Device	Std. Pass. Immobil. & Alarm
Parking Index Rating	Easy
Where Made	Okazaki/Mizushima, Japan
Fuel Factor	
MPG Rating (city/hwy)	Average-23/28
Driving Range (mi.)	Long-415
Fuel Type	Regular
Annual Fuel Cost	Average-$2,057
Gas Guzzler Tax	No
Greenhouse Gas Emissions (tons/yr.)	Average-6.7
Barrels of Oil Used per year	Average-12.2

How the Competition Rates

Competitors	Rating	Pg.
Toyota Highlander	2	246
Hyundai Santa Fe	9	160
Ford Explorer	6	138

Price Range	Retail	Markup
ES	$22,695	4%
SE 2WD	$23,995	4%
SE 4WD	$25,495	4%
GT 4WD	$28,595	4%

Safety Checklist

Crash Tests:
Frontal	Very Poor
Side	Very Poor

Airbags:
Head	Fr. & Rr. Roof Curtain
Torso	Front Pelvis/Torso from Seat
Pelvis	Front Pelvis/Torso from Seat
Roll Sensing	Yes
Knee Bolster	None

Crash Avoidance:
Frontal Collision Warning	None
Blind Spot Detection	None
Crash Imminent Braking	None
Lane Departure Warning	None

General:
Auto. Crash Notification	None
Day Running Lamps	Optional

Safety Belt/Restraint:
Dynamic Head Restraints	None
Adjustable Belt	Standard Front
Pretensioners	Standard Front

Mitsubishi Outlander

Specifications

Drive	FWD
Engine	2.4-liter I4
Transmission	CVT
Tow Rating (lbs.)	Very Low-1500
Head/Leg Room (in.)	Roomy-40.3/41.6
Interior Space (cu. ft.)	Average-100.4
Cargo Space (cu. ft.)	Very Roomy-36.2
Wheelbase/Length (in.)	105.1/183.7

Mitsubishi Outlander Sport

Ratings—10 Best, 1 Worst

Combo Crash Tests	4
Safety Features	5
Rollover	2
Preventive Maintenance	3
Repair Costs	4
Warranty	9
Fuel Economy	7
Complaints	–
Insurance Costs	3
OVERALL RATING	**4**

Mitsubishi Outlander Sport

Mitsubishi Outlander Sport

At-a-Glance

Status/Year Series Started	All New/2013
Twins	-
Body Styles	SUV
Seating	5
Anti-Theft Device	Std. Pass. Immobil. & Alarm
Parking Index Rating	Very Easy
Where Made	Normal, IL
Fuel Factor	
MPG Rating (city/hwy)	Good-24/31
Driving Range (mi.)	Very Long-444
Fuel Type	Regular
Annual Fuel Cost	Low-$1,926
Gas Guzzler Tax	No
Greenhouse Gas Emissions (tons/yr.)	Average-6.7
Barrels of Oil Used per year	Average-12.2

How the Competition Rates

Competitors	Rating	Pg.
Acura RDX		83
Hyundai Tucson	7	162
Subaru XV Crosstrek		238

Price Range

Price Range	Retail	Markup
ES 2WD Manual	$19,170	4%
ES 4WD	$21,770	4%
SE 2WD	$22,295	4%
SE 4WD	$23,695	4%

Safety Checklist

Crash Tests:
Frontal . . . . Average
Side . . . . Very Poor

Airbags:
Head . . . . Fr. & Rr. Roof Curtain
Torso . . . . Front Pelvis/Torso from Seat
Pelvis . . . . Front Pelvis/Torso from Seat
Roll Sensing . . . . Yes
Knee Bolster . . . . Standard Driver

Crash Avoidance:
Frontal Collision Warning . . . . None
Blind Spot Detection . . . . None
Crash Imminent Braking . . . . None
Lane Departure Warning . . . . None

General:
Auto. Crash Notification . . . . None
Day Running Lamps . . . . None

Safety Belt/Restraint:
Dynamic Head Restraints . . . . None
Adjustable Belt . . . . Standard Front
Pretensioners . . . . Standard Front

Mitsubishi Outlander Sport

Specifications

Drive	FWD
Engine	2.0-liter I4
Transmission	CVT
Tow Rating (lbs.)	–
Head/Leg Room (in.)	Average-39.4/41.6
Interior Space (cu. ft.)	Average-97.5
Cargo Space (cu. ft.)	Roomy-21.7
Wheelbase/Length (in.)	105.1/169.1

Ratings—10 Best, 1 Worst

Combo Crash Tests	–
Safety Features	2
Rollover	10
Preventive Maintenance	9
Repair Costs	2
Warranty	2
Fuel Economy	3
Complaints	7
Insurance Costs	3

OVERALL RATING — –

Nissan 370Z

Nissan 370Z

At-a-Glance

Status/Year Series Started Appearance Change/2010
Twins . . . . -
Body Styles . . . . Coupe, Convertible
Seating 2
Anti-Theft Device . . . . . Std. Pass. Immobil. & Alarm
Parking Index Rating . . . . .Very Easy
Where Made. Tochigi, Japan
Fuel Factor . . . .
  MPG Rating (city/hwy) Poor-18/26
  Driving Range (mi.) Average-397
  Fuel Type. . . . . .Premium
  Annual Fuel Cost . . . . High-$2,678
  Gas Guzzler Tax . . . . .No
  Greenhouse Gas Emissions (tons/yr.) High-8.7
  Barrels of Oil Used per year High-15.7

How the Competition Rates

Competitors	Rating	Pg.
Chevrolet Corvette		112
Subaru BRZ		233
Mazda MX-5 Miata		195

Price Range	Retail	Markup
Base Manual	$33,120	8%
Touring Coupe	$39,120	8%
Nismo	$43,020	8%
Touring Roadster	$45,470	8%

Safety Checklist

Crash Tests:
  Frontal . . . . –
  Side . . . . –
Airbags:
  Head . . . . .Front Roof Curtain
  Torso. . . . . .Front Pelvis/Torso from Seat
  Pelvis . . . . .Front Pelvis/Torso from Seat
  Roll Sensing . . . . No
  Knee Bolster . . . . None
Crash Avoidance:
  Frontal Collision Warning . . . . None
  Blind Spot Detection . . . . None
  Crash Imminent Braking . . . . None
  Lane Departure Warning . . . . None
General:
  Auto. Crash Notification . . . . None
  Day Running Lamps . . . . None
Safety Belt/Restraint:
  Dynamic Head Restraints . . . . . .Standard Front
  Adjustable Belt . . . . None
  Pretensioners . . . . .Standard Front

Nissan 370Z

Specifications

Drive. . . . . RWD
Engine 3.7-liter V6
Transmission . . . . 6-sp. Manual
Tow Rating (lbs.) . . . . –
Head/Leg Room (in.) Average-38.2/42.9
Interior Space (cu. ft.). . . . . .Very Cramped-51.6
Cargo Space (cu. ft.) . . . . .Very Cramped-6.9
Wheelbase/Length (in.) 100.4/167.2

Ratings—10 Best, 1 Worst

Combo Crash Tests	3
Safety Features	3
Rollover	8
Preventive Maintenance	9
Repair Costs	8
Warranty	2
Fuel Economy	9
Complaints	–
Insurance Costs	3
OVERALL RATING	**6**

Nissan Altima

Nissan Altima

At-a-Glance

Status/Year Series Started	All New/2013
Twins	-
Body Styles	Sedan
Seating	5
Anti-Theft Device	Std. Pass. Immobil. & Alarm
Parking Index Rating	Average
Where Made	Smyrna, TN / Canton, MS
Fuel Factor	
MPG Rating (city/hwy)	Very Good-27/38
Driving Range (mi.)	Very Long-559
Fuel Type	Regular
Annual Fuel Cost	Very Low-$1,657
Gas Guzzler Tax	No
Greenhouse Gas Emissions (tons/yr.)	Low-5.9
Barrels of Oil Used per year	Low-10.6

How the Competition Rates

Competitors	Rating	Pg.
Honda Accord	9	146
Kia Optima	7	176
Toyota Camry	4	243

Price Range

	Retail	Markup
Base	$21,500	4%
2.5L S	$22,500	7%
3.5L SL	$30,080	8%

Safety Checklist

Crash Tests:
Frontal . . . . Poor
Side . . . . Poor

Airbags:
Head . . . . Fr & Rr. Roof Curtain
Torso . . . . Front Pelvis/Torso from Seat
Pelvis . . . . Front Pelvis/Torso from Seat
Roll Sensing . . . . No
Knee Bolster . . . . None

Crash Avoidance:
Frontal Collision Warning . . . . None
Blind Spot Detection . . . . Optional
Crash Imminent Braking . . . . None
Lane Departure Warning . . . . None

General:
Auto. Crash Notification . . . . None
Day Running Lamps . . . . None

Safety Belt/Restraint:
Dynamic Head Restraints . . . . None
Adjustable Belt . . . . Standard Front
Pretensioners . . . . Standard Front

Nissan Altima

Specifications

Drive	FWD
Engine	2.5-liter I4
Transmission	CVT
Tow Rating (lbs.)	–
Head/Leg Room (in.)	Very Cramped-40/39.1
Interior Space (cu. ft.)	Average-101.9
Cargo Space (cu. ft.)	Cramped-15.4
Wheelbase/Length (in.)	109.3/191.5

Nissan Altima Coupe Compact

Ratings—10 Best, 1 Worst

Combo Crash Tests	–
Safety Features	2
Rollover	8
Preventive Maintenance	9
Repair Costs	8
Warranty	2
Fuel Economy	7
Complaints	–
Insurance Costs	1

OVERALL RATING — –

Nissan Altima Coupe

At-a-Glance

Status/Year Series Started. Unchanged/2008
Twins . . . . -
Body Styles . . . . .Coupe
Seating 5
Anti-Theft Device . . . . . . Std. Pass. Immobil. & Alarm
Parking Index Rating . . . . Easy
Where Made. . . . . Smyrna, TN
Fuel Factor. . . . .
  MPG Rating (city/hwy) Good-23/32
  Driving Range (mi.) . . . . Very Long-527
  Fuel Type . . . . .Regular
  Annual Fuel Cost . . . . Low-$1,954
  Gas Guzzler Tax . . . . .No
  Greenhouse Gas Emissions (tons/yr.). . Average-7.1
  Barrels of Oil Used per year Average-12.7

How the Competition Rates

Competitors	Rating	Pg.
Mitsubishi Lancer	6	205
Scion tC	8	229
Subaru Impreza	4	235

Price Range	Retail	Markup
2.5L S	$24,980	7%

Nissan Altima Coupe

Nissan Altima Coupe

Safety Checklist

Crash Tests:
  Frontal. . . . .–
  Side. . . . .–
Airbags:
  Head . . . . Fr. & Rr. Roof Curtain
  Torso. . . . . .Front Pelvis/Torso from Seat
  Pelvis . . . . .Front Pelvis/Torso from Seat
  Roll Sensing . . . . No
  Knee Bolster . . . . None
Crash Avoidance:
  Frontal Collision Warning . . . . None
  Blind Spot Detection . . . . None
  Crash Imminent Braking . . . . None
  Lane Departure Warning . . . . None
General:
  Auto. Crash Notification . . . . None
  Day Running Lamps . . . . Optional
Safety Belt/Restraint:
  Dynamic Head Restraints . . . . None
  Adjustable Belt . . . . .Standard Front
  Pretensioners . . . . .Standard Front

Nissan Altima Coupe

Specifications

Drive . . . . FWD
Engine 2.5-liter I4
Transmission . . . . .CVT
Tow Rating (lbs.) . . . . –
Head/Leg Room (in.) Roomy-39.7/42.5
Interior Space (cu. ft.). . . . . .Very Cramped-89.3
Cargo Space (cu. ft.) . . . . .Very Cramped-8.2
Wheelbase/Length (in.) 105.3/180.9

Ratings—10 Best, 1 Worst

Combo Crash Tests	–
Safety Features	6
Rollover	1
Preventive Maintenance	4
Repair Costs	4
Warranty	2
Fuel Economy	1
Complaints	3
Insurance Costs	10

OVERALL RATING — –

Nissan Armada

Nissan Armada

At-a-Glance

Status/Year Series Started	Unchanged/2004
Twins	-
Body Styles	SUV
Seating	7/8
Anti-Theft Device	Std. Pass. Immobil. & Alarm
Parking Index Rating	Very Hard
Where Made	Canton, MS
Fuel Factor	
MPG Rating (city/hwy)	Very Poor-12/18
Driving Range (mi.)	Average-395
Fuel Type	Regular
Annual Fuel Cost	Very High-$3,644
Gas Guzzler Tax	No
Greenhouse Gas Emissions (tons/yr.)	Very High-10.4
Barrels of Oil Used per year	Very High-23.5

How the Competition Rates

Competitors	Rating	Pg.
Chevrolet Suburban	7	119
Ford Expedition	4	137
Toyota Sequoia		252

Price Range	Retail	Markup
SV 2WD	$38,490	10%
SL 2WD	$43,940	10%
SL 4WD	$46,840	10%
Platinum 4WD	$53,950	10%

Safety Checklist

Crash Tests:
Frontal . . . . –
Side . . . . –
Airbags:
Head . . . . Fr. & Rr. Roof Curtain
Torso . . . . Front Pelvis/Torso from Seat
Pelvis . . . . Front Pelvis/Torso from Seat
Roll Sensing . . . . .Yes
Knee Bolster . . . . None
Crash Avoidance:
Frontal Collision Warning . . . . None
Blind Spot Detection . . . . None
Crash Imminent Braking . . . . None
Lane Departure Warning . . . . None
General:
Auto. Crash Notification . . . . None
Day Running Lamps . . . . None
Safety Belt/Restraint:
Dynamic Head Restraints . . . . . .Standard Front
Adjustable Belt . . . . . .Standard Front and Rear
Pretensioners . . . . .Standard Front

Nissan Armada

Specifications

Drive	RWD
Engine	.5.6-liter V8
Transmission	5-sp. Auto. w/Overdrive
Tow Rating (lbs.)	Very High-8200
Head/Leg Room (in.)	Roomy-41/41.8
Interior Space (cu. ft.)	Roomy-127.3
Cargo Space (cu. ft.)	Average-20
Wheelbase/Length (in.)	123.2/207.7

Ratings—10 Best, 1 Worst

Combo Crash Tests	–
Safety Features	4
Rollover	2
Preventive Maintenance	9
Repair Costs	9
Warranty	2
Fuel Economy	8
Complaints	10
Insurance Costs	1
OVERALL RATING	**–**

Nissan Cube

Nissan Cube

At-a-Glance

Status/Year Series Started. Unchanged/2009
Twins . . . . -
Body Styles . . . . Hatchback
Seating 5
Anti-Theft Device . . . . . Std. Pass. Immobil. & Alarm
Parking Index Rating . . . . .Very Easy
Where Made. . . . . Oppama, Japan
Fuel Factor. . . . .
  MPG Rating (city/hwy) Good-27/31
  Driving Range (mi.) Short-378
  Fuel Type . . . . .Regular
  Annual Fuel Cost . . . . Low-$1,795
  Gas Guzzler Tax . . . . .No
  Greenhouse Gas Emissions (tons/yr.). . Average-6.5
  Barrels of Oil Used per year Average-11.8

How the Competition Rates

Competitors	Rating	Pg.
Kia Soul	6	179
Mini Countryman		204
Scion xD		231

Price Range

	Retail	Markup
Base	$14,980	4%
S	$16,580	4%
SL	$18,680	4%

Nissan Cube

Safety Checklist

Crash Tests:
  Frontal. . . . .–
  Side. . . . .–
Airbags:
  Head . . . . Fr. & Rr. Roof Curtain
  Torso. . . . . .Front Pelvis/Torso from Seat
  Pelvis . . . . .Front Pelvis/Torso from Seat
  Roll Sensing . . . . No
  Knee Bolster . . . . None
Crash Avoidance:
  Frontal Collision Warning . . . . None
  Blind Spot Detection . . . . None
  Crash Imminent Braking . . . . None
  Lane Departure Warning . . . . None
General:
  Auto. Crash Notification . . . . None
  Day Running Lamps . . . . None
Safety Belt/Restraint:
  Dynamic Head Restraints . . . . . .Standard Front
  Adjustable Belt . . . . .Standard Front
  Pretensioners . . . . .Standard Front

Nissan Cube

Specifications

Drive. . . . . FWD
Engine 1.8-liter I4
Transmission . . . . .CVT
Tow Rating (lbs.) . . . . –
Head/Leg Room (in.) . . . . . . Very Roomy-42.6/42.4
Interior Space (cu. ft.). Average-97.7
Cargo Space (cu. ft.) . . . . .Very Cramped-11.4
Wheelbase/Length (in.) 99.6/156.7

Ratings—10 Best, 1 Worst

Combo Crash Tests	–
Safety Features	6
Rollover	1
Preventive Maintenance	4
Repair Costs	7
Warranty	2
Fuel Economy	1
Complaints	5
Insurance Costs	5
OVERALL RATING	**–**

Nissan Frontier

Nissan Frontier

At-a-Glance

Status/Year Series Started	Unchanged/2005
Twins	-
Body Styles	Pickup
Seating	5
Anti-Theft Device	Opt. Pass. Immobil. & Alarm
Parking Index Rating	Very Hard
Where Made	Canton, MS
Fuel Factor	
MPG Rating (city/hwy)	Very Poor-14/19
Driving Range (mi.)	Very Short-335
Fuel Type	Regular
Annual Fuel Cost	Very High-$3,240
Gas Guzzler Tax	No
Greenhouse Gas Emissions (tons/yr.)	Very High-11.6
Barrels of Oil Used per year	Very High-21.4

How the Competition Rates

Competitors	Rating	Pg.
Honda Ridgeline		155
Toyota Tacoma	1	254

Price Range

	Retail	Markup
S King Cab 2WD I4 Manual	$18,200	5%
SV Crew Cab 4WD SWB	$26,970	7%
PRO-4X	$29,320	8%
SL Crew Cab 4WD LWB	$32,080	8%

Safety Checklist

Crash Tests:
Frontal..–
Side...–
Airbags:
Head......................Fr & Rr. Roof Curtain
Torso...........Front Pelvis/Torso from Seat
Pelvis...........Front Pelvis/Torso from Seat
Roll Sensing.....................................Yes
Knee Bolster...................................None
Crash Avoidance:
Frontal Collision Warning...............None
Blind Spot Detection.....................None
Crash Imminent Braking................None
Lane Departure Warning...............None
General:
Auto. Crash Notification................None
Day Running Lamps.....................None
Safety Belt/Restraint:
Dynamic Head Restraints......Standard Front
Adjustable Belt.................Standard Front
Pretensioners.................Standard Front

Nissan Frontier

Specifications

Drive	4WD
Engine	4.0-liter V6
Transmission	5-sp. Automatic
Tow Rating (lbs.)	High-6100
Head/Leg Room (in.)	Roomy-40/42.4
Interior Space (cu. ft.)	Average-101.1
Cargo Space (cu. ft.)	Roomy-27.1
Wheelbase/Length (in.)	125.9/205.5

Ratings—10 Best, 1 Worst

Combo Crash Tests	1
Safety Features	4
Rollover	4
Preventive Maintenance	9
Repair Costs	8
Warranty	2
Fuel Economy	8
Complaints	9
Insurance Costs	5
OVERALL RATING	**5**

Nissan Juke

Nissan Juke

At-a-Glance

Status/Year Series Started	Unchanged/2011
Twins	-
Body Styles	SUV
Seating	5
Anti-Theft Device	Std. Pass. Immobil. & Alarm
Parking Index Rating	Easy
Where Made	Oppama, Japan
Fuel Factor	
MPG Rating (city/hwy)	Good-27/32
Driving Range (mi.)	Short-383
Fuel Type	Premium
Annual Fuel Cost	Low-$1,927
Gas Guzzler Tax	No
Greenhouse Gas Emissions (tons/yr.)	Average-6.3
Barrels of Oil Used per year	Average-11.4

How the Competition Rates

Competitors	Rating	Pg.
Kia Soul	6	179
Ford Escape	7	136
Scion xB		230

Price Range	Retail	Markup
S FWD	$19,990	5%
SV FWD	$22,110	5%
SV AWD	$23,760	6%
SL AWD	$26,650	6%

Safety Checklist

Crash Tests:
Frontal . . . . Very Poor
Side . . . . Very Poor

Airbags:
Head . . . . Fr. & Rr. Roof Curtain
Torso . . . . Front Pelvis/Torso from Seat
Pelvis . . . . Front Pelvis/Torso from Seat
Roll Sensing . . . . No
Knee Bolster . . . . None

Crash Avoidance:
Frontal Collision Warning . . . . None
Blind Spot Detection . . . . None
Crash Imminent Braking . . . . None
Lane Departure Warning . . . . None

General:
Auto. Crash Notification . . . . None
Day Running Lamps . . . . None

Safety Belt/Restraint:
Dynamic Head Restraints . . . . . . Standard Front
Adjustable Belt . . . . Standard Front
Pretensioners . . . . Standard Front

Nissan Juke

Specifications

Drive	FWD
Engine	1.6-liter I4
Transmission	CVT
Tow Rating (lbs.)	–
Head/Leg Room (in.)	Average-39.6/42.1
Interior Space (cu. ft.)	Very Cramped-86.7
Cargo Space (cu. ft.)	Very Cramped-10.5
Wheelbase/Length (in.)	99.6/162.4

Ratings—10 Best, 1 Worst

Combo Crash Tests	7
Safety Features	2
Rollover	7
Preventive Maintenance	8
Repair Costs	9
Warranty	2
Fuel Economy	10
Complaints	1
Insurance Costs	5
OVERALL RATING	**7**

Nissan Leaf

Nissan Leaf

At-a-Glance

Status/Year Series Started........ Unchanged/2011
Twins . . . . -
Body Styles . . . . Hatchback
Seating 5
Anti-Theft Device . . . . . . Std. Pass. Immobil. & Alarm
Parking Index Rating . . . . .Very Easy
Where Made. . . . . Oppama, Japan / Smyrna, TN
Fuel Factor . . . .
   MPG Rating (city/hwy) . . . . . . Very Good-106/92
   Driving Range (mi.) . . . . .Very Short-80
   Fuel Type . . . . Electricity
   Annual Fuel Cost . . . . .Very Low-$423
   Gas Guzzler Tax . . . . .No
   Greenhouse Gas Emissions (tons/yr.). Very Low-0.0
   Barrels of Oil Used per year . . . . Very Low-0.0

How the Competition Rates

Competitors	Rating	Pg.
Chevrolet Volt	9	122
Honda Insight		152
Toyota Prius	7	248

Price Range	Retail	Markup
SV	$35,200	4%
SL	$37,250	4%

Safety Checklist

Crash Tests:
   Frontal . . . . Average
   Side . . . . Very Good
Airbags:
   Head . . . . Fr. & Rr. Roof Curtain
   Torso. . . . . .Front Pelvis/Torso from Seat
   Pelvis . . . . .Front Pelvis/Torso from Seat
   Roll Sensing . . . . No
   Knee Bolster . . . . None
Crash Avoidance:
   Frontal Collision Warning . . . . None
   Blind Spot Detection . . . . None
   Crash Imminent Braking . . . . None
General:
   Lane Departure Warning . . . . None
   Auto. Crash Notification . . . . None
   Day Running Lamps . . . . None
Safety Belt/Restraint:
   Dynamic Head Restraints . . . . None
   Adjustable Belt . . . . .Standard Front
   Pretensioners . . . . .Standard Front

Nissan Leaf

Specifications

Drive. . . . . FWD
Engine . . . . 80.0 kW Electric
Transmission . . . . Single Speed Reducer
Tow Rating (lbs.) . . . . –
Head/Leg Room (in.) . . . . . . Very Roomy-41.2/42.1
Interior Space (cu. ft.). Cramped-90
Cargo Space (cu. ft.) Cramped-14.5
Wheelbase/Length (in.) 106.3/175

Ratings—10 Best, 1 Worst

Combo Crash Tests	2
Safety Features	4
Rollover	8
Preventive Maintenance	7
Repair Costs	6
Warranty	2
Fuel Economy	3
Complaints	9
Insurance Costs	3
OVERALL RATING	**4**

Nissan Maxima

Nissan Maxima

At-a-Glance

Status/Year Series Started. Unchanged/2009
Twins . . . . -
Body Styles . . . . .Sedan
Seating 5
Anti-Theft Device . . . . . . Std. Pass. Immobil. & Alarm
Parking Index Rating . . . . Average
Where Made. Smyrna, TN
Fuel Factor. . . . .
  MPG Rating (city/hwy) Poor-19/26
  Driving Range (mi.) Long-432
  Fuel Type. . . . . .Regular
  Annual Fuel Cost . . . . High-$2,380
  Gas Guzzler Tax . . . . .No
  Greenhouse Gas Emissions (tons/yr.) High-8.3
  Barrels of Oil Used per year High-15.0

How the Competition Rates

Competitors	Rating	Pg.
Chevrolet Impala	6	115
Honda Accord	9	146
Toyota Camry	4	243

Price Range	Retail	Markup
S	$32,780	9%
SV	$35,080	9%

Safety Checklist

Crash Tests:
  Frontal. . . . . .Very Poor
  Side. . . . . Poor
Airbags:
  Head . . . . .Fr & Rr. Roof Curtain
  Torso. . . . . .Front Pelvis/Torso from Seat
  Pelvis . . . . .Front Pelvis/Torso from Seat
  Roll Sensing . . . . No
  Knee Bolster . . . . None
Crash Avoidance:
  Frontal Collision Warning . . . . None
  Blind Spot Detection . . . . None
  Crash Imminent Braking. . . . . None
  Lane Departure Warning . . . . None
General:
  Auto. Crash Notification . . . . None
  Day Running Lamps . . . . None
Safety Belt/Restraint:
  Dynamic Head Restraints. . . . . .Standard Front
  Adjustable Belt . . . . .Standard Front
  Pretensioners . . . . .Standard Front

Nissan Maxima

Specifications

Drive. . . . . FWD
Engine 3.5-liter V6
Transmission . . . . .CVT
Tow Rating (lbs.) . . . . Very Low-1000
Head/Leg Room (in.) Roomy-38.5/43.8
Interior Space (cu. ft.). Cramped-95.8
Cargo Space (cu. ft.) Cramped-14.2
Wheelbase/Length (in.) 109.3/190.6

Ratings—10 Best, 1 Worst

Combo Crash Tests	1
Safety Features	6
Rollover	2
Preventive Maintenance	8
Repair Costs	4
Warranty	2
Fuel Economy	3
Complaints	8
Insurance Costs	10
OVERALL RATING	**3**

Nissan Murano

Nissan Murano

At-a-Glance

Status/Year Series Started........ Unchanged/2009
Twins . . . . -
Body Styles . . . . SUV
Seating 5
Anti-Theft Device . . . . . . Std. Pass. Immobil. & Alarm
Parking Index Rating . . . . Hard
Where Made. . . . . Kyushu, Japan
Fuel Factor . . . .
  MPG Rating (city/hwy) Poor-18/24
  Driving Range (mi.) Long-440
  Fuel Type . . . . .Regular
  Annual Fuel Cost . . . . High-$2,537
  Gas Guzzler Tax . . . . .No
  Greenhouse Gas Emissions (tons/yr.) High-9.1
  Barrels of Oil Used per year High-16.5

How the Competition Rates

Competitors	Rating	Pg.
Acura MDX	8	82
Honda Pilot	4	154
Toyota Highlander	2	246

Price Range

	Retail	Markup
S FWD	$29,290	9%
SV AWD	$34,460	9%
SL FWD	$36,400	9%
LE AWD	$39,900	9%

Safety Checklist

Crash Tests:
  Frontal . . . . .Very Poor
  Side . . . . .Very Poor
Airbags:
  Head . . . . Fr. & Rr. Roof Curtain
  Torso . . . . .Front Pelvis/Torso from Seat
  Pelvis . . . . .Front Pelvis/Torso from Seat
  Roll Sensing . . . . .Yes
  Knee Bolster . . . . None
Crash Avoidance:
  Frontal Collision Warning . . . . None
  Blind Spot Detection . . . . Optional
  Crash Imminent Braking . . . . None
  Lane Departure Warning . . . . None
General:
  Auto. Crash Notification . . . . None
  Day Running Lamps . . . . None
Safety Belt/Restraint:
  Dynamic Head Restraints . . . . . .Standard Front
  Adjustable Belt . . . . . .Standard Front and Rear
  Pretensioners . . . . .Standard Front

Nissan Murano

Specifications

Drive. . . . . AWD
Engine 3.5-liter V6
Transmission . . . . .CVT
Tow Rating (lbs.) Low-3500
Head/Leg Room (in.) . . . . . Very Roomy-40.1/43.6
Interior Space (cu. ft.). . . . . Very Roomy-140.4
Cargo Space (cu. ft.) Roomy-31.8
Wheelbase/Length (in.) 111.2/189.9

Ratings—10 Best, 1 Worst

Combo Crash Tests	5
Safety Features	6
Rollover	3
Preventive Maintenance	4
Repair Costs	6
Warranty	2
Fuel Economy	3
Complaints	–
Insurance Costs	10
OVERALL RATING	**5**

Nissan Pathfinder

Safety Checklist

Crash Tests:
Frontal............................Poor
Side.............................Good
Airbags:
Head..............Fr. & Rr. Roof Curtain
Torso..........Front Pelvis/Torso from Seat
Pelvis..........Front Pelvis/Torso from Seat
Roll Sensing.........................Yes
Knee Bolster......................None
Crash Avoidance:
Frontal Collision Warning............None
Blind Spot Detection................None
Crash Imminent Braking.............None
Lane Departure Warning............None
General:
Auto. Crash Notification............None
Day Running Lamps................None
Safety Belt/Restraint:
Dynamic Head Restraints......Standard Front
Adjustable Belt......Standard Front and Rear
Pretensioners.............Standard Front

Nissan Pathfinder

At-a-Glance

Status/Year Series Started...........All New/2013
Twins..............................Infiniti JX
Body Styles............................SUV
Seating................................7
Anti-Theft Device......Std. Pass. Immobil. & Alarm
Parking Index Rating....................Hard
Where Made......................Smyrna, TN
Fuel Factor.............................
  MPG Rating (city/hwy).........Poor-19/25
  Driving Range (mi.)...........Long-415
  Fuel Type.....................Regular
  Annual Fuel Cost............High-$2,415
  Gas Guzzler Tax..................No
  Greenhouse Gas Emissions (tons/yr.).....High-8.8
  Barrels of Oil Used per year..........High-15.7

How the Competition Rates

Competitors	Rating	Pg.
Chevrolet Equinox	5	114
Toyota Highlander	2	246
Volvo XC90		270

Price Range	Retail	Markup
S 2WD	$28,570	7%
SV 4WD	$33,920	8%
Silver Edition 2WD	$35,910	8%
LE V8 4WD	$43,250	8%

Specifications

Drive...................................4WD
Engine..........................3.5-liter V6
Transmission.........................CVT
Tow Rating (lbs.)..............Average-5000
Head/Leg Room (in.).....Very Cramped-41.1/38.5
Interior Space (cu. ft.).........Very Roomy-157.8
Cargo Space (cu. ft.).............Average-16
Wheelbase/Length (in.)........114.2/197.2

Nissan Quest

Ratings—10 Best, 1 Worst

Combo Crash Tests	–
Safety Features	4
Rollover	3
Preventive Maintenance	8
Repair Costs	5
Warranty	2
Fuel Economy	3
Complaints	1
Insurance Costs	5
OVERALL RATING	–

Nissan Quest

Nissan Quest

At-a-Glance

Status/Year Series Started........ Unchanged/2011
Twins . . . . -
Body Styles . . . . .Minivan
Seating 7
Anti-Theft Device . . . . . . Std. Pass. Immobil. & Alarm
Parking Index Rating . . . . Hard
Where Made. . . . . Kyushu, Japan
Fuel Factor . . . .
  MPG Rating (city/hwy) Poor-19/25
  Driving Range (mi.) Long-428
  Fuel Type. . . . . .Regular
  Annual Fuel Cost . . . . High-$2,415
  Gas Guzzler Tax .No
  Greenhouse Gas Emissions (tons/yr.) High-8.7
  Barrels of Oil Used per year High-15.7

How the Competition Rates

Competitors	Rating	Pg.
Chrysler Town and Country	5	125
Honda Odyssey	7	153
Toyota Sienna	3	253

Price Range

Price Range	Retail	Markup
S	$27,750	7%
SV	$31,050	9%
SL	$34,500	9%
LE	$41,350	9%

Safety Checklist

Crash Tests:
  Frontal. . . . .–
  Side. . . . .–
Airbags:
  Head . . . . Fr. & Rr. Roof Curtain
  Torso. . . . . .Front Pelvis/Torso from Seat
  Pelvis . . . . .Front Pelvis/Torso from Seat
  Roll Sensing . . . . No
  Knee Bolster . . . . None
Crash Avoidance:
  Frontal Collision Warning . . . . None
  Blind Spot Detection . . . . Optional
  Crash Imminent Braking . . . . None
  Lane Departure Warning . . . . None
General:
  Auto. Crash Notification . . . . None
  Day Running Lamps . . . . None
Safety Belt/Restraint:
  Dynamic Head Restraints . . . . . .Standard Front
  Adjustable Belt . . . . . .Standard Front and Rear
  Pretensioners . . . . .Standard Front

Nissan Quest

Specifications

Drive. . . . . FWD
Engine 3.5-liter V6
Transmission . . . . .CVT
Tow Rating (lbs.) Low-3500
Head/Leg Room (in.) . . . . . . Very Roomy-42.1/43.8
Interior Space (cu. ft.). . . . . Very Roomy-177.8
Cargo Space (cu. ft.) . . . . Very Roomy-37.1
Wheelbase/Length (in.) 118.1/200.8

Ratings—10 Best, 1 Worst

Combo Crash Tests	5
Safety Features	6
Rollover	3
Preventive Maintenance	8
Repair Costs	4
Warranty	2
Fuel Economy	5
Complaints	9
Insurance Costs	5
OVERALL RATING	**5**

Nissan Rogue

Nissan Rogue

At-a-Glance

Status/Year Series Started........ Unchanged/2008
Twins . . . . -
Body Styles . . . . SUV
Seating 5
Anti-Theft Device . . . . . . Std. Pass. Immobil. & Alarm
Parking Index Rating . . . . Average
Where Made. . . . . .Kyushu, Japan / Smyrna, TN
Fuel Factor . . . .
  MPG Rating (city/hwy) Average-22/27
  Driving Range (mi.) Short-382
  Fuel Type . . . . .Regular
  Annual Fuel Cost . . . . Average-$2,144
  Gas Guzzler Tax . . . . .No
  Greenhouse Gas Emissions (tons/yr.). High-7.6
  Barrels of Oil Used per year High-13.7

How the Competition Rates

Competitors	Rating	Pg.
Kia Sorento	3	178
Toyota Venza	3	256
Volvo XC60	9	269

Price Range	Retail	Markup
S FWD	$22,310	5%
S AWD	$23,610	5%
S FWD	$24,750	5%
S AWD	$26,050	5%

Safety Checklist

Crash Tests:
  Frontal . . . . .Poor
  Side. . . . . Good
Airbags:
  Head . . . . Fr. & Rr. Roof Curtain
  Torso. . . . . .Front Pelvis/Torso from Seat
  Pelvis . . . . .Front Pelvis/Torso from Seat
  Roll Sensing . . . . .Yes
  Knee Bolster . . . . None
Crash Avoidance:
  Frontal Collision Warning . . . . None
  Blind Spot Detection . . . . None
  Crash Imminent Braking . . . . None
  Lane Departure Warning . . . . None
General:
  Auto. Crash Notification . . . . None
  Day Running Lamps . . . . None
Safety Belt/Restraint:
  Dynamic Head Restraints . . . . . .Standard Front
  Adjustable Belt . . . . . .Standard Front and Rear
  Pretensioners . . . . .Standard Front

Nissan Rogue

Specifications

Drive . . . . AWD
Engine 2.5-liter I4
Transmission . . . . .CVT
Tow Rating (lbs.) . . . . Very Low-1000
Head/Leg Room (in.) Roomy-40.4/42.5
Interior Space (cu. ft.). Average-97.5
Cargo Space (cu. ft.) Roomy-28.9
Wheelbase/Length (in.) 105.9/183.3

Nissan Sentra

Ratings—10 Best, 1 Worst	
Combo Crash Tests	–
Safety Features	4
Rollover	6
Preventive Maintenance	8
Repair Costs	9
Warranty	2
Fuel Economy	10
Complaints	–
Insurance Costs	3
OVERALL RATING	**–**

Nissan Sentra

Nissan Sentra

At-a-Glance

Status/Year Series Started	All New/2013
Twins	-
Body Styles	Sedan
Seating	5
Anti-Theft Device	Std. Pass. Immobil. & Alarm
Parking Index Rating	Easy
Where Made	Canton, MS
Fuel Factor	
MPG Rating (city/hwy)	Very Good-30/39
Driving Range (mi.)	Long-442
Fuel Type	Regular
Annual Fuel Cost	Very Low-$1,537
Gas Guzzler Tax	No
Greenhouse Gas Emissions (tons/yr.)	Low-5.3
Barrels of Oil Used per year	Low-9.7

How the Competition Rates

Competitors	Rating	Pg.
Chevrolet Cruze	9	113
Honda Civic		148
Toyota Corolla	4	244

Price Range	Retail	Markup
Base	$17,430	4%
S	$18,180	7%
SL	$19,580	7%
SE-R Spec V Manual Trans.	$20,810	7%

Safety Checklist

Crash Tests:
Frontal...................................–
Side......................................–
Airbags:
Head...................Fr & Rr. Roof Curtain
Torso............Front Pelvis/Torso from Seat
Pelvis...........Front Pelvis/Torso from Seat
Roll Sensing..............................No
Knee Bolster...........................None
Crash Avoidance:
Frontal Collision Warning..............None
Blind Spot Detection...................None
Crash Imminent Braking................None
Lane Departure Warning................None
General:
Auto. Crash Notification...............None
Day Running Lamps....................None
Safety Belt/Restraint:
Dynamic Head Restraints......Standard Front
Adjustable Belt...............Standard Front
Pretensioners................Standard Front

Nissan Sentra

Specifications

Drive	FWD
Engine	1.8-liter I4
Transmission	CVT
Tow Rating (lbs.)	–
Head/Leg Room (in.)	Roomy-39.4/42.5
Interior Space (cu. ft.)	Cramped-95.9
Cargo Space (cu. ft.)	Cramped-15.1
Wheelbase/Length (in.)	106.3/182.1

Ratings—10 Best, 1 Worst

Combo Crash Tests	–
Safety Features	6
Rollover	2
Preventive Maintenance	4
Repair Costs	4
Warranty	2
Fuel Economy	1
Complaints	2
Insurance Costs	5

OVERALL RATING   –

Nissan Titan

Nissan Titan

At-a-Glance

Status/Year Series Started	Appearance Change/2004
Twins	-
Body Styles	Pickup
Seating	5
Anti-Theft Device	Opt. Pass. Immobil. & Alarm
Parking Index Rating	Very Hard
Where Made	Canton, MS
Fuel Factor	
MPG Rating (city/hwy)	Very Poor-12/17
Driving Range (mi.)	Short-387
Fuel Type	Regular
Annual Fuel Cost	Very High-$3,720
Gas Guzzler Tax	No
Greenhouse Gas Emissions (tons/yr.)	Very High-10.6
Barrels of Oil Used per year	Very High-23.5

How the Competition Rates

Competitors	Rating	Pg.
Chevrolet Silverado	7	117
Ford F-150	5	139
Honda Ridgeline		155

Price Range

	Retail	Markup
S King 2WD	$27,410	10%
SV King 4WD	$32,260	10%
SL Crew 2WD	$37,510	10%
SL Crew 4WD	$40,210	10%

Safety Checklist

Crash Tests:
Frontal	–
Side	–

Airbags:
Head	Fr & Rr. Roof Curtain
Torso	Front Pelvis/Torso from Seat
Pelvis	Front Pelvis/Torso from Seat
Roll Sensing	Yes
Knee Bolster	None

Crash Avoidance:
Frontal Collision Warning	None
Blind Spot Detection	None
Crash Imminent Braking	None
Lane Departure Warning	None

General:
Auto. Crash Notification	None
Day Running Lamps	None

Safety Belt/Restraint:
Dynamic Head Restraints	Standard Front
Adjustable Belt	Standard Front
Pretensioners	Standard Front

Nissan Titan

Specifications

Drive	RWD
Engine	5.6-liter V8
Transmission	5-sp. Automatic
Tow Rating (lbs.)	High-7400
Head/Leg Room (in.)	Roomy-41/41.8
Interior Space (cu. ft.)	Roomy-112.8
Cargo Space (cu. ft.)	–
Wheelbase/Length (in.)	139.8/224.6

Ratings—10 Best, 1 Worst

Combo Crash Tests	1
Safety Features	4
Rollover	4
Preventive Maintenance	9
Repair Costs	10
Warranty	2
Fuel Economy	8
Complaints	8
Insurance Costs	1
OVERALL RATING	**4**

Nissan Versa

Nissan Versa Hatchback

At-a-Glance

Status/Year Series Started	Unchanged/2006
Twins	-
Body Styles	Sedan, Hatchback
Seating	5
Anti-Theft Device	Opt. Pass. Immobil. & Alarm
Parking Index Rating	Very Easy
Where Made	Aguascalientes, Mexico
Fuel Factor	
MPG Rating (city/hwy)	Good-26/35
Driving Range (mi.)	Short-388
Fuel Type	Regular
Annual Fuel Cost	Very Low-$1,750
Gas Guzzler Tax	No
Greenhouse Gas Emissions (tons/yr.)	Low-6.1
Barrels of Oil Used per year	Average-11.0

How the Competition Rates

Competitors	Rating	Pg.
Honda Fit	4	151
Hyundai Accent	8	156
Toyota Yaris	5	257

Price Range

	Retail	Markup
S Manual	$10,990	4%
SV Automatic	$14,560	4%
SL Sedan	$15,560	4%
SL Hatchback	$18,390	4%

Safety Checklist

Crash Tests:
Frontal . . . . Very Poor
Side . . . . Very Poor
Airbags:
Head . . . . Fr & Rr. Roof Curtain
Torso . . . . Front Pelvis/Torso from Seat
Pelvis . . . . Front Pelvis/Torso from Seat
Roll Sensing . . . . No
Knee Bolster . . . . None
Crash Avoidance:
Frontal Collision Warning . . . . None
Blind Spot Detection . . . . None
Crash Imminent Braking . . . . None
Lane Departure Warning . . . . None
General:
Auto. Crash Notification . . . . None
Day Running Lamps . . . . None
Safety Belt/Restraint:
Dynamic Head Restraints . . . . . . Standard Front
Adjustable Belt . . . . Standard Front
Pretensioners . . . . Standard Front

Nissan Versa

Specifications

Drive	FWD
Engine	1.6-liter I4
Transmission	4-sp. Automatic
Tow Rating (lbs.)	–
Head/Leg Room (in.)	Average-39.8/41.8
Interior Space (cu. ft.)	Cramped-90
Cargo Space (cu. ft.)	Cramped-14.8
Wheelbase/Length (in.)	102.4/175.4

Ratings—10 Best, 1 Worst

Combo Crash Tests	–
Safety Features	6
Rollover	1
Preventive Maintenance	4
Repair Costs	8
Warranty	2
Fuel Economy	1
Complaints	3
Insurance Costs	10
OVERALL RATING	**–**

Nissan Xterra

Nissan Xterra

Nissan Xterra

At-a-Glance

Status/Year Series Started. Unchanged/2005
Twins . . . . -
Body Styles . . . . SUV
Seating 5
Anti-Theft Device . . . . . . Std. Pass. Immobil. & Alarm
Parking Index Rating . . . . Average
Where Made. . . . . Canton, MS
Fuel Factor . . . .
  MPG Rating (city/hwy) . . . . . .Very Poor-15/20
  Driving Range (mi.) . . . . .Very Short-357
  Fuel Type. . . . . .Regular
  Annual Fuel Cost . . . . Very High-$3,044
  Gas Guzzler Tax .No
  Greenhouse Gas Emissions (tons/yr.)Very High-11.0
  Barrels of Oil Used per year . . . . . . .Very High-20.1

How the Competition Rates

Competitors	Rating	Pg.
Hyundai Santa Fe	9	160
Toyota FJ Cruiser		245
Volvo XC90		270

Price Range	Retail	Markup
X 2WD	$24,260	6%
X 4WD	$26,310	6%
S 4WD	$28,300	6%
PRO-4X	$30,720	7%

Safety Checklist

Crash Tests:
  Frontal. . . . . –
  Side. . . . . –
Airbags:
  Head . . . . .Fr & Rr. Roof Curtain
  Torso. . . . . .Front Pelvis/Torso from Seat
  Pelvis . . . . .Front Pelvis/Torso from Seat
  Roll Sensing . . . . .Yes
  Knee Bolster . . . . None
Crash Avoidance:
  Frontal Collision Warning . . . . None
  Blind Spot Detection . . . . None
  Crash Imminent Braking . . . . None
  Lane Departure Warning . . . . None
General:
  Auto. Crash Notification . . . . None
  Day Running Lamps . . . . None
Safety Belt/Restraint:
  Dynamic Head Restraints . . . . . .Standard Front
  Adjustable Belt . . . . . .Standard Front and Rear
  Pretensioners . . . . .Standard Front

Nissan Xterra

Specifications

Drive. 4WD
Engine 4.0-liter V6
Transmission . . . . .5-sp. Automatic
Tow Rating (lbs.) Average-5000
Head/Leg Room (in.) Roomy-39.9/42.4
Interior Space (cu. ft.). Average-99.8
Cargo Space (cu. ft.) . . . . Very Roomy-36.3
Wheelbase/Length (in.) 106.3/178.7

Porsche Cayenne

Porsche Cayenne

Ratings—10 Best, 1 Worst

Combo Crash Tests	–
Safety Features	7
Rollover	4
Preventive Maintenance	4
Repair Costs	1
Warranty	8
Fuel Economy	2
Complaints	4
Insurance Costs	5
OVERALL RATING	**–**

Porsche Cayenne

At-a-Glance

Status/Year Series Started. Unchanged/2011
Twins . . . . Volkswagen Touareg
Body Styles . . . . SUV
Seating 5
Anti-Theft Device . Std. Pass. Immobil. & Active Alarm
Parking Index Rating . . . . Hard
Where Made. . . . . .Leipzig, Germany
Fuel Factor . . . .
  MPG Rating (city/hwy) . . . . .Very Poor-17/23
  Driving Range (mi.) Long-431
  Fuel Type. . . . . .Premium
  Annual Fuel Cost . . . . Very High-$2,905
  Gas Guzzler Tax . . . . .No
  Greenhouse Gas Emissions (tons/yr.) Very High-9.6
  Barrels of Oil Used per year High-17.3

How the Competition Rates

Competitors	Rating Pg.
Audi Q7	93
Infiniti FX	165
Land Rover Range Rover	180

Price Range

	Retail	Markup
Base	$48,200	
S	$65,000	
Hybrid	$69,000	
Turbo	$107,100	

Safety Checklist

Crash Tests:
  Frontal. . . . .–
  Side. . . . .–
Airbags:
  Head . . . . Fr. & Rr. Roof Curtain
  Torso. . . . . Fr. & Rr. Torso from Seat
  Pelvis . . . . None
  Roll Sensing . . . . .Yes
  Knee Bolster . . . . Standard Driver
Crash Avoidance:
  Frontal Collision Warning . . . . None
  Blind Spot Detection . . . . Optional
  Crash Imminent Braking. . . . . None
  Lane Departure Warning . . . . None
General:
  Auto. Crash Notification . . . . None
  Day Running Lamps . . . . Standard
Safety Belt/Restraint:
  Dynamic Head Restraints. . . . . None
  Adjustable Belt . . . . .Standard Front
  Pretensioners . . . . Standard

Porsche Cayenne

Specifications

Drive. . . . . AWD
Engine 3.6-liter V6
Transmission . . . . .8-sp. Automatic
Tow Rating (lbs.) . . . . .Very High-7716
Head/Leg Room (in.) . . . . . Very Roomy-39.57/67.1
Interior Space (cu. ft.). . . . .–
Cargo Space (cu. ft.) Roomy-23.7
Wheelbase/Length (in.) 114/190.8

Ratings—10 Best, 1 Worst

Combo Crash Tests	3
Safety Features	2
Rollover	1
Preventive Maintenance	1
Repair Costs	10
Warranty	–
Fuel Economy	2
Complaints	6
Insurance Costs	5
OVERALL RATING	**2**

Ram 1500

Ram 1500

At-a-Glance

Status/Year Series Started. Unchanged/2009
Twins . . . . -
Body Styles . . . . Pickup
Seating 5/6
Anti-Theft Device . . . . Std. Pass. Immobil.
Parking Index Rating . . . . .Very Hard
Where Made. . . . . Saltillo, Mexico / Warren, MI
Fuel Factor. . . . .
  MPG Rating (city/hwy) . . . . .Very Poor-17/25
  Driving Range (mi.) . . . . Very Long-516
  Fuel Type. . . . . .Regular
  Annual Fuel Cost . . . . High-$2,591
  Gas Guzzler Tax . . . . .No
  Greenhouse Gas Emissions (tons/yr.) High-9.1
  Barrels of Oil Used per year High-16.5

How the Competition Rates

Competitors	Rating	Pg.
Chevrolet Silverado	7	117
Ford F-150	5	139
Toyota Tundra	2	255

Price Range	Retail	Markup
Tradesman Reg Cab SWB 2WD	$22,590	7%
SLT Reg Cab SWB 4WD	$31,020	8%
Sport Quad Cab SWB 2WD	$36,430	8%
Laramie Longhorn Crew Cab 4WD	$47,420	9%

Safety Checklist

Crash Tests:
  Frontal. . . . . Average
  Side. . . . . Very Poor*
Airbags:
  Head . . . . .Front Roof Curtain
  Torso. . . . . Front Torso from Seat
  Pelvis . . . . None
  Roll Sensing .Yes
  Knee Bolster . . . . None
Crash Avoidance:
  Frontal Collision Warning . . . . None
  Blind Spot Detection . . . . None
  Crash Imminent Braking . . . . None
  Lane Departure Warning . . . . None
General:
  Auto. Crash Notification . . . . None
  Day Running Lamps. . . . . Optional
Safety Belt/Restraint:
  Dynamic Head Restraints. . . . . None
  Adjustable Belt . . . . .Standard Front
  Pretensioners . . . . .Standard Front

Ram 1500

Specifications

Drive. 4WD
Engine 5.7-liter V8
Transmission . . . . .6-sp. Automatic
Tow Rating (lbs.) High-6800
Head/Leg Room (in.) Roomy-41/41
Interior Space (cu. ft.). Roomy-116.4
Cargo Space (cu. ft.) . . . . Very Roomy-57.5
Wheelbase/Length (in.) 140.5/229

*Additional injury potential in side test. See footnote 4 on page 27.

Ratings—10 Best, 1 Worst

Combo Crash Tests	–
Safety Features	1
Rollover	10
Preventive Maintenance	10
Repair Costs	–
Warranty	2
Fuel Economy	6
Complaints	–
Insurance Costs	–
OVERALL RATING	**–**

Scion FR-S

Scion FR-S

At-a-Glance

Status/Year Series Started	All New/2013
Twins	Subaru BRZ
Body Styles	Coupe
Seating	4
Anti-Theft Device	Std. Pass. Immobil.
Parking Index Rating	Very Easy
Where Made	Gunma, Japan
Fuel Factor	
MPG Rating (city/hwy)	Average-22/30
Driving Range (mi.)	Very Short-330
Fuel Type	Regular
Annual Fuel Cost	Average-$2,058
Gas Guzzler Tax	No
Greenhouse Gas Emissions (tons/yr.)	Average-7.3
Barrels of Oil Used per year	Average-13.2

How the Competition Rates

Competitors	Rating	Pg.
Mazda MX-5 Miata		195
Nissan 370Z		208
Subaru BRZ		195

Price Range

	Retail	Markup
Manual	$24,200	5%
Automatic	$25,300	5%

Safety Checklist

Crash Tests:
Frontal . . . . –
Side . . . . –

Airbags:
Head . . . . Fr. & Rr. Roof Curtain
Torso . . . . None
Pelvis . . . . Front Pelvis/Torso from Seat
Roll Sensing . . . . No
Knee Bolster . . . . None

Crash Avoidance:
Frontal Collision Warning . . . . None
Blind Spot Detection . . . . None
Crash Imminent Braking . . . . None
Lane Departure Warning . . . . None

General:
Auto. Crash Notification . . . . None
Day Running Lamps . . . . Standard

Safety Belt/Restraint:
Dynamic Head Restraints . . . . None
Adjustable Belt . . . . None
Pretensioners . . . . Standard Front

Scion FR-S

Specifications

Drive	RWD
Engine	2.0-liter I4
Transmission	6-sp. Manual
Tow Rating (lbs.)	–
Head/Leg Room (in.)	Very Cramped-37.1/41.9
Interior Space (cu. ft.)	Very Cramped-76.5
Cargo Space (cu. ft.)	Very Cramped-6.9
Wheelbase/Length (in.)	101.2/166.7

Scion iQ Subcompact

Ratings—10 Best, 1 Worst

Combo Crash Tests	1
Safety Features	2
Rollover	4
Preventive Maintenance	–
Repair Costs	–
Warranty	2
Fuel Economy	10
Complaints	10
Insurance Costs	5
OVERALL RATING	**3**

Scion iQ

Scion iQ

At-a-Glance

Status/Year Series Started........ Unchanged/2011
Twins .... -
Body Styles .... Hatchback
Seating 4
Anti-Theft Device ....None
Parking Index Rating ....Very Easy
Where Made............. Takaoka City, Japan
Fuel Factor...................................
  MPG Rating (city/hwy) .... Very Good-36/37
  Driving Range (mi.) ....Very Short-310
  Fuel Type....................Regular
  Annual Fuel Cost .... Very Low-$1,412
  Gas Guzzler Tax ....No
  Greenhouse Gas Emissions (tons/yr.). Very Low-5.0
  Barrels of Oil Used per year .... Very Low-8.9

How the Competition Rates

Competitors	Rating	Pg.
Mazda Mazda2		189
Smart ForTwo		232
Fiat 500	8	133

Price Range

	Retail	Markup
Base	$15,265	5%

Safety Checklist

Crash Tests:
  Frontal..........................Very Poor
  Side..............................Very Poor
Airbags:
  Head .... Fr. & Rr. Roof Curtain
  Torso.............................. None
  Pelvis ....Front Pelvis/Torso from Seat
  Roll Sensing .... No
  Knee Bolster ....Standard Front
Crash Avoidance:
  Frontal Collision Warning .... None
  Blind Spot Detection .... None
  Crash Imminent Braking .... None
  Lane Departure Warning .... None
General:
  Auto. Crash Notification .... None
  Day Running Lamps .... None
Safety Belt/Restraint:
  Dynamic Head Restraints............ None
  Adjustable Belt .... None
  Pretensioners ....Standard Front

Scion iQ

Specifications

Drive.................................... FWD
Engine 1.3-liter I4
Transmission ....CVT
Tow Rating (lbs.) .... –
Head/Leg Room (in.) .....Very Cramped-37.7/40.9
Interior Space (cu. ft.).........Very Cramped-73.8
Cargo Space (cu. ft.) ....Very Cramped-3.5
Wheelbase/Length (in.) 78.7/120.1

Ratings—10 Best, 1 Worst

Combo Crash Tests	8
Safety Features	4
Rollover	7
Preventive Maintenance	10
Repair Costs	5
Warranty	2
Fuel Economy	6
Complaints	9
Insurance Costs	1
OVERALL RATING	**8**

Scion tC

Scion tC

Scion tC

At-a-Glance

Status/Year Series Started Unchanged/2011
Twins . . . . -
Body Styles . . . . .Coupe
Seating 5
Anti-Theft Device . . . . Std. Pass. Immobil.
Parking Index Rating . . . . Average
Where Made . . . . .Toyota City, Japan
Fuel Factor . . . .
 MPG Rating (city/hwy) Average-23/31
 Driving Range (mi.) Short-377
 Fuel Type . . . . .Regular
 Annual Fuel Cost . . . . Low-$1,977
 Gas Guzzler Tax . . . . .No
 Greenhouse Gas Emissions (tons/yr.) . . Average-7.1
 Barrels of Oil Used per year Average-12.7

How the Competition Rates

Competitors	Rating	Pg.
Mazda Mazda3	5	190
Mitsubishi Lancer	6	205
Subaru Impreza	4	235

Price Range	Retail	Markup
Base Manual	$18,725	5%
Base Automatic	$19,725	5%
Release Series 8.0 Manual	$21,815	5%
Release Series 8.0 Auto.	$22,865	5%

Safety Checklist

Crash Tests:
 Frontal . . . . Good
 Side . . . . Very Good
Airbags:
 Head . . . . Fr. & Rr. Roof Curtain
 Torso . . . . None
 Pelvis . . . . .Front Pelvis/Torso from Seat
 Roll Sensing . . . . No
 Knee Bolster . . . . .Standard Front
Crash Avoidance:
 Frontal Collision Warning . . . . None
 Blind Spot Detection . . . . None
 Crash Imminent Braking . . . . None
 Lane Departure Warning . . . . None
General:
 Auto. Crash Notification . . . . None
 Day Running Lamps . . . . None
Safety Belt/Restraint:
 Dynamic Head Restraints . . . . . .Standard Front
 Adjustable Belt . . . . None
 Pretensioners . . . . .Standard Front

Scion tC

Specifications

Drive . . . . FWD
Engine 2.5-liter I4
Transmission . . . . .6-sp. Automatic
Tow Rating (lbs.) . . . . –
Head/Leg Room (in.) . . . . .Very Cramped-37.7/41.8
Interior Space (cu. ft.) . . . . .Very Cramped-88.4
Cargo Space (cu. ft.) . . . . Very Roomy-34.5
Wheelbase/Length (in.) 106.3/174

Ratings—10 Best, 1 Worst

Combo Crash Tests	–
Safety Features	1
Rollover	3
Preventive Maintenance	8
Repair Costs	8
Warranty	2
Fuel Economy	5
Complaints	4
Insurance Costs	1

OVERALL RATING — –

Scion xB

Scion xB

At-a-Glance

Status/Year Series Started	Unchanged/2008
Twins	-
Body Styles	Hatchback
Seating	5
Anti-Theft Device	None
Parking Index Rating	Very Easy
Where Made	Iwata, Japan
Fuel Factor	
MPG Rating (city/hwy)	Average-22/28
Driving Range (mi.)	Very Short-341
Fuel Type	Regular
Annual Fuel Cost	Average-$2,113
Gas Guzzler Tax	No
Greenhouse Gas Emissions (tons/yr.)	High-7.6
Barrels of Oil Used per year	High-13.7

How the Competition Rates

Competitors	Rating	Pg.
Kia Soul	6	179
Nissan Cube		212
Toyota Yaris	5	257

Price Range	Retail	Markup
Manual	$16,300	5%
Automatic	$17,250	5%

Scion xB

Safety Checklist

Crash Tests:
Frontal	–
Side	–

Airbags:
Head	Fr. & Rr. Roof Curtain
Torso	None
Pelvis	Front Pelvis/Torso from Seat
Roll Sensing	No
Knee Bolster	None

Crash Avoidance:
Frontal Collision Warning	None
Blind Spot Detection	None
Crash Imminent Braking	None
Lane Departure Warning	None

General:
Auto. Crash Notification	None
Day Running Lamps	None

Safety Belt/Restraint:
Dynamic Head Restraints	None
Adjustable Belt	Standard Front
Pretensioners	Standard Front

Scion xB

Specifications

Drive	FWD
Engine	2.4-liter I4
Transmission	4-sp. Automatic
Tow Rating (lbs.)	–
Head/Leg Room (in.)	Cramped-40/40.8
Interior Space (cu. ft.)	Average-100.8
Cargo Space (cu. ft.)	Very Cramped-11.6
Wheelbase/Length (in.)	102.4/167.3

Scion xD

Ratings—10 Best, 1 Worst

Combo Crash Tests	–
Safety Features	3
Rollover	5
Preventive Maintenance	10
Repair Costs	7
Warranty	2
Fuel Economy	8
Complaints	9
Insurance Costs	3
OVERALL RATING	**–**

Scion xD

At-a-Glance

Status/Year Series Started Unchanged/2008
Twins . . . . -
Body Styles . . . . Hatchback
Seating 5
Anti-Theft Device . . . . .None
Parking Index Rating . . . . Easy
Where Made. . . . . Takaoka City, Japan
Fuel Factor . . . .
  MPG Rating (city/hwy) Good-27/33
  Driving Range (mi.) . . . . Very Short-324
  Fuel Type. . . . . .Regular
  Annual Fuel Cost . . . . Very Low-$1,750
  Gas Guzzler Tax . . . . .No
  Greenhouse Gas Emissions (tons/yr). Very Low-5.0
  Barrels of Oil Used per year Average-11.4

How the Competition Rates

Competitors	Rating	Pg.
Hyundai Accent	8	156
Kia Rio	8	177
Suzuki SX4	1	240

Price Range	Retail	Markup
Manual	$15,745	5%
Automatic	$16,545	5%

Safety Checklist

Crash Tests:
  Frontal. . . . .–
  Side. . . . .–
Airbags:
  Head . . . . Fr. & Rr. Roof Curtain
  Torso. . . . . Front Torso from Seat
  Pelvis . . . . None
  Roll Sensing . . . . No
  Knee Bolster . . . . None
Crash Avoidance:
  Frontal Collision Warning . . . . None
  Blind Spot Detection . . . . None
  Crash Imminent Braking . . . . None
  Lane Departure Warning . . . . None
General:
  Auto. Crash Notification . . . . None
  Day Running Lamps . . . . None
Safety Belt/Restraint:
  Dynamic Head Restraints. . . . . .Standard Front
  Adjustable Belt . . . . .Standard Front
  Pretensioners . . . . .Standard Front

Scion xD

Specifications

Drive. . . . . FWD
Engine 1.8-liter I4
Transmission . . . . .4-sp. Automatic
Tow Rating (lbs.) . . . . –
Head/Leg Room (in.) . . . . .Very Cramped-38.9/40.3
Interior Space (cu. ft.). . . . . . . .Very Cramped-84.5
Cargo Space (cu. ft.) . . . . .Very Cramped-10.5
Wheelbase/Length (in.) 96.9/154.7

Ratings—10 Best, 1 Worst

Ratings	
Combo Crash Tests	–
Safety Features	3
Rollover	1
Preventive Maintenance	5
Repair Costs	4
Warranty	1
Fuel Economy	10
Complaints	4
Insurance Costs	3
OVERALL RATING	**–**

Smart ForTwo

Smart ForTwo

At-a-Glance

Status/Year Series Started Appearance Change/2008 Twins . . . . -
Body Styles . . . . Coupe, Convertible
Seating 2
Anti-Theft Device . Std. Active Immobil. & Pass. Alarm
Parking Index Rating . . . . .Very Easy
Where Made. . . . . .Hambach, France
Fuel Factor . . . .
  MPG Rating (city/hwy) . . . . Very Good-34/38
  Driving Range (mi.) . . . . .Very Short-311
  Fuel Type . . . . .Regular
  Annual Fuel Cost . . . . Very Low-$1,442
  Gas Guzzler Tax . . . . .No
  Greenhouse Gas Emissions (tons/yr.). Low-5.1
  Barrels of Oil Used per year Low-9.1

How the Competition Rates

Competitors	Rating	Pg.
Fiat 500	8	133
Ford Fiesta	4	140
Scion iQ	3	228

Price Range	Retail	Markup
pure Coupe	$12,490	8%
passion Coupe	$14,890	8%
passion Cabriolet	$17,890	8%

Safety Checklist

Crash Tests:
  Frontal . . . . –
  Side . . . . –
Airbags:
  Head . . . . .Front Roof Curtain
  Torso. . . . . Front Torso from Seat
  Pelvis . . . . None
  Roll Sensing . . . . No
  Knee Bolster . . . . .Standard Front
Crash Avoidance:
  Frontal Collision Warning . . . . None
  Blind Spot Detection . . . . None
  Crash Imminent Braking . . . . None
  Lane Departure Warning . . . . None
General:
  Auto. Crash Notification . . . . Optional
  Day Running Lamps . . . . Optional
Safety Belt/Restraint:
  Dynamic Head Restraints. . . . . None
  Adjustable Belt . . . . None
  Pretensioners . . . . Standard

Smart ForTwo

Specifications

Drive. . . . . FWD
Engine 0.9-liter I3
Transmission . . . . .5-sp. Manual
Tow Rating (lbs.) . . . . –
Head/Leg Room (in.) Cramped-39.7/41.2
Interior Space (cu. ft.). . . . . .Very Cramped-37.6
Cargo Space (cu. ft.) . . . . .Very Cramped-7.8
Wheelbase/Length (in.) 73.5/106.1

Ratings—10 Best, 1 Worst

Combo Crash Tests	–
Safety Features	2
Rollover	10
Preventive Maintenance	10
Repair Costs	–
Warranty	2
Fuel Economy	6
Complaints	–
Insurance Costs	–
OVERALL RATING	**–**

Subaru BRZ

Subaru BRZ

At-a-Glance

Status/Year Series Started	All New/2013
Twins	Scion FR-S
Body Styles	Coupe
Seating	4
Anti-Theft Device	Std. Pass. Immobil.
Parking Index Rating	Very Easy
Where Made	Gunma, Japan
Fuel Factor	
MPG Rating (city/hwy)	Average-22/30
Driving Range (mi.)	Very Short-330
Fuel Type	Premium
Annual Fuel Cost	Average-$2,238
Gas Guzzler Tax	No
Greenhouse Gas Emissions (tons/yr.)	Average-7.3
Barrels of Oil Used per year	Average-13.2

How the Competition Rates

Competitors	Rating	Pg.
Nissan 370Z		208
Mazda MX-5 Miata		195
Scion FR-S		227

Price Range

	Retail	Markup
Premium Manual	$25,495	5%
Premium Automatic	$26,595	5%
Limited Manual	$27,495	5%
Limited Automatic	$28,595	5%

Safety Checklist

Crash Tests:
- Frontal . . . . –
- Side . . . . –

Airbags:
- Head . . . . Fr. & Rr. Roof Curtain
- Torso . . . . Front Pelvis/Torso from Seat
- Pelvis . . . . Front Pelvis/Torso from Seat
- Roll Sensing . . . . No
- Knee Bolster . . . . None

Crash Avoidance:
- Frontal Collision Warning . . . . None
- Blind Spot Detection . . . . None
- Crash Imminent Braking . . . . None
- Lane Departure Warning . . . . None

General:
- Auto. Crash Notification . . . . None
- Day Running Lamps . . . . Standard

Safety Belt/Restraint:
- Dynamic Head Restraints . . . . None
- Adjustable Belt . . . . None
- Pretensioners . . . . Standard Front

Subaru BRZ

Specifications

Drive	RWD
Engine	2.0-liter I4
Transmission	6-sp. Manual
Tow Rating (lbs.)	–
Head/Leg Room (in.)	Very Cramped-37.1/41.9
Interior Space (cu. ft.)	Very Cramped-76.5
Cargo Space (cu. ft.)	Very Cramped-6.9
Wheelbase/Length (in.)	101.2/166.7

Ratings—10 Best, 1 Worst

Combo Crash Tests	4
Safety Features	6
Rollover	3
Preventive Maintenance	4
Repair Costs	7
Warranty	2
Fuel Economy	5
Complaints	8
Insurance Costs	1
OVERALL RATING	**3**

Subaru Forester

Subaru Forester

At-a-Glance

Status/Year Series Started	Unchanged/2009
Twins	-
Body Styles	SUV
Seating	5
Anti-Theft Device	Std. Pass. Immobil. & Active Alarm
Parking Index Rating	Very Easy
Where Made	Gunma, Japan
Fuel Factor	
MPG Rating (city/hwy)	Average-21/27
Driving Range (mi.)	Average-394
Fuel Type	Regular
Annual Fuel Cost	Average-$2,205
Gas Guzzler Tax	No
Greenhouse Gas Emissions (tons/yr.)	High-8.0
Barrels of Oil Used per year	High-14.3

How the Competition Rates

Competitors	Rating	Pg.
Hyundai Tucson	7	234
Mazda CX-5	6	193
Toyota RAV4		251

Price Range	Retail	Markup
X Manual	$21,295	6%
X Premium	$24,795	6%
X Limited	$26,995	7%
XT Touring	$29,995	7%

Safety Checklist

Crash Tests:
Frontal	Good
Side	Very Poor

Airbags:
Head	Fr. & Rr. Roof Curtain
Torso	Front Pelvis/Torso from Seat
Pelvis	Front Pelvis/Torso from Seat
Roll Sensing	Yes
Knee Bolster	None

Crash Avoidance:
Frontal Collision Warning	None
Blind Spot Detection	None
Crash Imminent Braking	None
Lane Departure Warning	None

General:
Auto. Crash Notification	None
Day Running Lamps	Standard

Safety Belt/Restraint:
Dynamic Head Restraints	Standard Front
Adjustable Belt	Standard Front
Pretensioners	Standard Front

Subaru Forester

Specifications

Drive	AWD
Engine	2.5-liter I4
Transmission	4-sp. Automatic
Tow Rating (lbs.)	Low-2400
Head/Leg Room (in.)	Very Roomy-41.6/43.1
Interior Space (cu. ft.)	Roomy-107.6
Cargo Space (cu. ft.)	Roomy-33.9
Wheelbase/Length (in.)	103/179.5

Subaru Impreza   Compact

Ratings—10 Best, 1 Worst

Combo Crash Tests	3
Safety Features	3
Rollover	9
Preventive Maintenance	5
Repair Costs	8
Warranty	2
Fuel Economy	8
Complaints	6
Insurance Costs	1
OVERALL RATING	**4**

Subaru Impreza

Subaru Impreza

At-a-Glance

Status/Year Series Started. Unchanged/2012
Twins . . . . -
Body Styles . . . . Sedan, Hatchback
Seating 5
Anti-Theft Device . Std. Pass. Immobil. & Active Alarm
Parking Index Rating . . . . Easy
Where Made. . . . . Gunma, Japan
Fuel Factor. . . . .
  MPG Rating (city/hwy) Good-25/34
  Driving Range (mi.) Average-412
  Fuel Type. . . . . .Regular
  Annual Fuel Cost . . . . Low-$1,813
  Gas Guzzler Tax . . . . .No
  Greenhouse Gas Emissions (tons/yr.). . Average-6.5
  Barrels of Oil Used per year Average-11.8

How the Competition Rates

Competitors	Rating	Pg.
Honda Civic		148
Mazda Mazda3	5	190
Mitsubishi Lancer	6	205

Price Range	Retail	Markup
Base Sedan Manual	$17,895	5%
Sport Limited Wagon	$22,995	6%
WRX Limited Wagon Manual	$29,295	6%
WRX STi Limited Sedan	$38,645	6%

Safety Checklist

Crash Tests:
  Frontal. . . . . Poor
  Side. . . . . Poor
Airbags:
  Head . . . . Fr. & Rr. Roof Curtain
  Torso. . . . . .Front Pelvis/Torso from Seat
  Pelvis . . . . .Front Pelvis/Torso from Seat
  Roll Sensing . . . . No
  Knee Bolster . . . . Standard Driver
Crash Avoidance:
  Frontal Collision Warning . . . . None
  Blind Spot Detection . . . . None
  Crash Imminent Braking . . . . None
  Lane Departure Warning . . . . None
General:
  Auto. Crash Notification . . . . None
  Day Running Lamps . . . . Standard
Safety Belt/Restraint:
  Dynamic Head Restraints . . . . None
  Adjustable Belt . . . . .Standard Front
  Pretensioners . . . . .Standard Front

Subaru Impreza

Specifications

Drive. . . . . AWD
Engine 2.0-liter I4
Transmission . . . . .5-sp. Manual
Tow Rating (lbs.) . . . . –
Head/Leg Room (in.) . . . . . . Very Roomy-39.8/43.5
Interior Space (cu. ft.). Cramped-96.9
Cargo Space (cu. ft.) . . . . . Very Cramped-12
Wheelbase/Length (in.) 104.1/180.3

235

Ratings—10 Best, 1 Worst

Combo Crash Tests	3
Safety Features	5
Rollover	8
Preventive Maintenance	2
Repair Costs	7
Warranty	2
Fuel Economy	7
Complaints	4
Insurance Costs	1
OVERALL RATING	**3**

Subaru Legacy

At-a-Glance

Status/Year Series Started	Unchanged/2010
Twins	-
Body Styles	Sedan
Seating	5
Anti-Theft Device	Std. Pass. Immobil. & Active Alarm
Parking Index Rating	Average
Where Made	Lafayette, IN
Fuel Factor	
MPG Rating (city/hwy)	Good-24/32
Driving Range (mi.)	Very Long-500
Fuel Type	Regular
Annual Fuel Cost	Low-$1,903
Gas Guzzler Tax	No
Greenhouse Gas Emissions (tons/yr.)	Average-6.7
Barrels of Oil Used per year	Average-12.2

How the Competition Rates

Competitors	Rating	Pg.
Chevrolet Malibu	9	116
Ford Fusion		143
Mazda Mazda6	4	192

Price Range

	Retail	Markup
Base Manual	$20,295	6%
Premium	$22,495	6%
Limited	$25,894	6%
3.6R Limited	$28,895	7%

Subaru Legacy

Safety Checklist

Crash Tests:
- Frontal . . . . Poor
- Side . . . . Poor

Airbags:
- Head . . . . Fr. & Rr. Roof Curtain
- Torso . . . . Front Pelvis/Torso from Seat
- Pelvis . . . . Front Pelvis/Torso from Seat
- Roll Sensing . . . . No
- Knee Bolster . . . . None

Crash Avoidance:
- Frontal Collision Warning . . . . Optional
- Blind Spot Detection . . . . None
- Crash Imminent Braking . . . . Optional
- Lane Departure Warning . . . . Optional

General:
- Auto. Crash Notification . . . . None
- Day Running Lamps . . . . Standard

Safety Belt/Restraint:
- Dynamic Head Restraints . . . . None
- Adjustable Belt . . . . Standard Front
- Pretensioners . . . . Standard Front

Subaru Legacy

Check Surroundings Before Backing Up

Specifications

Drive	AWD
Engine	2.5-liter I4
Transmission	6-sp. Manual
Tow Rating (lbs.)	—
Head/Leg Room (in.)	Very Roomy-40.3/43
Interior Space (cu. ft.)	Average-103
Cargo Space (cu. ft.)	Cramped-14.7
Wheelbase/Length (in.)	108.3/187.2

Ratings—10 Best, 1 Worst	
Combo Crash Tests	3
Safety Features	7
Rollover	3
Preventive Maintenance	2
Repair Costs	8
Warranty	2
Fuel Economy	7
Complaints	3
Insurance Costs	3
OVERALL RATING	**2**

Subaru Outback

Subaru Outback

At-a-Glance

Status/Year Series Started Appearance Change/2010
Twins . . . . -
Body Styles . . . . Station Wagon
Seating 5
Anti-Theft Device . Std. Pass. Immobil. & Active Alarm
Parking Index Rating . . . . Average
Where Made. .Lafayette, IN
Fuel Factor. . . . .
  MPG Rating (city/hwy) Good-24/30
  Driving Range (mi.) . . . . Very Long-488
  Fuel Type. . . . . .Regular
  Annual Fuel Cost . . . . Low-$1,951
  Gas Guzzler Tax . . . . .No
  Greenhouse Gas Emissions (tons/yr.) . . Average-7.1
  Barrels of Oil Used per year Average-12.7

How the Competition Rates

Competitors	Rating	Pg.
Audi Allroad	9	91
Toyota Venza	3	256
Volkswagen Jetta	6	261

Price Range	Retail	Markup
Base Manual	$23,495	6%
Premium	$25,995	6%
Limited	$29,095	7%
3.6R Limited	$32,095	7%

Safety Checklist

Crash Tests:
  Frontal. . . . . Poor
  Side. . . . . Poor
Airbags:
  Head . . . . Fr. & Rr. Roof Curtain
  Torso. . . . . .Front Pelvis/Torso from Seat
  Pelvis . . . . .Front Pelvis/Torso from Seat
  Roll Sensing . . . . .Yes
  Knee Bolster . . . . None
Crash Avoidance:
  Frontal Collision Warning . . . . Optional
  Blind Spot Detection . . . . None
  Crash Imminent Braking . . . . Optional
  Lane Departure Warning . . . . Optional
General:
  Auto. Crash Notification . . . . None
  Day Running Lamps . . . . Standard
Safety Belt/Restraint:
  Dynamic Head Restraints. . . . . None
  Adjustable Belt . . . . .Standard Front
  Pretensioners . . . . .Standard Front

Subaru Outback

Specifications

Drive. . . . . AWD
Engine 2.5-liter I4
Transmission . . . . .6-sp. Manual
Tow Rating (lbs.) . . . . —
Head/Leg Room (in.) . . . . Very Roomy-40.8/43
Interior Space (cu. ft.). Roomy-105.4
Cargo Space (cu. ft.) . . . . Very Roomy-34.3
Wheelbase/Length (in.) 107.9/189

Subaru XV Crosstrek

Ratings—10 Best, 1 Worst

Combo Crash Tests	–
Safety Features	5
Rollover	3
Preventive Maintenance	5
Repair Costs	8
Warranty	2
Fuel Economy	8
Complaints	–
Insurance Costs	5
OVERALL RATING	**–**

Subaru XV Crosstrek

Subaru XV Crosstrek

At-a-Glance

Status/Year Series Started	All New/2013
Twins	-
Body Styles	SUV
Seating	5
Anti-Theft Device	Std. Pass. Immobil. & Active Alarm
Parking Index Rating	Easy
Where Made	Gunma, Japan
Fuel Factor	
MPG Rating (city/hwy)	Good-25/33
Driving Range (mi.)	Very Long-446
Fuel Type	Regular
Annual Fuel Cost	Low-$1,833
Gas Guzzler Tax	No
Greenhouse Gas Emissions (tons/yr.)	Average-6.5
Barrels of Oil Used per year	Average-11.8

How the Competition Rates

Competitors	Rating	Pg.
Hyundai Tucson	7	162
Jeep Compass	1	171
Toyota RAV4		251

Price Range	Retail	Markup
Premium Manual	$21,995	5%
Premium w/Moonroof	$23,995	6%
Limited	$24,495	6%
Limited w/Moonroof & Nav	$26,495	6%

Safety Checklist

Crash Tests:
Frontal . . . . –
Side . . . . –

Airbags:
Head . . . . Fr. & Rr. Roof Curtain
Torso . . . . Front Pelvis/Torso from Seat
Pelvis . . . . Front Pelvis/Torso from Seat
Roll Sensing . . . . .Yes
Knee Bolster . . . . Standard Driver

Crash Avoidance:
Frontal Collision Warning . . . . None
Blind Spot Detection . . . . None
Crash Imminent Braking . . . . None
Lane Departure Warning . . . . None

General:
Auto. Crash Notification . . . . None
Day Running Lamps . . . . Standard

Safety Belt/Restraint:
Dynamic Head Restraints . . . . None
Adjustable Belt . . . . .Standard Front
Pretensioners . . . . .Standard Front

Subaru XV Crosstrek

Specifications

Drive	AWD
Engine	2.0-liter I4
Transmission	5-sp. Manual
Tow Rating (lbs.)	–
Head/Leg Room (in.)	Very Roomy-39.8/43.5
Interior Space (cu. ft.)	Very Cramped-75.2
Cargo Space (cu. ft.)	Roomy-22.3
Wheelbase/Length (in.)	103.7/175.2

Ratings—10 Best, 1 Worst

Combo Crash Tests	–
Safety Features	6
Rollover	7
Preventive Maintenance	5
Repair Costs	2
Warranty	3
Fuel Economy	6
Complaints	10
Insurance Costs	3
OVERALL RATING	**–**

Suzuki Kizashi

At-a-Glance

Status/Year Series Started. Unchanged/2010
Twins . . . . -
Body Styles . . . . .Sedan
Seating 5
Anti-Theft Device . . . . . . Std. Pass. Immobil. & Alarm
Parking Index Rating . . . . .Very Easy
Where Made. . . . . Sagara, Japan
Fuel Factor . . . .
  MPG Rating (city/hwy) Average-23/30
  Driving Range (mi.) Long-427
  Fuel Type . . . . .Regular
  Annual Fuel Cost . . . . Low-$2,002
  Gas Guzzler Tax . . . . .No
  Greenhouse Gas Emissions (tons/yr.) . . Average-7.1
  Barrels of Oil Used per year Average-12.7

How the Competition Rates

Competitors	Rating	Pg.
Mazda Mazda3	5	190
Mitsubishi Lancer	6	205
Subaru Impreza	4	235

Price Range	Retail	Markup
Base Manual	$19,999	4%
SE Automatic	$21,749	4%
GTS AWD	$27,199	4%
SLS	$28,999	4%

Suzuki Kizashi

Safety Checklist

Crash Tests:
  Frontal. . . . .–
  Side. . . . .–
Airbags:
  Head . . . . Fr. & Rr. Roof Curtain
  Torso. . . . . Fr. & Rr. Pelvis/Torso from Seat
  Pelvis . . . . Fr. & Rr. Pelvis/Torso from Seat
  Roll Sensing . . . . No
  Knee Bolster . . . . None
Crash Avoidance:
  Frontal Collision Warning . . . . None
  Blind Spot Detection . . . . Standard
  Crash Imminent Braking . . . . None
  Lane Departure Warning . . . . None
General:
  Auto. Crash Notification . . . . None
  Day Running Lamps . . . . Standard
Safety Belt/Restraint:
  Dynamic Head Restraints . . . . None
  Adjustable Belt . . . . .Standard Front
  Pretensioners . . . . .Standard Front

Suzuki Kizashi

Specifications

Drive. . . . . FWD
Engine 2.4-liter I4
Transmission . . . . .CVT
Tow Rating (lbs.) . . . . –
Head/Leg Room (in.) Average-39.3/41.7
Interior Space (cu. ft.). Cramped-92.1
Cargo Space (cu. ft.). Cramped-13.3
Wheelbase/Length (in.) 106.3/183.1

Ratings—10 Best, 1 Worst

Combo Crash Tests	2
Safety Features	5
Rollover	5
Preventive Maintenance	1
Repair Costs	3
Warranty	3
Fuel Economy	6
Complaints	3
Insurance Costs	1
OVERALL RATING	**1**

Suzuki SX4 Crossover

At-a-Glance

Status/Year Series Started........ Unchanged/2007
Twins .... -
Body Styles .... Sedan, Hatchback
Seating 5
Anti-Theft Device .... None
Parking Index Rating .... Very Easy
Where Made .... Sagara, Japan
Fuel Factor
  MPG Rating (city/hwy) Average-23/29
  Driving Range (mi.) ...... Very Short-335
  Fuel Type .... Regular
  Annual Fuel Cost .... Low-$2,029
  Gas Guzzler Tax .... No
  Greenhouse Gas Emissions (tons/yr.) .. Average-7.3
  Barrels of Oil Used per year Average-13.2

How the Competition Rates

Competitors	Rating	Pg.
Honda Fit	4	151
Hyundai Accent	8	156
Kia Rio	8	177

Price Range

Price Range	Retail	Markup
Sedan Manual	$13,699	4%
LE Popular Sedan	$17,849	4%
Premium Hatchback	$19,175	4%
Tech Hatchback	$20,449	4%

Suzuki SX4 Sedan

Safety Checklist

Crash Tests:
  Frontal .... Poor
  Side .... Very Poor
Airbags:
  Head .... Fr. & Rr. Roof Curtain
  Torso .... Fr. & Rr. Pelvis/Torso from Seat
  Pelvis .... Fr. & Rr. Pelvis/Torso from Seat
  Roll Sensing .... No
  Knee Bolster .... None
Crash Avoidance:
  Frontal Collision Warning .... None
  Blind Spot Detection .... None
  Crash Imminent Braking .... None
  Lane Departure Warning .... None
General:
  Auto. Crash Notification .... None
  Day Running Lamps .... Standard
Safety Belt/Restraint:
  Dynamic Head Restraints .... None
  Adjustable Belt .... Standard Front
  Pretensioners .... Standard Front

Suzuki SX4 Sportback

Specifications

Drive .... FWD
Engine 2.0-liter I4
Transmission .... CVT
Tow Rating (lbs.) .... –
Head/Leg Room (in.) Average-40/41.4
Interior Space (cu. ft.) Cramped-90
Cargo Space (cu. ft.) ...... Very Cramped-7
Wheelbase/Length (in.) 98.4/176.8

Ratings—10 Best, 1 Worst	4Runner	GX
Combo Crash Tests	4	–
Safety Features	8	8
Rollover	1	1
Preventive Maintenance	8	7
Repair Costs	3	7
Warranty	1	6
Fuel Economy	2	1
Complaints	9	8
Insurance Costs	8	8
OVERALL RATING	**4**	

Toyota 4Runner

Lexus GX460

At-a-Glance

Status/Year Series Started	Unchanged/2006
Twins	Lexus GX
Body Styles	SUV
Seating	5/7
Anti-Theft Device	Std. Pass. Immobil. & Opt. Pass. Alarm
Parking Index Rating	Average
Where Made	Tahara, Japan
Fuel Factor	
MPG Rating (city/hwy)	Very Poor-17/21
Driving Range (mi.)	Long-428
Fuel Type	Regular
Annual Fuel Cost	Very High-$2,767
Gas Guzzler Tax	No
Greenhouse Gas Emissions (tons/yr.)	High-7.9
Barrels of Oil Used per year	Very High-18.3

How the Competition Rates

Competitors	Rating	Pg.
Ford Explorer	6	138
Honda Pilot	4	154
Nissan Pathfinder	5	218

Price Range	Retail	Markup
SR5 2WD	$31,340	9%
SR5 4WD	$33,215	9%
Trail Edition	$37,005	9%
Limited 4WD	$40,880	9%

Safety Checklist

Crash Tests:

Frontal	Poor
Side	Average

Airbags:

Head	Fr. & Rr. Roof Curtain
Torso	None
Pelvis	Front Pelvis/Torso from Seat
Roll Sensing	Yes
Knee Bolster	Standard Front

Crash Avoidance:

Frontal Collision Warning	None
Blind Spot Detection	None
Crash Imminent Braking	None
Lane Departure Warning	None

General:

Auto. Crash Notification	Optional
Day Running Lamps	Standard

Safety Belt/Restraint:

Dynamic Head Restraints	Standard Front
Adjustable Belt	Standard Front
Pretensioners	Standard Front

Toyota 4Runner

Specifications

Drive	4WD
Engine	4.0-liter V6
Transmission	5-sp. Automatic
Tow Rating (lbs.)	Average-5000
Head/Leg Room (in.)	Average-39.3/41.7
Interior Space (cu. ft.)	Average-97.3
Cargo Space (cu. ft.)	Very Roomy-47.2
Wheelbase/Length (in.)	109.8/189.9

Ratings—10 Best, 1 Worst

Combo Crash Tests	–
Safety Features	8
Rollover	8
Preventive Maintenance	9
Repair Costs	3
Warranty	1
Fuel Economy	5
Complaints	–
Insurance Costs	8
OVERALL RATING	**–**

Toyota Avalon

At-a-Glance

Status/Year Series Started	All New/2013
Twins	-
Body Styles	Sedan
Seating	5
Anti-Theft Device	Std. Pass. Immobil. & Alarm
Parking Index Rating	Hard
Where Made	Georgetown, KY
Fuel Factor	
MPG Rating (city/hwy)	Average-21/31
Driving Range (mi.)	Long-418
Fuel Type	Regular
Annual Fuel Cost	Average-$2,094
Gas Guzzler Tax	No
Greenhouse Gas Emissions (tons/yr.)	Average-7.3
Barrels of Oil Used per year	High-13.7

How the Competition Rates

Competitors	Rating	Pg.
Chevrolet Impala	6	115
Ford Fusion		143
Nissan Altima	7	209

Price Range

Price Range	Retail	Markup
Base	$33,195	11%
Limited	$36,435	11%

Toyota Avalon

Safety Checklist

Crash Tests:
Frontal . . . . –
Side . . . . –
Airbags:
Head . . . . Fr. & Rr. Roof Curtain
Torso . . . . None
Pelvis . . . . Fr & Rr. Pelvis/Torso from Seat
Roll Sensing . . . . No
Knee Bolster . . . . Standard Front
Crash Avoidance:
Frontal Collision Warning . . . . Optional
Blind Spot Detection . . . . Optional
Crash Imminent Braking . . . . Optional
Lane Departure Warning . . . . None
General:
Auto. Crash Notification . . . . Optional
Day Running Lamps . . . . Standard
Safety Belt/Restraint:
Dynamic Head Restraints . . . . None
Adjustable Belt . . . . Standard Front
Pretensioners . . . . Standard Front

Toyota Avalon

Specifications

Drive	FWD
Engine	3.5-liter V6
Transmission	6-sp. Automatic
Tow Rating (lbs.)	Very Low-1000
Head/Leg Room (in.)	Average-39/42.1
Interior Space (cu. ft.)	Roomy-103.6
Cargo Space (cu. ft.)	Average-16
Wheelbase/Length (in.)	111/195.2

Toyota Camry

Toyota Camry

Ratings—10 Best, 1 Worst

Combo Crash Tests	1
Safety Features	6
Rollover	8
Preventive Maintenance	6
Repair Costs	4
Warranty	1
Fuel Economy	8
Complaints	8
Insurance Costs	5
OVERALL RATING	**4**

Toyota Camry

At-a-Glance

Status/Year Series Started	Unchanged/2012
Twins	-
Body Styles	Sedan
Seating	5
Anti-Theft Device	Std. Pass. Immobil. & Opt. Pass. Alarm
Parking Index Rating	Average
Where Made	Georgetown, KY
Fuel Factor	
MPG Rating (city/hwy)	Good-25/35
Driving Range (mi.)	Very Long-488
Fuel Type	Regular
Annual Fuel Cost	Low-$1,793
Gas Guzzler Tax	No
Greenhouse Gas Emissions (tons/yr.)	Average-6.7
Barrels of Oil Used per year	Average-12.2

How the Competition Rates

Competitors	Rating	Pg.
Chevrolet Malibu	9	116
Ford Fusion		143
Honda Accord	9	146

Price Range	Retail	Markup
L	$22,055	9%
SE	$23,220	10%
Hybrid XLE	$27,400	9%
XLE V6	$30,115	10%

Safety Checklist

Crash Tests:
Frontal . . . . .Very Poor
Side . . . . .Very Poor
Airbags:
Head . . . . Fr. & Rr. Roof Curtain
Torso . . . . None
Pelvis . . . . Fr & Rr. Pelvis/Torso from Seat
Roll Sensing . . . . No
Knee Bolster . . . . .Standard Front
Crash Avoidance:
Frontal Collision Warning . . . . None
Blind Spot Detection . . . . Optional
Crash Imminent Braking . . . . None
Lane Departure Warning . . . . None
General:
Auto. Crash Notification . . . . Optional
Day Running Lamps . . . . Standard
Safety Belt/Restraint:
Dynamic Head Restraints . . . . None
Adjustable Belt . . . . .Standard Front
Pretensioners . . . . .Standard Front

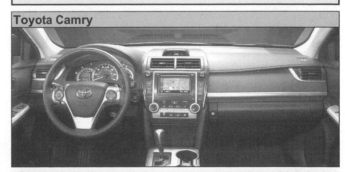

Toyota Camry

Specifications

Drive	FWD
Engine	2.5-liter I4
Transmission	6-sp. Automatic
Tow Rating (lbs.)	Very Low-1000
Head/Leg Room (in.)	Cramped-38.8/41.6
Interior Space (cu. ft.)	Average-102.7
Cargo Space (cu. ft.)	Cramped-15.4
Wheelbase/Length (in.)	109.3/189.2

Ratings—10 Best, 1 Worst

Combo Crash Tests	5
Safety Features	3
Rollover	6
Preventive Maintenance	9
Repair Costs	7
Warranty	1
Fuel Economy	8
Complaints	2
Insurance Costs	1
OVERALL RATING	**4**

Toyota Corolla

Toyota Corolla

At-a-Glance

Status/Year Series Started	Unchanged/2009
Twins	-
Body Styles	Sedan
Seating	5
Anti-Theft Device	Std. Pass. Immobil.
Parking Index Rating	Easy
Where Made	Cambridge, Ontario
Fuel Factor	
MPG Rating (city/hwy)	Good-26/34
Driving Range (mi.)	Short-384
Fuel Type	Regular
Annual Fuel Cost	Very Low-$1,770
Gas Guzzler Tax	No
Greenhouse Gas Emissions (tons/yr.)	Average-6.3
Barrels of Oil Used per year	Average-11.4

How the Competition Rates

Competitors	Rating	Pg.
Honda Civic		148
Mazda Mazda3	5	190
Volkswagen Jetta	6	262

Price Range	Retail	Markup
Base Manual	$16,230	6%
Base Automatic	$17,060	6%
LE	$18,180	8%
S	$19,060	8%

Safety Checklist

Crash Tests:
Frontal	Average
Side	Poor

Airbags:
Head	Fr. & Rr. Roof Curtain
Torso	Front Torso from Seat
Pelvis	None
Roll Sensing	No
Knee Bolster	None

Crash Avoidance:
Frontal Collision Warning	None
Blind Spot Detection	None
Crash Imminent Braking	None
Lane Departure Warning	None

General:
Auto. Crash Notification	None
Day Running Lamps	Standard

Safety Belt/Restraint:
Dynamic Head Restraints	Standard Front
Adjustable Belt	Standard Front
Pretensioners	Standard Front

Toyota Corolla

Specifications

Drive	FWD
Engine	1.8-liter I4
Transmission	4-sp. Automatic
Tow Rating (lbs.)	Very Low-1500
Head/Leg Room (in.)	Cramped-38.8/41.7
Interior Space (cu. ft.)	Cramped-92.1
Cargo Space (cu. ft.)	Very Cramped-12.3
Wheelbase/Length (in.)	102.4/180

Toyota FJ Cruiser — Mid-Size SUV

Ratings—10 Best, 1 Worst

Combo Crash Tests	–
Safety Features	5
Rollover	1
Preventive Maintenance	8
Repair Costs	5
Warranty	1
Fuel Economy	2
Complaints	2
Insurance Costs	1
OVERALL RATING	**–**

Toyota FJ Cruiser

Toyota FJ Cruiser

At-a-Glance

Status/Year Series Started........ Unchanged/2007
Twins . . . . -
Body Styles . . . . SUV
Seating 5
Anti-Theft Device . . . . Std. Pass. Immobil.
Parking Index Rating . . . . .Very Hard
Where Made. . . . . Kyushu, Japan
Fuel Factor . . . .
  MPG Rating (city/hwy) . . . . . . .Very Poor-17/20
  Driving Range (mi.) . . . . .Very Short-346
  Fuel Type. . . . . .Regular
  Annual Fuel Cost . . . . .Very High-$2,822
  Gas Guzzler Tax . . . . .No
  Greenhouse Gas Emissions (tons/yr.). High-8.2
  Barrels of Oil Used per year . . . . . . .Very High-18.3

How the Competition Rates

Competitors	Rating	Pg.
Jeep Wrangler		174
Volkswagen Touareg		265
Nissan Xterra		224

Price Range

	Retail	Markup
2WD Automatic	$26,880	8%
4WD Manual	$28,060	8%
4WD Automatic	$28,470	8%

Safety Checklist

Crash Tests:
  Frontal. . . . .–
  Side. . . . .–
Airbags:
  Head . . . . Fr. & Rr. Roof Curtain
  Torso. . . . . Front Torso from Seat
  Pelvis . . . . None
  Roll Sensing . . . . .Yes
  Knee Bolster . . . . None
Crash Avoidance:
  Frontal Collision Warning . . . . None
  Blind Spot Detection . . . . None
  Crash Imminent Braking. . . . . None
  Lane Departure Warning . . . . None
General:
  Auto. Crash Notification . . . . None
  Day Running Lamps . . . . Standard
Safety Belt/Restraint:
  Dynamic Head Restraints. . . . . .Standard Front
  Adjustable Belt . . . . .Standard Front
  Pretensioners . . . . .Standard Front

Toyota FJ Cruiser

Specifications

Drive. 4WD
Engine 5.0-liter V6
Transmission . . . . .5-sp. Automatic
Tow Rating (lbs.) Average-4700
Head/Leg Room (in.) . . . . Very Roomy-41.3/41.9
Interior Space (cu. ft.). . . . . –
Cargo Space (cu. ft.) Roomy-27.9
Wheelbase/Length (in.) 105.9/183.9

Toyota Highlander

Ratings—10 Best, 1 Worst

Combo Crash Tests	3
Safety Features	6
Rollover	3
Preventive Maintenance	7
Repair Costs	2
Warranty	1
Fuel Economy	2
Complaints	6
Insurance Costs	8
OVERALL RATING	**2**

Toyota Highlander

At-a-Glance

Status/Year Series Started	Unchanged/2008
Twins	-
Body Styles	SUV
Seating	7
Anti-Theft Device	Opt. Pass. Immobil. & Alarm
Parking Index Rating	Hard
Where Made	Princeton, IN
Fuel Factor	
MPG Rating (city/hwy)	Very Poor-17/22
Driving Range (mi.)	Very Short-364
Fuel Type	Regular
Annual Fuel Cost	High-$2,717
Gas Guzzler Tax	No
Greenhouse Gas Emissions (tons/yr.)	High-7.7
Barrels of Oil Used per year	High-17.3

How the Competition Rates

Competitors	Rating	Pg.
Audi Q5		92
Honda Pilot	4	154
Nissan Murano	3	217

Price Range

	Retail	Markup
Base 2WD 4cyl	$28,870	10%
SE 4WD	$35,860	10%
Limited 4WD	$39,250	10%
Limited Hybrid	$46,170	9%

Safety Checklist

Crash Tests:
Frontal . . . . Very Poor
Side . . . . Average

Airbags:
Head . . . . Fr. & Rr. Roof Curtain
Torso . . . . None
Pelvis . . . . Front Pelvis/Torso from Seat
Roll Sensing . . . . Yes
Knee Bolster . . . . Standard Driver

Crash Avoidance:
Frontal Collision Warning . . . . None
Blind Spot Detection . . . . None
Crash Imminent Braking . . . . None
Lane Departure Warning . . . . None

General:
Auto. Crash Notification . . . . None
Day Running Lamps . . . . Optional

Safety Belt/Restraint:
Dynamic Head Restraints . . . . . . Standard Front
Adjustable Belt . . . . Standard Front
Pretensioners . . . . Standard Front

Toyota Highlander

Specifications

Drive	4WD
Engine	3.5-liter V6
Transmission	5-sp. Automatic
Tow Rating (lbs.)	Very Low-2000
Head/Leg Room (in.)	Very Roomy-40.6/43.2
Interior Space (cu. ft.)	Very Roomy-145.7
Cargo Space (cu. ft.)	Very Cramped-10.3
Wheelbase/Length (in.)	109.8/188.4

Ratings—10 Best, 1 Worst

Combo Crash Tests	–
Safety Features	3
Rollover	5
Preventive Maintenance	9
Repair Costs	6
Warranty	1
Fuel Economy	7
Complaints	3
Insurance Costs	5
OVERALL RATING	**–**

Toyota Matrix

Toyota Matrix

At-a-Glance

Status/Year Series Started	Unchanged/2009
Twins	-
Body Styles	Hatchback
Seating	5
Anti-Theft Device	Std. Pass. Immobil.
Parking Index Rating	Easy
Where Made	Cambridge, Ontario
Fuel Factor	
MPG Rating (city/hwy)	Good-25/32
Driving Range (mi.)	Short-366
Fuel Type	Regular
Annual Fuel Cost	Low-$1,855
Gas Guzzler Tax	No
Greenhouse Gas Emissions (tons/yr.)	Average-6.5
Barrels of Oil Used per year	Average-11.8

How the Competition Rates

Competitors	Rating	Pg.
Chevrolet Cruze	9	113
Mazda Mazda3	5	190
Volkswagen Golf		260

Price Range

	Retail	Markup
Base Manual	$19,275	6%
Base Automatic	$20,115	6%
S	$21,455	8%
S AWD	$22,415	8%

Safety Checklist

Crash Tests:

Frontal	–
Side	–

Airbags:

Head	Fr. & Rr. Roof Curtain
Torso	Front Torso from Seat
Pelvis	None
Roll Sensing	No
Knee Bolster	None

Crash Avoidance:

Frontal Collision Warning	None
Blind Spot Detection	None
Crash Imminent Braking	None
Lane Departure Warning	None

General:

Auto. Crash Notification	None
Day Running Lamps	Standard

Safety Belt/Restraint:

Dynamic Head Restraints	Standard Front
Adjustable Belt	Standard Front
Pretensioners	Standard Front

Toyota Matrix

Specifications

Drive	FWD
Engine	1.8-liter I4
Transmission	4-sp. Automatic
Tow Rating (lbs.)	Very Low-1500
Head/Leg Room (in.)	Roomy-40.5/41.6
Interior Space (cu. ft.)	Cramped-94.2
Cargo Space (cu. ft.)	Average-19.8
Wheelbase/Length (in.)	102.4/171.9

Ratings—10 Best, 1 Worst

Combo Crash Tests	7
Safety Features	7
Rollover	6
Preventive Maintenance	9
Repair Costs	7
Warranty	1
Fuel Economy	10
Complaints	1
Insurance Costs	3
OVERALL RATING	**7**

Toyota Prius

Toyota Prius

At-a-Glance

Status/Year Series Started	Unchanged/2010
Twins	-
Body Styles	Hatchback
Seating	5
Anti-Theft Device	Std. Pass. Immobil.
Parking Index Rating	Very Easy
Where Made	Toyota City, Japan
Fuel Factor	
MPG Rating (city/hwy)	Very Good-51/48
Driving Range (mi.)	Very Long-590
Fuel Type	Regular
Annual Fuel Cost	Very Low-$1,037
Gas Guzzler Tax	No
Greenhouse Gas Emissions (tons/yr.)	Very Low-3.0
Barrels of Oil Used per year	Very Low-6.6

How the Competition Rates

Competitors	Rating	Pg.
Chevrolet Volt	9	122
Ford C-MAX		134
Honda Insight		152

Price Range

Price Range	Retail	Markup
I	$23,015	5%
III	$25,565	7%
V	$29,805	7%
Plug-In Hybrid Advanced	$39,525	4%

Safety Checklist

Crash Tests:
Frontal .... Good
Side .... Average

Airbags:
Head .... Fr. & Rr. Roof Curtain
Torso .... Front Torso from Seat
Pelvis .... None
Roll Sensing .... No
Knee Bolster .... Standard Driver

Crash Avoidance:
Frontal Collision Warning .... Optional
Blind Spot Detection .... None
Crash Imminent Braking .... Optional
Lane Departure Warning .... Optional

General:
Auto. Crash Notification .... Optional
Day Running Lamps .... Standard

Safety Belt/Restraint:
Dynamic Head Restraints ...... Standard Front
Adjustable Belt .... Standard Front
Pretensioners .... Standard Front

Toyota Prius

Specifications

Drive	FWD
Engine	1.8-liter I4
Transmission	ECVT
Tow Rating (lbs.)	–
Head/Leg Room (in.)	Average-38.6/42.5
Interior Space (cu. ft.)	Cramped-93.7
Cargo Space (cu. ft.)	Average-21.6
Wheelbase/Length (in.)	106.3/176.4

Ratings—10 Best, 1 Worst

Combo Crash Tests	–
Safety Features	2
Rollover	6
Preventive Maintenance	9
Repair Costs	7
Warranty	1
Fuel Economy	10
Complaints	–
Insurance Costs	5

OVERALL RATING —

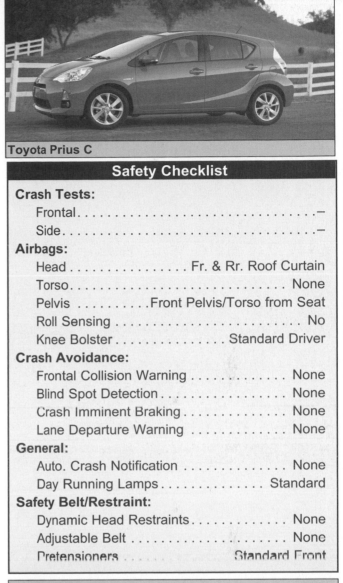

Toyota Prius C

Toyota Prius C

At-a-Glance

Status/Year Series Started	Unchanged/2012
Twins	-
Body Styles	Hatchback
Seating	5
Anti-Theft Device	Opt. Pass. Immobil.
Parking Index Rating	Very Easy
Where Made	Toyota City, Japan
Fuel Factor	
MPG Rating (city/hwy)	Very Good-53/46
Driving Range (mi.)	Very Long-471
Fuel Type	Regular
Annual Fuel Cost	Very Low-$1,037
Gas Guzzler Tax	No
Greenhouse Gas Emissions (tons/yr.)	Very Low-3.0
Barrels of Oil Used per year	Very Low-6.6

How the Competition Rates

Competitors	Rating	Pg.
Ford C-MAX		134
Honda Insight		152
Nissan Leaf	7	215

Price Range

	Retail	Markup
One	$18,950	5%
Two	$19,900	6%
Three	$21,635	7%
Four	$23,230	7%

Safety Checklist

Crash Tests:
Frontal	–
Side	–

Airbags:
Head	Fr. & Rr. Roof Curtain
Torso	None
Pelvis	Front Pelvis/Torso from Seat
Roll Sensing	No
Knee Bolster	Standard Driver

Crash Avoidance:
Frontal Collision Warning	None
Blind Spot Detection	None
Crash Imminent Braking	None
Lane Departure Warning	None

General:
Auto. Crash Notification	None
Day Running Lamps	Standard

Safety Belt/Restraint:
Dynamic Head Restraints	None
Adjustable Belt	None
Pretensioners	Standard Front

Toyota Prius C

Specifications

Drive	FWD
Engine	1.5-liter I4
Transmission	ECVT
Tow Rating (lbs.)	–
Head/Leg Room (in.)	Cramped-38.6/41.7
Interior Space (cu. ft.)	Very Cramped-87
Cargo Space (cu. ft.)	Average-17
Wheelbase/Length (in.)	100.4/157.3

Ratings—10 Best, 1 Worst

Combo Crash Tests	–
Safety Features	4
Rollover	5
Preventive Maintenance	9
Repair Costs	7
Warranty	1
Fuel Economy	10
Complaints	–
Insurance Costs	5
OVERALL RATING	**–**

Toyota Prius V

At-a-Glance

Status/Year Series Started	Unchanged/2012
Twins	-
Body Styles	Hatchback
Seating	5
Anti-Theft Device	Std. Pass. Immobil.
Parking Index Rating	Easy
Where Made	Toyota City, Japan
Fuel Factor	
MPG Rating (city/hwy)	Very Good-44/40
Driving Range (mi.)	Very Long-501
Fuel Type	Regular
Annual Fuel Cost	Very Low-$1,222
Gas Guzzler Tax	No
Greenhouse Gas Emissions (tons/yr.)	Very Low-3.5
Barrels of Oil Used per year	Very Low-7.8

How the Competition Rates

Competitors	Rating	Pg.
Ford C-MAX		134
Honda Insight		152
Mazda Mazda5		191

Price Range

	Retail	Markup
Two	$26,550	7%
Three	$27,315	7%
Five	$30,140	7%

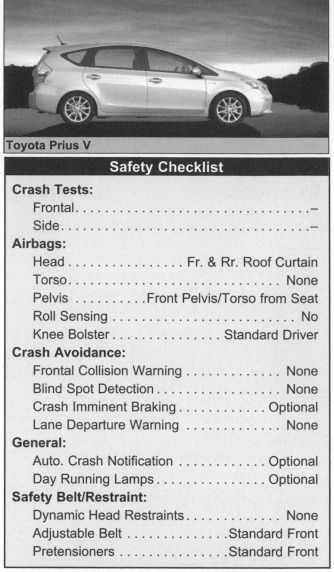

Toyota Prius V

Safety Checklist

Crash Tests:
Frontal . . . . –
Side . . . . –
Airbags:
Head . . . . Fr. & Rr. Roof Curtain
Torso . . . . None
Pelvis . . . . Front Pelvis/Torso from Seat
Roll Sensing . . . . No
Knee Bolster . . . . Standard Driver
Crash Avoidance:
Frontal Collision Warning . . . . None
Blind Spot Detection . . . . None
Crash Imminent Braking . . . . Optional
Lane Departure Warning . . . . None
General:
Auto. Crash Notification . . . . Optional
Day Running Lamps . . . . Optional
Safety Belt/Restraint:
Dynamic Head Restraints . . . . None
Adjustable Belt . . . . Standard Front
Pretensioners . . . . Standard Front

Toyota Prius V

Specifications

Drive	FWD
Engine	1.8-liter I4
Transmission	ECVT
Tow Rating (lbs.)	–
Head/Leg Room (in.)	Average-40/41.3
Interior Space (cu. ft.)	Cramped-97
Cargo Space (cu. ft.)	Very Roomy-34
Wheelbase/Length (in.)	109.4/181.7

Ratings—10 Best, 1 Worst

Combo Crash Tests	–
Safety Features	5
Rollover	2
Preventive Maintenance	8
Repair Costs	2
Warranty	1
Fuel Economy	5
Complaints	–
Insurance Costs	8
OVERALL RATING	–

Toyota RAV4

Toyota RAV4

Safety Checklist

Crash Tests:
Frontal . . . . –
Airbags:
Side . . . . –
Head . . . . Fr. & Rr. Roof Curtain
Torso . . . . None
Pelvis . . . . Front Pelvis/Torso from Seat
Roll Sensing . . . . Yes
Knee Bolster . . . . Standard Driver
Crash Avoidance:
Frontal Collision Warning . . . . None
Blind Spot Detection . . . . Optional
Crash Imminent Braking . . . . None
Lane Departure Warning . . . . Optional
General:
Auto. Crash Notification . . . . None
Day Running Lamps . . . . Optional
Safety Belt/Restraint:
Dynamic Head Restraints . . . . None
Adjustable Belt . . . . Standard Front
Pretensioners . . . . Standard Front

At-a-Glance

Status/Year Series Started . . . . All New/2013
Twins . . . . -
Body Styles . . . . SUV
Seating 5/7
Anti-Theft Device . . . . Std. Pass. Immobil.
Parking Index Rating . . . . Easy
Where Made . . . . Woodstock, Ontario / Tahara, Japan
Fuel Factor . . . .
  MPG Rating (city/hwy) Average-21/27
  Driving Range (mi.) Short-371
  Fuel Type . . . . Regular
  Annual Fuel Cost . . . . Average-$2,205
  Gas Guzzler Tax . . . . No
  Greenhouse Gas Emissions (tons/yr.) High-7.6
  Barrels of Oil Used per year High-13.7

Toyota RAV4

How the Competition Rates

Competitors	Rating	Pg.
Ford Escape	7	136
Honda CR-V	7	150
Hyundai Tucson	7	162

Price Range

Price Range	Retail	Markup
Base 2WD 4cyl	$22,650	7%
Sport 2WD 4cyl	$24,350	7%
Sport 4WD 4cyl	$25,750	7%
Limited 4WD V6	$28,650	7%

Specifications

Drive 4WD
Engine 2.5-liter I4
Transmission . . . . 4-sp. Automatic
Tow Rating (lbs.) . . . . Very Low-1500
Head/Leg Room (in.) Roomy-40.8/41.8
Interior Space (cu. ft.) . . . . Very Roomy-144.5
Cargo Space (cu. ft.) . . . . . . Very Cramped-12.3
Wheelbase/Length (in.) 104.7/181.9

Ratings—10 Best, 1 Worst

Combo Crash Tests	–
Safety Features	6
Rollover	1
Preventive Maintenance	7
Repair Costs	3
Warranty	1
Fuel Economy	1
Complaints	7
Insurance Costs	8

OVERALL RATING   –

Toyota Sequoia

At-a-Glance

Status/Year Series Started Unchanged/2008
Twins . . . . -
Body Styles . . . . SUV
Seating 8
Anti-Theft Device . . . . . . Std. Pass. Immobil. & Alarm
Parking Index Rating . . . . Very Hard
Where Made. . . . . Princeton, IN
Fuel Factor . . . .
  MPG Rating (city/hwy) . . . . . . .Very Poor-13/17
  Driving Range (mi.) Short-384
  Fuel Type. . . . . .Regular
  Annual Fuel Cost . . . . Very High-$3,539
  Gas Guzzler Tax . . . . .No
  Greenhouse Gas Emissions (tons/yr.)Very High-10.2
  Barrels of Oil Used per year . . . . . . Very High-23.5

How the Competition Rates

Competitors	Rating	Pg.
Audi Q7		93
Chevrolet Tahoe	8	120
Nissan Armada		211

Price Range

Price Range	Retail	Markup
SR5 2WD	$41,995	10%
SR5 4WD FFV	$45,180	10%
Limited 4WD	$54,665	10%
Platinum 4WD FFV	$62,570	10%

![Toyota Sequoia]

Toyota Sequoia

Safety Checklist

Crash Tests:
  Frontal. . . . .–
  Side. . . . .–
Airbags:
  Head . . . . Fr. & Rr. Roof Curtain
  Torso. . . . . Front Torso from Seat
  Pelvis . . . . None
  Roll Sensing . . . . .Yes
  Knee Bolster . . . . .Standard Front
Crash Avoidance:
  Frontal Collision Warning . . . . None
  Blind Spot Detection . . . . Optional
  Crash Imminent Braking . . . . None
  Lane Departure Warning . . . . None
General:
  Auto. Crash Notification . . . . None
  Day Running Lamps . . . . Optional
Safety Belt/Restraint:
  Dynamic Head Restraints . . . . None
  Adjustable Belt . . . . . .Standard Front and Rear
  Pretensioners . . . . .Standard Front

Toyota Sequoia

Specifications

Drive 4WD
Engine 5.7-liter V8
Transmission . . . . 6-sp. Automatic
Tow Rating (lbs.) High-7100
Head/Leg Room (in.) . . . . .Very Cramped-34.8/42.5
Interior Space (cu. ft.). . . . . –
Cargo Space (cu. ft.) Average-18.9
Wheelbase/Length (in.) 122/205.1

Ratings—10 Best, 1 Worst

Combo Crash Tests	5
Safety Features	6
Rollover	5
Preventive Maintenance	4
Repair Costs	2
Warranty	1
Fuel Economy	3
Complaints	3
Insurance Costs	8
OVERALL RATING	**3**

Toyota Sienna

Toyota Sienna

At-a-Glance

Status/Year Series Started	Unchanged/2004
Twins	-
Body Styles	Minivan
Seating	7/8
Anti-Theft Device	Opt. Pass. Immbobil. & Alarm
Parking Index Rating	Hard
Where Made	Princeton, IN
Fuel Factor	
MPG Rating (city/hwy)	Poor-18/25
Driving Range (mi.)	Average-412
Fuel Type	Regular
Annual Fuel Cost	High-$2,498
Gas Guzzler Tax	No
Greenhouse Gas Emissions (tons/yr.)	High-8.7
Barrels of Oil Used per year	High-15.7

How the Competition Rates

Competitors	Rating	Pg.
Dodge Grand Caravan	5	131
Honda Odyssey	7	153
Volkswagen Routan		263

Price Range

Price Range	Retail	Markup
L 7 -Pass FWD	$26,435	8%
LE 8-Pass FWD	$29,985	8%
XLE 7-Pass AWD	$35,800	9%
Limited 7-Pass AWD	$41,325	9%

Safety Checklist

Crash Tests:
Frontal . . . . Poor
Side . . . . Average
Airbags:
Head . . . . Fr. & Rr. Roof Curtain
Torso . . . . Front Torso from Seat
Pelvis . . . . None
Roll Sensing . . . . No
Knee Bolster . . . . Standard Driver
Crash Avoidance:
Frontal Collision Warning . . . . None
Blind Spot Detection . . . . Optional
Crash Imminent Braking . . . . Optional
Lane Departure Warning . . . . None
General:
Auto. Crash Notification . . . . Optional
Day Running Lamps . . . . Optional
Safety Belt/Restraint:
Dynamic Head Restraints . . . . . . Standard Front
Adjustable Belt . . . . Standard Front
Pretensioners . . . . Standard Front

Toyota Sienna

Specifications

Drive	FWD
Engine	3.5-liter V6
Transmission	6-sp. Automatic
Tow Rating (lbs.)	Low-3500
Head/Leg Room (in.)	Average-41/40.5
Interior Space (cu. ft.)	Very Roomy-164
Cargo Space (cu. ft.)	Very Roomy-39.1
Wheelbase/Length (in.)	119.3/200.2

Ratings—10 Best, 1 Worst	
Combo Crash Tests	2
Safety Features	3
Rollover	2
Preventive Maintenance	8
Repair Costs	5
Warranty	1
Fuel Economy	1
Complaints	6
Insurance Costs	5
OVERALL RATING	**1**

Toyota Tacoma

Toyota Tacoma

At-a-Glance

Status/Year Series Started	Unchanged/2009
Twins	-
Body Styles	Pickup
Seating	4
Anti-Theft Device	Opt. Pass. Immobil.
Parking Index Rating	Very Hard
Where Made	San Antonio, TX
Fuel Factor	
MPG Rating (city/hwy)	Very Poor-16/21
Driving Range (mi.)	Short-378
Fuel Type	Regular
Annual Fuel Cost	Very High-$2,871
Gas Guzzler Tax	No
Greenhouse Gas Emissions (tons/yr.)	Very High-10.2
Barrels of Oil Used per year	Very High-18.3

How the Competition Rates

Competitors	Rating	Pg.
Honda Ridgeline		155
Nissan Frontier		213

Price Range	Retail	Markup
Base Reg. Cab 2WD Manual	$17,525	6%
Prerunner Dbl. Cab 2WD Auto.	$24,510	8%
Base Access Cab 4WD V6 Auto.	$26,585	7%
Base Dbl. Cab 4WD LWB V6 Auto.	$28,085	8%

Safety Checklist

Crash Tests:
Frontal.........................Very Poor
Side...............................Poor
Airbags:
Head.....................Front Roof Curtain
Torso................Front Torso from Seat
Pelvis.............................None
Roll Sensing........................Yes
Knee Bolster.......................None
Crash Avoidance:
Frontal Collision Warning..............None
Blind Spot Detection.................None
Crash Imminent Braking................None
Lane Departure Warning...............None
General:
Auto. Crash Notification...............None
Day Running Lamps................Standard
Safety Belt/Restraint:
Dynamic Head Restraints...............None
Adjustable Belt................Standard Front
Pretensioners................Standard Front

Toyota Tacoma

Specifications

Drive	4WD
Engine	4.0-liter V6
Transmission	5-sp. Automatic
Tow Rating (lbs.)	Low-3500
Head/Leg Room (in.)	Average-40/41.7
Interior Space (cu. ft.)	Very Cramped-88.7
Cargo Space (cu. ft.)	Very Roomy-38
Wheelbase/Length (in.)	127.4/208.1

Ratings—10 Best, 1 Worst

Combo Crash Tests	5
Safety Features	4
Rollover	2
Preventive Maintenance	7
Repair Costs	3
Warranty	1
Fuel Economy	1
Complaints	8
Insurance Costs	5
OVERALL RATING	**2**

Toyota Tundra

Toyota Tundra

At-a-Glance

Status/Year Series Started	Unchanged/2007
Twins	-
Body Styles	Pickup
Seating	5/6
Anti-Theft Device	Opt. Pass. Immobil. & Alarm
Parking Index Rating	Very Hard
Where Made	San Antonio, TX
Fuel Factor	
MPG Rating (city/hwy)	Very Poor-14/19
Driving Range (mi.)	Average-391
Fuel Type	Regular
Annual Fuel Cost	Very High-$3,234
Gas Guzzler Tax	No
Greenhouse Gas Emissions (tons/yr.)	Very High-9.5
Barrels of Oil Used per year	Very High-20.6

How the Competition Rates

Competitors	Rating	Pg.
Ford F-150	5	139
Nissan Titan		222
Ram 1500	2	226

Price Range

	Retail	Markup
Reg. Cab 2WD V6	$25,355	8%
Dbl. Cab 4WD 5.7L V8	$32,005	8%
Crew Max 4WD 4.6 V8	$33,585	8%
Platinum Crew Max 4WD 5.7L FFV	$48,070	8%

Safety Checklist

Crash Tests:
Frontal . . . . Very Poor
Side . . . . Very Good

Airbags:
Head . . . . Front Roof Curtain
Torso . . . . Front Torso from Seat
Pelvis . . . . None
Roll Sensing . . . . Yes
Knee Bolster . . . . Standard Front

Crash Avoidance:
Frontal Collision Warning . . . . None
Blind Spot Detection . . . . None
Crash Imminent Braking . . . . None
Lane Departure Warning . . . . None

General:
Auto. Crash Notification . . . . None
Day Running Lamps . . . . Optional

Safety Belt/Restraint:
Dynamic Head Restraints . . . . None
Adjustable Belt . . . . None
Pretensioners . . . . Standard Front

Toyota Tundra

Specifications

Drive	4WD
Engine	5.7-liter V8
Transmission	6-sp. Auto. w/Overdrive
Tow Rating (lbs.)	Very High-9800
Head/Leg Room (in.)	Roomy-40.2/42.5
Interior Space (cu. ft.)	Very Roomy-131
Cargo Space (cu. ft.)	Very Roomy-42
Wheelbase/Length (in.)	145.7/228.7

Ratings—10 Best, 1 Worst

Combo Crash Tests	7
Safety Features	4
Rollover	4
Preventive Maintenance	4
Repair Costs	2
Warranty	1
Fuel Economy	4
Complaints	6
Insurance Costs	5
OVERALL RATING	**3**

Toyota Venza

At-a-Glance

Status/Year Series Started	Unchanged/2009
Twins	-
Body Styles	SUV
Seating	5
Anti-Theft Device	Std. Pass. Immobil. & Opt. Pass. Alarm
Parking Index Rating	Very Hard
Where Made	Georgetown, KY
Fuel Factor	
MPG Rating (city/hwy)	Poor-20/26
Driving Range (mi.)	Average-395
Fuel Type	Regular
Annual Fuel Cost	Average-$2,305
Gas Guzzler Tax	No
Greenhouse Gas Emissions (tons/yr.)	High-8.0
Barrels of Oil Used per year	Very High-18.3

How the Competition Rates

Competitors	Rating	Pg.
Chevrolet Equinox	5	114
Honda Pilot	4	154
Nissan Murano	3	217

Price Range

	Retail	Markup
LE FWD 4cyl	$27,700	9%
LE FWD V6	$29,250	9%
XLE AWD V6	$34,630	10%
Ltd. AWD V6	$38,870	10%

Toyota Venza

Safety Checklist

Crash Tests:
Frontal . . . . Good
Side . . . . Good
Airbags:
Head . . . . Fr. & Rr. Roof Curtain
Torso . . . . Front Torso from Seat
Pelvis . . . . None
Roll Sensing . . . . No
Knee Bolster . . . . Standard Driver
Crash Avoidance:
Frontal Collision Warning . . . . None
Blind Spot Detection . . . . None
Crash Imminent Braking . . . . None
Lane Departure Warning . . . . None
General:
Auto. Crash Notification . . . . None
Day Running Lamps . . . . Standard
Safety Belt/Restraint:
Dynamic Head Restraints . . . . . Standard Front
Adjustable Belt . . . . Standard Front
Pretensioners . . . . Standard Front

Toyota Venza

Specifications

Drive	FWD
Engine	2.7-liter I4
Transmission	6-sp. Automatic
Tow Rating (lbs.)	Very Low-1000
Head/Leg Room (in.)	Very Cramped-39.6/40.2
Interior Space (cu. ft.)	Roomy-108
Cargo Space (cu. ft.)	Very Roomy-36.2
Wheelbase/Length (in.)	109.3/189

Toyota Yaris

Ratings—10 Best, 1 Worst

Combo Crash Tests	4
Safety Features	2
Rollover	5
Preventive Maintenance	9
Repair Costs	10
Warranty	1
Fuel Economy	9
Complaints	–
Insurance Costs	3
OVERALL RATING	**5**

Toyota Yaris

Toyota Yaris

At-a-Glance

Status/Year Series Started	Unchanged/2012
Twins	-
Body Styles	Hatchback
Seating	5
Anti-Theft Device	-
Parking Index Rating	Very Easy
Where Made	Kanto Jidosha/ Takaoka City, Japan
Fuel Factor	
MPG Rating (city/hwy)	Very Good-30/37
Driving Range (mi.)	Very Short-364
Fuel Type	Regular
Annual Fuel Cost	Very Low-$1,569
Gas Guzzler Tax	No
Greenhouse Gas Emissions (tons/yr.)	Very Low-4.5
Barrels of Oil Used per year	Low-10.3

How the Competition Rates

Competitors	Rating	Pg.
Honda Fit	4	151
Kia Rio	8	177
Nissan Versa	4	223

Price Range

	Retail	Markup
L 2-Door Manual	$14,370	4%
L 4-Door	$15,395	4%
LE	$16,430	4%
SE	$17,280	4%

Safety Checklist

Crash Tests:
Frontal . . . . Average
Side . . . . Average

Airbags:
Head . . . . Fr & Rr. Roof Curtain
Torso . . . . None
Pelvis . . . . Front Pelvis/Torso from Seat
Roll Sensing . . . . No
Knee Bolster . . . . Standard Driver

Crash Avoidance:
Frontal Collision Warning . . . . None
Blind Spot Detection . . . . None
Crash Imminent Braking . . . . None
Lane Departure Warning . . . . None

General:
Auto. Crash Notification . . . . None
Day Running Lamps . . . . None

Safety Belt/Restraint:
Dynamic Head Restraints . . . . None
Adjustable Belt . . . . None
Pretensioners . . . . Standard Front

Toyota Yaris

Toyota Yaris

Specifications

Drive	FWD
Engine	1.5-liter I4
Transmission	4-sp. Automatic
Tow Rating (lbs.)	–
Head/Leg Room (in.)	Cramped-39.3/40.6
Interior Space (cu. ft.)	Very Cramped-85.1
Cargo Space (cu. ft.)	Cramped-15.6
Wheelbase/Length (in.)	98.9/153.5

Ratings—10 Best, 1 Worst

Combo Crash Tests	6
Safety Features	1
Rollover	8
Preventive Maintenance	8
Repair Costs	3
Warranty	7
Fuel Economy	5
Complaints	1
Insurance Costs	5
OVERALL RATING	**5**

Volkswagen Beetle

At-a-Glance

Status/Year Series Started........ Unchanged/2012
Twins . . . . -
Body Styles . . . . Coupe, Convertible
Seating 4
Anti-Theft Device . . . . . . Std. Pass. Immobil. & Alarm
Parking Index Rating . . . . .Very Easy
Where Made. . . . . .Puebla, Mexico
Fuel Factor. . . . .
  MPG Rating (city/hwy) Average-22/29
  Driving Range (mi.) . . . . Very Short-358
  Fuel Type . . . . .Regular
  Annual Fuel Cost . . . . Average-$2,085
  Gas Guzzler Tax . . . . .No
  Greenhouse Gas Emissions (tons/yr.). . Average-7.3
  Barrels of Oil Used per year Average-13.2

How the Competition Rates

Competitors	Rating	Pg.
Scion xD	3	231
Chevrolet Sonic	10	118
Suzuki SX4	1	240

Price Range

	Retail	Markup
2.5 L Manual	$19,795	4%
TDI Manual	$23,295	4%
TDI Automatic	$24,395	4%
2.0T	$24,495	4%

Volkswagen Beetle

Safety Checklist

Crash Tests:
  Frontal. . . . . Average
  Side. . . . . Good
Airbags:
  Head . . . . Front Head/Torso from Seat
  Torso. . . . . Front Head/Torso from Seat
  Pelvis . . . . None
  Roll Sensing . . . . No
  Knee Bolster . . . . None
Crash Avoidance:
  Frontal Collision Warning . . . . None
  Blind Spot Detection . . . . None
  Crash Imminent Braking . . . . None
  Lane Departure Warning . . . . None
General:
  Auto. Crash Notification . . . . None
  Day Running Lamps . . . . Standard
Safety Belt/Restraint:
  Dynamic Head Restraints . . . . None
  Adjustable Belt . . . . None
  Pretensioners . . . . .Standard Front

Volkswagen Beetle

Specifications

Drive. . . . . FWD
Engine 2.5-liter I5
Transmission . . . . .6-sp. Automatic
Tow Rating (lbs.) . . . . –
Head/Leg Room (in.) Cramped-39.4/41.3
Interior Space (cu. ft.). . . . . .Very Cramped-85.1
Cargo Space (cu. ft.). Cramped-15.4
Wheelbase/Length (in.) 99.9/168.4

Ratings—10 Best, 1 Worst	
Combo Crash Tests	–
Safety Features	3
Rollover	9
Preventive Maintenance	8
Repair Costs	5
Warranty	7
Fuel Economy	6
Complaints	7
Insurance Costs	5
OVERALL RATING	**–**

Volkswagen CC

At-a-Glance

Status/Year Series Started Appearance Change/2009	
Twins	-
Body Styles	Sedan
Seating	5
Anti-Theft Device	Std. Pass. Immobil. & Alarm
Parking Index Rating	Average
Where Made	Ewden, Germany
Fuel Factor	
MPG Rating (city/hwy)	Average-22/31
Driving Range (mi.)	Very Long-468
Fuel Type	Premium
Annual Fuel Cost	Average-$2,211
Gas Guzzler Tax	No
Greenhouse Gas Emissions (tons/yr.)	Average-7.3
Barrels of Oil Used per year	Average-13.2

How the Competition Rates

Competitors	Rating	Pg.
Acura TSX		85
Subaru Legacy	3	236
Toyota Camry	4	243

Price Range	Retail	Markup
Sport Manual	$30,250	4%
Luxury	$35,355	4%
VR6 Luxury	$37,730	4%
VR6 4Motion	$41,420	4%

Volkswagen CC

Safety Checklist

Crash Tests:
Frontal . . . . –
Side . . . . –

Airbags:
Head . . . . Fr & Rr. Roof Curtain
Torso . . . . Front Pelvis/Torso from Seat
Pelvis . . . . Front Pelvis/Torso from Seat
Roll Sensing . . . . No
Knee Bolster . . . . None

Crash Avoidance:
Frontal Collision Warning . . . . None
Blind Spot Detection . . . . None
Crash Imminent Braking . . . . None
Lane Departure Warning . . . . None

General:
Auto. Crash Notification . . . . None
Day Running Lamps . . . . Standard

Safety Belt/Restraint:
Dynamic Head Restraints . . . . None
Adjustable Belt . . . . Standard Front
Pretensioners . . . . Standard

Volkswagen CC

Specifications

Drive	FWD
Engine	2.0-liter I4
Transmission	6-sp. Automatic
Tow Rating (lbs.)	–
Head/Leg Room (in.)	Very Cramped-37.4/41.6
Interior Space (cu. ft.)	Cramped-93.6
Cargo Space (cu. ft.)	Cramped-13.2
Wheelbase/Length (in.)	106.7/188.9

Ratings—10 Best, 1 Worst

Combo Crash Tests	–
Safety Features	4
Rollover	6
Preventive Maintenance	9
Repair Costs	6
Warranty	7
Fuel Economy	7
Complaints	2
Insurance Costs	1

OVERALL RATING   –

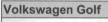
Volkswagen Golf

At-a-Glance

Status/Year Series Started........	Unchanged/2010
Twins	-
Body Styles	Hatchback
Seating	5
Anti-Theft Device	Std. Pass. Immobil. & Alarm
Parking Index Rating	Very Easy
Where Made........................	Wolfgang, Germany
Fuel Factor..................................	
MPG Rating (city/hwy)	Good-24/31
Driving Range (mi.)	Short-387
Fuel Type..................................	Regular
Annual Fuel Cost	Low-$1,926
Gas Guzzler Tax	No
Greenhouse Gas Emissions (tons/yr.)..	Average-7.1
Barrels of Oil Used per year	Average-12.7

How the Competition Rates

Competitors	Rating	Pg.
Mazda Mazda3	5	190
Subaru Impreza	4	235
Toyota Matrix		247

Price Range

Price Range	Retail	Markup
Base 2-Door Manual	$17,995	4%
TDI 2-Door Manual	$24,235	4%
TDI 2-Door Automatic	$25,335	4%
TDI 4-Door Automatic	$26,035	4%

Volkswagen Golf

Safety Checklist

Crash Tests:
Frontal. . . . .–
Side. . . . .–
Airbags:
Head . . . . .Fr & Rr. Roof Curtain
Torso. . . . . .Front Pelvis/Torso from Seat
Pelvis . . . . .Front Pelvis/Torso from Seat
Roll Sensing . . . . No
Knee Bolster . . . . Standard
Crash Avoidance:
Frontal Collision Warning . . . . None
Blind Spot Detection . . . . None
Crash Imminent Braking . . . . None
Lane Departure Warning . . . . None
General:
Auto. Crash Notification . . . . None
Day Running Lamps . . . . Standard
Safety Belt/Restraint:
Dynamic Head Restraints. . . . . None
Adjustable Belt . . . . .Standard Front
Pretensioners . . . . .Standard Front

Volkswagen Golf

Specifications

Drive.	FWD
Engine	2.5-liter I5
Transmission	6-sp. Manual
Tow Rating (lbs.)	–
Head/Leg Room (in.)	Cramped-39.3/41.2
Interior Space (cu. ft.).	Cramped-93.5
Cargo Space (cu. ft.)	Cramped-15.2
Wheelbase/Length (in.)	101.5/165.4

Ratings—10 Best, 1 Worst	
Combo Crash Tests	5
Safety Features	3
Rollover	7
Preventive Maintenance	9
Repair Costs	6
Warranty	7
Fuel Economy	7
Complaints	3
Insurance Costs	3
OVERALL RATING	**6**

Volkswagen Jetta

Volkswagen Jetta Sport Wagen

At-a-Glance

Status/Year Series Started	Unchanged/2011
Twins	-
Body Styles	Sedan, Wagon
Seating	5
Anti-Theft Device	Std. Pass. Immobil. & Alarm
Parking Index Rating	Easy
Where Made	Puebla, Mexico
Fuel Factor	
MPG Rating (city/hwy)	Good-24/31
Driving Range (mi.)	Short-387
Fuel Type	Regular
Annual Fuel Cost	Low-$1,926
Gas Guzzler Tax	No
Greenhouse Gas Emissions (tons/yr.)	Average-7.1
Barrels of Oil Used per year	Average-12.7

How the Competition Rates

Competitors	Rating	Pg.
Ford Focus	6	142
Honda Civic		148
Toyota Corolla	4	244

Price Range	Retail	Markup
Base Manual	$15,545	4%
S	$17,775	4%
SEL	$22,895	4%
TDI Wagon	$26,640	4%

Safety Checklist

Crash Tests:
Frontal . . . . Good
Side . . . . Poor
Airbags:
Head . . . . .Fr & Rr. Roof Curtain
Torso . . . . .Front Pelvis/Torso from Seat
Pelvis . . . . .Front Pelvis/Torso from Seat
Roll Sensing . . . . No
Knee Bolster . . . . None
Crash Avoidance:
Frontal Collision Warning . . . . None
Blind Spot Detection . . . . None
Crash Imminent Braking . . . . None
Lane Departure Warning . . . . None
General:
Auto. Crash Notification . . . . None
Day Running Lamps . . . . Standard
Safety Belt/Restraint:
Dynamic Head Restraints . . . . None
Adjustable Belt . . . . .Standard Front
Pretensioners . . . . .Standard Front

Volkswagen Jetta

Specifications

Drive	FWD
Engine	2.5-liter I5
Transmission	6-sp. Automatic
Tow Rating (lbs.)	–
Head/Leg Room (in.)	Very Cramped-38.2/41.2
Interior Space (cu. ft.)	Cramped-94.1
Cargo Space (cu. ft.)	Cramped-15.5
Wheelbase/Length (in.)	104.4/182.2

Ratings—10 Best, 1 Worst

Combo Crash Tests	9
Safety Features	3
Rollover	8
Preventive Maintenance	8
Repair Costs	6
Warranty	7
Fuel Economy	6
Complaints	8
Insurance Costs	3
OVERALL RATING	**9**

Volkswagen Passat

Volkswagen Passat

At-a-Glance

Status/Year Series Started. Unchanged/2012
Twins . . . . -
Body Styles . . . . .Sedan
Seating 5
Anti-Theft Device . . . . . . Std. Pass. Immobil. & Alarm
Parking Index Rating . . . . Average
Where Made. . . . . Chattanooga, TN
Fuel Factor. . . . .
  MPG Rating (city/hwy) Average-22/31
  Driving Range (mi.) . . . . Very Long-468
  Fuel Type. . . . . .Regular
  Annual Fuel Cost . . . . Average-$2,033
  Gas Guzzler Tax . . . . .No
  Greenhouse Gas Emissions (tons/yr.). . Average-7.3
  Barrels of Oil Used per year Average-13.2

How the Competition Rates

Competitors	Rating	Pg.
Honda Accord	9	146
Hyundai Sonata	9	161
Nissan Altima	7	209

Price Range

Price Range	Retail	Markup
S Manual	$20,845	4%
SE 2.0 TDI	$25,045	4%
SEL	$28,259	2%
SEL 3.6L	$33,525	4%

Safety Checklist

Crash Tests:
  Frontal. . . . . Very Good
  Side. . . . . Good
Airbags:
  Head . . . . .Fr & Rr. Roof Curtain
  Torso. . . . . .Front Pelvis/Torso from Seat
  Pelvis . . . . .Front Pelvis/Torso from Seat
  Roll Sensing . . . . No
  Knee Bolster . . . . None
Crash Avoidance:
  Frontal Collision Warning . . . . None
  Blind Spot Detection . . . . None
  Crash Imminent Braking . . . . None
General:
  Lane Departure Warning . . . . None
  Auto. Crash Notification . . . . None
  Day Running Lamps . . . . Standard
Safety Belt/Restraint:
  Dynamic Head Restraints. . . . . None
  Adjustable Belt . . . . .Standard Front
  Pretensioners . . . . Standard

Volkswagen Passat

Specifications

Drive. . . . . FWD
Engine 2.5-liter I5
Transmission . . . . .6-sp. Automatic
Tow Rating (lbs.) . . . . –
Head/Leg Room (in.) Cramped-38.3/42.4
Interior Space (cu. ft.). Average-102
Cargo Space (cu. ft.) Cramped-15.9
Wheelbase/Length (in.) 110.4/191.6

Ratings—10 Best, 1 Worst

Combo Crash Tests	–
Safety Features	8
Rollover	3
Preventive Maintenance	9
Repair Costs	6
Warranty	7
Fuel Economy	2
Complaints	1
Insurance Costs	8
OVERALL RATING	**–**

Volkswagen Routan

At-a-Glance

Status/Year Series Started........ Unchanged/2009
Twins . . . . -
Body Styles . . . . .Minivan
Seating 7
Anti-Theft Device . . . . . . Std. Pass. Immobil. & Alarm
Parking Index Rating . . . . .Very Hard
Where Made. . . . . Windsor, Ontario
Fuel Factor. . . . .
  MPG Rating (city/hwy) . . . . .Very Poor-17/25
  Driving Range (mi.) Average-397
  Fuel Type. . . . . .Regular
  Annual Fuel Cost . . . . High-$2,591
  Gas Guzzler Tax . . . . .No
  Greenhouse Gas Emissions (tons/yr.) High-9.1
  Barrels of Oil Used per year High-16.5

How the Competition Rates

Competitors	Rating	Pg.
Dodge Grand Caravan	5	131
Mazda Mazda5		191
Toyota Sienna	3	253

Price Range

	Retail	Markup
S	$27,020	4%
SE	$32,010	4%
SEL	$37,890	4%
SEL Premium	$44,280	4%

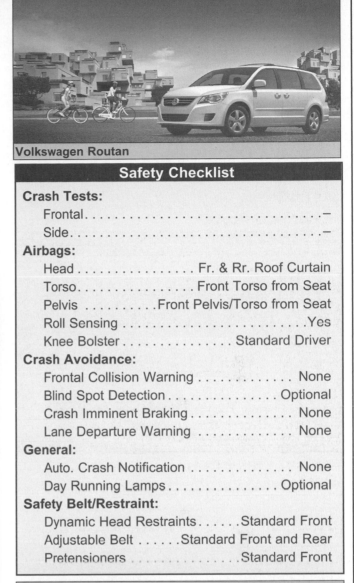
Volkswagen Routan

Safety Checklist

Crash Tests:
  Frontal. . . . .–
  Side. . . . .–
Airbags:
  Head . . . . Fr. & Rr. Roof Curtain
  Torso. . . . . Front Torso from Seat
  Pelvis . . . . .Front Pelvis/Torso from Seat
  Roll Sensing . . . . .Yes
  Knee Bolster . . . . Standard Driver
Crash Avoidance:
  Frontal Collision Warning . . . . None
  Blind Spot Detection . . . . Optional
  Crash Imminent Braking . . . . None
  Lane Departure Warning . . . . None
General:
  Auto. Crash Notification . . . . None
  Day Running Lamps . . . . Optional
Safety Belt/Restraint:
  Dynamic Head Restraints . . . . . .Standard Front
  Adjustable Belt . . . . . .Standard Front and Rear
  Pretensioners . . . . .Standard Front

Volkswagen Routan

Specifications

Drive. . . . . FWD
Engine 3.6-liter V6
Transmission . . . . .6-sp. Automatic
Tow Rating (lbs.) . . . . Very Low-2000
Head/Leg Room (in.) . . . . .Very Cramped-37.2/40.6
Interior Space (cu. ft.). . . . . Very Roomy-163.5
Cargo Space (cu. ft.) Roomy-32.7
Wheelbase/Length (in.) 121.4/202.5

Ratings—10 Best, 1 Worst

Combo Crash Tests	2
Safety Features	5
Rollover	2
Preventive Maintenance	8
Repair Costs	6
Warranty	7
Fuel Economy	4
Complaints	4
Insurance Costs	8
OVERALL RATING	**4**

Volkswagen Tiguan

At-a-Glance

Status/Year Series Started	Unchanged/2009
Twins	-
Body Styles	SUV
Seating	5
Anti-Theft Device	Std. Pass. Immobil. & Alarm
Parking Index Rating	Average
Where Made	Wolfgang, Germany
Fuel Factor	
MPG Rating (city/hwy)	Poor-21/26
Driving Range (mi.)	Short-386
Fuel Type	Premium
Annual Fuel Cost	High-$2,434
Gas Guzzler Tax	No
Greenhouse Gas Emissions (tons/yr.)	High-8.0
Barrels of Oil Used per year	High-14.3

How the Competition Rates

Competitors	Rating	Pg.
Hyundai Tucson	7	162
Subaru Forester	3	234
Toyota RAV4		251

Price Range

Price Range	Retail	Markup
S Manual	$22,995	4%
SE	$29,160	4%
SE 4Motion	$31,115	4%
SEL 4Motion	$36,820	4%

Volkswagen Tiguan

Safety Checklist

Crash Tests:

Frontal	Very Poor
Side	Average

Airbags:

Head	Fr & Rr. Roof Curtain
Torso	Front Pelvis/Torso from Seat
Pelvis	Front Pelvis/Torso from Seat
Roll Sensing	Yes
Knee Bolster	None

Crash Avoidance:

Frontal Collision Warning	None
Blind Spot Detection	None
Crash Imminent Braking	None
Lane Departure Warning	None

General:

Auto. Crash Notification	None
Day Running Lamps	Standard

Safety Belt/Restraint:

Dynamic Head Restraints	None
Adjustable Belt	Standard Front
Pretensioners	Standard Front

Volkswagen Tiguan

Specifications

Drive	FWD
Engine	2.0-liter I4
Transmission	6-sp. Automatic
Tow Rating (lbs.)	Low-2200
Head/Leg Room (in.)	Very Cramped-39.1/40.1
Interior Space (cu. ft.)	Cramped-95.4
Cargo Space (cu. ft.)	Roomy-23.8
Wheelbase/Length (in.)	102.5/174.5

Ratings—10 Best, 1 Worst

Combo Crash Tests	–
Safety Features	5
Rollover	3
Preventive Maintenance	9
Repair Costs	1
Warranty	7
Fuel Economy	2
Complaints	5
Insurance Costs	5

OVERALL RATING — –

Volkswagen Touareg

Volkswagen Touareg

At-a-Glance

Status/Year Series Started	Unchanged/2011
Twins	Porsche Cayenne
Body Styles	SUV
Seating	5
Anti-Theft Device	Std. Pass. Immobil. & Alarm
Parking Index Rating	Hard
Where Made	Bratislava, Slovakia
Fuel Factor	
MPG Rating (city/hwy)	Very Poor-17/23
Driving Range (mi.)	Very Long-509
Fuel Type	Premium
Annual Fuel Cost	Very High-$2,905
Gas Guzzler Tax	No
Greenhouse Gas Emissions (tons/yr.)	Very High-9.6
Barrels of Oil Used per year	High-17.3

How the Competition Rates

Competitors	Rating	Pg.
Acura MDX	8	82
BMW X5	6	100
Volvo XC90		270

Price Range

	Retail	Markup
Sport VR6	$43,425	5%
LUX TDI	$52,930	5%
Executive VR6	$55,155	5%
Hybrid	$62,055	5%

Safety Checklist

Crash Tests:
Frontal	–
Side	–

Airbags:
Head	Fr & Rr. Roof Curtain
Torso	Front Pelvis/Torso from Seat
Pelvis	Front Pelvis/Torso from Seat
Roll Sensing	Yes
Knee Bolster	None

Crash Avoidance:
Frontal Collision Warning	None
Blind Spot Detection	None
Crash Imminent Braking	None
Lane Departure Warning	None

General:
Auto. Crash Notification	None
Day Running Lamps	Standard

Safety Belt/Restraint:
Dynamic Head Restraints	None
Adjustable Belt	Standard Front
Pretensioners	Standard

Volkswagen Touareg

Specifications

Drive	AWD
Engine	3.6-liter V6
Transmission	8-sp. Automatic
Tow Rating (lbs.)	Very High-7716
Head/Leg Room (in.)	Average-39.6/41.4
Interior Space (cu. ft.)	Roomy-103.6
Cargo Space (cu. ft.)	Roomy-32.1
Wheelbase/Length (in.)	113.9/188.8

Ratings—10 Best, 1 Worst

Combo Crash Tests	–
Safety Features	4
Rollover	9
Preventive Maintenance	5
Repair Costs	6
Warranty	10
Fuel Economy	4
Complaints	10
Insurance Costs	10
OVERALL RATING	**–**

Volvo C70

At-a-Glance

Status/Year Series Started........ Unchanged/2006
Twins . . . . -
Body Styles . . . . Coupe, Convertible
Seating 4
Anti-Theft Device .Std. Pass. Immobil. & Active Alarm
Parking Index Rating . . . . Hard
Where Made. . . . . Udevalla, Sweden
Fuel Factor . . . .
  MPG Rating (city/hwy) Poor-19/28
  Driving Range (mi.) . . . . Very Short-353
  Fuel Type. . . . . Regular
  Annual Fuel Cost . . . . Average-$2,316
  Gas Guzzler Tax . . . . No
  Greenhouse Gas Emissions (tons/yr.). High-8.3
  Barrels of Oil Used per year High-15.0

How the Competition Rates

Competitors	Rating	Pg.
Audi A4	10	87
BMW 3 Series	10	95
Acura ILX	8	81

Price Range	Retail	Markup
T5 Convertible	$40,990	6%

Volvo C70

Safety Checklist

Crash Tests:
  Frontal. . . . .–
  Side. . . . .–
Airbags:
  Head . . . . .Front Door Curtain
  Torso. . . . . .Front Torso from Seat
  Pelvis . . . . None
  Roll Sensing . . . . .Yes
  Knee Bolster . . . . None
Crash Avoidance:
  Frontal Collision Warning . . . . None
  Blind Spot Detection . . . . Optional
  Crash Imminent Braking . . . . None
  Lane Departure Warning . . . . None
General:
  Auto. Crash Notification . . . . None
  Day Running Lamps . . . . Standard
Safety Belt/Restraint:
  Dynamic Head Restraints . . . . None
  Adjustable Belt . . . . None
  Pretensioners . . . . Standard

Volvo C70

Specifications

Drive. . . . . FWD
Engine 2.5-liter I5
Transmission . . . . .5-sp. Automatic
Tow Rating (lbs.) . . . . Very Low-2000
Head/Leg Room (in.) Cramped-38.2/42.3
Interior Space (cu. ft.). . . . . Very Cramped-84
Cargo Space (cu. ft.) Cramped-12.8
Wheelbase/Length (in.) 103.9/181.7

Ratings—10 Best, 1 Worst	
Combo Crash Tests	10
Safety Features	9
Rollover	8
Preventive Maintenance	6
Repair Costs	5
Warranty	10
Fuel Economy	3
Complaints	5
Insurance Costs	5
OVERALL RATING	**10**

Volvo S60

Volvo S60

At-a-Glance

Status/Year Series Started	Unchanged/2011
Twins	-
Body Styles	Sedan
Seating	5
Anti-Theft Device	Std. Pass. Immobil. & Active Alarm
Parking Index Rating	Average
Where Made	Ghent, Belgium
Fuel Factor	
MPG Rating (city/hwy)	Poor-18/25
Driving Range (mi.)	Short-367
Fuel Type	Regular
Annual Fuel Cost	High-$2,498
Gas Guzzler Tax	No
Greenhouse Gas Emissions (tons/yr.)	High-8.7
Barrels of Oil Used per year	High-15.7

How the Competition Rates

Competitors	Rating	Pg.
Acura TL	5	84
Hyundai Sonata	9	161
Infiniti EX		164

Price Range	Retail	Markup
T5 FWD	$31,750	6%
T5 AWD	$33,750	6%
T6 AWD	$40,450	6%
T6 R AWD	$43,900	6%

Safety Checklist

Crash Tests:

Frontal	Very Good
Side	Good

Airbags:

Head	Fr & Rr. Roof Curtain
Torso	Front Pelvis/Torso/Shoulder from Seat
Pelvis	Front Pelvis/Torso from Seat
Roll Sensing	Yes
Knee Bolster	None

Crash Avoidance:

Frontal Collision Warning	Optional
Blind Spot Detection	Optional
Crash Imminent Braking	Standard
Lane Departure Warning	Optional

General:

Auto. Crash Notification	None
Day Running Lamps	Standard

Safety Belt/Restraint:

Dynamic Head Restraints	None
Adjustable Belt	Standard Front
Pretensioners	Standard

Volvo S60

Specifications

Drive	FWD
Engine	2.5-liter I5
Transmission	6-sp. Automatic
Tow Rating (lbs.)	—
Head/Leg Room (in.)	Cramped-38.3/41.9
Interior Space (cu. ft.)	Cramped-92
Cargo Space (cu. ft.)	Cramped-14
Wheelbase/Length (in.)	109.3/182.2

Ratings—10 Best, 1 Worst

Combo Crash Tests	–
Safety Features	7
Rollover	7
Preventive Maintenance	6
Repair Costs	6
Warranty	10
Fuel Economy	4
Complaints	7
Insurance Costs	8

OVERALL RATING   –

Volvo S80

Volvo S80

At-a-Glance

Status/Year Series Started. Unchanged/2008
Twins . . . . -
Body Styles . . . . .Sedan
Seating 5
Anti-Theft Device . Std. Pass. Immobil. & Active Alarm
Parking Index Rating . . . . Average
Where Made. . . . . Torslanda, Sweden
Fuel Factor. . . . .
  MPG Rating (city/hwy) Poor-19/28
  Driving Range (mi.) Average-411
  Fuel Type. . . . . .Regular
  Annual Fuel Cost . . . . Average-$2,316
  Gas Guzzler Tax . . . . .No
  Greenhouse Gas Emissions (tons/yr.) High-8.0
  Barrels of Oil Used per year High-14.3

How the Competition Rates

Competitors	Rating	Pg.
BMW 7 Series		97
Cadillac XTS	8	109
Infiniti M	6	168

Price Range	Retail	Markup
FWD 3.2	$38,950	6%
AWD T6	$42,950	6%

Safety Checklist

Crash Tests:
  Frontal. . . . . –
  Side. . . . . –
Airbags:
  Head . . . . .Fr & Rr. Roof Curtain
  Torso. . . . . .Front Pelvis/Torso from Seat
  Pelvis . . . . .Front Pelvis/Torso from Seat
  Roll Sensing . . . . No
  Knee Bolster . . . . None
Crash Avoidance:
  Frontal Collision Warning . . . . Optional
  Blind Spot Detection . . . . Optional
  Crash Imminent Braking . . . . Standard
  Lane Departure Warning . . . . Optional
General:
  Auto. Crash Notification . . . . None
  Day Running Lamps . . . . Standard
Safety Belt/Restraint:
  Dynamic Head Restraints . . . . None
  Adjustable Belt . . . . .Standard Front
  Pretensioners . . . . Standard

Volvo S80

Specifications

Drive. . . . . FWD
Engine 3.2-liter I6
Transmission . . . . .6-sp. Automatic
Tow Rating (lbs.) . . . . –
Head/Leg Room (in.) . . . . .Very Cramped-37.8/41.9
Interior Space (cu. ft.). Average-98
Cargo Space (cu. ft.) Cramped-14.9
Wheelbase/Length (in.) 111.6/191

Ratings—10 Best, 1 Worst

Combo Crash Tests	10
Safety Features	9
Rollover	3
Preventive Maintenance	6
Repair Costs	4
Warranty	10
Fuel Economy	2
Complaints	4
Insurance Costs	10
OVERALL RATING	**9**

Volvo XC60

Volvo XC60

At-a-Glance

Status/Year Series Started........ Unchanged/2009
Twins . . . . -
Body Styles . . . . SUV
Seating 5
Anti-Theft Device . Std. Pass. Immobil. & Active Alarm
Parking Index Rating . . . . Hard
Where Made. . . . . Ghent, Belgium
Fuel Factor . . . .
  MPG Rating (city/hwy) . . . . .Very Poor-17/23
  Driving Range (mi.) . . . . .Very Short-356
  Fuel Type. . . . . .Regular
  Annual Fuel Cost . . . . High-$2,671
  Gas Guzzler Tax . . . . .No
  Greenhouse Gas Emissions (tons/yr.). High-9.1
  Barrels of Oil Used per year High-16.5

How the Competition Rates

Competitors	Rating	Pg.
Acura MDX	8	82
Infiniti FX		165
BMW X5	6	100

Price Range	Retail	Markup
3.2 FWD	$34,200	6%
3.2 AWD	$36,200	6%
T6 AWD	$40,450	6%
T6 R AWD	$44,650	6%

Safety Checklist

Crash Tests:
  Frontal. . . . . Very Good
  Side. . . . . Very Good
Airbags:
  Head . . . . .Fr & Rr. Roof Curtain
  Torso. . . Front Pelvis/Torso/Shoulder from Seat
  Pelvis . . . . .Front Pelvis/Torso from Seat
  Roll Sensing . . . . .Yes
  Knee Bolster . . . . None
Crash Avoidance:
  Frontal Collision Warning . . . . Optional
  Blind Spot Detection . . . . Optional
  Crash Imminent Braking . . . . Standard
  Lane Departure Warning . . . . Optional
General:
  Auto. Crash Notification . . . . None
  Day Running Lamps . . . . Standard
Safety Belt/Restraint:
  Dynamic Head Restraints . . . . None
  Adjustable Belt . . . . .Standard Front
  Pretensioners . . . . Standard

Volvo XC60

Specifications

Drive. . . . . AWD
Engine 3.0-liter I6
Transmission . . . . .6-sp. Automatic
Tow Rating (lbs.) Low-3300
Head/Leg Room (in.) Cramped-39/41.2
Interior Space (cu. ft.). Average-99
Cargo Space (cu. ft.) . . . . Very Roomy-34
Wheelbase/Length (in.) 109.2/182.2

Ratings—10 Best, 1 Worst

Combo Crash Tests	–
Safety Features	5
Rollover	2
Preventive Maintenance	4
Repair Costs	3
Warranty	10
Fuel Economy	2
Complaints	4
Insurance Costs	10

OVERALL RATING — –

Volvo XC90

Volvo XC90

At-a-Glance

Status/Year Series Started........ Unchanged/2003
Twins . . . . -
Body Styles . . . . SUV
Seating 7
Anti-Theft Device . Std. Pass. Immobil. & Active Alarm
Parking Index Rating . . . . .Very Hard
Where Made. . . . . Torslanda, Sweden
Fuel Factor. . . . .
  MPG Rating (city/hwy) . . . . .Very Poor-16/22
  Driving Range (mi.) Short-385
  Fuel Type. . . . . .Regular
  Annual Fuel Cost . . . . Very High-$2,821
  Gas Guzzler Tax . . . . .No
  Greenhouse Gas Emissions (tons/yr.) High-7.9
  Barrels of Oil Used per year . . . . Very High-18.3

How the Competition Rates

Competitors	Rating	Pg.
BMW X5	6	100
Infiniti FX		165
Mercedes-Benz M-Class		200

Price Range

Price Range	Retail	Markup
3.2 FWD	$39,500	6%
3.2 AWD	$41,500	6%
3.2 R FWD	$42,300	6%
3.2 R AWD	$44,300	6%

Safety Checklist

Crash Tests:
  Frontal. . . . .–
  Side. . . . .–
Airbags:
  Head . . . . Fr. & Rr. Roof Curtain
  Torso. . . . . .Front Pelvis/Torso from Seat
  Pelvis . . . . None
  Roll Sensing . . . . .Yes
  Knee Bolster . . . . None
Crash Avoidance:
  Frontal Collision Warning . . . . None
  Blind Spot Detection . . . . Optional
  Crash Imminent Braking . . . . None
  Lane Departure Warning . . . . None
General:
  Auto. Crash Notification . . . . None
  Day Running Lamps. . . . . Standard
Safety Belt/Restraint:
  Dynamic Head Restraints. . . . . None
  Adjustable Belt . . . . . .Standard Front and Rear
  Pretensioners . . . . Standard

Volvo XC90

Specifications

Drive. . . . . .AWD
Engine 3.2-liter V6
Transmission . . . . .6-sp. Automatic
Tow Rating (lbs.) Average-5000
Head/Leg Room (in.) Cramped-39.7/41
Interior Space (cu. ft.). Average-100.9
Cargo Space (cu. ft.) . . . . .Very Cramped-8.8
Wheelbase/Length (in.) 112.6/189.3

Use this page to keep some notes on the choices you are considering. Include any comments your friends make, statements made by the dealer that may be important later, and your own personal reactions to the car and the test drive. After you've looked at 4 or 5 cars, it's easy to mix up the details.

MAKE/MODEL: **PRICE RANGE:**   **PAGE:**

PROS: CONS:

NOTES:

MAKE/MODEL: **PRICE RANGE:**   **PAGE:**

PROS: CONS:

NOTES:

MAKE/MODEL: **PRICE RANGE:**   **PAGE:**

PROS: CONS:

NOTES: